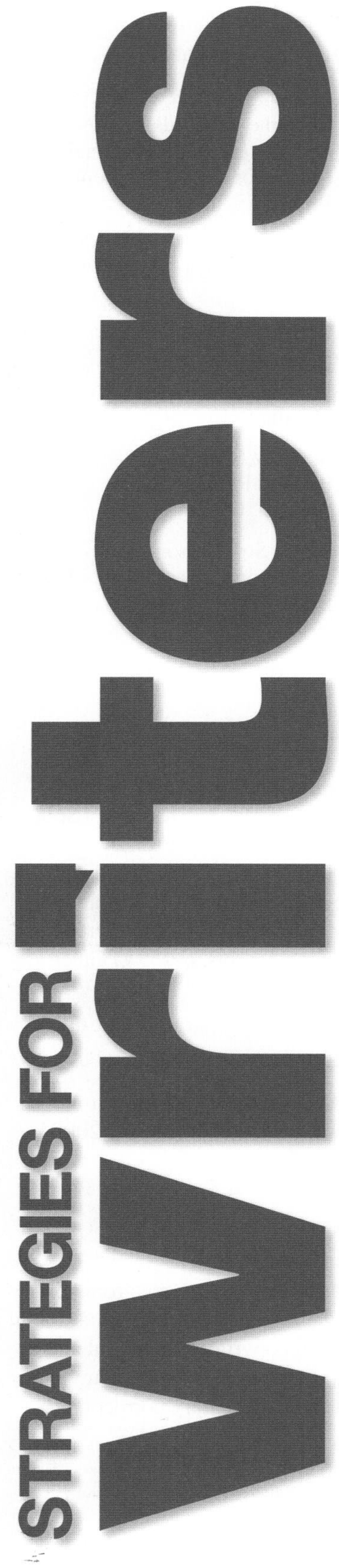

7

Senior Author

Rebecca Bowers Sipe, Ed.D.
Eastern Michigan University

Consulting Authors

Julie Coiro, Ph.D.
University of Rhode Island

Amy Humphreys, Ed.M., NBCT
Educational Consultant

Sara B. Kajder, Ph.D.
University of Pittsburgh

Mark Overmeyer, M.A.
Cherry Creek School District, Colorado

Senior Consultant

James Scott Miller

ZB Zaner-Bloser

Program Reviewers

Zaner-Bloser wishes to thank these educators who reviewed portions of this program and provided comments prior to publication.

Joe Anspaugh
Shelbyville Middle School
Shelbyville, IN

Michele Barto, Ed.D.
Fairleigh Dickinson University
Madison, NJ

Jackie Blosser
Lima City Schools
Lima, OH

Kim Bondy
South Arbor Academy
Ypsilanti, MI

Kelly Caravelli
Meadowbrook Middle School
Poway, CA

Cathy Cassy
St. Louis Public Schools
St. Louis, MO

Penny Clare
Educational Consultant
Lee, NH

Mary Dunton
Literacy Consultant
Sparks, NV

Emily Gleason
Beaverton School District
Beaverton, OR

Denise Gray, Ed.D.
Whiteriver Elementary School
Whiteriver, AZ

Laura Hall
Walton Charter Academy
Pontiac, MI

Donna Jett
Rockwood South Middle School
Fenton, MO

Christine Johnson, Ed.D.
Boonton Public Schools
Boonton, NJ

Dr. Roma Morris
Columbia School District
Columbia, MS

Rosanne Richards
Southern Nevada Regional Professional Development Program
North Las Vegas, NV

Sharlene E. Ricks
Alpine School District
American Fork, UT

Debbie Rutherford
Independent National Consultant
Omaha, NE

Melinda Springli
Lawton Public Schools
Lawton, OK

Kerry Stephenson
Pendleton County School District
Butler, KY

Photography: Cover ©McPhoto/Blickwinkel/age fotostock; Interior models, Tom Dubanowich; Stopwatch image © Royalty-Free/Corbis; p. 3 © Richard Cumins/Corbis; p. 9 © Michael St. Mauer Sheil/Corbis; pp. 28, 29 © Mystery Spot postcards; p. 133, © Phil Schermeister/Corbis; p. 191 © Free Agents Limited/Corbis; p. 213 © Lois Ellen Frank/Corbis, © Carlos Hernandez/cultura/Corbis; p. 237 © Michael Springer/Getty Images; p. 238 © Jake Wyman/Photographer's Choice/Getty Images; p. 263 © Walter Bibikow/JAI/Corbis; pp. 313, 315 © U.S. Space & Rocket Center. Space Camp® is a registered trademark of Alabama. pp. 333, 334 © Stone Mountain Park. Used with permission. All rights reserved. p. 383 © Michael DeYoung/Corbis; p. 409 © Gary W. Carter/Corbis; p. 427 © Sanford/Agliolo/Corbis; p. 455 © Galen Rowell/Corbis

Art Credits: pp. 4, 30, 52, 134, 156, 188, 264, 286, 310, 384, 406, 428 Illustrated Alaskan Moose Studio; pp. 55, 56, 57, 70, 80, 81 Charles Shaw; pp. 82, 214, 336, 456, 477 Chris Vallo; pp. 267, 444, 453, 454 Marilyn Rodgers Bahney Paselsky

Literature Credits: pp. 192–193 *The Structure That Never Sleeps* by Kim Williams © 2000 by Highlights for Children, Inc., Columbus, Ohio; p. 200–201 *What's So Hot About Spices?* by Gail Jarrow and Paul Sherman © 2000 by Highlights for Children, Inc., Columbus, Ohio

ISBN 978-0-7367-7282-2

Zaner-Bloser, Inc.
1-800-421-3018
www.zaner-bloser.com
Printed in the United States of America 12 13 14 15 19840 6 5 4 3 2

SUSTAINABLE FORESTRY INITIATIVE
Certified Chain of Custody
Promoting Sustainable Forestry
www.sfiprogram.org
SFI-00993

Hi, there! We're your *Strategies for Writers* Writing Partners!

We're here to guide you step-by-step through the stages of the writing process: Prewrite, Draft, Revise, Edit, and Publish.

In each unit, we'll focus on one mode of writing: **narrative, informative/ explanatory, argument,** or **descriptive**.

Have you ever wondered what makes a good personal narrative? Or what the elements of a cause-and-effect report are? How about some reasons for writing a summary or an observation report? We'll answer those questions and more.

We'll focus on these six traits of effective writing: **Ideas, Organization, Voice, Word Choice, Sentence Fluency,** and **Conventions**. We'll explain how to apply the traits to each genre of writing, and we'll show you how the traits work together.

In each chapter, we'll first review a model writing sample. Then we'll use a rubric to score the model. Rubrics are a great way to know exactly what is expected as you plan and evaluate your writing. After that, it's your turn to write!

Narrative writing

Table of Contents

Informative/Explanatory writing

Table of Contents

Argument writing

Table of Contents

Descriptive writing

Table of Contents

Appendices

Appendix A: Grammar Practice

Table of Contents

Appendix B: Rubrics

Narrative writing tells a story to the reader.

Hi, there! I'm Nina. I'm learning to write narratives at school, and I really think I'm going to like it. I share stories, both real and made up, with my friends and family all the time. They always tell me I should write them down, and I can't wait to get started!

IN THIS UNIT

- Personal Narrative
- E-Mail
- Historical Episode
- SCIENCE CONNECTION Play
- Writing for a Test

Name: Nina
Home: Nevada
Hobbies: reading, history, sketching buildings, traveling with Dad
Favorite Books: *Castle* and *Pyramid* by David Macaulay
Favorite Foods: tacos and fried chicken

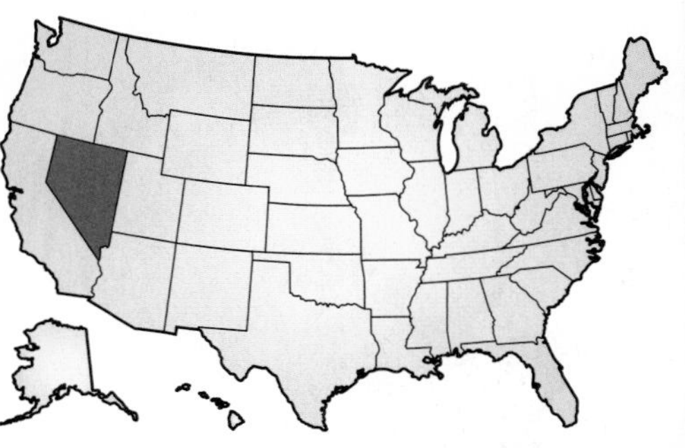

What's a Personal Narrative?

It's a true story about an event that really happened to me. I think this kind of writing is fun because I get to write about something interesting, exciting, or even sad from my own life.

What's in a Personal Narrative?

Narrator
That's me! The narrator is the person who is telling the story. I've experienced many things that I'd like to tell people. Now I'll be able to share one of my stories with an audience!

Sequence
This is the order in which things happened. I'll describe the events of my story as they happened because I want my reader to understand the big picture, from beginning to end.

Tone
Tone is how I want my story to sound and how I want my readers to feel. I can change the tone depending on what I'm writing about. It sounds tricky, but it isn't. I might use short sentence patterns to build suspense, powerful verbs to create drama, or descriptive language to create a mysterious, sad, or funny tone.

The 5 W's
These are the details that tell the **who, what, when, where,** and **why** of my story. I'll use all of these in my story, but I have to remember to keep each detail vivid and true!

Why write a Personal Narrative?

There are plenty of reasons to write a personal narrative. I listed some here. I hope they will help me as I think about what I want to write.

Entertainment

Entertaining the reader is one good reason to write a personal narrative. Sometimes something happens to me that is so funny, exciting, or sad that I just want to share it with someone else.

Personal Reflection

Writing helps me reflect, or make sense out of the things I remember. Reflecting can help me understand how I've been affected by something I've experienced.

Information

Sometimes I might experience something that would be useful for others to read about. I can write my account in order to educate, instruct, or inform my reader.

Summary

Some things I've experienced would make long and complicated stories. Often there are many smaller details that lead up to one main event, so it's important for me to summarize only the details my reader really needs to know. It's also good to practice using my summarization skills, especially since I'll use them a lot in school.

Linking Narrative Writing Traits to a Personal Narrative

In this chapter, you will write a story about an experience you want to share. This type of narrative writing is called a personal narrative. Nina will guide you through the stages of the writing process: Prewrite, Draft, Revise, Edit, and Publish. In each stage, Nina will show you important writing strategies that are linked to the Narrative Writing Traits below.

Narrative Writing Traits

- a single, focused topic with relevant, engaging details that develop the experiences or events
- a narrator or characters that bring the story to life

- well-structured and logical event sequences, often in chronological order, that guide the reader through the story
- an engaging beginning and a satisfying conclusion that reflects on the story's events
- a variety of transition words that signal time or setting changes

- a voice that is appropriate for the audience and purpose
- dialogue that, if used, is realistic and helps develop the characters and story

- precise, descriptive words and phrases

- a variety of sentences that flow and are a pleasure to read aloud

- no or few errors in grammar, usage, mechanics, and spelling

Before you write, read Melanie Van der Hoff's personal narrative on the next three pages. Then use the personal narrative rubric on pages 10–11 to decide how well she did. (You might want to look back at What's in a Personal Narrative? on page 4, too!)

A Journey Back in Time

by Melanie Van der Hoff

Narrator

The older people in our family used to talk often about World War II. The years were passing, but the men's memories of fighting to free Europe remained strong. Then the movie *Saving Private Ryan* came out in 1998, and Uncle Harry knew he had to go back to see France again. I was lucky enough to be one of the family members who went with him that year. The area that our visit would primarily focus on was the Normandy Beaches. About 150 miles to the west of Paris, these beaches were the landing spot in June 1944 for 175,000 British, American, and Canadian forces. They had crossed the English Channel from Britain in boats and planes. Their goal was to retake Europe from Nazi Germany. Uncle Harry was one of the soldiers who made the landing.

Who
What
Why
Where
When
Sequence

The journey back in time began when our plane landed in Paris. This beautiful city became the headquarters for our trip. From a small hotel in the district called the Latin Quarter, it was an easy Metro, or subway, ride to the city's main attractions. We strolled along the Seine River, stood in line for the elevators to the top of the Eiffel Tower, and saw the *Mona Lisa* at the Louvre Museum. But these sights, though impressive, were not the real reason for our trip.

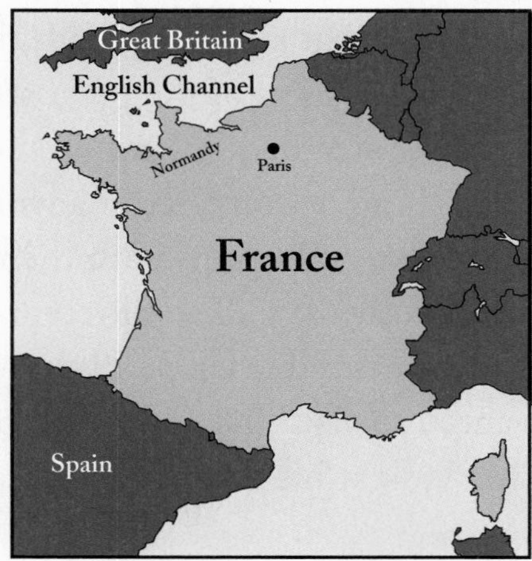

Sequence

On the fourth day, we rented a car and set out for our true destination. Meandering north through the French countryside, we saw ancient, sleepy villages as well as some with a more modern appearance. Uncle Harry explained that these newer-looking towns had probably been bombed out during the war and then rebuilt. Within a few hours, we were approaching the invasion area.

Our guidebooks and maps traced out a quiet route along the coast. From our car, we saw the remains of German artillery in two different areas. The ancient, rusting hulks, once so threatening to the Allied invaders, sat placidly in the sun. We joined the few tourists walking around one site, touching the artillery, and looking out to the sea. Uncle Harry did not want to get out of the car, though. He was saving his strength for the two things he had really come to see.

The first of these was the area called Omaha Beach. A long, open stretch of land, this was the main invasion area for the American forces. I recalled the chaotic scenes from *Saving Private Ryan,* the soldiers shouting and dying everywhere, the boats and artillery all around. What a contrast with the quiet scene on the day we visited! Few, if any, signs of the great struggle remained. There was a family camping area nearby, and on the beach lay groups of teenagers sunbathing. I wondered if anyone in their families had ever shared wartime recollections with them. Uncle Harry shook his head almost sorrowfully. "It's all so different now," he whispered.

I wondered if Uncle Harry was ready for the other site he had wanted to visit: the American cemetery overlooking Omaha Beach. One look at his determined face, though, gave us our answer.

The American cemetery is one of the most impressive sites you will ever see. More than 9,000 soldiers killed on invasion day or soon after are buried there. The white crosses, interrupted now and then by Stars of David, are lined up in rows as far as one can see. The simple birth and death dates engraved on the grave markers tell nothing of the agony those soldiers endured. And some graves are not even identified. Engraved on these headstones are the words "HERE RESTS IN HONORED GLORY A COMRADE IN ARMS KNOWN BUT TO GOD."

Tone

Uncle Harry had never given us the particulars, but we knew that several of his close buddies had died on Omaha Beach. Now we asked him if he wanted to look for any of their graves. Too choked up with emotion to speak, Uncle Harry stood at the memorial in the center of the cemetery and shook his head no. He had done his duty just by going there. And it felt as if, by accompanying him and bearing witness to what he had endured, we had done our duty, too.

Rubric

Use this 6-point rubric to plan and evaluate a personal narrative.

	6	5	4
Ideas	The narrative orients the reader to and focuses on one event. Memorable description of the 5 W's develops the experience and answers the audience's questions.	The narrative focuses on one event. Many interesting details mention the 5 W's and answer the reader's questions.	The narrative focuses on one event and is clear more often than not. Some quality details include some of the 5 W's.
Organization	Ideas are organized to unfold naturally and logically. The lead engages the reader.	Ideas are organized logically. The lead is strong.	The overall organization works. The lead is functional.
Voice	The writer makes a strong connection with the reader by using first-person point of view and a personal tone.	The writer connects with the reader by using first-person point of view and a personal tone.	The writer fails to connect with the reader in the beginning. The voice is distant or too formal.
Word Choice	Precise words and phrases convey the experience and bring the story to life.	Vivid words and phrases help the reader form mental images of the story.	Some catchy words or phrases are used. Some descriptions are vague, but the overall meaning is still clear.
Sentence Fluency	Variety in sentence length and beginnings is striking. The narrative flows smoothly.	There is noticeable variety in sentence length and beginnings. The writing has a rhythm when read out loud.	There is some variety in sentence length and beginnings. The writing is easy to read.
Conventions	Conjunctions are used correctly in compound sentences, and all sentences are complete.	Minor errors with conjunctions and sentence construction do not interfere with the meaning.	There are noticeable errors with conjunctions and sentence construction, but they don't distract the reader.
+Presentation	Visuals (photographs or illustrations) are used effectively.		

3	2	1	
The narrative is often not focused. The details are general or vague and do not answer the 5 W's.	The narrative is not clear. Broad details do little to enhance the writing.	The writing lacks details. The focus is missing.	Ideas
The organization is confusing in places. The lead is not designed to catch the reader's interest.	The organization is difficult to follow throughout. The lead may be missing or confusing.	The reader feels lost. The lead is missing.	Organization
The writer's voice is often hard to relate to. The voice is rarely personal.	There is just a hint of the writer's voice. The voice isn't a good match for the audience or purpose.	The writer's voice is absent. The reader does not know who is writing the story.	Voice
Many words are too general and don't create clear descriptions.	The writing contains very few descriptions. Descriptive words that are used are tired and unclear.	Most of the words are dull and general. The reader cannot form clear mental images. The words simply fill the page and don't speak to the reader.	Word Choice
Sentence beginnings are repetitive, and there is little variety in length.	Little variety in the sentences makes the story hard to read aloud.	The story is difficult to read even with practice. Sentences are repetitive or incomplete.	Sentence Fluency
Noticeable errors with conjunctions and sentence construction cause the reader to reread parts of the story.	Many mistakes with conjunctions and sentence construction make the writing hard to read.	Frequent, serious mistakes with conjunctions and sentence construction make the writing almost impossible to read.	Conventions

See Appendix B for 4-, 5-, and 6-point narrative rubrics.

Using the Personal Narrative Rubric to Study the Model

Did you notice that the model on pages 7–9 points out some key elements of a personal narrative? As she wrote "A Journey Back in Time," Melanie Van der Hoff used these elements to help her describe a personal experience. She also used the 6-point rubric on pages 10–11 to plan, draft, revise, and edit the writing. A rubric is a great tool to evaluate writing during the writing process.

Now let's use the same rubric to score the model. To do this, we'll focus on each trait separately, starting with Ideas. We'll use the top descriptor for each trait (column 6), along with examples from the model, to help us understand how the traits work together. How would you score Melanie on each trait?

- **The narrative orients the reader to and focuses on one event.**
- **Memorable description of the 5 W's develops the experience and answers the audience's questions.**

Melanie's narrative focuses on one event—a family trip to France. She answers many of the 5 W's in the very first paragraph, such as *who* (Uncle Henry and family), *where* (France), *what* (a trip to France), and even *why* (for Uncle Harry to revisit where he once fought in WWII).

[from the writing model]

Then the movie *Saving Private Ryan* came out in 1998, and Uncle Harry knew he had to go back to see France again. I was lucky enough to be one of the family members who went with him that year.

- **Ideas are organized to unfold naturally and logically.**
- **The lead engages the reader.**

Melanie's opening made me feel as though I was sitting around a table with her family, about to hear stories from long ago. The lead grabbed my attention and I was excited to read on. Melanie also organizes each part of her narrative in a logical order, which makes it easy to read and understand.

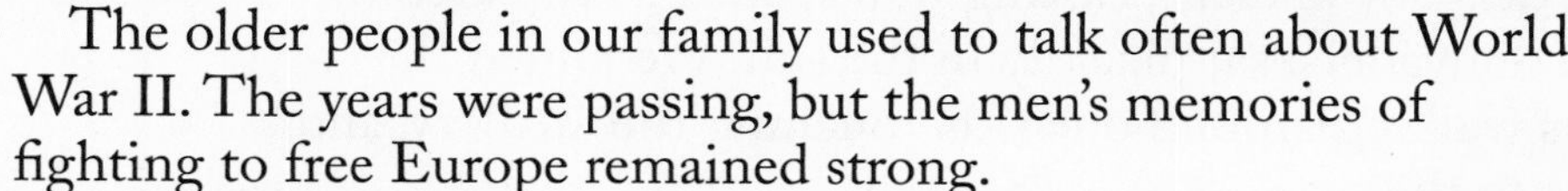

The older people in our family used to talk often about World War II. The years were passing, but the men's memories of fighting to free Europe remained strong.

- **The writer makes a strong connection with the reader by using first-person point of view and a personal tone.**

It was easy to connect with Melanie's narrative because she uses first-person point of view (*I, we*) and a personal tone. However, she keeps her voice respectful and serious, which is appropriate when considering her narrative's theme.

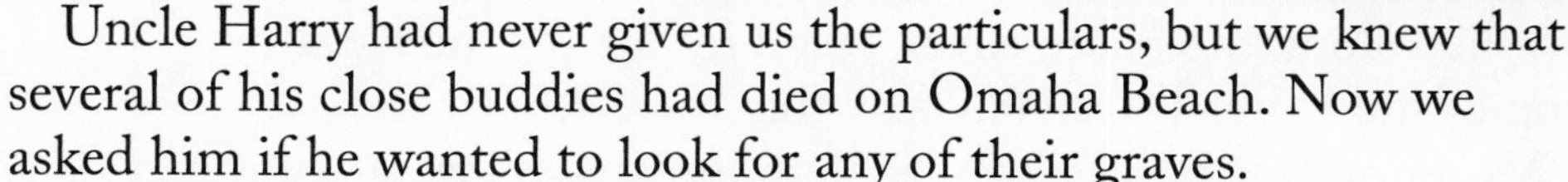

Uncle Harry had never given us the particulars, but we knew that several of his close buddies had died on Omaha Beach. Now we asked him if he wanted to look for any of their graves.

- **Precise words and phrases convey the experience and bring the story to life.**

Melanie uses so many precise and colorful descriptions of her family trip that I can picture each scene in my mind like a movie. She uses adjectives that are specific, creative, and appropriate for her subject. They make her narrative really come alive for me.

[from the writing model]

From our car, we saw the remains of German artillery in two different areas. The ancient, rusting hulks, once so threatening to the Allied invaders, sat placidly in the sun. We joined the few tourists walking around one site, touching the artillery, and looking out to the sea.

- **Variety in sentence length and beginnings is striking.**
- **The narrative flows smoothly.**

At first I wondered why Melanie's narrative flows so smoothly, why it is so easy to read and understand. But then I realized that she uses well-constructed sentences of varying lengths and with different types of beginnings, and this makes all the difference.

[from the writing model]

We strolled along the Seine River, stood in line for the elevators to the top of the Eiffel Tower, and saw the *Mona Lisa* at the Louvre Museum. But these sights, though impressive, were not the real reason for our trip.

Conventions

- **Conjunctions are used correctly in compound sentences, and all sentences are complete.**

Melanie obviously proofread her work carefully—I did not find any incomplete sentences. She also uses conjunctions such as *and* and *but* correctly in each of her compound sentences. I get distracted when reading narratives full of mistakes, so I really appreciate her hard work before publishing.

[from the writing model]

Uncle Harry had never given us the particulars, but we knew that several of his close buddies had died on Omaha Beach. Now we asked him if he wanted to look for any of their graves.

+Presentation Visuals (photographs or illustrations) are used effectively.

My Turn!

I'm going to write a personal narrative, too. Follow along to see how I use good writing strategies. I'm going to use the rubric to help me write.

Prewrite

Focus on **Ideas**

The Rubric Says The narrative orients the reader to and focuses on one event.

Writing Strategy List things the audience should know about the topic.

My dad took me to see the Mystery Spot in California. Right away, I knew I wanted to design buildings as cool as this.

When my teacher asked us to write a personal narrative, I chose the Mystery Spot. There is so much I could say, but I wanted to focus on things my audience would want and need to know. I made notes listing important points. That was my strategy. Here are my notes.

Notes About the Mystery Spot

- ✔ first visited Mystery Spot two years ago with Dad
- ✔ a couple of miles from downtown Santa Cruz, California
- ✔ Mystery Spot is on a hill, in the redwoods
- ✔ stand on 2 x 4s, smaller person looks taller (Dad and a kid)
- ✔ board sticking out of window—does the ball roll up?
- ✔ floor at 30-degree angle; pendulum easier to push one way than the other
- ✔ not really gravity—Dad got the answers
- ✔ psychologist from U. of California checked out Mystery Spot
- ✔ angles, tilts, and hill create optical illusions (define)
- ✔ loved the Mystery Spot, and loved the explanation
- ✔ made me want to be a creative builder, too

Pick an event that you want to tell others about. Gather information by making notes on what you saw.

Prewrite

Focus on **Organization**

The Rubric Says Ideas are organized to unfold naturally and logically.

Writing Strategy Make a 5 W's Chart.

Before I write, I'll fill out a 5 W's chart. With all my information organized, it will be easy to keep all the events in a logical order as I write. I want the narration to flow naturally from one idea or event to the next.

Writer's Term

5 W's Chart

A **5 W's Chart** organizes information by asking and answering the questions *What* happened? *Who* was there? *Why* did it happen? *When* did it happen? *Where* did it happen?

5 W's Chart

What happened?
- visited Mystery Spot
- stood on 2 x 4s
- smaller person looks taller; board sticking out of window
- floor at 30-degree angle; pendulum
- Mystery Spot made me want to design buildings

Who was there?
- Dad and I

Why did it happen?
- not really gravity—Dad got the answers
- psychologist from U. of Cal. checked out Mystery Spot
- angles, tilts, and hill create optical illusions (define)

When did it happen?
- first visited two years ago

Where did it happen?
- on a hill, a couple of miles outside of Santa Cruz, in the redwoods

Reflect

Why does including all of the 5 W's make a good narrative?

Apply

Organize your ideas by using your own notes to make a 5 W's Chart.

Draft

Focus on Ideas

The Rubric Says The narrative orients the reader to and focuses on one event. Memorable description of the 5 W's develops the experience and answers the audience's questions.

Writing Strategy Use the 5 W's chart to stay focused and answer the audience's questions.

I'm going to use my 5 W's Chart to write my draft. The rubric says to focus on one event, and to use memorable details to answer the 5 W's. Well, my chart is already complete, so now I'll use it as a guide while writing to keep me focused on the main topic.

I'll open my narrative by describing where I went (Santa Cruz, California) and what I did there (visited the Mystery Spot). I'll use loads of interesting and vivid details to help the reader visualize my trip. The rest of the 5 W's will be answered throughout my narrative. I'll worry about spelling and grammar later. Right now I just need to get started!

Proofreading Marks

- Indent
- Make uppercase
- Make lowercase
- Add something
- Take out something
- Add a period
- New paragraph
- Spelling error

[DRAFT]

[starts with something to think about]

[where, when, who, what]

A Visit That Inspired Me

I've heard the saying that you can't learn everything you need to know in your own backyard. I'm not sure that's exactly true. I do think you can lern a lot of things on trips to interesting places, though. When I first visited the Mystery Spot two years ago with my dad, we were traveling to California. I learned two important things. One is that buildings can be designed in very interesting ways. The other is that I might want to desing some interesting buildings myself.

The Mystery Spot is just a few miles from downtown Santa Cruz, in the middle of some redwoods. Dad and I had noticed it on our way into the city. Then the desk clerk at our motel told us that we should stop there, that it was really worth seeing. So the next day we decided to make a special trip to the Spot. The signs along the road made it easy to find the place.

Reflect

What do you think? Do the introductory details grab and hold your interest?

Apply

Write a draft using interesting details from your 5 W's Chart to grab your audience's attention.

Revise

Focus on Organization

The Rubric Says Ideas are organized to unfold naturally and logically.

Writing Strategy Reorder sentences that seem out of place.

I thought the sentences in my narrative were organized well when I read it over. They take the reader through the story in a logical order. However, in the paragraph about the ball rolling up the board, I can see that if I change the order of the sentences just a little, this scene would make a lot more sense.

[DRAFT]

The area where things began to get really bazaar was the cabin. This structure looked old and wore down. Filled with surprises. When we walked up to the cabin, ~~the guide rolled a ball down the long board~~. We saw a long board sticking out a front window. It was pretty obvious that the end sticking out was higher than the end resting inside. Then the guide rolled a ball down the board. The ball went a little way it stopped and rolled right back up! What was going on here?

[reordered sentences]

Apply

Are your sentences in a logical order? If not, rearrange them to make sure they make sense to the audience.

Revise

Focus on 

The Rubric Says The writer makes a strong connection with the reader by using first-person point of view and a personal tone.

Writing Strategy Use personal pronouns (*I*, *me*) to connect with the readers.

My job as a narrator is to help my reader fully connect with and understand my story. I use first-person pronouns throughout my narrative, but I did find an area where my voice is a bit too formal. I will make some revisions now to create a more casual tone.

[DRAFT]

[used casual tone]

The Mystery Spot is a pretty small area, only about 150 feet in diameter. You have to climb a hill to reach it, and the tour guides promise that ~~puzzling events~~ strange things will start happening the minute you step into it. These guides are not ~~misleading~~ lying.

Reflect

What do you think about Nina's revisions? Is her tone more casual and easier to connect with now?

Apply

Use first person and a casual tone to connect with the reader.

Revise

Focus on **Word Choice**

The Rubric Says Precise words and phrases convey the experience and bring the story to life.

Writing Strategy Choose precise and interesting words and phrases for effect.

I want my reader to feel as excited as I felt when I visited the Mystery Spot. But some sections of my draft are boring. I'll add some precise and interesting words to liven things up, just as the rubric says.

[DRAFT]

[added specific phrases] → from work

A few days later, Dad come home ^from work^ with some answers. One of his coworkers told him that a psychologist from the University of California had checked out the place. He discovered that all the strange things we had experienced are based on optical illusions ^, or sights that appear different from what they really are^. Remember that the Mystery Spot was built on a hill. That, along with the ^crazy^ angles and ^tilted^ walls, confuses people into thinking things is not level—when they actually are.

[added interesting words]

Apply

Add specific and interesting words to your draft to bring your story to life.

Edit

Focus on **Conventions**

The Rubric Says Conjunctions are used correctly in compound sentences, and all sentences are complete.

Writing Strategy Make sure all sentences are complete.

Writer's Term

Sentence Fragment

A **sentence fragment** is a group of words that begins with a capital letter and ends with a period or other end punctuation but does not state a complete thought.

Writer's Term

Run-on Sentence

A **run-on sentence** is two simple sentences that are run together and not joined correctly.

I'm almost done! Now I just have to check my spelling, punctuation, and capitalization. The rubric says all sentences should be complete, and conjunctions should be used properly. I'll keep my eyes open for these things, too.

[DRAFT]

[corrected sentence fragment]

The area where things began to get really ~~bazaar~~ bizarre was the cabin. This structure looked old and wore[n] down, but it was ~~. F~~filled with surprises.

Reflect

What do you think? How did Nina do with her grammar, spelling, and punctuation? Can you find any incomplete sentences?

Apply

Conventions

Your turn! Check your draft for spelling, punctuation, and capitalization. Make sure all sentences are complete and conjunctions are used properly.

For more practice fixing incomplete sentences and using conjunctions correctly, use the exercises on the next two pages.

Sentence Fragments, Run-ons, and Comma Splices

Know the Rule

Correct a **sentence fragment** in one of these ways:

- Add a subject, a predicate, or both.
  Example: Dad and I made a visit to the Mystery Spot.
- Attach the fragment to a related sentence.
  Example: Dad and I planned a special trip, a visit to the Mystery Spot.

Correct a **run-on sentence** or a **comma splice** (when two independent clauses are joined by only a comma) in one of these ways:

- Combine the sentences with both a comma and a conjunction such as *and, but, or,* or *for.*
  Example: I loved the Mystery Spot**, and** I wanted to go back soon.
- Combine the sentences with a semicolon.
  Example: I loved the Mystery Spot**;** I wanted to go back soon.
- Write two separate sentences.
  Example: I loved the Mystery Spot**.** I wanted to go back soon.

Practice the Rule

Number a sheet of paper from 1–10. Write **F** for each sentence fragment. Write **RO** for each run-on sentence. Write **CS** for each comma splice. For each fragment, write **S** if the subject is missing or **P** if the predicate is missing.

1. Architecture, a topic of interest to many people.
2. Very high structures particularly interesting.
3. The very earliest skyscrapers in the 1880s.
4. City real estate was very expensive, it was cheaper to build up than to build out.
5. Some call Chicago the home of the skyscraper others say New York.
6. Famous skyscrapers in both Chicago and New York.
7. The Sears Tower in Chicago has a new name it is called the Willis Tower.
8. The Empire State Building has 102 stories the Willis Tower has 110 stories.
9. The invention of elevators meant that buildings could become taller, taller buildings were built.
10. The tallest building in the world.

Coordinating Conjunctions

Know the Rule

Coordinating conjunctions (*and, but, or*) connect words or groups of words (including independent clauses) that are closely related. They can be used to fix run-on sentences, sentence fragments, and comma splices.

Example: This morning I made strawberry pancakes, **and** then I went for a long walk.

Example: Father told us we could go to the movies, **but** there are no movies playing that we would like to see.

Practice the Rule

Read each incomplete sentence below. Then on a separate piece of paper, rewrite each one using the correct coordinating conjunction.

1. It doesn't matter if your favorite music is classical, ______ if you prefer listening to hip hop.
2. It's a simple, everyday thing, ______ music has the power to stir your imagination.
3. For example, listen closely to this piano music, ______ then tell me what you envision in your mind.
4. The music might sound to you like a storm approaching, ______ it might sound like the raging ocean crashing against barren cliffs.
5. One hundred people might all envision one hundred different scenes, ______ remember, there are no wrong answers in this kind of an exercise.
6. I like to listen to music when I work, ______ some people find music too distracting.
7. They start paying too much attention to the music, ______ then their imagination takes over.
8. They get lost in the images in their mind, ______ they lose track of their work.
9. Music is as old as humankind, ______ it constantly renews itself with each generation.
10. Some people don't believe it, ______ having music in your life is beneficial in many ways.

Publish

+Presentation

Publishing Strategy Publish the narrative in a class diary.

Presentation Strategy Use photographs or illustrations to help tell the story.

That was fun to write, and it will be even more fun to share. I think I'll publish my personal narrative in our class diary so my classmates can share in the mystery of the Mystery Spot. I'll use some photographs from my trip to give even more details of my adventure. I'll be sure to place the photos near the appropriate text to avoid confusion. I'll be sure my work is neat and readable, whether I write it by hand or use a computer. I'll also need to read it one last time to make sure it includes all the items on my checklist.

My Final Checklist

Did I—

- ✔ fix any incomplete sentences?
- ✔ correctly use coordinating conjunctions?
- ✔ use helpful and properly placed photographs or illustrations?
- ✔ neatly handwrite or type my paper?
- ✔ put my name on each page of my narrative?

Apply

Make a checklist to check your personal narrative. Then make a final draft to publish.

A VISIT THAT INSPIRED ME

by Nina

I've heard the saying that you can't learn everything you need to know in your own backyard. I'm not sure that's exactly true. I do think you can learn a lot of things on trips to interesting places, though. When I first visited the Mystery Spot two years ago with my dad, we were traveling in California. I learned two important things. One is that buildings can be designed in very interesting ways. The other is that I might want to design some interesting buildings myself.

The Mystery Spot is just a few miles from downtown Santa Cruz, in the middle of some redwoods. Dad and I had noticed it on our way into the city. Then the desk clerk at our motel told us that we should stop there, that it was really worth seeing. So the next day we decided to make a special trip to the Spot. The signs along the road made it easy to find the place.

The Mystery Spot is a pretty small area, only about 150 feet in diameter. You have to climb a hill to reach it, and the tour guides promise that strange things will start happening the minute you step into it. These guides are not lying. For example, one of the first things you see is 2 × 4s that stretch across two pieces of concrete. Our guide asked for volunteers to stand at each end of a 2 × 4. My dad and a kid several inches shorter volunteered, and then they traded places. It looked like the kid was taller than my dad! I could tell right away that I was going to like this place.

The area where things began to get really bizarre was the cabin. This structure looked old and worn down, but it was filled with surprises.

When we walked up to the cabin, we saw a long board sticking out a front window. It was pretty obvious that the end sticking out was higher than the end resting inside. Then the guide rolled a ball down the board. The ball went a little way, but it stopped and rolled right back up! What was going on here? Could it be that the laws of gravity didn't work in this place?

The inside of the cabin was just as strange. The floor seemed to be pitched at about a 30-degree angle, and it was very hard to walk there. People seemed as if they were tilted in all directions and could fall over at any minute, and a few people held on to the railings because they were feeling dizzy. Another weird thing was the pendulum, which hung from the ceiling. You could push it in both directions, but it was much easier to push it to one side of the cabin than to the other.

I was finding the Mystery Spot totally fascinating, but I was also wondering what was going on. Our guide kept talking about strange gravitational forces, but my logical mind was telling me that this didn't quite make sense.

A few days later, Dad came home from work with some answers. One of his coworkers told him that a psychologist from the University of California had checked out the place. He discovered that all the strange things we had experienced are based on optical illusions, or sights that appear different from what they really are. Remember that the Mystery Spot was built on a hill. That, along with the crazy angles and tilted walls, confuses people into thinking things are not level—when they actually are.

I loved the Mystery Spot. After I heard this explanation, I loved it even more. It showed me that people could design houses or other buildings to create all sorts of impressions. They aren't exactly optical illusions, but there must be ways to make small rooms seem bigger and tall buildings seem even higher. I thought about some of the drawings I've done in industrial arts class. Maybe I could learn to combine my ideas into plans for some really neat buildings.

Reflect

What do you think? Did Nina use all the traits of a good personal narrative? Check her writing against the rubric. Then use the rubric to check the personal narrative you wrote!

What's an E-Mail?

It's an electronic message I send to someone I know. I like to send e-mail because I can just click the send button and the message is delivered right away!

What's in an E-Mail?

Sender
I'm the sender, the person who is writing the message. Instead of talking to someone on the phone, I can write an e-mail they can read when they're ready!

"E-Mail Etiquette"
E-mail etiquette is using the most polite, most accepted, or clearest way to write an e-mail. For example, I include a subject line and make sure my spelling and grammar are correct—even in a friendly e-mail.

Tone
I use a friendly and lively tone when I'm writing an e-mail. That doesn't mean I get sloppy! Nor does it mean that I'm not serious. After a friendly greeting, I get right to the point, and I avoid using slang words.

Organization
I make sure to use multiple paragraphs in my e-mail, and I give information in an order that makes sense. E-mail is a quick, friendly way to share information, but if it's not in any kind of order, the person who receives it will have no idea what I'm talking about!

Why write an E-Mail?

There are lots of reasons to write an e-mail. Here are some of the most common reasons. I have sent e-mail for all of them.

Give Information

Sometimes an e-mail is the best way to give information. I can send an e-mail to educate, instruct, or inform my reader.

Stay in Touch

Sometimes I write e-mails to let people know how and what I'm doing. I send e-mails to friends, family members, and even to my teacher, who always writes back.

Make Plans

Often e-mails are used to set up social events and meetings. For example, our band director can send e-mails to every member of the marching band if he needs to change practice times. He can e-mail all of us at once! I like to send e-mail invitations to weekend sleepovers. I can invite six friends by pressing just one button!

Linking Narrative Writing Traits to an E-Mail

In this chapter, you will send a message electronically. This type of writing is called an e-mail. Nina will guide you through the stages of the writing process: Prewrite, Draft, Revise, Edit, and Publish. In each stage, Nina will show you important writing strategies that are linked to the Narrative Writing Traits below.

Narrative Writing Traits

	• a single, focused topic with relevant, engaging details that develop the experiences or events • a narrator or characters that bring the story to life
	• well-structured and logical event sequences, often in chronological order, that guide the reader through the story • an engaging beginning and a satisfying conclusion that reflects on the story's events • a variety of transition words that signal time or setting changes
	• a voice that is appropriate for the audience and purpose • dialogue that, if used, is realistic and helps develop the characters and story
	• precise, descriptive words and phrases
	• a variety of sentences that flow and are a pleasure to read aloud
	• no or few errors in grammar, usage, mechanics, and spelling

Before you write, read Mary Kubik's e-mail on the next page. Then use the e-mail rubric on pages 34–35 to decide how well she did. (You might want to look back at What's in an E-Mail? on page 30, too!)

E-Mail Model

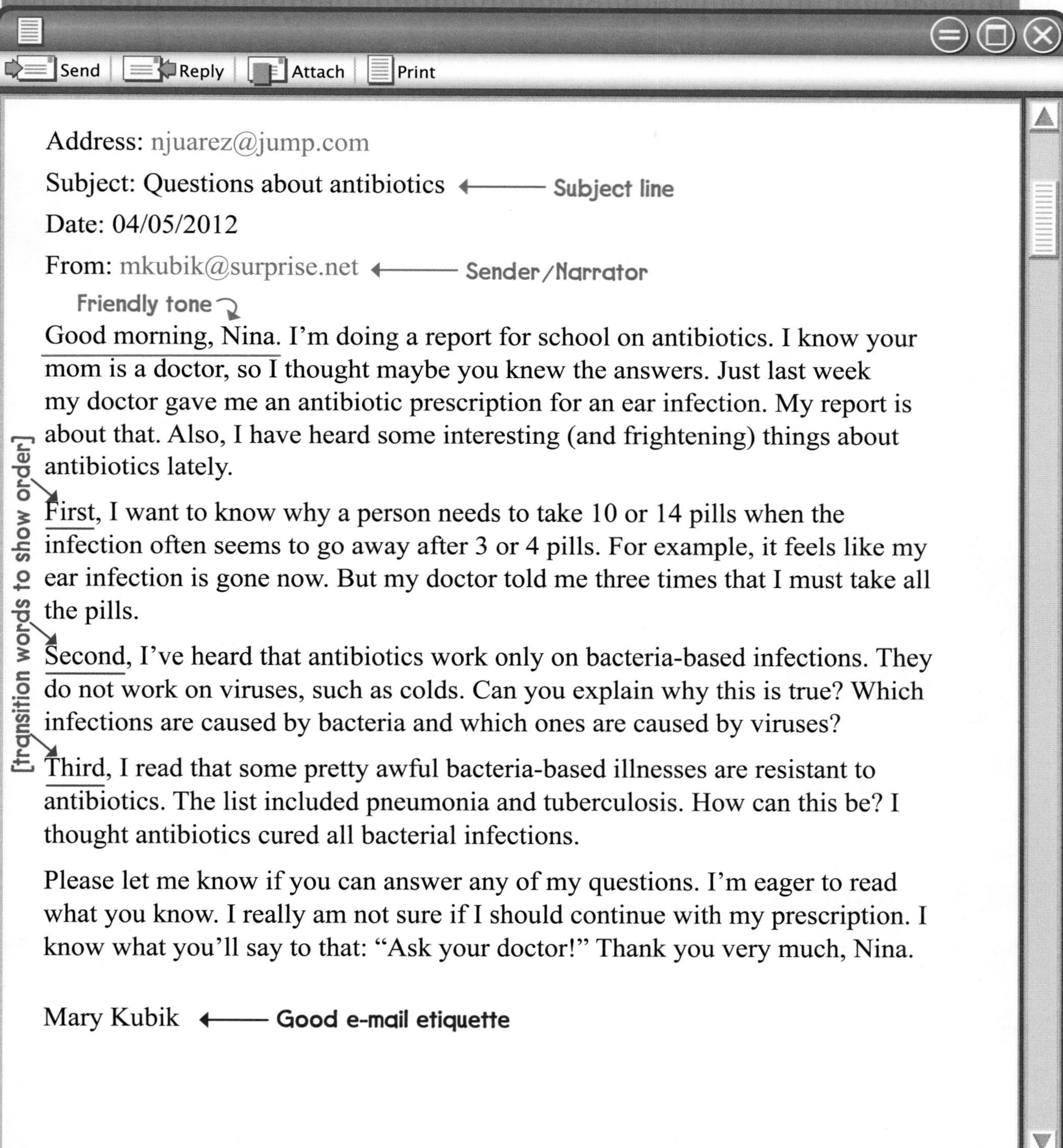

Send | Reply | Attach | Print

Address: njuarez@jump.com

Subject: Questions about antibiotics

Date: 04/05/2012

From: mkubik@surprise.net

Good morning, Nina. I'm doing a report for school on antibiotics. I know your mom is a doctor, so I thought maybe you knew the answers. Just last week my doctor gave me an antibiotic prescription for an ear infection. My report is about that. Also, I have heard some interesting (and frightening) things about antibiotics lately.

First, I want to know why a person needs to take 10 or 14 pills when the infection often seems to go away after 3 or 4 pills. For example, it feels like my ear infection is gone now. But my doctor told me three times that I must take all the pills.

Second, I've heard that antibiotics work only on bacteria-based infections. They do not work on viruses, such as colds. Can you explain why this is true? Which infections are caused by bacteria and which ones are caused by viruses?

Third, I read that some pretty awful bacteria-based illnesses are resistant to antibiotics. The list included pneumonia and tuberculosis. How can this be? I thought antibiotics cured all bacterial infections.

Please let me know if you can answer any of my questions. I'm eager to read what you know. I really am not sure if I should continue with my prescription. I know what you'll say to that: "Ask your doctor!" Thank you very much, Nina.

Mary Kubik

Rubric

Use this 6-point rubric to plan and evaluate an e-mail.

	6	5	4
Ideas	The writer's main idea is clear and focused. The details are relevant and striking.	The main idea is clear. The details are relevant and clear.	The main idea is clear. Some of the details are interesting, but a few may be irrelevant.
Organization	Details are presented in an order that makes sense. A variety of transitions smoothly connect the details and guide the reader.	Details are presented in a logical order. Transitions connect details and guide the reader.	The organization of details makes the writing easy to follow. Transitions are present.
Voice	The writer's voice enhances the writing and connects with the reader. The tone is respectful and friendly.	The writer's voice connects with the reader most of the time. It may sound too informal in places.	The writer's voice sounds too casual. Exclamations and words in capital letters "scream" at the reader.
Word Choice	The writing is precise and free of informal or slang words.	The writing is precise in most places and does not use slang. One or two informal words may be present.	Some vague or general words are used. Some overly informal or slang words are used.
Sentence Fluency	All sentences are complete and correct. They flow well and are enjoyable to read.	There may be a sentence fragment or run-on sentence. The writing flows well.	Some sentence fragments or other problems are present. They are distracting in places.
Conventions	All verb tenses are correct. The writing is easy to understand.	The writing contains a few verb tense errors, but the reader must hunt for them.	Verb tense errors are noticeable but don't confuse the reader.

+Presentation The e-mail is accurately typed and has extra space between paragraphs.

3	2	1	
The main idea is somewhat clear. The details are very general.	The main idea is unclear. Details are sketchy.	The writing is too sketchy to have a main idea.	Ideas
Many details are out of order. Transitions may or may not be present.	The writing is hard to follow because there is no logical order. Transitions are unclear or missing.	The writing is confusing. Transitions are missing.	Organization
The writer's voice lacks character and fades in and out.	The writer's voice is difficult to find at times. The voice may not be a good match for the audience or purpose.	The writer's voice is missing.	Voice
The language is unclear and/or too informal in many places. Some slang words are used.	Most of the language is vague, unclear, and too informal, and many slang expressions are used.	The language is so vague that it's hard to follow; the tone is too informal and filled with slang.	Word Choice
Several sentence fragments, run-ons, or other problems are confusing for the reader at times.	Many sentence fragments, run-ons, and other problems make the writing difficult to read.	So many sentences are incorrect that the writing is nearly impossible to understand.	Sentence Fluency
Noticeable errors in verb tense confuse the reader.	The writing contains many errors in verb tenses and is difficult to read.	The writing is filled with serious errors in verb tenses that impede reading.	Conventions

See Appendix B for 4-, 5-, and 6-point narrative rubrics.

Using the E-Mail Rubric to Study the Model

Did you notice that the model on page 33 points out some key elements of an e-mail? As she wrote her e-mail, Mary Kubik used these elements to help her. She also used the 6-point rubric on pages 34–35 to plan, draft, revise, and edit the writing. A rubric is a great tool to evaluate writing during the writing process.

Now let's use the same rubric to score the model. To do this, we'll focus on each trait separately, starting with Ideas. We'll use the top descriptor for each trait (column 6), along with examples from the model, to help us understand how the traits work together. How would you score Mary on each trait?

- **The writer's main idea is clear and focused.**
- **The details are relevant and striking.**

I like how Mary gets right to the point. She states her purpose almost immediately, and then provides helpful, relevant supporting details to explain further.

[from the writing model]

Good morning, Nina. I'm doing a report for school on antibiotics. I know your mom is a doctor, so I thought maybe you knew the answers. Just last week my doctor gave me an antibiotic prescription for an ear infection. My report is about that. Also, I have heard some interesting (and frightening) things about antibiotics lately.

- **Details are presented in an order that makes sense for the topic.**
- **A variety of transitions smoothly connect the details and guide the reader.**

Mary asks several questions, but because she uses transition words (such as *first*, *second*, and *third*), I was able to follow along without feeling lost. The order of the questions makes sense to me and helps me follow details about a topic I don't know much about.

[from the writing model] 

First, I want to know why a person needs to take 10 or 14 pills when the infection often seems to go away after 3 or 4 pills. For example, it feels like my ear infection is gone now.

- **The writer's voice enhances the writing and connects with the reader.**
- **The tone is respectful and friendly.**

Mary's voice is serious, which suits her topic, yet friendly and respectful. She uses words like *please* and *thank you*, which everyone loves to hear. Who wouldn't want to respond when asked like that?

[from the writing model] 

Please let me know if you can answer any of my questions. I'm eager to read what you know. I really am not sure if I should continue with my prescription. I know what you'll say to that: "Ask your doctor!" Thank you very much, Nina.

- **The writing is precise and free of informal or slang words.**

Mary uses words accurately. She doesn't waste time with slang or informal speech, which only weakens her purpose and distances the reader. Reading her e-mail was fun, and responding will be, too!

[from the writing model]

Second, I've heard that antibiotics work only on bacteria-based infections. They do not work on viruses, such as colds. Can you explain why this is true? Which infections are caused by bacteria and which ones are caused by viruses?

- **All sentences are complete and correct.**
- **They flow well and are enjoyable to read.**

Mary uses sentences that are complete and properly constructed. She uses both short and long sentences, which helps her writing flow naturally. I enjoyed reading her e-mail.

[from the writing model]

Third, I read that some pretty awful bacteria-based illnesses are resistant to antibiotics. The list included pneumonia and tuberculosis. How can this be?

- All verb tenses are correct.
- The writing is easy to understand.

Mary's spelling is great—and so is her punctuation and grammar. I couldn't find any errors in her e-mail! She also uses past and past participle verb forms correctly.

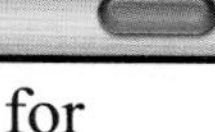

[from the writing model]

Just last week my doctor gave me an antibiotic prescription for an ear infection. . . . Also, I have heard some interesting (and frightening) things about antibiotics lately.

+Presentation The e-mail is accurately typed and has extra space between paragraphs.

My Turn!

I'm going to write an e-mail about something I want to know more about. I'm going to use the rubric and good writing strategies. Read on to see what I do!

Prewrite

Focus on **Ideas**

The Rubric Says **The writer's main idea is clear and focused. The details are relevant and striking.**

Writing Strategy **List the main idea or purpose for writing. Then list relevant details that support it.**

Hmmm...who am I going to send an e-mail to? And what will I write about? I know! I've been wondering why people from different places use different words for things, even when they all speak English. That will be my main idea. I'll e-mail my fourth grade teacher, Ms. Jackson. She knows a lot about words and languages. But first I'll list all of the important supporting details to make sure my purpose is crystal clear.

E-Mail Assignment

Main Idea: People from different places speak different dialects of English.

Details:

- ✔ new kids at school from different places use unfamiliar words
- ✔ Abby is from the South
- ✔ Jill is from Maine
- ✔ where did *wicked* come from
- ✔ also, *tote* and *I'm fixing to*
- ✔ announcers on TV sound perfect—why?
- ✔ English is not the same everywhere, I guess
- ✔ send to Ms. Jackson, my fourth-grade teacher
- ✔ get Ms. Jackson's e-mail address from home

Apply

Write down the main idea for an e-mail you want to write. Then make a list of details to cover in the e-mail.

Prewrite

Focus on **Organization**

The Rubric Says Details are presented in an order that makes sense for the topic.

Writing Strategy Make a Main Idea Table.

Writer's Term

Main Idea Table

A **Main Idea Table** shows how a main idea is supported by details.

OK, I've got my main idea and lots of supporting details. Now I need to organize those details in a way that makes the most sense for my purpose. I'll use a Main Idea Table. This will help me organize my information into good paragraphs, too.

MAIN IDEA TABLE

Main Idea: People from different places speak different dialects of English.

Supporting Detail	Supporting Detail	Supporting Detail	Supporting Detail	Supporting Detail
Dialect is words and phrases that are used in specific places.	Jill from Maine says, "Those pancakes were wicked good."	Abby from the South says, "I'm fixing to" and "tote."	Evening starts right after lunch.	TV announcers don't even have accents.

Reflect

Did Nina organize her details well? Do her details support her main idea?

Apply

Make a Main Idea Table to organize your supporting details.

Draft

Focus on **Organization**

The Rubric Says Details are presented in an order that makes sense for the topic. A variety of transitions smoothly connect the details and guide the reader.

Writing Strategy Use transition words to help your reader follow along.

Writer's Term

E-Mail Etiquette

E-mail etiquette is the polite or accepted way to write an e-mail message. For good e-mail etiquette, do the following:

1. Write a clear subject line.
2. Include a salutation.
3. Do not use emoticons (such as ☺ or ☹) unless you are writing to a really good friend.
4. Do not use all capital letters.

Well, it's time to start writing. I need to present my questions and details the right way, or things might get confusing. The rubric says to present the details in a logical way, and to use a variety of transitions to guide the reader. If I write, "I have several questions about dialect," then Ms. Jackson will know to expect more than one question. Then phrases like *First of all* and *My second question is* will help her follow along. Transitions help the reader move from paragraph to paragraph without feeling lost.

E-mail etiquette is also very important. Ms. Jackson was my teacher, but she is not a friend my own age. I won't use emoticons and abbreviations in this e-mail; that would seem disrespectful, and she wouldn't take my questions seriously. I'll write my draft first and then worry about grammar and spelling later.

Proofreading Marks

- Indent
- Make uppercase
- Make lowercase
- Add something
- Take out something
- Add a period
- New paragraph
- Spelling error

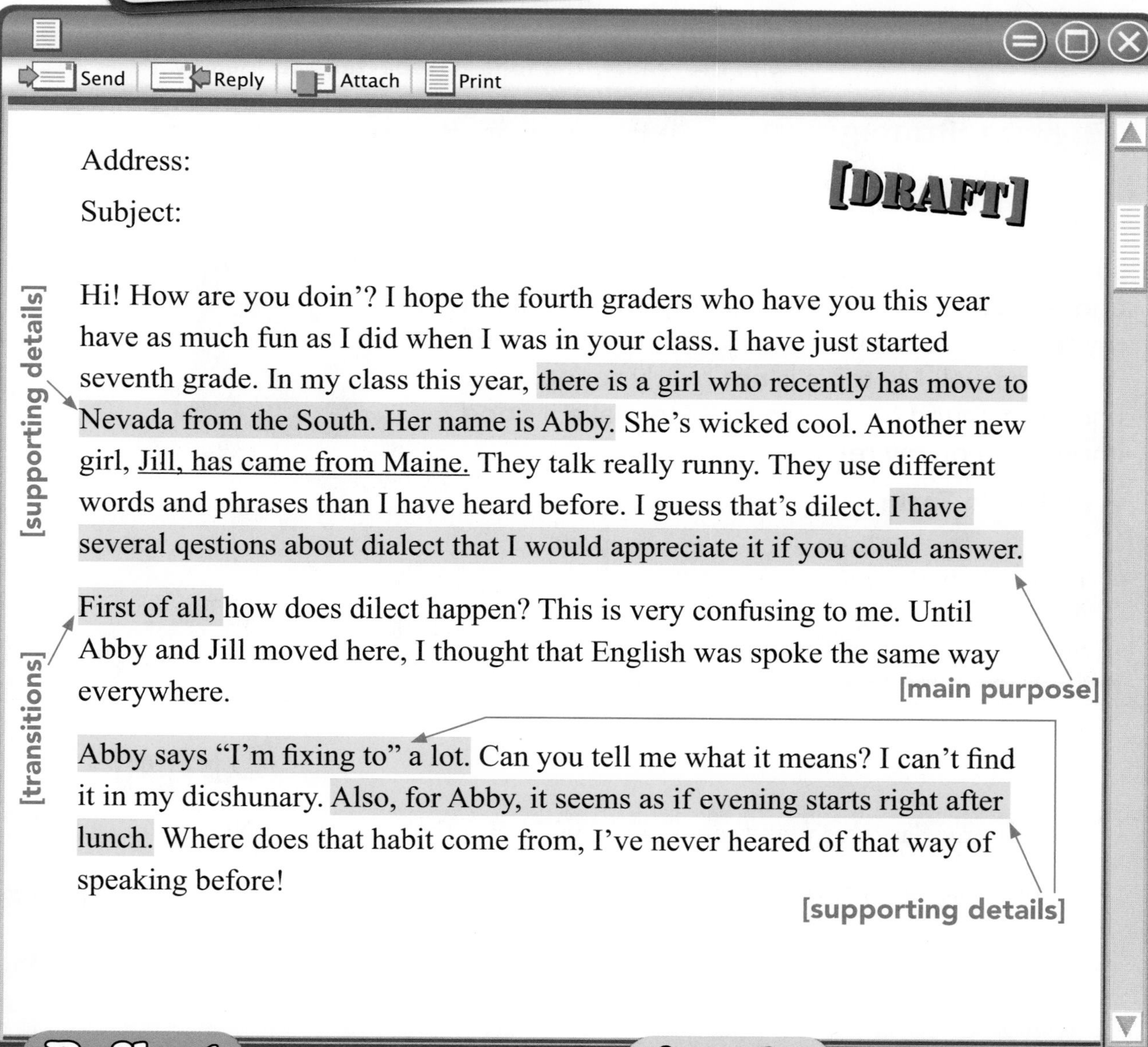
Send Reply Attach Print

Address:

Subject:

[DRAFT]

Hi! How are you doin'? I hope the fourth graders who have you this year have as much fun as I did when I was in your class. I have just started seventh grade. In my class this year, there is a girl who recently has move to Nevada from the South. Her name is Abby. She's wicked cool. Another new girl, Jill, has came from Maine. They talk really runny. They use different words and phrases than I have heard before. I guess that's dilect. I have several qestions about dialect that I would appreciate it if you could answer.

First of all, how does dilect happen? This is very confusing to me. Until Abby and Jill moved here, I thought that English was spoke the same way everywhere.

Abby says "I'm fixing to" a lot. Can you tell me what it means? I can't find it in my dicshunary. Also, for Abby, it seems as if evening starts right after lunch. Where does that habit come from, I've never heared of that way of speaking before!

Reflect

Has Nina explained her main purpose clearly? Are her details in a logical order?

Apply

List your details in a logical order and connect them with a variety of transitions.

Revise

Focus on 

The Rubric Says The writer's voice enhances the writing and connects with the reader. The tone is respectful and friendly.

Writing Strategy Make sure the tone is appropriate for the topic and reader.

Now for some revision. The rubric says my voice should enhance the writing, connect with the reader, and remain respectful and friendly. Ms. Jackson was my teacher, not a close friend. I think my tone might be too casual. My topic is not overly serious, but I need to sound more respectful to make a good impression on my reader.

Writer's Term

Tone

Tone is how the writing sounds. A writer's tone can be serious, funny, sarcastic, or objective.

In my class this year, there is a girl who recently has move to Nevada from the South. Her name is Abby. ~~She's wicked cool.~~

[kept appropriate tone]

Apply

Keep your voice friendly, but appropriate for your topic and intended reader.

Revise

Focus on **Word Choice**

The Rubric Says The writing is precise and free of informal or slang words.

Writing Strategy Avoid the use of slang.

Writer's Term

Spell Check

Spell check is a function on your computer. It checks the spelling of every word in the document. Be careful, though, because sometimes it suggests words different from the one you're trying to write. If you can't tell which way is correct, look the word up in a dictionary.

I'm going to look at the rubric again. I see that I need to make sure I didn't use any informal or slang words. I can see some spelling errors already. I will fix those right away. Do you see any slang or informal words? Check out my draft and see if I caught the same things you did.

[replaced slang]

~~Hi! How are you doin'?~~ Hello, Ms. Jackson. I hope the fourth graders who have you this year have as much fun as I did when I was in your class. I have just started seventh grade. In my class this year, there is a girl who recently has move to Nevada from the South. Her name is Abby. ~~She's wicked cool.~~

Reflect

Is Nina's draft better now? Did she get rid of slang? Do you think Ms. Jackson will enjoy reading Nina's e-mail?

Apply

Check your draft for slang. Then fix all the spelling errors you can find. Spell check really helps with that.

Revise

Focus on 

The Rubric Says All sentences are complete and correct. They flow well and are enjoyable to read.

Writing Strategy Check every sentence.

To make sure my writing flows smoothly, I'll check that each sentence is complete and accurate. I'll also make sure I've followed proper e-mail etiquette. For instance, I see some SHOUTING. I'll also delete all emoticons, which are just for casual e-mails to friends.

[DRAFT]

[fixed sentence fragment]

I've also noticed that announcers on TV don't talk like Southerners. , People from Maine, ~~OR~~ or people from Nevada. Why does their speech sound so perfect?

[took out SHOUTING] [delete emoticons]

I'm beginning to think that English is ~~VERY~~ very complicated. ~~☺~~ Please answer ~~me~~ my e-mail and help me figure it out.

Nina Juarez [inserted full name]

Apply

Fix any incomplete sentences.
Be sure to use good e-mail etiquette.

Edit

The Rubric Says All verb tenses are correct. The writing is easy to understand.

Writing Strategy Check for and fix any incorrect shifts in verb tense.

Writer's Term

Past and Past Participle Forms of Verbs

The **past tense form of a verb** tells about something that happened in the past. The past tense form does not have a helping verb. The **past participle form of a verb** needs a helping verb, such as *have, has, had, is,* or *was*. Many verbs, called irregular verbs, have different past and past participle forms.

The last step is to proofread my e-mail to check my grammar, spelling, and punctuation. The rubric also says to make sure all verb tenses are correct. I will carefully proofread my e-mail one last time.

[DRAFT]

First of all, how does dialect happen? When Jill says things to people like "Those pancakes were wicked good," they have no idea what she means. And there are things I say that Jill has never ~~heared~~ heard before. This is very confusing to me. Until Abby and Jill moved here, I thought that English was spoken the same way everywhere.

[corrected past participle form of verb]

Reflect

Did Nina catch all her errors in punctuation and grammar? How did she do with her verb forms?

Apply

Conventions

Review your draft for punctuation, grammar, and spelling errors. Check that all verb tenses are used correctly.

For more practice with past, past participle, and perfect verb forms, see the next two pages.

Past and Past Participle Verb Forms

Know the Rule

A past tense verb tells about an action that happened in the past. The past participle tells about an action that was completed in the past but may have continued over a period of time.

Past tense form of a verb: I **gave** my teacher a printout from the dialect website.

Past participle form of a verb: She **has given** me a lot of support for my dialect project.

Incorrect: She **has gave** me a lot of support for my dialect project.

This table gives the **present, past**, and **past participle forms** of a few common verbs. If you are not sure of the correct form of a verb, check a dictionary.

Forms of Verbs

Present	Past	Past Participle
go	went	(has, have) gone
write	wrote	(has, have) written
speak	spoke	(has, have) spoken

Practice the Rule

Read each sentence. If the verb is incorrect, rewrite the verb correctly on a separate sheet of paper. If the verb is correct, write **Correct**.

1. English is spoke different ways in different countries.
2. My pen pal in Britain may have wrote you a letter about his family's car.
3. He may have chosen to use some words that are unfamiliar to you.
4. He wrote that the boot had been damaged in an accident.
5. Would you have knew which part of the car was the boot?
6. Then he wrote that he have visited his aunt in her flat.
7. Who knew that a flat is an apartment?
8. I has spoken with my pen pal on the phone only once.
9. He has promised to make a list of fun British dialect for me to learn.
10. I have agree to do the same for him and include it in my next letter.

The Perfect Tenses

Know the Rule

The **present perfect tense** (*have eaten*) shows action that started in the past and was recently completed or is still happening. The **past perfect tense** (*had eaten*) shows action that was completed by a certain time in the past. The **future perfect tense** (*will have eaten*) shows action that will be complete by a certain time in the future. To form **perfect tenses,** use a form of *have* with the **past participle** of a verb.

Practice the Rule

Read each sentence. If the verb is incorrect, rewrite the verb correctly on a separate sheet of paper. If the verb is correct, write **Correct**.

1. I had wrote to my cousin, Tess, several times over the school year about our upcoming summer vacation together.
2. Tess had responded within an hour each and every time!
3. These days, I am so busy with the holidays, I have forgotten to stay in touch.
4. But just now, I have sended a long e-mail, explaining why I have been so busy.
5. Tess is such a great pen pal, I am sure she will have written back by bedtime tonight.
6. Tess and I have spent three summer vacations together.
7. I has always enjoyed her company when we have gotten together.
8. Before our first vacation together, Tess has spent her summers going to camp.
9. She has told me that she did not enjoy camp at all.
10. By the time next school year rolls around, I had enjoyed a great summer with Tess.

Publish

+Presentation

Publishing Strategy Send my e-mail to the appropriate person.

Presentation Strategy Check my typing and add spaces between paragraphs.

I'm finished! I not only neatly typed my e-mail using block-style paragraphs, but I also left extra space between paragraphs to make reading easier on the eyes. Now I could share my e-mail with a friend or my language arts class, but I think sending it to Ms. Jackson is the most important thing to do. I hope she will write back with some information about dialect soon. But before I hit the Send button, I will read through my e-mail one last time to make sure it includes all the items on my final checklist.

My Final Checklist

Did I—

- ✔ fix all of my spelling, grammar, and punctuation errors?
- ✔ properly use all past and past participle verb forms?
- ✔ properly use all perfect tense verb forms?
- ✔ leave extra space between each paragraph?

Apply

Make a checklist to go over your e-mail. Then make the corrections you need and publish a final copy. Then it's time to hit that send button!

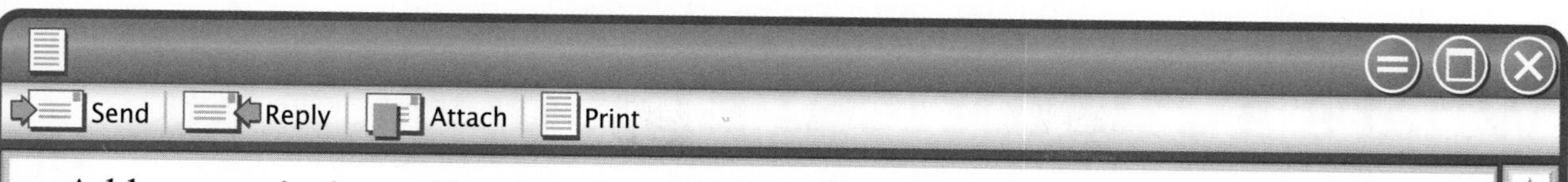

Address: msjackson@harriettubmanelementary.org

Subject: Questions about dialect

Date: 09/07/2012

From: njuarez@jump.com

Hello, Ms. Jackson. I hope the fourth graders who have you this year have as much fun as I did when I was in your class. I have just started seventh grade. In my class this year, there is a girl who recently moved to Nevada from the South. Her name is Abby. Another new girl, Jill, has come from Maine. They talk really funny. They use different words and phrases than I have heard before. I have several questions about dialect that I would appreciate it if you could answer.

First of all, how does dialect happen? When Jill says things to people like "Those pancakes were wicked good," they have no idea what she means. And there are things I say that Jill has never heard before. This is very confusing to me. Until Abby and Jill moved here, I thought that English was spoken the same way everywhere.

Another example that I have collected is that Abby says "I'm fixing to" a lot. Can you tell me what it means? I can't find it in my dictionary. Also, for Abby, it seems as if evening starts right after lunch. Where does that habit come from? I've never heard of that way of speaking before!

Abby also says she "totes" things instead of carrying them. Is that why we have tote bags? Do people say "tote" in a lot of other places?

I've also noticed that announcers on TV don't talk like Southerners, people from Maine, or people from Nevada. Why does their speech sound so perfect?

I'm beginning to think that English is very complicated. Please answer my e-mail and help me figure it out.

Nina Juarez

Reflect

How do you like it? Did Nina use all the traits of a good e-mail? Check it against the rubric to find out. Then use the rubric to check your own e-mail.

What's a Historical Episode?

It's a story about something that happened in the past. It can make the reader feel as if he or she were right there when the episode was happening. I'm excited about trying this kind of writing because I can pretend that I'm there!

What's in a Historical Episode?

Historical Details
These are the parts of the story that come from history. I'll have to read up on the setting and gather information—and keep track of where my facts come from, too.

Sequence
This is the order in which events happen. I'll need to tell the story so that it has a beginning and middle that lead naturally to the conclusion.

Dialogue
This is conversation between characters in the episode. It will be fun to make up what the people in my story are saying to each other. I'll have to make the dialogue sound realistic to help develop a believable and engaging story.

Third-Person Point of View
This is when the narrator of the story is not a character. I won't use the words *I, me, my, you, your, we, us,* or *our*. Instead, I'll use *he, she, they,* and *them*. I'll be an all-knowing, invisible narrator!

Why write a Historical Episode?

I can think of a whole bunch of reasons to write a historical episode. Here's a list of a few. I hope it will help me decide what I want to write about.

Information

Writing about history is a fun way to give people knowledge of the past. It can be more fun to read a historical episode with characters and dialogue than to read history from a textbook.

Personal Exploration

I like to find out how people in the past solved their problems. Did they have problems that were similar to mine? I also like to imagine what I would experience if I traveled to another place and time.

Lessons From the Past

Some events in the past teach important lessons about today. By including relevant, factual details, I can show what we have in common with the past so maybe we can avoid struggles they had back then.

Entertainment

Historical episodes can be very entertaining. They can be exciting, sad, or funny. They can also introduce characters who are larger than life, with interesting personalities.

Linking Narrative Writing Traits to a Historical Episode

In this chapter, you will write a story about something that happened in the past. This type of narrative writing is called a historical episode. Nina will guide you through the stages of the writing process: Prewrite, Draft, Revise, Edit, and Publish. In each stage, Nina will show you important writing strategies that are linked to the Narrative Writing Traits below.

Narrative Writing Traits

	• a single, focused topic with relevant, engaging details that develop the experiences or events • a narrator or characters that bring the story to life
	• well-structured and logical event sequences, often in chronological order, that guide the reader through the story • an engaging beginning and a satisfying conclusion that reflects on the story's events • a variety of transition words that signal time or setting changes
	• a voice that is appropriate for the audience and purpose • dialogue that, if used, is realistic and helps develop the characters and story
	• precise, descriptive words and phrases
	• a variety of sentences that flow and are a pleasure to read aloud
	• no or few errors in grammar, usage, mechanics, and spelling

Before you write, read Art Foley's historical episode on the next three pages. Then use the historical episode rubric on pages 58–59 to decide how well he did. (You might want to look back at What's in a Historical Episode? on page 52, too!)

Wanted: A Boat to India

by Art Foley

Beginning

Third-person narrator

Marco Polo was beginning to wonder if he was ever going to get to Cathay. His father and uncle had returned to Venice from that country in the Far East, laden with spices, gold, and other rich treasures. Marco had been excited when the men said he could accompany them on this next trip, but so far things had not gone smoothly. They had traveled far out of their way to avoid a war in Armenia. They had struggled across a vast, hot desert in Persia, where packs of bandits roamed around terrorizing travelers. Then the other day their own party had been attacked by one of these bandit hordes, and they had been lucky to escape alive.

Historical details

Now, though, they were finally at Hormuz, at the edge of the sea.

"It's as hot here as it was in the desert," Marco said to himself. "But maybe our luck will change. Maybe we will be able to hire a boat that will get us at least as far as India."

Marco accompanied Niccolò and Maffeo, his father and uncle, when they went down to the harbor. Along with them went Omar, a trader from Hormuz who had recently done business with them. Omar, a tall man with a broad face and easy smile, assured them that they would have no trouble getting a boat.

Middle

"Look at all the ships in this harbor," he insisted. "These captains and their crews cross back and forth to India every week. They will fall all over themselves trying to get your business."

The Polos looked around a little doubtfully. The harbor was indeed filled with boats. Their crooked triangular sails swayed slightly as a hot breeze rippled through them. All but two or three of the boats, though, looked far too small to make the crossing.

"Talk to that captain over there," Niccolò told Omar, "and ask if we can see his boat."

Dialogue

"An excellent choice," Omar praised him. "This man has been a captain for over twenty years with never a mishap."

Even as they approached the boat, however, the Polos began to get apprehensive. Like all the others, it had only one mast, one rudder, and one sail.

"Ask the captain how his ship can be seaworthy," Maffeo told Omar. "What happens if that single mast snaps in the wind? And what holds the boards together? I don't see any iron nails."

"Of course there aren't any nails," Omar responded. "Shipbuilders around here use wooden pegs, which work quite well. They stitch the planks together with strong threads made of coconut fibers. And the masts are lightweight and very flexible. I think perhaps you are worrying too much."

Maffeo reminded Omar that Venice, the city where the Polos lived, was known for its merchants sailing to distant ports. He and his brother had seen a good ship or two in their day.

"These ships are lightweight and flexible," Omar continued, almost as if he hadn't heard them. "They are well suited to ride the storms of the Indian Ocean."

Marco was getting a little tired of listening to this haggling. "These boats don't look so bad to me," he thought. "Isn't it important for us to try to move along?"

Marco looked up at the boat owner, who was gesturing to him to climb aboard. As soon as he did, a foul odor assailed his nose. "Could you ask the captain what causes that terrible smell?" he called down to Omar.

"It's the fish oil," Omar explained. "Shipbuilders in this region use the oil instead of tar to caulk the seams of the boat. And really, the oil, despite the bad smell, does its job quite well. These ships are lightweight and flexible, and. . . "

Historical details

By this time, all the Polos, even Marco, had had enough. They just could not believe that small, flimsy boats like these, held together with wooden pegs and fish oil, could get them safely to their destination. They thanked their friend Omar for his help, nodded politely to the captain, and walked away.

I guess we haven't gotten rid of our bad luck yet, thought Marco. We will have to find another way to continue eastward.

Conclusion

Rubric

Use this 6-point rubric to plan and evaluate a historical episode.

	6	5	4
Ideas	Rich, well-researched historical details add authenticity. The details are relevant and striking.	Historical details add authenticity to the writing. The writing makes sense.	The writing contains some interesting details, but more information would help.
Organization	The story is well organized, ending with a conclusion that follows naturally from the story events. A variety of transitions guide the reader through the story.	The story has a clear beginning, middle, and ending. Transitions connect ideas.	The story is organized into a beginning, middle, and ending. Transitions are present.
Voice	Third-person narration is used consistently in an original way. Realistic-sounding dialogue develops the characters.	Third-person narration is used consistently. Dialogue sounds realistic for the most part.	Point of view is incon-sistent. Sometimes the reader cannot tell who is speaking. Dialogue is sometimes stiff.
Word Choice	Precise words, such as powerful verbs, capture the action and convey the events clearly.	Strong verbs show the action in the story. Verbs used in speaker tags show action.	Some verbs are strong and others are ordinary or repetitious. Vague words are present.
Sentence Fluency	An exceptional variety of sentences move the story along smoothly. The story is enjoyable to read.	A variety of sentence beginnings and lengths are noticeable. The story is easy to read.	There is some variety in sentence beginnings and length. Some sections may be choppy to read.
Conventions	The writer has used different sentence structure correctly to enhance meaning.	A few errors in sentence structure require a careful look to find them.	The reader will notice a few errors in sentence structure that don't interfere with writing.
+Presentation	Illustrations are thoughtfully integrated with the writing.		

	3	2	1
Ideas	Some parts of the writing are unclear. Details are present but are very general.	Details are vague. The main idea is unclear.	The writing has no focus. Details are missing, vague, or poorly researched.
Organization	The writing structure doesn't help the reader follow the story. Some transitions are missing.	Lack of organization makes the story difficult to follow. Transitions are missing or are incorrect.	Transitions are missing. The story doesn't have an introduction and just stops without a logical ending.
Voice	The writer's voice comes and goes. Dialogue is unrealistic and may be confusing.	The writer's voice is unclear or absent from the writing. Dialogue is missing or confusing.	The writer's voice is absent from the writing. No dialogue is present.
Word Choice	Weak verbs are evident in the writing, along with vague words or more language than is necessary.	Verbs are missing from the writing. The message is not clear.	Words and phrases are vague or unclear. The meaning is also unclear.
Sentence Fluency	Some sentences have the same beginnings. Lack of variety in sentence length or structure makes some sections dull.	Many sentences are incomplete, and other problems are evident. The writing may need to be reread for meaning.	Many sentence problems make the writing difficult to read throughout.
Conventions	Many errors in sentence structure require the reader to slow down. The message may not be clear.	Frequent, serious errors in sentence structure make the writing hard to read.	The message is unclear throughout because of serious errors in sentence structure.

See Appendix B for 4-, 5-, and 6-point narrative rubrics.

Using the Historical Episode Rubric to Study the Model

Did you notice that the model on pages 55–57 points out some key elements of a historical episode? As he wrote "Wanted: A Boat to India," Art Foley used these elements to help him describe a historical event. He also used the 6-point rubric on pages 58–59 to plan, draft, revise, and edit the writing. A rubric is a great tool to evaluate writing during the writing process.

Now let's use the same rubric to score the model. To do this, we'll focus on each trait separately, starting with Ideas. We'll use the top descriptor for each trait (column 6), along with examples from the model, to help us understand how the traits work together. How would you score Art on each trait?

- **The writer's main idea is clear and focused.**
- **The details are relevant and striking.**

I love how Art immediately introduces the historical event he is writing about, and in such a creative way—I can't help but want to continue reading. His details are vivid and authentic, providing me with a clear and accurate vision of the events he is describing.

[from the writing model]

Marco Polo was beginning to wonder if he was ever going to get to Cathay. His father and uncle had returned to Venice from that country in the Far East, laden with spices, gold, and other rich treasures.

- **The story is well organized, ending with a conclusion that follows naturally from the story events.**
- **A variety of transitions guide the reader through the story.**

Art uses transitions like *Now* and *By this time* to help me understand time passing or a shift in scenes. The entire episode flows naturally and ends with a satisfying conclusion.

[from the writing model]

By this time, all the Polos, even Marco, had had enough. They just could not believe that small, flimsy boats like these, held together with wooden pegs and fish oil, could get them safely to their destination. They thanked their friend Omar for his help, nodded politely to the captain, and walked away.

- **Third-person narration is used consistently in an original way.**
- **Realistic-sounding dialogue develops the characters.**

Art uses third-person point of view (*he, his, they,* and *them*) throughout his writing. The dialogue Art uses is very realistic; he includes words and phrases used during Marco Polo's time. This helped me get a good feel for the characters who are speaking.

[from the writing model]

"Look at all the ships in this harbor," he insisted. "These captains and their crews cross back and forth to India every week. They will fall all over themselves trying to get your business."

- **Precise words, such as powerful verbs, capture the action and convey the events clearly.**

Art uses the most creative and precise verbs in his historical episode, which made reading his piece fun. Words like *gesturing* and *assailed* are strong and clear. From the description, the scene that played in my mind as I read was clear and animated.

[from the writing model]

Marco looked up at the boat owner, who was gesturing to him to climb aboard. As soon as he did, a foul odor assailed his nose. "Could you ask the captain what causes that terrible smell?" he called down to Omar.

- **An exceptional variety of sentences move the story along smoothly.**
- **The story is enjoyable to read.**

Art uses questions to make the story more interesting and to help us know what is going on in Marco Polo's mind. The questions really made me wonder what was going to happen next!

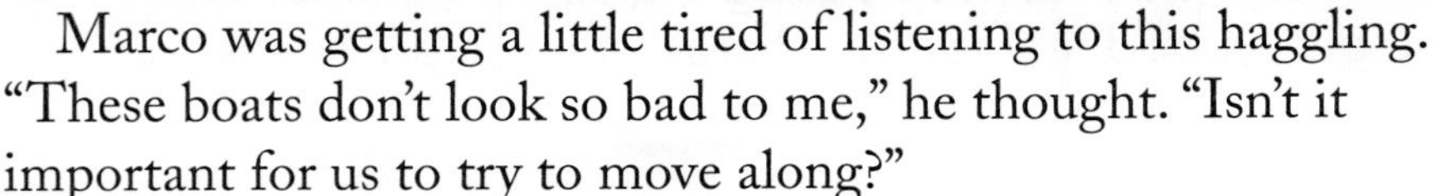

Marco was getting a little tired of listening to this haggling. "These boats don't look so bad to me," he thought. "Isn't it important for us to try to move along?"

- **The writer has used different sentence structures correctly to enhance meaning.**

I can't find any spelling, punctuation, or capitalization errors in Art's story. He uses several different sentence structures, including quotations. Each type of sentence is used correctly. Take a look at this example of dialogue.

[from the writing model]

"Talk to that captain over there," Niccolò told Omar, "and ask if we can see his boat."

"An excellent choice," Omar praised him.

Presentation Illustrations are thoughtfully integrated with the writing.

My Turn!

I want to do as well as Art Foley did as I write my historical episode. I'm glad I can lean on the rubric as a guide. I can't wait to get started. Follow along and see how I do.

Prewrite

Focus on Ideas

The Rubric Says Rich, well-researched historical details add authenticity.

Writing Strategy Gather historical information from several references, including primary sources.

I've thought a lot about what historical period I want to write about. We've been reading in our social studies class about the slave trade in Africa in the 1700s and 1800s. I decided I want to write a story set in that time. I'll use the strategy of getting information about the period from reference sources.

I'll start with an encyclopedia to get an overview. Then I'll go to the Internet. Maybe I'll be lucky to find a great primary source, such as a slave's actual story of being captured and transported across the ocean. (You can't always find a primary source, but I'll try hard to find one.) And I'll keep track of the sources I use.

Writer's Term

Historical Period

A **historical period** is a time gone by. Colonial America, the Victorian age, and the 1980s are all historical periods.

Writer's Term

Primary Source

A **primary source** is a person or book that provides a firsthand account of the information. For example, a primary source about a war would be the journal, diary, or letter of a person who experienced the war firsthand.

Here are two good ways to find primary sources:

- **Talk to an older person that you know.** The person may have firsthand experiences or letters from older friends or relatives to share.
- **Use the Internet.** Enter your topic idea in a good search engine used in your school. Be sure you use only reliable websites.

As I did my research, I took notes on anything that I thought could be used in a story. Here are a few of my notes from my primary source, the narrative by captured slave Olaudah Equiano.

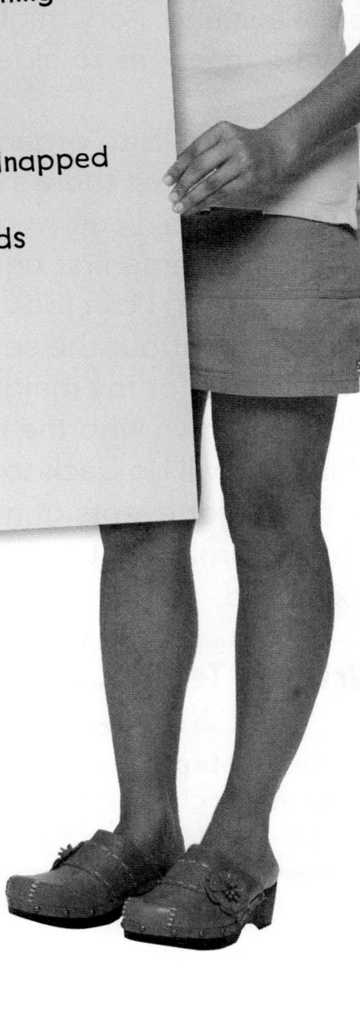

Slave trade in Africa—1700s and 1800s/Olaudah's capture

- ✔ families lived in fenced compounds, more than one building
- ✔ meals—goat stew, plantains, yams
- ✔ made clothes, rugs, etc., on hand & foot loom
- ✔ when adults working in the fields, children often watching as lookouts from trees
- ✔ kidnapping pretty common
- ✔ Olaudah heard of prisoners shackled in dungeons
- ✔ kidnappers snuck over walls of family compound, kidnapped Olaudah and his sister
- ✔ covered their mouths, carried them off into the woods

Story ideas

- ✔ Africa during slave trade—1760
- ✔ African family living in compound—family life
- ✔ brother and sister at home
- ✔ kidnappers in an African village

Apply

Gather information from references and primary sources, and jot down some story ideas. Keep track of where you found your information.

Prewrite

Focus on **Organization**

The Rubric Says The story is well organized, ending with a conclusion that follows naturally from the story events.

Writing Strategy Make a Story Map.

When I finished my research, I had a lot of information! Before I can use it in a story, I have to think of a simple plot I can develop without getting confused with all the details. I think a good, exciting story might be about an African girl who manages to hide from some slave traders.

My strategy is to organize my ideas with a Story Map. Since there's no set order for filling in a Story Map, I can write in the plot/problem and the outcome first because I know what they are. Then I can look through my notes for information about the setting and fill that in. I need names for my major characters and also will write down who the minor characters will be.

Finally I will go back to my notes to get ideas for the major events of my episode. This is actually turning out to be a little easier than I expected.

Writer's Term

Story Map

A **Story Map** organizes the setting, major and minor characters, plot and problem, major events, and outcome of the story.

STORY MAP

Setting

Where small village, not far from the coast in West Africa

When 1760

Major Characters Binta, a 12-year-old African girl; Diallo, her 10-year-old brother

Minor Characters three slave traders; Binta and Diallo's mother

Plot/Problem

A girl and her brother have to get away from some slave traders.

Event 1	Event 2	Event 3
Binta and Diallo are left alone as their parents go to work in the fields.	Traders come into their village and toward their family compound.	The girl and her brother look for a place to hide.

Outcome

The girl and her brother avoid being captured.

Reflect

What do you think about Nina's Story Map? Did she cover all of the story elements?

Apply

Make a Story Map that organizes the parts of your historical episode.

Draft

Focus on **Voice**

The Rubric Says Third-person narration is used consistently in an original way.

Writing Strategy Maintain consistency in style and tone.

Writer's Term

Point of View

Point of view tells the reader who is telling the story. Writers use **first person** to tell about their own experiences and to show that they are part of the story. Writers use **third person** to tell about the experiences of others and to show that they are not part of the story.

As I write my draft, I need to think about who is telling the story. I know from the rubric that my story should be written in the third-person point of view. This means that I should write as if a narrator is telling the story. This is someone who is not part of the story and not one of the characters. So I need to make sure I don't use the word *I*. Instead, I'll use *he, she,* or *they* as I write about the characters. To help my reader follow along, it's also important to keep my style and tone consistent throughout my writing.

Right now I just need to get my ideas on paper. Later I can polish my writing when I check for correct spelling, punctuation, and grammar.

Proofreading Marks

⊐ Indent	Take out something
≡ Make uppercase	⊙ Add a period
/ Make lowercase	¶ New paragraph
∧ Add something	(sp) Spelling error

A Daring Escape

by Nina

[DRAFT]

[used third-person point of view]

Binta was a twelve-year-old girl. She lived in a small village in West Africa. She loved her parents and her brothers and sisters, and they had many happy times together. But Binta was always afraid.

There were many things that frighten Binta. When she had to light the fire to cook the family's food. She was afraid that she could not do household chores well enough. Most of all, she was afraid to be left alone when the older people left went out to work in the fields. In that year, 1760, everybody knew that there were slave traders around. They kidnaped healthy-looking young people and sold them. A man from the villige had travel down the river. He came back and told everyone about a traders' fort.

One morning, Binta's mother was going out to work in the field as usual. Watch your little brother carefully, she said, and make sure he stays inside our compond walls.Your father has heard that there are traders around."

All at once Binta got very afraid, but she tried hard not to show it. She promised that "she would take good care of her brother."

The morning went by and nothing happened. Every half hour or so, Binta had Diallo, her brother, climb the tall silk-cotton tree in their

[DRAFT]

yard to look for kidnappers, but except for the birds' screetches, the forest around the village was quiet. Binta was starting to relax in the afternoon when she sent Diallo up the tree one more time.

He had climb about ten feet when he came scrambling back down. He had a terrifyed look on his face. "Sister, there are two men and a woman sneaking up to the village"! he whispered. "What shall we do?"

Binta was as frightened as her brother. For a minute she stood paralyzed. Then she could hear the kidnappers' careless talk.

"It is my impression that there are not any adults in the vicenity," one muttered to the others. "Let us attempt to locate some children."

"That is an excellent plan," said the woman's voice. "We shall examine what is behind that nearby wall. Be silent as we approach."

Binta and Diallo could hear the rustle of dry branches as the kidnappers came closer to the walls around their family compound.

"If they climb over, they're going to get us," said Diallo.

"But if we try to go out through the gate, they'll see us anyway," Binta replied. It seemed as if. There was no escape.

Binta had an idea. She remembered the place behind her mother's quarters where they used to burrow under the fence. "If we can

[DRAFT]

get through there now, maybe we can hide in the forest until the kidnappers go away."

The small opening was on the opposite side of the compound from where the kidnappers were approaching. So Binta and Diallo had time to make their escape. Diallo went under first, then helped his sister squeeze through. Their compound was close enough to the forest that it was easy to get there and hide.

From their spot behind some low, thick bushes, Binta and Diallo could hear the kidnappers messing up their family compound.

"I'm sure there were children here a minute ago," said the woman. "Where do you suppose they went?"

"Forget it," one of the men replied. "Let's try somewhere else."

Binta and Diallo stayed in the woods for a long time. Finally, when they heard their parents returning, they went back to the compound.

"Why were you outside?" Binta's mother said to her. "I told you to keep your brother safe from harm."

"That's just what I did, Mother," Binta replied. And as she thought about it, she knew she had reason to be proud. She had been afraid, but she did what she had to do anyway.

Reflect

Read Nina's draft. How well did she use third-person point of view?

Apply

Write a draft using third-person point of view. Double-check to see that you are using it correctly.

Revise

Focus on Ideas

The Rubric Says Rich, well-researched historical details add authenticity. The writing is clear, focused, and well-paced.

Writing Strategy Add historical details to make the story authentic.

Well, I let my writing partner, Brandon, read my finished draft. He really liked the faster pace of my story, which enhances the excitement and drama of the episode. But he thought my story would be more authentic if I used more historical details at the beginning. I went back to my notes, found a little more information, and added it to my paper.

Writer's Term

Historical Detail

A **historical detail** is a fact that is correct in its relationship to a certain time or place in history.

[DRAFT]

[historical details]

There were many things that frighten Binta. When she had to light the fire to cook the family's ~~food~~ dinner of goat stew, plantains, and yams. She was afraid that ~~she could not do household chores~~ her cloth weaving on the hand-and-foot loom was not done well enough.

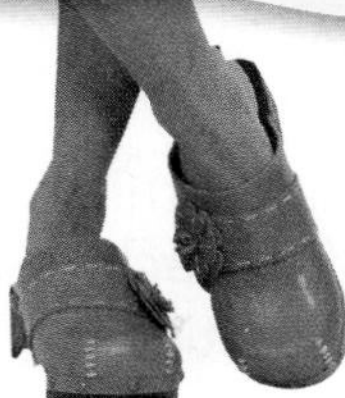

Revise

Focus on Word Choice

The Rubric Says Precise words, such as powerful verbs, capture the action and convey the events clearly.

Writing Strategy Replace weak verbs with strong ones.

The rubric reminds me to use precise and powerful verbs to show action. I went back and reread my writing to see if I could find any verbs that needed strengthening. I want my readers to "see" my story unfold in their minds as if they were watching a movie. The more specific the verb, the more powerful the connection will be between the reader and my story.

I guess *messing up* is not a very strong or accurate description of what is truly happening in the scene below. I will revise that sentence now. What do you think of my new verb?

[DRAFT]

[used powerful verb]

From their spot behind some low, thick bushes, Binta and Diallo could hear the kidnappers ~~messing up~~ ransacking their family compound.

Reflect

What do you think of Nina's revision? Can you "see" this scene better now?

Apply

Use precise words, including powerful verbs, to clearly describe your episode for your reader.

Revise

The Rubric Says An exceptional variety of sentences move the story along smoothly. The story is enjoyable to read.

Writing Strategy Use different kinds of sentences.

I'm going to look at my sentences. I know using a variety of sentences helps my writing flow smoothly and makes reading more enjoyable for my reader. I will use a question here to mix things up a bit.

[DRAFT]

Binta had an idea. ~~She remembered the place behind her mother's quarters where they used to burrow under the fence.~~ "If we can get through there now, maybe we can hide in the forest until the kidnappers go away."

[added question] "Remember that place behind Mother's quarters where we used to burrow under the fence?

Apply

Do you have any questions in your historical episode? Try putting in a few to add to the drama.

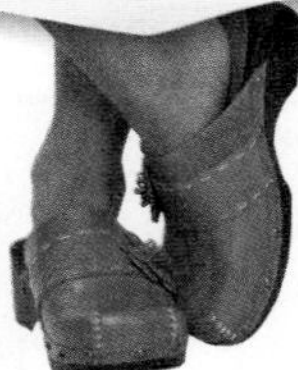

Edit

Focus on **Conventions**

The Rubric Says The writer has used different sentence structures correctly to enhance meaning.

Writing Strategy Check to see that punctuation is correct.

Writer's Term

Quotation

A **quotation** restates the exact words of a speaker or writer. A quotation is placed within quotation marks and is credited to the speaker or writer.

It's time to look for errors in my episode. I've used all kinds of sentence structures to enhance my story, including quotations. But I sometimes forget a comma or a quotation mark, so I need to check for those. Here's a quotation that's missing some punctuation. I'll go and fix it now.

[DRAFT]

One morning, Binta's mother was going out to work in the field as usual. "Watch your little brother carefully," she said, "and make sure he stays inside our ~~compond~~ compound walls. Your father has heard that there are traders around."

[added quotation marks]

Reflect

What do you think of the edits? Could you find any punctuation mistakes that Nina did not catch and fix? How do Nina's edits help you better enjoy her historical episode?

Apply

Conventions

Edit your draft for spelling, grammar, and punctuation errors. Pay extra attention to quotations.

For more practice with punctuation, use the exercises on the next two pages.

Punctuation of Quotations

Know the Rule

A **direct quotation** is the exact words of a speaker. It is enclosed in quotation marks. A comma separates the speaker's words from the rest of the sentence.

Example: "I really liked your book," Marion said.

An **indirect quotation** is a retelling of the speaker's words.

Example: Marion said that she enjoyed my book.

Here are some rules for using quotation marks:

- Begin and end a direct quotation with quotation marks.
- If a direct quotation is a sentence, begin it with a capital letter. If it is part of a sentence, do not use a capital letter.
- Place a comma, period, question mark, or exclamation mark that ends a quote inside the quotation marks.
- If a quotation is divided, enclose both parts within quotation marks.
- Do not use quotation marks around an indirect quotation. In an indirect quotation, the speaker's words are often preceded by the word *that*.

Practice the Rule

Find the quotation error in each sentence below. Then write the corrected sentences on a separate sheet of paper.

1. "I really like reading historical fiction, don't you"? Antonio asked his friend Laura.
2. "Yes, said Laura. Some of the stories we read in literature class were really good."
3. "I liked *Number the Stars,* by Lois Lowry, a lot" she said.
4. Isn't that the story about the family that protects their friends from the Nazis during World War II?" Mai Li asked.
5. Laura answered "Yes, and it certainly made that period of history come alive for me."
6. Antonio responded that "he enjoyed reading tales about King Arthur and his knights."
7. "Mai Li said, I'm not sure if those count as historical fiction or fantasy."
8. "Laura said that she enjoyed reading fantasy as much as she enjoyed historical fiction."

Hyphens and Parentheses

Know the Rule

Hyphens and **parentheses** are used to make writing more clear. Use a hyphen to

- separate syllables in a word when you must break the word at the end of a line of text.
- link the parts of some compound words, such as *twelve-year-old.*
- link some word pairs or groups of words that precede a noun and act as an adjective, such as *well-known actor.*
- link the parts of numbers (written as words) between twenty-one and ninety-nine.

Use parentheses to set off an explanation or example, especially when the information is not essential to the sentence (nonrestrictive).

Example: Sushi (raw fish served in a roll of rice) must be prepared with care.

Practice the Rule

Copy the following sentences on a separate piece of paper. Then add hyphens and parentheses as needed to make each sentence correct.

1. Today is Nana's my grandmother's birthday, and we are heading to her favorite restaurant, The Piper's Den.
2. This family owned business has been located on High Street for over thirty five years.
3. Nana always orders eggplant parmesan an Italian dish of eggplant, sauce, and cheese.
4. Some of the world's most delicious food comes from Italy—a country in the Medi terranean section of Europe.
5. The chef at The Piper's Den has known Nana since he was twenty one.
6. Nana used to be the editor in chief of a famous cooking magazine.
7. The chef brought out cannoli and tiramisu well known Italian desserts as a birthday treat for Nana.
8. This was truly the best way to celebrate Nana's eighty sixth birthday!

Publish

+Presentation

Publishing Strategy Include the historical episode in the hallway display case.

Presentation Strategy Add illustrations that support and enhance the story.

Now it's time to publish my historical episode. I'm so proud of this piece. My teacher wants students to hang their finished work in the class's hallway display, so it needs to be neatly written or typed. I think if I add a few illustrations to enhance my story—just like in a book—that would be perfect. I'll be sure my illustrations do not conflict with the story's details. First I want to read it through one last time and make sure it includes all the items on my final checklist.

My Final Checklist

Did I—

- ✔ correctly use all punctuation, including quotation marks, hyphens, and parentheses?
- ✔ correct all my spelling and grammar errors?
- ✔ add neatly drawn illustrations to support and enhance my story?
- ✔ neatly handwrite or type my historical episode for presentation?

Apply

Make a final checklist to check your historical episode. Then make a final draft to publish.

A Daring Escape

by Nina Juarez

Binta was a twelve-year-old girl. She lived in a small village in West Africa. She loved her parents and her brothers and sisters, and they had many happy times together. But Binta was always afraid.

There were many things that frightened Binta. She was afraid when she had to light the fire to cook the family's dinner of goat stew, plantains, and yams. She was afraid that her cloth weaving on the hand-and-foot loom was not done well enough. Most of all, she was afraid to be left alone when the older people went out to work in the fields. In that year, 1760, everybody knew that there were slave traders around. They kidnapped healthy-looking young people and sold them. A man from the village had traveled down the river. He came back and told everyone about a traders' fort where prisoners were shackled together and led, crying for mercy, into a dark underground dungeon.

One morning, Binta's mother was going out to work in the field as usual. "Watch your little brother carefully," she said, "and make sure he stays inside our compound walls. Your father has heard that there are traders around."

All at once Binta got very afraid, but she tried hard not to show it. She promised her mother that she would take good care of her brother.

The morning went by, and nothing happened. Every half hour or so, Binta had Diallo, her brother, climb the tall silk-cotton tree in their yard to look for kidnappers, but except for the birds' screeches, the forest around the village was quiet. Binta was starting to relax in the afternoon when she sent Diallo up the tree one more time.

He had climbed only about ten feet when he came scrambling back down. He had a terrified look on his face. "Sister, there are two men and a woman sneaking up to the village!" he whispered. "What shall we do?"

Binta was as frightened as her brother. For a minute she stood paralyzed. Then she could hear the kidnappers' careless talk.

"It looks like there aren't any adults around," one muttered to the others. "Let's find us some children."

"Good idea," said the woman's voice. "Let's see what's behind that wall over there. Be quiet now."

Binta and Diallo could hear the rustle of dry branches as the kidnappers came closer to the walls around their family compound.

"If they climb over, they're going to get us," said Diallo.

"But if we try to go out through the gate, they'll see us anyway," Binta replied. It seemed as if there was no escape.

Suddenly, Binta had an idea. "Remember that place behind Mother's quarters where we used to burrow under the fence? If we can get through there now, maybe we can hide in the forest until the kidnappers go away."

The small opening was on the opposite side of the compound from where the kidnappers were approaching. So Binta and Diallo had time to make their escape. Diallo went under first. Then he helped his sister squeeze through. Their compound was close enough to the forest that it was easy to get there and hide.

From their spot behind some low, thick bushes, Binta and Diallo could hear the kidnappers ransacking their family compound.

"I'm sure there were children here a minute ago," said the woman. "Where do you suppose they went?"

"Forget it," one of the men replied. "Let's try somewhere else."

Binta and Diallo stayed in the woods for a long time. Finally, when they heard their parents returning, they went back to the compound.

"Why were you outside?" Binta's mother said to her. "I told you to keep your brother safe from harm."

"That's just what I did, Mother," Binta replied. And as she thought about it, she knew she had reason to be proud. She had been afraid, but she did what she had to do anyway.

Reflect

How did Nina do? Did she use all the traits of a good historical episode in her writing? Check it against the rubric. Don't forget to use the rubric to check your own historical episode.

What's a Play?

It's a story—typically acted out on a stage by actors—told almost entirely through dialogue. I think writing a play and seeing it performed will be exciting!

What's in a Play?

Plot
The plot is made up of all the events arranged by the author to develop the story line or idea. Important parts of the plot are the introduction, rising action, climax, falling action, and resolution.

Conflict
This is the challenge or problem that the main character must somehow overcome. The conflict is the force that drives the plot toward the resolution.

Characters
As there is limited time to develop characters, plays usually focus on a small number of characters. The plot revolves around the main character, or *protagonist*. The character or force that opposes the protagonist is called the *antagonist*.

Scene
Scenes show time and location. Different backgrounds or props can be used to show a change of scene. This helps the audience follow the plot.

Stage Directions
These are written instructions, set apart from the dialogue in parentheses, for each character to follow. Stage directions may tell actors where to walk or how to say their lines.

Why write a Play?

There are plenty of reasons to write a play. Below, I've explained some of the most common. I'm sure one will inspire me as I get ready to write my own play.

Personal Enjoyment

There is something magical about creating characters and "watching" how they behave in a story. With a play, you get to literally watch your characters come to life. They speak the lines you've given them, and they move as you've instructed. This is going to be fun!

Entertainment

I love telling stories through writing. But writing a play has an extra benefit—I can watch others act out my story. I get to share a story, message, or information in a different and interesting way. I might even want to play one of the characters!

Share Information

Writing a play is a creative way to share a message or information with an audience. Sure, writing essays or short stories is effective, but using live actors and a stage can get information out there in a powerful and engaging way.

Linking Narrative Writing Traits to a Play

In this chapter, you will write a story to be performed. This type of narrative writing is called a play. Nina will guide you through the stages of the writing process: Prewrite, Draft, Revise, Edit, and Publish. In each stage, Nina will show you important writing strategies that are linked to the Narrative Writing Traits below.

Narrative Writing Traits

 Ideas	• a single, focused topic with relevant, engaging details that develop the experiences or events • a narrator or characters that bring the story to life
 Organization	• well-structured and logical event sequences, often in chronological order, that guide the reader through the story • an engaging beginning and a satisfying conclusion that reflects on the story's events • a variety of transition words that signal time or setting changes
 Voice	• a voice that is appropriate for the audience and purpose • dialogue that, if used, is realistic and helps develop the characters and story
 Word Choice	• precise, descriptive words and phrases
 Sentence Fluency	• a variety of sentences that flow and are a pleasure to read aloud
 Conventions	• no or few errors in grammar, usage, mechanics, and spelling

Before you write, read Aleem Martel's play on the next three pages. Then use the play rubric on pages 88–89 to decide how well he did. You might want to look back at What's in a Play? on page 82, too!

Play Model

THE BIRTH OF OXYGEN

by Aleem Martel

characters

Characters

Antoine Lavoisier, a French scientist

Marie-Anne, Antoine Lavoisier's wife and assistant

Pierre-Simon Leplace, Antoine Lavoisier's colleague

stage directions

scene

Scene 1: *It is the late 1770s. Lavoisier is sitting at a long desk in his personal library at his home in Paris, France. Books and loose papers are scattered all over his desk. Sconces are lit on the walls—it is in the middle of the night.*

Lavoisier: (*bent over his books, quill in his right hand, his left elbow on the desk, his left hand supporting his forehead*) This cannot be! I simply do *not* accept it! This phantom element—phlogiston—blast it! It does not exist. (*Marie-Anne softly enters the room.*)

Marie-Anne: Love…it is three in the morning. I know you are on the verge of discovery, but when will you rest your weary mind?

Lavoisier: I cannot rest now, Marie-Anne, I'm almost done. Let me be.

Marie-Anne: Why not wait until tomorrow, when Monsieur Leplace and I are at your call in the laboratory?

Lavoisier: You do not understand, good wife. This phlogiston—it taunts me. Yes, I agree with the notion that there is an element present during combustion, an element aiding the process and altering all that burns, but phlogiston? Johann Joachim Becher's theory of a colorless, tasteless, odorless, and weightless substance found in all combustible materials is pure lunacy! (*He slams his fist down on the desk.*) But where does that lost mass go? It *must* go somewhere! It can't just…just disappear. This is unknown territory in the science world. Yet, I am so close….

conflict

plot

Scene 2: *Lavoisier, wearing a long white laboratory coat, is frantically moving about his laboratory, setting up a number of large and strangely shaped vessels.*

Lavoisier: Marie-Anne, when did Pierre-Simon say he would arrive?

Marie-Anne: Monsieur Leplace will be here any moment, my love.

(*A finely-dressed man rushes into the room. Lavoisier remains busy.*)

Lavoisier: Pierre-Simon! You have finally arrived! Not a moment to lose. I've had a breakthrough, and today you and I will make scientific history!

Pierre-Simon Leplace: (*putting on a long white laboratory coat and then standing at the end of the lab table*) I *knew* you were on the verge of discovery! But before we begin—please tell me what you are thinking. Remember—I am forever a student of science.

Lavoisier: (*continues to set up apparatus while talking*) You are familiar with the insane idea of phlogiston. You know that I have never agreed with Becher's theory. And yet, I too believed there was *something* universal that perhaps fueled the act of combustion.

Pierre-Simon: Yes. According to Becher, this stuff, this *phlogiston* (*the word is spoken scornfully*) is released into the air when a substance burns, and it has neither mass, nor odor, nor color. Ridiculous! But *what* allows combustion to occur?

Lavoisier: Well, today we shall burn this substance here (*points to a pile of powder in an enclosed vessel*), but we shall do so within enclosed vessels. This enclosed system will allow us to trap all released gases, which shall enable us to weigh them, evaluate them, and document the results. I believe that although a combusted substance appears to lose mass, this mass is simply *transferred* into something else, my guess—a gas.

Pierre-Simon: (*puts hand to forehead*) Of course! It's so simple, yet revolutionary. To the experiment!

Lavoisier: (*turns to his wife*) Marie-Anne, please document these next critical hours. Should we meet with success, this information shall be then put into a paper to be released to the scientific community. The death of phlogiston is near!

Scene 3: *Marie-Anne is writing at the desk in the library. Pierre-Simon is standing behind her, while Lavoisier is pacing the length of the room.*

Lavoisier: In conclusion, our experiments have proven the presence of an invisible element that aids the act of combustion. This element is *not* phlogiston, for it has mass. It should be noted that the combusted material did lose mass. However, this loss in mass matched exactly the mass of the gases collected in the second enclosed vessel. This proves that even during a violent reaction such as burning, matter is not created or destroyed—it is simply transformed. I have named the gaseous element aiding the combustion process *oxygen.*

Pierre-Simon: Remarkable! We must tell our scientific peers at once!

Marie-Anne: (*She gathers up the papers and hands them to Lavoisier.*) Your endless nights have served you well. Your restless mind can now find peace.

Lavoisier: Dear wife, this is not the end. It is merely a slight distraction. But make no mistake, this discovery—this birth of oxygen—is but the dawn of a new scientific day. And I plan on leading the way! (*Lavoisier exits the room.*)

Pierre-Simon: How does it feel, Marie-Anne, to be married to the Father of Modern Chemistry? Well, we are off to tell the world! Wish us well, for we will need it. (*Pierre-Simon leaves the room. Marie-Anne watches him leave, then places her hand on her forehead and slowly shakes her head from side to side. The lights dim.*)

The End

Rubric

Use this 6-point rubric to plan and evaluate a play.

	6	5	4
Ideas	Dialogue and stage directions clearly develop plot, characters, and setting. Details are accurate.	Dialogue and stage directions develop the story. Most details are accurate.	Dialogue develops the story. More stage directions are needed. Most details are accurate.
Organization	The play is organized and well paced. A logical sequence of events builds tension toward the climax and provides a resolution at the end.	The play is organized and well paced. Most of the events build tension toward the climax and provide a resolution at the end.	The play is organized but not well paced. Some of the events build tension toward the climax, and there is an identifiable resolution.
Voice	The dialogue sounds believable and reveals the characters' personalities.	Most of the dialogue sounds believable. One character's voice may need to be stronger.	Some of the dialogue sounds believable. Characters' personalities emerge now and again.
Word Choice	Precise language, such as specific nouns and powerful verbs, energize the play.	Specific nouns and strong verbs are used in the play.	Specific nouns and strong verbs are used most of the time.
Sentence Fluency	A variety of sentences adds interest. Fragments, if used, are effective.	Most of the sentences add interest. Fragments, if used, are effective.	Some of the sentences are varied. Fragments, if used, are effective.
Conventions	Sentences are punctuated correctly. Conjunctions are used correctly.	Most sentences are punctuated correctly. Most conjunctions are used correctly.	Several sentences are not punctuated correctly. One or two conjunctions are used incorrectly.

+Presentation The format makes the play easy to follow.

3	2	1	
Dialogue and stage directions do not develop the story enough. Most details are accurate.	Dialogue or stage directions are not clear. Details may not be accurate or relevant.	Dialogue and stage directions are not used to develop the story. Details are vague.	Ideas
The play is organized but not well paced. Events simply occur, but they do not lead to a clear climax or resolution.	The play is poorly organized. The climax is vague, and there is no clear resolution.	The writing is not organized. Both the climax and resolution are missing.	Organization
The dialogue sounds unrealistic in places. There is little sense of the characters' personalities.	The dialogue is very weak. There is no sense of the characters' personalities.	Dialogue is weak and confusing to follow.	Voice
Nouns and verbs are ordinary. They do not bring energy to the play.	Vague or misleading nouns and verbs confuse the reader.	Words are weak or used incorrectly.	Word Choice
Most of the sentences are not varied. Fragments, if used, are effective.	Sentences are not varied. Fragments are not used intentionally.	Sentences are written incorrectly, causing the reader to struggle to understand the meaning.	Sentence Fluency
Many errors are repeated and cause confusion. Conjunctions may be missing or used incorrectly.	Serious errors interfere with meaning. Most sentences are written incorrectly.	The writing has not been edited.	Conventions

See Appendix B for 4-, 5-, and 6-point narrative rubrics.

Using the Play Rubric to Study the Model

Did you notice that the model on pages 85–87 points out some key elements of a play? As he wrote "The Birth of Oxygen," Aleem Martel used these elements to help him explain a scientific topic in the form of a play. He also used the 6-point rubric on pages 88–89 to plan, draft, revise, and edit the writing. A rubric is a great tool to evaluate writing during the writing process.

Now let's use the same rubric to score the model. To do this, we'll focus on each trait separately, starting with Ideas. We'll use the top descriptor for each trait (column 6), along with examples from the model, to help us understand how the traits work together. How would you score Aleem on each trait?

- **Dialogue and stage directions clearly develop plot, characters, and setting.**
- **Details are accurate.**

Aleem uses both stage directions and dialogue to paint vivid and powerful scenes. Each character's unique personality becomes clear through both body language and dialogue. I can also envision the rooms in which the action takes place. Aleem was even careful to use props and language appropriate for the time period.

[from the writing model]

Lavoisier: (*bent over his books, quill in his right hand, his left elbow on the desk, his left hand supporting his forehead*) This cannot be! I simply do *not* accept it! This phantom element—phlogiston—blast it! It does not exist.

- **The play is organized and well paced.**
- **A logical sequence of events builds tension toward the climax and provides a resolution at the end.**

Aleem opens his play with a bang. I am instantly engaged and can't wait to see if and how Lavoisier succeeds. I like the fast pace of each scene, too. Each event is clear and efficiently moves the reader toward the climax. At the end, the resolution is very satisfying.

[from the writing model]

Lavoisier: Marie-Anne, when did Pierre-Simon say he would arrive?

Marie-Anne: Monsieur Leplace will be here any moment, my love.

(*A finely dressed man rushes into the room. Lavoisier remains busy.*)

Lavoisier: Pierre-Simon! You have finally arrived! Not a moment to lose. I've had a breakthrough, and today you and I will make scientific history!

- **The dialogue sounds believable and reveals the characters' personalities.**

As I read the play, I could almost hear the characters' voices inside my head. The dialogue cleverly reveals aspects of their personalities, which helps me feel connected to the plot as a whole. Believable dialogue makes it easy to emotionally connect with the characters.

[from the writing model]

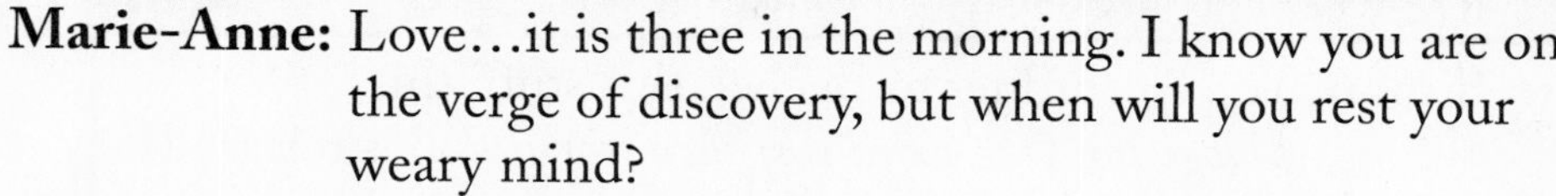

Marie-Anne: Love…it is three in the morning. I know you are on the verge of discovery, but when will you rest your weary mind?

Lavoisier: I cannot rest now, Marie-Anne, I'm almost done. Let me be.

Marie-Anne: Why not wait until tomorrow, when Monsieur Leplace and I are at your call in the laboratory?

- **Precise language, such as specific nouns and powerful verbs, energize the play.**

What powerful nouns and verbs Aleem uses in this play! Words like *taunts, notion, combustion,* and *lunacy* all add power and life to the story. These words add zeal to the plot and keep the audience or reader engaged.

[from the writing model]

Lavoisier: You do not understand, good wife. This phlogiston—it taunts me. Yes, I agree with the notion that there is an element present during combustion, an element aiding the process and altering all that burns, but phlogiston? Johann Joachim Becher's theory of a colorless, tasteless, odorless, and weightless substance found in all combustible materials is pure lunacy!

- **A variety of sentences adds interest.**
- **Fragments, if used, are effective.**

I like how Aleem uses a variety of sentence structures. He mixes up short and long sentences to create a sort of rhythm that is easy to both listen to and read. This variety also keeps the dialogue realistic and interesting.

[from the writing model]

Pierre-Simon: Yes. According to Becher, this stuff, this *phlogiston* (*the word is spoken scornfully*) is released into the air when a substance burns, and it has neither mass, nor odor, nor color. Ridiculous! But *what* allows combustion to occur?

- **Sentences are punctuated correctly.**
- **Conjunctions are used correctly.**

I've read Aleem's play several times and still can't find any spelling, grammar, or punctuation errors. He even uses conjunctions correctly! I want my play to be just as powerful and accurate as Aleem's, so I'll work hard and pay close attention to my conventions.

[from the writing model]

Lavoisier: Well, today we shall burn this substance here (*points to a pile of powder in an enclosed vessel*), but we shall do so within enclosed vessels. This enclosed system will allow us to trap all released gases, which shall enable us to weigh them, evaluate them, and document the results.

Presentation The format makes the play easy to follow.

My Turn!

Now it's my turn to write a play. I'll use the rubric and good writing strategies to help me. Read on to see how I do it.

Prewrite

Focus on **Ideas**

The Rubric Says Dialogue and stage directions clearly develop plot, characters, and setting. Details are accurate.

Writing Strategy Plan the plot and research details.

It's Science Week at my school, and this year we've been asked to dramatize a special moment in science. We can choose a specific discovery, a science-related event, or even a conversation between two or more scientists. Of course, all dialogue will be fictional, but the play must be based on scientific facts.

My first task is to decide on a plot, or what my play will be about. Then I'll do some research to gather accurate information. Next I'll decide on my list of characters and where the action will take place, or the setting. I'll take notes on all my ideas as I go.

Notes About the Science Play

- ✔ topic: Marie Curie
- ✔ born in Poland—moved to Paris to pursue education
- ✔ married Pierre Curie; worked together in lab
- ✔ used Henri Becquerel's work on uranium as background for their work on radiation
- ✔ discovered and named polonium (1898), radium (1898), radioactivity
- ✔ won two Nobel Prizes for her work in science (1903 & 1911)
- ✔ met with great prejudice because she was a woman
- ✔ characters—Marie, Pierre, maybe Henri?
- ✔ setting—in the lab. They were always there!

Apply

Research a science-related topic. Take notes and decide on your list of characters and setting.

Prewrite

Focus on **Organization**

The Rubric Says The play is organized and well paced. A logical sequence of events builds tension toward the climax and provides a resolution at the end.

Writing Strategy Use a Story Map to logically and effectively sequence events.

Writer's Term

Story Map

A **Story Map** is a graphic organizer that helps you plan the major aspects, such as a list of characters and the conflict, of your story.

Now that I've decided on my plot, characters, and setting, it's time to develop the plot. I'll use a Story Map to help me pace the events from beginning to end.

Story Map

Setting	Inside the Curies' lab and office	
Major Character(s)	Marie Curie, Pierre Curie	
Minor Character(s)	A telegram delivery boy	
Theme	Marie's discoveries and her struggle to be taken seriously in the field of science	
Conflict	To overcome the prejudice against women and get credit for her discoveries	
Plot		
Event 1	**Event 2**	**Event 3**
April 1898, Marie discovers polonium	December 1898, Marie discovers radium	1903, Marie and Pierre receive the Nobel Prize in Physics (climax)
Resolution Pierre given his own lab; Marie becomes its Director of Research; she breaks down barriers against women in science		

Reflect

How will this Story Map help Nina stay on track as she writes her draft?

Apply

Complete a Story Map to help you sequence the events of your play.

Draft

Focus on **Word Choice**

The Rubric Says Precise language, such as specific nouns and powerful verbs, energize the play.

Writing Strategy Use specific nouns and powerful verbs.

We've all heard the phrase "show me, don't tell me." It's a great line to keep in mind while writing a play. I want my audience to connect with my characters on an emotional level. To do so, my characters will really have to *show* how they feel through their dialogue and actions. Using specific nouns and powerful verbs will help.

Using a few well-selected words can be so much more effective than a string of vague, weak words. For example, *He clutched at his empty belly* is so much more powerful than, *The man was very hungry*. As I write, I'll be sure to choose descriptive and specific words.

Now it's time to draft my play. I'll use my Story Map to keep me on track. I won't worry too much about spelling, grammar, or punctuation at first. I know I'll fix any mistakes in my final copy. Right now, I just need to focus on writing my play.

Proofreading Marks

- Indent
- Make uppercase
- Make lowercase
- Add something
- Take out something
- Add a period
- New paragraph
- Spelling error

[DRAFT]

What a Woman Can Do

by Nina

Characters

Marie Curie, a scientist

Pierre Curie, Marie's husband and scientific partner

Delivery Boy

[used specific nouns and powerful verbs]

Scene 1 *(Both Marie and Pierre are working in their laboratory. Scientific apparatis is spread out along a long table. Pierre is bent over some equipment. Marie is carefully measuring something and then taking notes.)*

[used specific nouns and powerful verbs]

Marie: *(walks over to Pierre while looking at her notebook)* Pierre, I am getting the same figures again! I've replicated my work for a third time and the results are still the same

Pierre: *(sharply looks up, eyes wide with excitement)* You have discovered an unknown more powerful than Henri Becquerel's uranium?

Reflect

How well has Nina used specific nouns and powerful verbs? Where could she strengthen her language?

Apply

Write a draft of your play using your Story Map as a guide. Remember to include powerful, specific language.

Revise

Focus on **Ideas**

The Rubric Says Dialogue and stage directions clearly develop plot, characters, and setting.

Writing Strategy Write dialogue and stage directions that inform the reader.

In a play, it's the dialogue that informs the audience of the plot, conflict, and setting. I worked hard at writing dialogue that is not only realistic but also informative. Of course, stage directions help out, too. I put a lot of thought into my stage directions to make every movement on stage count. As I was reading over my play, I found a spot where Marie's lines don't really reflect her feelings of insecurity. I'll add some stage directions and revise her lines to make things clearer.

[used revealing stage directions and dialogue]

(nods) Yes. It's all here in the numbers.

Marie: At first I believed I was just incorrectly duplicating Becquerel's experiments with uranium. But I've conducted the same experiment over and over. and yet... (shaking her head and closing her notebook)

Apply

Use stage directions and dialogue to inform your audience of characters' personalities, setting, and plot development.

Revise

Focus on **Organization**

The Rubric Says The play is organized and well paced. A logical sequence of events builds tension toward the climax and provides a resolution at the end.

Writing Strategy Follow the Story Map.

It's my job to pace the events of the plot logically and effectively. When more information is being given, the pace should be slower to allow the audience time to process everything. As the action rises, the pace should quicken. The climax is the part of the play in which the audience should be at the edge of their seats. I thought there could be more action to build the excitement around the climax, so I added some stage directions to tighten the pace.

Writer's Term

Rising Action The pace of the story's events quickens. Tension within the plot is building.

Climax The tension between the protagonist and the antagonist has peaked.

Resolution The conflict is resolved and the end of the story is near.

[DRAFT]

(Quickly turning to Pierre.)

Marie: ^ Pierre! It's from the Royal Swedish Academy of Sciences. What could this mean?

Pierre: Open it and see! It's been five years since our discoveries. Too long for anyone to challenge us now. (He ^quickly stands and walks to Marie's side. Marie and Pierre then silently read the letter together. ^The delivery boy strains to secretly read it over their shoulders.)

[added action to climax]

Reflect

How has Nina effectively used events to build tension toward the climax?

Apply

Organize the events of your play effectively. Build tension toward the climax and slow things down during the resolution.

Revise

Focus on **Sentence Fluency**

The Rubric Says A variety of sentences adds interest. Fragments, if used, are effective.

Writing Strategy Vary sentence patterns for meaning, reader or listener interest, and style.

Most of the time, complete sentences are the rule when you write. However, in a piece of writing that contains a lot of dialogue, such as a play, effective fragments are fine. After all, people do use sentence fragments when they're speaking naturally. As long as a fragment makes sense and fits the character, it's OK to use. Plus, using all kinds of sentence patterns keeps the dialogue lively and the audience interested.

[DRAFT]

Pierre: (*sharply looks up, eyes wide with excitement*) ~~You have discovered an~~ An unknown more powerful than Henri Becquerel's uranium?

[used sentence fragment]

Apply

To keep dialogue realistic and interesting, use a few effective fragments throughout your play. Make sure they are clear, though.

Edit

Focus on **Conventions**

The Rubric Says Sentences are punctuated correctly. Conjunctions are used correctly.

Writing Strategy Check the use of conjunctions to join sentences.

My play's almost done! Now I need to carefully read it over and fix any spelling, punctuation, and capitalization mistakes. I'll also look for places where I can use a conjunction to change two sentences into one compound-complex sentence. A variety of sentences keeps writing interesting.

Writer's Term

Types of Sentences
All sentences fall into just four types: simple, compound, complex, and compound-complex. Be sure the punctuation makes the meaning of the sentences clear.

[DRAFT]

Marie: That was *our* work, Pierre! Now you must suffer because your partner is a woman—and your wife as well? I tell you—I'm sick of it all. It's been years since we've published our findings. Although The scientific world seemed to accept it as fact, There is still no word from the Academy, and there is No funding for further research?!

[formed a compound-complex sentence]

Reflect

How is Nina's editing? Can you find any mistakes she might have missed? Has she used all conjunctions correctly?

Apply Conventions

Check your draft for spelling, punctuation, and capitalization. Make sure you've used conjunctions and pronouns correctly.

For more practice identifying complex and compound-complex sentences, use the exercises on the next two pages.

Grammar, Usage & Mechanics

Simple and Compound Sentences

Know the Rule

A **simple sentence** is made up of a subject and a predicate and expresses only one complete thought. It is an independent clause.

Example: The dog barked loudly.

A **compound sentence** is made of two closely related independent clauses. (The two clauses can be joined by a comma and a coordinating conjunction (*and, but, or, so, for,* or *yet*) or by a semicolon (;).

Example: The dog barked loudly, but no one was home to hear.

Practice the Rule

On a separate sheet of paper, write whether each sentence is simple or compound. For compound sentences, write the conjunction or punctuation that joins the clauses.

1. We planned a surprise party for Mother, but she suspected nothing.
2. I had to send out invitations.
3. Mother is allergic to wheat, so Father ordered a gluten-free birthday cake.
4. For dinner we're serving homemade soup, or perhaps some people will prefer the chili.
5. Auntie Linda offered to take care of the balloons and streamers.
6. Uncle Richard made a beautiful birthday banner; he forgot it at his house, which is over an hour away!
7. Everything was set up just in time for the party to begin.
8. Mother arrived home from work promptly at 6:30.
9. When she entered the room, Father turned on the lights, and everyone else jumped up to shout, "Surprise!"
10. Mother let out a cry of surprise and joy.

Complex Sentences

Know the Rule

A dependent clause must be joined with an independent clause to make sense. A sentence made up of an independent clause and a dependent clause is a **complex sentence**. A dependent clause often begins with a subordinating conjunction such as *although, because, if, as,* or *when*. If a dependent clause begins a sentence, it is followed by a comma.

Example: Although they were cold and drenched, the marching band played throughout halftime.

A sentence that has at least two independent clauses and one or more dependent clauses is a compound-complex sentence.

Example: When you are no longer thirsty, please rinse out your canteen and place it back on the shelf above the water pump.

Practice the Rule

On a separate sheet of paper, write whether each sentence is a complex sentence or a compound-complex sentence.

1. While I'm much younger, my elderly neighbor and I have become great friends.
2. Mr. Morrison, although he is almost 90 years old, walks me to my bus stop each morning, and then he walks me back home each afternoon.
3. When it gets hot in summer, we often stay inside to play checkers, or he'll sit and tell me stories about his life.
4. When he gets tired, he gently tells me it's time for his afternoon nap.
5. As we've planned, Mr. Morrison and I are going to a baseball game tomorrow morning.
6. Mr. Morrison said he had a surprise for me, and just before the game started, he gave me a team jersey.
7. If our team is victorious, we plan on celebrating with a banana split back at my house.
8. Sometime while the seventh inning was being played, we knew we'd lost the game, yet we still hoped for the best.
9. When I think back on it, I'll know that day spent with Mr. Morrison was one of my favorites.
10. Whether it rains or shines, Mr. Morrison and I do fun things together, and I'm so lucky he lives right next door.

Publish

+Presentation

Publishing Strategy Perform the play.

Presentation Strategy Prepare the play on the computer.

I had so much fun writing this play, and I'll have even more fun watching it live. My play was chosen to be performed for my school during Science Week! Later, we may make a podcast of the play. I'll use my computer to prepare the play. Characters' names should be in dark print and followed by a colon, stage directions should be in italics, and plenty of white space should be between lines. These features make it easier to read and perform a play. But first I'll make sure I've done everything on my final checklist.

My Final Checklist

Did I—

- ✔ use conjunctions correctly in complex and compound-complex sentences?
- ✔ check for spelling, grammar, and punctuation mistakes?
- ✔ type my play neatly?
- ✔ use bold type, italics, and white space to make my play easy to read and perform?

Apply

Make a checklist to check your play. Then make a final copy that's ready to be read and performed!

WHAT A WOMAN CAN DO

by Nina

Characters

Marie Curie, a scientist

Pierre Curie, Marie's husband and scientific partner

Delivery Boy

Scene 1: *Both Marie and Pierre are working in their laboratory. Scientific apparatus is spread out along a long table. Pierre is bent over some equipment. Marie is carefully measuring something and then taking notes.*

Marie: (*walks over to Pierre while looking at her notebook*) Pierre, I am getting the same figures again! I've replicated my work for a third time and the results are still the same.

Pierre: (*sharply looks up, eyes wide with excitement*) An unknown more powerful than Henri Becquerel's uranium?

Marie: (*nods*) Yes. It's all here in the numbers. At first I believed I was just incorrectly duplicating Becquerel's experiments with uranium. But I've conducted the same experiment over and over and yet.... (*shaking her head and closing her notebook*)

Pierre: Do not doubt your qualifications as a chemist and physicist, Marie. You are, by far, one of the most brilliant scientific minds at work right now in Paris.

Marie: How I wish your support affected the world outside our laboratory walls! I grow weary of having to prove my discoveries over and over again, merely because I am a woman. And then—to have others still insinuate that I am merely repeating what *you* truly discovered. (*sarcastically*) A woman! How could a woman discover anything of scientific value!

Pierre: I know you constantly meet with resistance and indifference in our field of study, but they are fools. Put their doubts far from your mind. Tell me—what have you found?

Marie: (*Sighing deeply, she picks up her notebook, opens it, and calmly reads her notes aloud.*) "April 1898—Today I have recorded the exact numbers yet again. Both substances pitchblende and chalcolite are more powerful, emit more particles, than uranium. Determined to isolate more powerful element. Have done so. Results show a new, unrecorded element." (*hands Pierre her notebook*)

Pierre: What a discovery, Marie! You've done it! Let's isolate this new element one more time together, for prudence's sake. No one will dispute your clean and precise work. What name will you give this new element?

Marie: Polonium—after my motherland, Poland. (*The lights fade with both working at Marie's end of the table.*)

SCENE 2: *Marie and Pierre are both working in the laboratory. Even more equipment is set up along the table. Both are carefully watching their experiments and taking notes.*

Marie: Can you believe our fortune, Pierre? Discovering yet *another* new element only eight months after our first?

Pierre: (*walks over to Marie's side*) Fortune has nothing to do with it! Our devotion, our brilliant teamwork, and your fearlessness in a male-dominated field—these are the true elements that have led us to this very moment.

Marie: I've been thinking. This new element—it's so powerful. It literally *radiates* particles. It should be named *radium.*

Pierre: Brilliant! It's true. As an element—it's so active. It has such an effect on its surroundings. One could say an element as such displays *radioactivity.*

Marie: Let's begin writing our paper to release to our scientific peers. I do not want others to claim this discovery for themselves. Woman or not—I've completed this work with my very heart and hands. I do not wish to be robbed at this point in time.

Pierre: I could not agree more. To our office! (*Both leave the laboratory as lights dim.*)

Scene 3: *Marie and Pierre are in their office. Two small desks face each other to form one large desk. Pierre is sitting at his desk, watching Marie as she paces back and forth from her desk to a large bookcase on the other side of the office. Piles of books cover both desks and areas of the floor as well.*

Pierre: Marie, please sit. You've got to let it go.

Marie: What was I thinking? I should have known!

Pierre: (*shaking his head*) It's the Academy that's wrong. They are fools if they refuse to take your work seriously.

Marie: That was *our* work, Pierre! Now you must suffer because your partner is a woman—and your wife as well? I tell you—I'm sick of it all. It's been years since we've published our findings. Although the scientific world seemed to accept it as fact, there is still no word from the Academy, and no funding for further research!

Pierre: We have always found a way. Still do. I have no desire to be rich and famous.

Marie: Nor do I—you know that, Pierre! But just think of what research could be completed with proper funding. Think of the many struggling scientists we know—all on the verge of their own discoveries. The world may never know, never benefit, if they can't fund their own work.

(*There's a knock at the door. Marie opens the door, and a delivery boy hands her an envelope.*)

Delivery Boy: (*standing straight and speaking officially*) Special telegram for Madame Marie Curie.

Marie: (*quickly turning to Pierre*) Pierre! It's from the Royal Swedish Academy of Sciences. What could this mean?

Pierre: Open it and see! It's been five years since our discoveries. Too long for anyone to challenge us now. (*He quickly stands and walks to Marie's side. Marie and Pierre then silently read the letter together. The delivery boy strains to secretly read it over their shoulders.*)

Delivery Boy: (*no longer sounding official*) But what does it mean? What does it say?

Marie: It means we've done it! We—Pierre, myself, and Henri Becquerel—have been awarded the Nobel Prize for Physics! We all are being recognized for our work with radiation. (*Marie and Pierre embrace as the lights dim. The delivery boy moves to front of stage. One spotlight shines on him.*)

Delivery Boy: Marie and Pierre went on to share their award money with other scientists and friends in need. They used some of the money to fund their own research as well. Pierre was then offered a professorship and his own laboratory. Marie was made the Director of Research for Pierre's new lab. In 1911, Marie was awarded the Nobel Prize for Chemistry for her work with polonium and radium. She was not only the first *woman* to receive a Nobel Prize, but she was also the first *person* to be awarded two Nobel Prizes. Marie's research and accomplishments paved the way for women in physics and chemistry.

Reflect

How did Nina do? Did she use all the traits of a good play in her writing? Check it against the rubric. Don't forget to use the rubric to check your own play, too.

Narrative test writing

Read the Writing Prompt

When you take a writing test, you'll be given a writing prompt. Most writing prompts have three parts:

Setup This part of the writing prompt gives you the background information you need to get ready to write.

Task This part of the writing prompt tells you exactly what you are supposed to write: a personal narrative describing your experience of learning a new skill.

Scoring Guide This section tells how your writing will be scored. To do well on the test, you should make sure you do everything on the list.

Remember the rubrics you used earlier in the unit? When you take a writing test, you don't always have all of the information that's on a rubric. However, the scoring guide is a lot like a rubric. It lists everything you need to think about to write a good paper. Like the rubrics you've used in this unit, many scoring guides are based on these six important traits of writing:

Think about a time when you learned a new skill. Maybe it was a new sport or a new hobby that you had never done before.

Write a personal narrative describing your experience of learning a new skill.

Be sure your writing

- uses appropriate narrative techniques, such as dialogue and description, to develop the story.
- is well organized with events that unfold naturally from beginning to end.
- uses a voice that is appropriate for the audience and purpose.
- captures the action with powerful verbs.
- has a variety of sentences.
- contains correct grammar, punctuation, capitalization, and spelling.

Writing Traits
in the Scoring Guide

The scoring guide in the prompt on page 111 has been made into this chart. Does it remind you of the rubrics you've used? Not all prompts include all the writing traits, but this one does. Use the scoring guide to do your best writing. Remember to write neatly and put your name on each page.

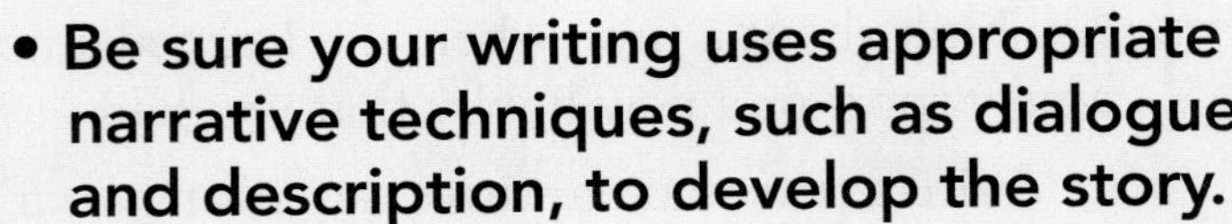

- **Be sure your writing uses appropriate narrative techniques, such as dialogue and description, to develop the story.**

- **Be sure your writing is well organized with events that unfold naturally from beginning to end.**

- **Be sure your writing uses a voice that is appropriate for the audience and purpose.**

- **Be sure your writing captures the action with powerful verbs.**

- **Be sure your writing has a variety of sentences.**

- **Be sure your writing contains correct grammar, punctuation, capitalization, and spelling.**

Look at Nick Vaughan's story on the next page. Did he follow the scoring guide?

Climbing Higher

by Nick Vaughan

The climbers around here call it "Red Rock," a rust-colored boulder near my home that's about two stories high and always seems to have a small crowd of climbers ascending and descending it. Now it was my turn. I'd had fun at indoor climbing gyms, but now I was ready to finally conquer Red Rock. One summer morning, I joined three other students and our instructor, Paul, to learn to rock climb outdoors.

Paul, who was in his twenties, was lean and tan from spending a lot of time rock climbing. He explained to the group that the safest way to start outdoors was top-roping. That's where a rope secured to the top of a boulder is attached to the body harness worn by both the climber and the belayer, who is the person on the ground who helps let out and pull in rope.

With my harness adjusted, Paul gave me some pointers on climbing. "Use your legs and not your arms," Paul said. "Stand straight up with your legs to get higher; don't pull yourself up with your arms." He eased my fears by reminding me that top-roping was safe. "Well, relatively safe," he added.

With my heart pumping fast, I started up the rock. I hugged the wall tightly as my hands clung onto the crevices. Then, as Paul instructed, I lifted my legs up to reach the next level. As I climbed, I could feel beads of sweat starting to form on my forehead.

Once, my foot missed the crevice I was trying to use, and I started to slip. My heart raced. I hung on as hard as I could. My belayer, a college student named Sarah, pulled the rope taut so I wouldn't fall. "Belay!" she yelled. After what seemed like minutes, my foot finally found the crevice. "On belay!" I yelled back, to let her know I was OK and ready to keep going.

Even though Red Rock was only a couple stories high, I was still nervous. I tried not to look down but instead focused on reaching the top. With each step higher, the top of the rock was closer, and my fears were further away.

At last, I made it. My arms and legs were trembling, but I had done it and I was proud. I had finally conquered Red Rock.

Using the Scoring Guide to Study the Model

Now we'll use the scoring guide to check Nick's writing test, "Climbing Higher." Let's see how well his story meets each of the six writing traits.

- **The writing uses appropriate narrative techniques, such as dialogue and description, to develop the story.**

Nick does a great job helping me envision Red Rock and his first experience climbing it. His vivid descriptions and dramatic dialogue held my interest throughout the story.

> The climbers around here call it "Red Rock," a rust-colored boulder near my home that's about two stories high and always seems to have a small crowd of climbers ascending and descending it.

> My belayer, a college student named Sarah, pulled the rope taut so I wouldn't fall. "Belay!" she yelled.

- **The writing is well organized with events that unfold naturally from beginning to end.**

Nick's writing moves smoothly from point to point. When I reached the end, I didn't feel that I had missed any part of the story.

> At last, I made it. My arms and legs were trembling, but I had done it and I was proud. I had finally conquered Red Rock.

- **The voice is appropriate for the audience and purpose.**

Nick's purpose is to entertain and inspire other readers his own age. His voice reflects this well. It was easy to connect with his writing, and I felt ready to face my own fears after reading "Climbing Higher."

Even though Red Rock was only a couple stories high, I was still nervous. I tried not to look down but instead focused on reaching the top. With each step higher, the top of the rock was closer, and my fears were further away.

- **The writing captures the action with powerful verbs.**

Nick uses a lot of powerful verbs that helped create a strong image in my mind as I read. I could really "see" what was happening, and my attention was held from beginning to end.

With my heart pumping fast, I started up the rock. I hugged the wall tightly as my hands clung onto the crevices. Then, as Paul instructed, I lifted my legs up to reach the next level. As I climbed, I could feel beads of sweat starting to form on my forehead.

Using the Scoring Guide to Study the Model

- A variety of sentences are used.

I like how Nick uses a variety of sentences. Mixing shorter sentences with longer sentences helps the writing flow and makes reading the story more enjoyable.

Once, my foot missed the crevice I was trying to use, and I started to slip. My heart raced. I hung on as hard as I could. My belayer, a college student named Sarah, pulled the rope taut so I wouldn't fall.

- The writing contains correct grammar, punctuation, capitalization, and spelling.

From what I could tell, Nick uses correct capitalization, punctuation, spelling, and grammar. Don't forget to check for mistakes in your own work. If you know you often misspell words, for instance, you should pay close attention to spelling. Editing for grammar and mechanics throughout the writing process will help you avoid errors on your final test.

Planning My Time

Before giving us a writing test prompt, my teacher tells us how much time we'll have to complete the test. Since I'm already familiar with the writing process, I can think about how much total time I need and then divide it into the different parts of the writing process. If the test takes an hour, here's how I can organize my time. Planning your time will help you, too!

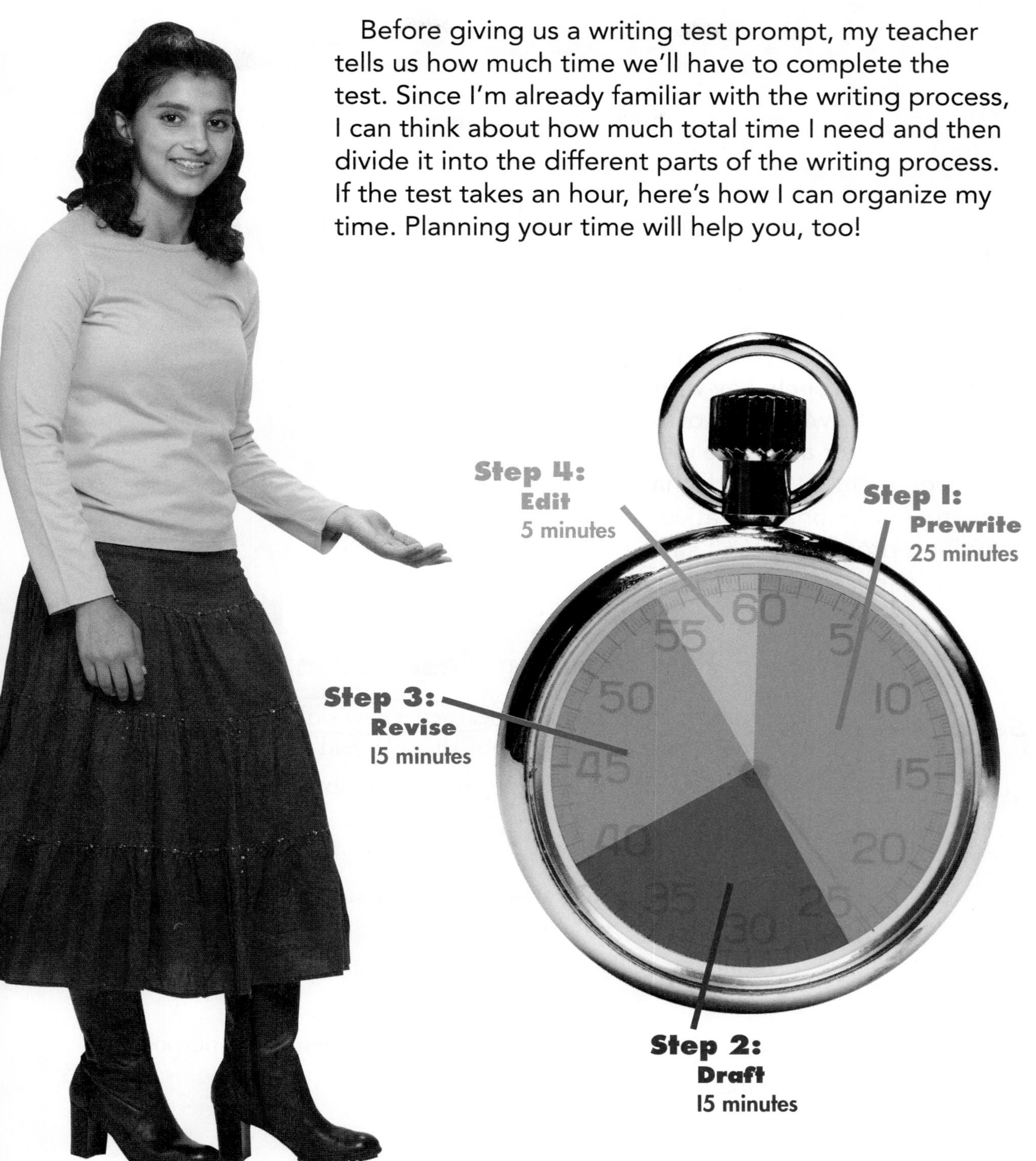

Prewrite

Focus on **Ideas**

Writing Strategy Study the writing prompt to find out what to do.

As soon as I get my writing prompt, I study it so that I'll know exactly what I'm supposed to do. A writing prompt often has three parts, but the parts aren't usually labeled. Locate and label the setup, task, and scoring guide on your writing prompt, as I did on mine below. Circle key words in the setup and in the task that tell what kind of writing you need to do and who your audience will be. I circled my topic in green. Then I circled what kind of writing I'll be doing (a personal narrative) in orange. Since the writing prompt doesn't say who the audience is, I'll write my story for my teacher.

My Writing Test Prompt

Setup — Remember a time when you learned a new skill or talent. Maybe it was a new sport or a new hobby that you had never done before.

Task — Write a personal narrative describing your experience of learning a new skill.

Scoring Guide — Be sure your writing

- uses appropriate narrative techniques, such as dialogue and description, to develop the story.
- is well organized with events that unfold from beginning to end.
- has a voice that is appropriate for the audience and purpose.
- captures the action with powerful verbs.
- has a variety of sentences.
- contains correct grammar, punctuation, capitalization, and spelling.

Think about how the scoring guide relates to the six writing traits you've studied in the rubrics. All of the traits might not be included in every scoring guide, but you need to remember them all to write a good narrative.

Ideas

- **Be sure your writing uses appropriate narrative techniques, such as dialogue and description, to develop the story.**

I'll need to come up with an entertaining story and use clear, descriptive language to create a vivid picture for my reader.

Organization

- **Be sure your writing is well organized with events that unfold naturally from beginning to end.**

I'll keep my story well organized and complete, and I'll use transitions to smoothly guide my reader from one event to the next.

Voice

- **Be sure your writing uses a voice that is appropriate for the audience and purpose.**

I'll use a voice that is not too formal, but not too casual either. I want my reader to connect with my story and also believe it.

Word Choice

- **Be sure your writing captures the action with powerful verbs.**

I can think of lots of powerful verbs to describe the action in my story and hold my reader's attention. This will be fun!

Sentence Fluency

- **Be sure your writing has a variety of sentences.**

I can add variety to my writing by using different kinds of sentences. This will help my writing flow better.

Conventions

- **Be sure your writing contains correct grammar, punctuation, capitalization, and spelling.**

I will pay close attention to my grammar and mechanics as I write.

Prewrite

Focus on **Ideas**

Writing Strategy Respond to the task.

Before you begin to write, you should always gather information. When you write to take a test, you can get information from the writing prompt. I'll take another look at the task now, since this is the part of the writing prompt that explains what I'm supposed to write. There isn't much time to rewrite, so it's really important to think about how you'll respond *before* you begin to write!

The writing prompt says to remember a time when I learned a new skill. I wrote down some notes about my idea to help.

Task — Write a personal narrative describing your experience of learning a new skill.

Notes

- ✔ I learned to in-line skate last year.
- ✔ It was a pretty exciting day!
- ✔ I fell a few times.

Apply

Before you start writing your story for a test, you should already know how you are going to respond to the task.

Prewrite

Focus on **Organization**

Writing Strategy Choose a graphic organizer.

I'll begin by organizing my ideas. First I'll choose a useful graphic organizer. I know that a really good graphic organizer for a personal narrative is a 5 W's Chart. It'll help me organize my story by answering the following questions: *What* happened? *Who* was there? *Why* did it happen? *When* did it happen? *Where* did it happen? Take a look at how I filled out this 5 W's Chart.

What happened?
- I learned to in-line skate.
- I fell three times—luckily, I was wearing pads and a helmet.
- Dad held onto me at first; then I was able to skate on my own. He said it was a lot like ice skating, which I know how to do, and he was right.
- I had to learn to stop.

Who was there?
- Just my dad and I

Why did it happen?
- I got in-line skates for my birthday and couldn't wait to try them out.
- I've always wanted to learn how to in-line skate.
- Dad's a good teacher because he used to play Roller Hockey.

When did it happen?
- The day after my 12th birthday; I couldn't wait any longer.

Where did it happen?
- We went to the parking lot at my dad's office on a Saturday—he wanted me to have plenty of room to skate.

Reflect

Did Nina answer all the questions with enough detail in her graphic organizer?

Apply

Use a graphic organizer to help you recall the important details for a personal narrative.

Prewrite

Focus on **Organization**

Writing Strategy Check the graphic organizer against the scoring guide.

You won't have much time for revisions during a test. That's why prewriting is a good idea! I'll check my 5 W's Chart against the scoring guide in the writing prompt before I start writing.

What happened?
- I learned to in-line skate.
- I fell three times—luckily, I was wearing pads and a helmet.
- Dad held onto me at first; then I was able to skate on my own. He said it was a lot like ice skating, which I know how to do, and he was right.
- I had to learn to stop.

Who was there?
- Just my dad and I

Why did it happen?
- I got in-line skates for my birthday and couldn't wait to try them out.
- I've always wanted to learn how to in-line skate.
- Dad's a good teacher because he used to play Roller Hockey.

When did it happen?
- The day after my 12th birthday; I couldn't wait any longer.

Where did it happen?
- We went to the parking lot at my dad's office on a Saturday—he wanted me to have plenty of room to skate.

Ideas

- **Be sure your writing uses appropriate narrative techniques, such as dialogue and description, to develop the story.**

I'll include lots of details from my 5 W's chart, as well as some dialogue, to "paint" a vivid picture of my story's events.

Organization

- **Be sure your writing is well organized with events that unfold naturally from beginning to end.**

I'll describe events as they happened by using transition words such as *next* and *then*. I won't skip around and confuse my reader.

Voice

- **Be sure your writing uses a voice that is appropriate for the audience and purpose.**

I'll keep my voice casual and use first-person point of view.

Word Choice

- **Be sure your writing captures the action with powerful verbs.**

I'll need to remember to use powerful verbs to give my writing energy.

Sentence Fluency

- **Be sure your writing has a variety of sentences.**

I'll keep this in mind as I write my draft.

- **Be sure your writing contains correct grammar, punctuation, capitalization, and spelling.**

When I go back and edit my draft, I'll make sure the grammar and mechanics are correct.

Reflect

Why is it important to check your graphic organizer before you begin writing?

Apply

Reread the scoring guide in the writing prompt before you start to write to be sure you know just what to do.

Draft

Focus on **Ideas**

Writing Strategy

Entertain the reader with lively, descriptive details and dialogue.

As I look back at the scoring guide, I'm reminded that I want to write a story that's interesting and entertaining. I'll use my 5 W's chart as a guide as I write my draft. I'll add lots of vivid details and even some interesting dialogue to liven things up.

Time to Roll

by Nina

For my birthday, I got a pair of in-line skates. I couldn't wait to get them on. But I didn't know how to skate. Fortunately, my dad, who used to play Roller Hockey, agreed to teach me. He had a plan: the next day, Saturday, he and I would head out to his office parking lot so that I could finally learn how to in-line skate! [entertaining, descriptive detail]

As we headed to his office that Saturday morning, I couldn't wait to get my skates on and go! My dad told me to be patient and gave me some pointers. He told me that in-line skating was a lot like ice skating, which I already knew how to do. He asked me if I was nervous. "I am not nervous at all," I said, "I am ready to skate." [interesting dialogue]

One skate around the parking lot and I knew I wasn't quite ready to skate. Giant oak trees lined the edge of the parking lot. You see,

Proofreading Marks

- Indent
- Make uppercase
- / Make lowercase
- ∧ Add something
- Take out something
- Add a period
- New paragraph
- (sp) Spelling error

[DRAFT]

stopping in Ice Skates and stopping in In-line Skates are two different things. I forgot to ask my dad how to stop until it was too late Before I hit his car, I fell to the ground, right on my hands! Fortunately, I was wearing a helmet and pads on my knees, elbows, and wrists.

Dad explained that to stop, I just had to lean back on my heels, where the stoppers were. For the next try, my dad suggested I hold on to him, just to get a feel for things without failing. Slowly, I skated with him.

[more dialogue]

"Try to stop." he instructed me. I lifted my toes and gently pressed. I came to a stop.

[entertaining, descriptive details]

He let me go on my own and had me practice turns. Uh-oh! My legs got a little crisscrossed once and I took another spill, legs tanlged and all. I was a still a little wobbly, but with every turn around the parking lot I began to feel more confident.

I fell once more, but that was because I'd gotten my speed up so much that I panicked when it was time to stop, but I was now an In-line Skater, ready to go out on my own and glide somewhat gracefully with my friends.

Reflect

What do you think? What makes Nina's story entertaining?

Apply

To help enliven your personal narrative, include fun, descriptive details and dialogue that make your story stand out!

Revise

Focus on **Organization**

Writing Strategy

Use transition words to clarify sequence.

I'll read my paper again for organization. The scoring guide says my writing should flow naturally from beginning to end. I know transition words connect ideas and help my writing flow. I found a spot that could be more clear, so I'll use some transitions to help my readers understand the sequence of events.

[added transition words]

Next ~~He~~ he let me go on my own and had me practice turns. Uh-oh! My legs got a little crisscrossed once and I took another spill, legs tanlged and all. When I got back up, I was a still a little wobbly, but with every turn around the parking lot I began to feel more confident.

Reflect

Is Nina's story easier to follow now that she's added some transition words?

Apply

Use transition words to help the reader follow your story.

Revise

Focus on **Voice**

Writing Strategy Connect with the readers.

The scoring guide says my voice should be appropriate for my audience and purpose. I'm sharing a personal experience, so first person is a great way to connect with my reader. But I found some dialogue that's too formal. What do you think of my revision?

[DRAFT]

He told me that in-line skating was a lot like ice skating, which I already knew how to do. He asked me if I was nervous. "~~I am not nervous at all~~ Nope," I said, "~~I am~~ I'm ready to skate!"

[used casual voice]

Reflect

Is it easier to connect with this scene now that Nina has revised the voice?

Apply

Use a voice that's appropriate for both your purpose and audience.

Revise

Focus on **Word Choice**

Writing Strategy Use powerful verbs to give the writing energy.

With my draft written, I'll read it to see if anything is missing. The scoring guide says to use powerful verbs. So I'll go back through and find some areas where I can change the verbs to be more powerful and exciting.

[DRAFT]

One ~~skate~~ whirl around the parking lot and I knew I wasn't quite ready to skate. Giant oak trees lined the edge of the parking lot. You see, stopping in Ice Skates and stopping in In-line Skates is a little bit different. I forgot to ask my dad how to stop until it was too late Before I hit his car, I ~~fell~~ tumbled to the ground, right on my hands!

[added powerful verbs]

Apply

Sometimes just changing a weaker verb to a more powerful one can add drama to your story.

Edit

Focus on **Conventions**

Writing Strategy Check the grammar, punctuation, capitalization, and spelling.

The scoring guide says to use correct grammar, punctuation, capitalization, and spelling. I made sure to leave enough time to do that.

FINAL DRAFT

Time to Roll

by Nina

the present I'd been wanting all year—

For my birthday, I got a pair of in-line skates. I couldn't wait to get

One problem, though:

them on. ~~But~~ I didn't know how to skate. Fortunately, my dad, who used to play Roller Hockey, agreed to teach me. He had a plan. The next day, Saturday, he and I would head out to his office parking lot so that I could finally learn how to in-line skate!

As we headed to his office that Saturday morning, I couldn't wait to get my skates on and go! My dad told me to be patient and gave me some pointers. He told me that in-line skating was a lot like ice skating, which I already knew how to do. He asked me if I was nervous. "Nope ~~I am not nervous at all~~," I said, "I'm ~~I am~~ ready to skate!"

One whirl ~~skate~~ around the parking lot and I knew I wasn't quite ready to skate. ~~Giant oak trees lined the edge of the parking lot.~~ You see,

Apply

It's important to check your grammar, punctuation, capitalization, and spelling every time you write for a test.

stopping in Ice Skates and stopping in In-line Skates are two different things. I forgot to ask my dad how to stop until it was too late! Before I hit his car, I tumbled to the ground, right on my hands! Fortunately, I was wearing a helmet and pads on my knees, elbows, and wrists.

Dad explained that to stop, I just had to lean back on my heels, where the stoppers were. For the next try, my dad suggested I hold onto him, just to get a feel for things without falling. Slowly, I skated with him.

"Try to stop," he instructed me. I lifted my toes and gently pressed. I came to a stop.

Next he let me go on my own and had me practice turns. Uh-oh! My legs got a little crisscrossed once and I took another spill, legs tangled and all. When I got back up, I was still a little wobbly, but with every turn around the parking lot I began to feel more confident.

I once more, but that was because I'd gotten my speed up so much that I panicked when it was time to stop. But I was now an in-line skater, ready to go out on my own and glide somewhat gracefully with my friends.

Reflect

Did Nina miss anything? Check her story against the scoring guide. Remember to use the scoring guide in your writing prompt to check your own writing anytime you take a test!

Guess what? We're finished! That wasn't bad at all! Here are some important tips to remember when you write for a test.

TEST TIPS

1. **Study the writing prompt before you start to write.** Most writing prompts have three parts: the setup, the task, and the scoring guide. The parts probably won't be labeled. You'll have to figure them out for yourself!
2. **Make sure you understand the task before you start to write.**
   - Read all three parts of the writing prompt carefully.
   - Circle key words in the task part of the writing prompt that tell what kind of writing you need to do. The task might also identify your audience.
   - Make sure you know how you'll be graded.
   - Say the assignment to yourself in your own words.
3. **Keep an eye on the clock.** Decide how much time you will spend on each part of the writing process and try to stick to your schedule. Don't spend so much time on prewriting that you don't have enough time to write.
4. **Reread your writing. Compare it to the scoring guide at least twice.** Remember the rubrics you have used all year? A scoring guide on a writing test is like a rubric. It can help you keep in mind what's important.
5. **Plan, plan, plan!** You don't get much time to revise during a test, so planning is more important than ever.
6. **Write neatly.** Remember: If the people who score your test can't read your writing, it doesn't matter how good your essay is!

Informative/ Explanatory writing explains something to the reader.

Hi, I'm Emily. In school, I'm learning about how to give my readers information through my writing. I might need to write a report to share what I have learned about a topic, or I might need to explain how to do or make something. I'm excited to try this kind of writing. I think it will help me become a better writer and thinker.

IN THIS UNIT

- Cause-and-Effect Report
- Research Report
- Summary: Response to Literature
- SOCIAL STUDIES CONNECTION ▶ Problem-Solution Essay
- Writing for a Test

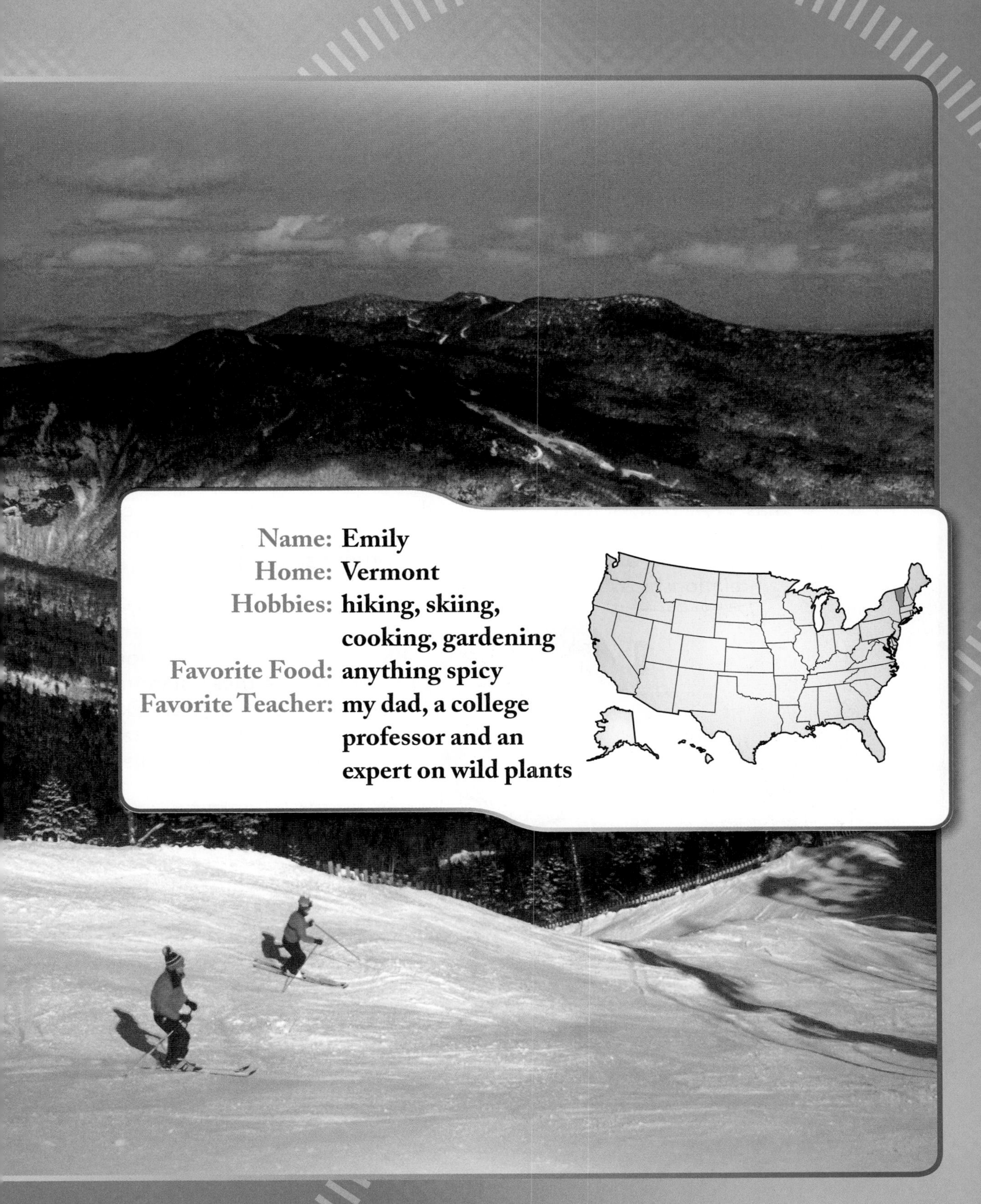
Name: Emily
Home: Vermont
Hobbies: hiking, skiing, cooking, gardening
Favorite Food: anything spicy
Favorite Teacher: my dad, a college professor and an expert on wild plants

What's a Cause-and-Effect Report?

It's a type of writing that deals with reasons (causes) that lead to specific results (effects). I think this kind of writing will be fun because I can pretend to be a detective who's looking for clues!

What's in a Cause-and-Effect Report?

Cause and Effect
These are the main reasons for the report. Every action, or cause, has a reaction, or effect. A cause-and-effect report focuses on cause-and-effect relationships.

Thesis Statement
This statement explains the main cause-and-effect relationship that the author wants to prove. A clear thesis statement can serve as the writer's starting point.

Supporting Evidence
Plenty of details should support the thesis statement in a cause-and-effect report. Details can include statistics, quotations, or real-life examples.

Transition Words and Phrases
Transition words and phrases connect important ideas in a cause-and-effect report. The writer often uses terms such as *because, if, so,* and *then* to let the reader know that one thing causes or results in another.

Why write a Cause-and-Effect Report?

There are plenty of reasons to write a cause-and-effect report. I listed some here, since I'm still thinking about why I want to write.

Make Connections
A cause-and-effect report tells readers about a connection they may not have known about. It breaks down an event, showing how it happened and connecting it to a specific cause.

Solve a Problem
A cause-and-effect report often answers the question "Why?" It also helps readers explore a problem and better understand it.

Entertain
A cause-and-effect report can be entertaining. Details can be lively and written in an upbeat tone. Think about some of the science shows you've seen on TV. Many of them explore cause-and-effect relationships in an exciting, interesting way, just like some reports.

Encourage Change
Sometimes it's hard to make a change until the causes and effects are explained. For example, if you want to put an end to a bad habit, you should first try to understand the causes and effects of your habit.

Linking Informative/Explanatory Writing Traits to a Cause-and-Effect Report

In this chapter, you will write to explain how one thing causes another. This type of informative/explanatory writing is called a cause-and-effect report. Emily will guide you through the stages of the writing process: Prewrite, Draft, Revise, Edit, and Publish. In each stage, Emily will show you important writing strategies that are linked to the Informative/Explanatory Writing Traits below.

Informative/Explanatory Writing Traits

- a clear, focused thesis
- relevant facts and concrete details that support and develop the thesis

- a strong introduction, body, and conclusion
- paragraphs that have a topic sentence and supporting details
- appropriate and varied transitions that connect ideas and show relationships

- appropriate voice and tone for the purpose and audience

- precise language
- domain-specific vocabulary that is used correctly and explained as necessary

- clear sentences whose structure supports the purpose

- no or few errors in grammar, usage, mechanics, and spelling

Before you write, read Dennis Nilssen's cause-and-effect report on the next page. Then use the cause-and-effect report rubric on pages 138–139 to decide how well he did. (You might want to look back at What's in a Cause-and-Effect Report? on page 134, too!)

Cause-and-Effect Report Model

The Perils of Sleep Deprivation

by Dennis Nilssen

How much sleep is enough? Experts agree that just about everyone needs eight hours a night. And how long do most people sleep? The average is fewer than seven hours. About one third of adults get fewer than six and a half hours per night. People may laugh off their sleep needs, saying that there aren't enough hours in the day to get everything done. But not getting enough sleep can harm a person's health and safety—as well as that of others—in many ways.

Thesis Statement

Have you ever heard the saying "A tired worker is only half a worker"? Everyone knows that sleepy workers can be a real problem in the workplace. They often get to work late. They don't contribute at meetings because they are too tired to pay attention. If they work with heavy equipment, they can easily injure themselves. If they are surgeons or pilots, they may botch surgeries or cause plane crashes. Consider the Chernobyl nuclear reactor accident and the Exxon Valdez oil spill. Both of these environmental catastrophes may have been the result of a worker not having enough sleep.

Transition Words and Phrases

Some doctors think that a constant lack of sleep can damage a person's health. There is no conclusive proof yet, but certain tests have shown that sleep deprivation can strongly change a person's metabolism (the biological process by which the body turns food into energy). Lack of sleep can alter the rate at which the body is able to re-energize and replenish itself. Sleep deprivation may even cause diabetes. In young people, it may also trigger conditions related to old age. Tests on sleep deprivation have also been done with laboratory rats. The results have shown that the less sleep an animal gets, the less able it is to ward off infections. The same may be true of humans.

Cause and Effect

Supporting Evidence

The most dangerous sleepy person, however, may be the sleepy driver. This is because nearly 100,000 traffic accidents per year are due, in part, to drowsy drivers. More than 1,500 passengers and drivers lose their lives each year in such accidents.

It is clear that lack of sleep results in all kinds of problems. If you are a six-hours-a-night person, do yourself a favor: Start going to bed and getting up at reasonable times. Your days will be much better!

Rubric

Use this 6-point rubric to plan and evaluate a cause-and-effect report.

	6	5	4
Ideas	The thesis statement is concise and clear. The writing provides relevant facts and concrete details that anticipate the reader's questions.	The thesis statement is clear. Many relevant facts and concrete details satisfy the reader's interest.	The thesis statement can be found easily. Several facts and concrete details help inform the reader.
Organization	Paragraphs are organized by cause and effect. The ideas in each paragraph are ordered logically.	Paragraphs are organized by cause and effect. Most ideas are ordered logically.	Paragraphs are largely organized by cause and effect. Some ideas are out of logical order within paragraphs.
Voice	The writer consistently uses a formal style.	The writer uses a formal style with very few breaks in style.	The writer uses a formal style in much of the essay.
Word Choice	Jargon, if used, is correct and explained.	One or two jargon terms are not clearly explained.	Some jargon terms may be used incorrectly or not clearly explained.
Sentence Fluency	Transitions are used effectively to vary sentence structure, resulting in smooth sentence flow and cohesion among ideas.	Transitions vary sentence structure, aiding sentence flow and cohesion among ideas in most of the essay.	Transitions are lacking or weak in a few places. Better transitions would improve flow and cohesion.
Conventions	Correct use of commas and apostrophes enhances the clarity of the writing.	Commas and apostrophes appear in the writing with minor errors that are easily overlooked.	Noticeable errors with commas and apostrophes don't interfere with meaning.
+Presentation	The fonts are legible and limited in number.		

3	2	1	
The thesis statement is not clear. Some facts are unrelated to the thesis, and details are vague or lacking.	The thesis statement is present but hard to understand. The facts and details are vague and mostly unrelated.	No thesis statement is present. The essay reads like a random collection of vague details.	Ideas
Paragraphs are sometimes organized by cause and effect. The order of ideas within paragraphs is sometimes unclear.	Paragraphs are not organized by cause and effect. The order of ideas within paragraphs is hard to follow.	The writing is not organized into paragraphs. The order of ideas is impossible to follow.	Organization
The writer's style wavers between formal and informal.	The writer's style is mostly informal.	The writer's style is impossible to discern.	Voice
Some jargon terms are used incorrectly or not explained at all.	Several jargon terms are used incorrectly. Explanations are missing.	All jargon used in the report is incorrect, unexplained, or both.	Word Choice
Transitions are lacking or weak in several places, resulting in poor sentence flow and lack of cohesion.	Few transitions are used. Sentence flow is choppy, leading to confusion of ideas.	No transitions are used. Sentences are impossible to follow, and ideas are unconnected.	Sentence Fluency
Noticeable errors with commas and apostrophes make the reader slow down to read.	Frequent errors with commas and apostrophes force the reader to reread sections of the report.	Many serious errors with commas and apostrophes interfere with the meaning.	Conventions

See Appendix B for 4-, 5-, and 6-point informative/explanatory rubrics.

Using the Cause-and-Effect Report Rubric to Study the Model

Did you notice that the model on page 137 points out some key elements of a cause-and-effect report? As he wrote "The Perils of Sleep Deprivation," Dennis Nilssen used these elements to help him describe the effects of a cause. He also used the 6-point rubric on pages 138–139 to plan, draft, revise, and edit the writing. A rubric is a great tool to evaluate writing during the writing process.

Now let's use the same rubric to score the model. To do this, we'll focus on each trait separately, starting with Ideas. We'll use the top descriptor for each trait (column 6), along with examples from the model, to help us understand how the traits work together. How would you score Dennis on each trait?

- **The thesis statement is concise and clear.**
- **The writing provides relevant facts and concrete details that anticipate the reader's questions.**

Dennis clearly introduces his thesis statement in the very first paragraph. Then, in the following paragraphs, he answers readers' possible questions about why sleep deprivation is a problem. By the end, I had a strong understanding of why sleep is so important.

[from the writing model]

Some doctors think that a constant lack of sleep can damage a person's health. There is no conclusive proof yet, but certain tests have shown that sleep deprivation can strongly change a person's metabolism (the biological process by which the body turns food into energy).

- **Paragraphs are organized by cause and effect.**
- **The ideas in each paragraph are ordered logically.**

I like how Dennis introduces a cause and then lists some of the related effects. This method just makes sense to me and really helped me understand the information.

[from the writing model]

Everyone knows that sleepy workers can be a real problem in the workplace. They often get to work late. They don't contribute at meetings because they are too tired to pay attention.

- **The writer consistently uses a formal style.**

Dennis understands the possible severe consequences of too little sleep, and he wants his reader to understand, too. His style throughout his writing is formal, which helps get the message across.

[from the writing model]

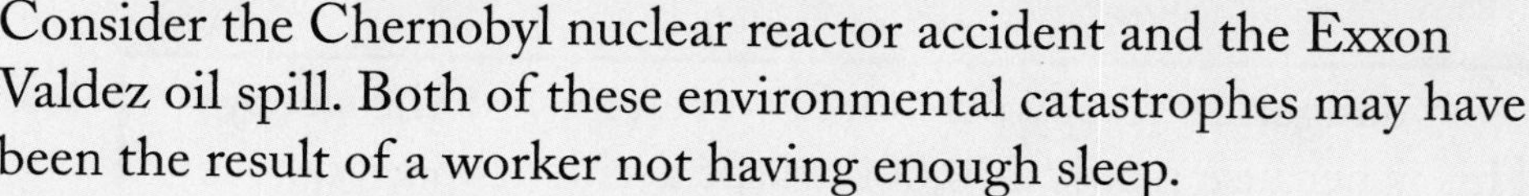
Consider the Chernobyl nuclear reactor accident and the Exxon Valdez oil spill. Both of these environmental catastrophes may have been the result of a worker not having enough sleep.

- **Jargon, if used, is correct and explained.**

I'm glad Dennis clearly explains all jargon right after using the difficult term. If I didn't know what the word meant, I wouldn't fully understand or enjoy his paper.

[from the writing model]

There is no conclusive proof yet, but certain tests have shown that sleep deprivation can strongly change a person's metabolism (the biological process by which the body turns food into energy). Lack of sleep can alter the rate at which the body is able to re-energize and replenish itself.

- **Transitions are used effectively to vary sentence structure, resulting in smooth sentence flow and cohesion among ideas.**

Dennis does a great job of using transitions like *however* and *in part* to create sentence variety. His sentences flow together smoothly, and I can see how his ideas are connected. When ideas have cohesion, they fit together well.

[from the writing model]

The most dangerous sleepy person, however, may be the sleepy driver. This is because nearly 100,000 traffic accidents per year are due, in part, to drowsy drivers. More than 1,500 passengers and drivers lose their lives each year in such accidents.

- **Correct use of commas and apostrophes enhances the clarity of the writing.**

Dennis uses commas and apostrophes correctly throughout his report. All contractions and possessive nouns are written accurately, and commas are used to help separate several independent clauses in one sentence.

[from the writing model]

People may laugh off their sleep needs, saying that there aren't enough hours in the day to get everything done. But not getting enough sleep can harm a person's health and safety—as well as that of others—in many ways.

Presentation The fonts are legible and limited in number.

My Turn!

I'm going to write a cause-and-effect report of my own. I'll follow the rubric and use good writing strategies. Read on to see how I do it!

Prewrite

Focus on **Ideas**

The Rubric Says The thesis statement is concise and clear.

Writing Strategy Do research and take notes about a cause-effect relationship in nature.

Living near mountains can teach you a thing or two about high altitudes. There's less oxygen high up and you need to ascend a mountain gradually to allow your body to adjust. But what, exactly, *can* happen? To find the answer, I looked at science texts and websites that I knew were reliable and appropriate. I found three specific effects of altitude on humans. Here are my notes.

1. high altitude pulmonary edema (fluid in lungs)
- tightness in the chest, feeling of suffocation, cough
- skin may turn colors, thinking becomes unclear, may even die
- go down, seek medical help

2. high altitude cerebral edema (brain tissue swells, fluid leaks)
- loss of coordination, confused mental functions, could lead to death
- could happen after about a week at high altitude
- go down right away, get treatment

3. acute mountain sickness (pretty common)
- generally get it over 10,000 feet
- headaches, dizziness, shortness of breath, sometimes nausea
- usually feel better when adjusted to level of altitude

Select a natural event and do research on it. Then take notes.

Prewrite

Focus on **Organization**

The Rubric Says Paragraphs are organized by cause and effect.

Writing Strategy Make a Cause-and-Effect Chain to organize the ideas.

The rubric says my paragraphs should be organized by cause and effect. The better organized my notes are, the easier it will be to write well-organized paragraphs. A Cause-and-Effect Chain is the perfect organizer for this task.

Writer's Term

Cause-and-Effect Chain

Sometimes one cause has several effects. An effect can also become a cause of another effect. When this happens, you can use a **Cause-and-Effect Chain** to show the causes of certain effects.

Cause-and-Effect Chain

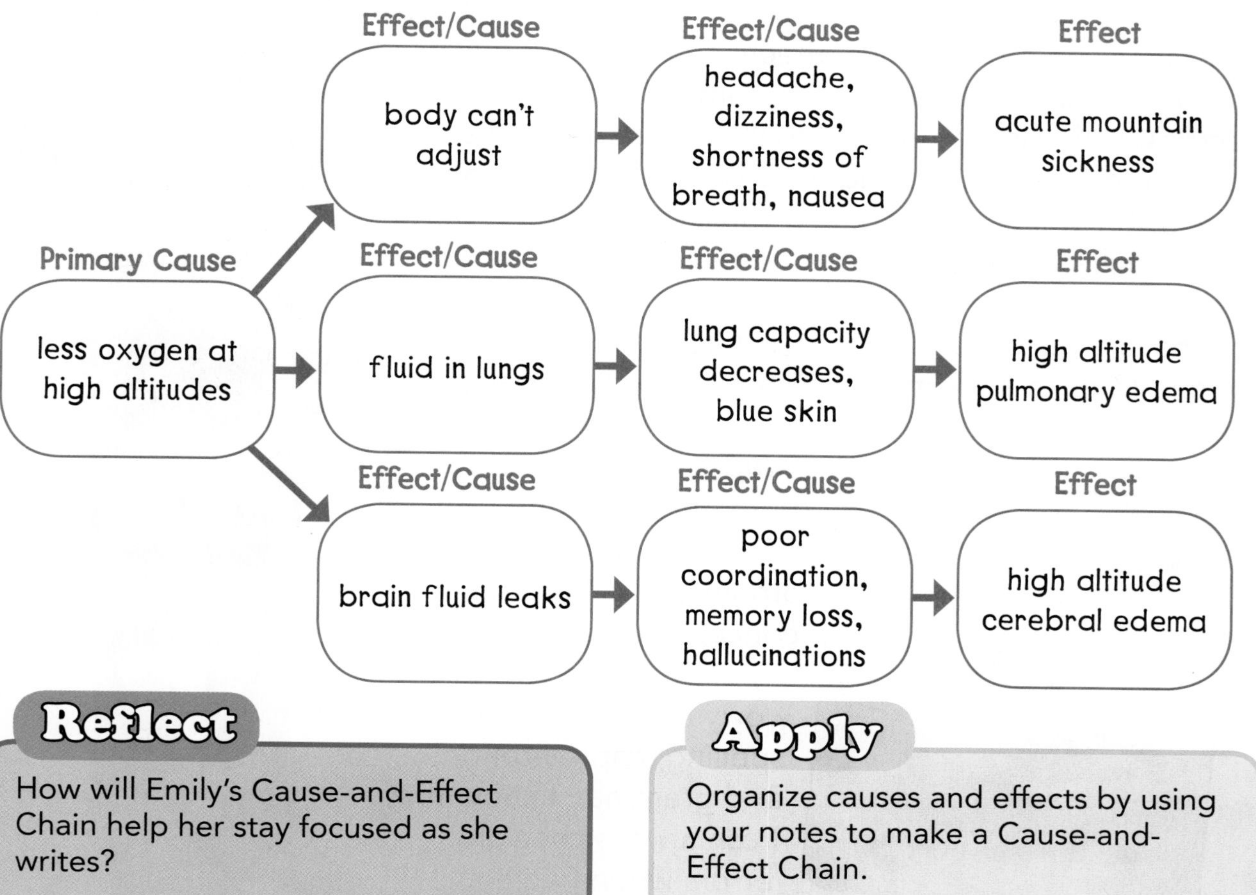

Reflect

How will Emily's Cause-and-Effect Chain help her stay focused as she writes?

Apply

Organize causes and effects by using your notes to make a Cause-and-Effect Chain.

Draft

Focus on **Ideas**

The Rubric Says The thesis statement is concise and clear.

Writing Strategy Include a concise thesis statement that reflects the purpose for writing.

Writer's Term

Thesis Statement

The **thesis statement** briefly states the purpose or main idea of an essay or a report.

The main purpose of my report is to explain that high altitudes can have serious effects on health. I'll follow the rubric and write a thesis statement to get that idea across. A thesis statement usually comes in the first paragraph so that the audience understands the point the writer will be making. In a cause-and-effect report, the thesis statement focuses on the cause-and-effect relationship to be discussed.

I have a good thesis statement in mind, so now I'll use my Cause-and-Effect Chain to help me organize the rest of my report. I think it will be easiest to devote one paragraph to each of the three effects on the right-hand side of my graphic organizer. As I draft, I'll concentrate on getting my ideas down without worrying too much about spelling, capitalization, and grammar. I know that I can always check for errors when I edit.

Proofreading Marks

- Indent
- Make uppercase
- Make lowercase
- Add something
- Take out something
- Add a period
- New paragraph
- Spelling error

[DRAFT]

What High Altitudes Can Do to You

When I was younger, my family vacationed in the mountains of Colorado. A few of us didn't feel well for the first several days, especially after a hiking trip. I knew there was less oxygen high up, but could that actually make us feel ill? After researching the topic, I've learned that high altitudes can have some pretty serious effects on people.

[concise thesis statement]

One effect is a condition called acute mountain sickness. Some people get sick with this when they hike up around 10,000 feet. The symptoms include headache, dizziness, shortness of breath, and sometimes, nausea. Talk about feeling miserable! Most of the time, hikers are able to continue climbing because they get used to the heights after a couple of days. And if they climb at a moderite pace, they are usually all right. But climbers have to be careful. If they climb too high too quickly, their conditions can get worse.

Reflect

Does Emily's thesis statement reflect her reason for writing?

Apply

It's time to start your draft. Be sure to include a brief thesis statement that explains your purpose.

Revise

Focus on **Organization**

The Rubric Says The ideas in each paragraph are ordered logically.

Writing Strategy Make sure the ideas are in order.

I think I did a great job ordering the ideas in my paragraphs! I wrote a topic sentence for each paragraph, and then wrote several, logically ordered supporting sentences to follow. But now that I reread my draft, I see that the ideas in my conclusion need to be reordered to make more sense.

[DRAFT]

[reordered ideas]

People must be careful and observant when they're at heights that are unusual for them. But altitude sickness does not always cause serious problems.

Apply

Make sure your ideas are logically ordered in each paragraph.

Revise

Focus on  Voice

The Rubric Says The writer consistently uses a formal style.

Writing Strategy Maintain consistency in style and tone.

The rubric says I should be consistent in using a formal style. My writing style is created from the choices I make in using words, phrases, and sentence structures. My tone is the attitude I convey to the reader; it shows how I feel about the subject. My style choices set the tone of the essay.

Now that I think about it, using a formal style makes a lot of sense for this essay because I take altitude sickness very seriously. To make sure I'm using a formal style consistently to set the tone, I'll remove casual language and rewrite any sentences that are incomplete or incorrect.

[DRAFT]

The symptoms include headache, dizziness, shortness of breath, and sometimes, nausea. ~~Talk about feeling miserable!~~ Most of the time, hikers are able to continue climbing because they get used to the heights after a couple of days.

[deleted casual style]

Reflect

What do you think? How would the deleted sentence affect Emily's credibility if she had not removed it?

Apply

Use a serious style to keep your writing credible and strong.

Revise

Focus on **Word Choice**

The Rubric Says Jargon, if used, is correct and explained.

Writing Strategy Clearly explain unfamiliar terms and jargon.

Writer's Term

Jargon

Jargon is the language used by a group of people to describe their profession, trade, or hobby. One group (such as nurses or horseback riders) might not understand the jargon used by another group (such as athletes or skydivers). For this reason, whenever jargon is used, it should always be carefully explained.

I'm concerned that the reader will be unfamiliar with some of the words I've used in my report. The rubric says to make sure all jargon is clearly explained, so I'll reread my draft now, looking for words that need further clarification.

[DRAFT]

Finally, high altitude cerebral edema can occur after about a week spent at high altitude. ^ Because the brain is affected, symptoms may include

High altitude cerebral edema is the name of a condition in which the brain's fluid begins to leak out, causing a swelling in brain tissue.

[explained jargon]

Make sure to explain all unfamiliar terms and jargon.

Edit

Focus on **Conventions**

The Rubric Says Correct use of commas and apostrophes enhances the clarity of the writing.

Writing Strategy Check the use of commas and apostrophes.

Writer's Term

Apostrophes

Use an **apostrophe** to form singular and plural possessives. Also use an apostrophe to replace the missing letter(s) in a contraction.

I know that punctuation mistakes will confuse my reader and make reading my work difficult. I'll fix any errors with commas and apostrophes now.

[DRAFT]

[corrected a plural possessive]

[corrected a singular possessive]

As the lungs' capacity ~~decreeses~~ decreases, a person's skin may turn blue. Other possible effects of lessened lung capacity are coughing and chest tightness, or a feeling of suffocation. If the edema isn't treated, a person can die from it. That's why it's important to descend from high altitude and get medical help at the first signs of edema.

[corrected a contraction]

Reflect

How do Emily's edits help her writing make more sense and flow better?

Apply

Conventions

Edit your draft for spelling, punctuation, and capitalization, making sure apostrophes and commas are used correctly.

For more practice with apostrophes and commas, use the exercises on the next two pages.

Apostrophes

Know the Rule

Apostrophes are used to form possessive nouns and contractions.

- Singular nouns and plural nouns not ending in *s* form the possessive by adding *'s*.
  Examples: friend (friend**'s**) children (children**'s**)
- Singular nouns ending in *s* form the possessive by adding *'s*.
  Examples: James (James**'s**) bus (bus**'s**)
- Plural nouns ending in *s* form the possessive by adding an apostrophe.
  Examples: trees (trees**'**) buses (buses**'**)
- An apostrophe replaces the missing letter or letters in a contraction.
  Examples: do + not = don't I + would = I'd
- Use an apostrophe to form the contraction of *it is*, but do not use an apostrophe to form the possessive of *it*.
  Example: The cat hurt **its** paw, but **it's** going to be OK.

Practice the Rule

On a separate sheet of paper, rewrite the sentences using correct punctuation.

1. Its difficult to predict who will suffer from high altitude sickness.
2. Peoples reactions are different at different levels.
3. But youre probably going to get sick if you go too high too soon.
4. As altitude increases, the airs oxygen level decreases.
5. A persons body has to adjust.
6. The bodys response could be headache, nausea, or interrupted sleep.
7. Ive never had altitude sickness myself, but it doesnt sound like much fun at all.
8. Its a risk everyone takes if they want to climb mountains.
9. Its less likely youll get altitude sickness if you take time to let your body get used to higher elevations.
10. Climbers physical condition may also make a difference in whether theyll get sick.

Commas

Know the Rule

Commas tell a reader where to pause. A comma is used to separate an **introductory word**, such as *yes* or *well*, from the rest of the sentence.

Example: No, I don't think I'll be going out tonight.

A comma is also used to separate **independent clauses** in a compound sentence and to separate a **noun of direct address** from the rest of a sentence. A noun of direct address names a person who is being spoken to.

Example: Every Tuesday night is pasta night at my house, and this week we've invited the neighbors over to share.

Example: Jincy, would you like to study together after school?

Practice the Rule

Copy the following sentences onto a separate sheet of paper, adding commas where they are needed.

1. Doris can you remember where you put your glasses?
2. Well I certainly haven't seen them for days!
3. I know you need them for reading but will you be all right driving home?
4. Oh no I think I see what happened to your glasses.
5. Yes I do believe the dog has them and has chewed them quite thoroughly.
6. Oh dear I can see they're mostly intact but can you actually use them?
7. These are your glasses Doris and they are in need of some serious repair!
8. It's kind of you to forgive me but I insist on paying to have them fixed.
9. I know a good optical shop but it won't be open until tomorrow morning.
10. Indeed I'll be happy to bring your glasses there as soon as I can.

Publish +Presentation

Publishing Strategy Submit my report to the school website.

Presentation Strategy Use a limited number of clear fonts.

I'm finished with my cause-and-effect report, and I can't wait to publish it! I've decided to submit my paper to the school website. That means I'll have to type my paper on a computer. I like using a computer because it lets me keep good margins, and I love choosing cool fonts. But I'll be sure to use only one or two clear fonts to keep things readable. I'll choose one font for the title and one for the body of my paper. Before I submit it, I also need to check it one last time against my final checklist.

My Final Checklist

Did I—

✔ use apostrophes in contractions and possessives correctly?

✔ use commas correctly?

✔ use only a few clear fonts for my paper?

✔ correct all spelling, grammar, and punctuation mistakes?

Apply

Check your cause-and-effect report against this checklist. Then make a final copy to publish.

What High Altitudes Can Do to You

by Emily

When I was younger, my family vacationed in the mountains of Colorado. A few of us didn't feel well for the first several days, especially after a hiking trip. I knew there was less oxygen high up, but could that actually make us feel ill? After researching the topic, I've learned that high altitudes can have some pretty serious effects on people.

One effect is a condition called acute mountain sickness. Some people get sick with this when they hike up around 10,000 feet. The symptoms include headache, dizziness, shortness of breath, and sometimes, nausea. Most of the time, hikers are able to continue climbing because they get used to the heights after a couple of days. And if they climb at a moderate pace, they are usually all right. But climbers have to be careful. If they climb too high too quickly, their conditions can get worse.

High altitude pulmonary edema is another effect that high altitude can have on a person. *Pulmonary* refers to the lungs, and *edema* refers to bleeding. High altitude can cause fluid to develop in the lungs. This can prevent oxygen from getting into the blood. As the lungs' capacity decreases, a person's skin may turn blue. Other possible effects of lessened lung capacity are coughing and chest tightness, or a feeling of suffocation. If the edema isn't treated, a person can die from it. That's why it's important to descend from high altitude and get medical help at the first signs of edema.

Finally, high altitude cerebral edema can occur after about a week spent at high altitude. High altitude cerebral edema is the name of a condition in which the brain's fluid begins to leak out, causing a swelling in brain tissue. Because the brain is affected, symptoms may include poor coordination, memory loss, and hallucinations. Once these symptoms are noticed, sufferers should immediately descend and seek medical help. Otherwise, death is possible.

Altitude sickness does not always cause serious problems. But people must be careful and observant when they're at heights that are unusual for them.

Reflect

Did Emily use all the traits of a good cause-and-effect report? Check her writing against the rubric, and don't forget to use the rubric to check your own work, too.

What's a Research Report?

A research report contains information that a writer discovers after asking questions, researching answers, and explaining discoveries about a specific topic. I like learning about new stuff, so I can't wait to get started!

What's in a Research Report?

Topic
A research report focuses on one main topic. When I write my report, I'll choose a topic that's interesting to me. Then, I can have fun while doing my research!

Structure
This is the way the report is organized. A good research report should include a strong introduction, body, and conclusion. It should also include a list of my sources.

Quotes
Concrete details from experts can add credibility to research writing. That's why it's important to include quotations in a research report.

Paraphrased Information
Writers paraphrase information when they use their own words to restate what someone else has said. It's important to paraphrase and give credit to my sources so that I can avoid plagiarism—stealing someone else's ideas or words.

Why write a Research Report?

I don't know yet why I want to write a research report, but here are a few reasons I'm thinking about.

Learning About a Topic
Doing research is a way to find out more about a topic. I bet I'll learn a lot in the process of writing my research report.

Public Service
Sometimes a research report includes public service information that can help people. For example, I once read a report on severe weather conditions, and now I know how to stay safe during a storm.

Entertainment
A research report can be entertaining. For instance, it would be kind of fun to do research on how to join the circus!

Researching Sources
Writing a research report can help me learn how to judge sources. If I see the same information in several different sources, I can probably trust the authors. Then I can look for more sources written by the same authors.

Linking Informative/Explanatory Writing Traits to a **Research Report**

In this chapter, you will write to inform your readers about an important topic. This type of informative/explanatory writing is called a research report. Emily will guide you through the stages of the writing process: Prewrite, Draft, Revise, Edit, and Publish. In each stage, Emily will show you important writing strategies that are linked to the Informative/Explanatory Writing Traits below.

Informative/Explanatory Writing Traits

- a clear, focused thesis
- relevant facts and concrete details that support and develop the thesis

- a strong introduction, body, and conclusion
- paragraphs that have a topic sentence and supporting details
- appropriate and varied transitions that connect ideas and show relationships

- appropriate voice and tone for the purpose and audience

- precise language
- domain-specific vocabulary that is used correctly and explained as necessary

- clear sentences whose structure supports the purpose

- no or few errors in grammar, usage, mechanics, and spelling

Before you write, read Isabel Sandoval's research report on the next three pages. Then use the research report rubric on pages 162–163 to decide how well she did. (You might want to look back at What's in a Research Report? on page 156, too!)

Research Report Model

The Weight Problem in America

by Isabel Sandoval

Structure: Introduction

Next time you're in a crowd, take a look around you. If the crowd is typical, many people are probably heavier than they should be. Weight has become a real health concern in America. This paper will present several facts and discuss some of the causes of overweight Americans. It will also suggest possible ways to overcome this epidemic.

Topic

Are all overweight Americans unhealthy or unfit? No. Muscular people weigh more than others who look about the same size. This is because muscle is heavier than fat. Also, pregnant women weigh more than they normally do, but this doesn't mean they're unfit. And some people are naturally heavier than others, but again, this doesn't always mean they're unhealthy. However, many people are seriously overweight, and these are the ones at risk for health problems.

Here are some figures to think about: More than 97 million Americans are overweight. According to the American Obesity Association, about 39 million of these are obese, which means they are more than 30 pounds overweight. Obesity is the cause of some 300,000 deaths in this country every year. It is also a risk factor in many ailments, including heart disease, arthritis, diabetes, high cholesterol, and cancer.

Obesity is not unknown in other countries; however, it is a much bigger problem in the United States. Consider Sam Moore, who moved here from Sierra Leone in 1998. His story is fairly common: "When I first came," Sam told writer Lawrence Lindner, "I was around 165 [pounds]. Now I'm looking at close to 200. It creeps up on you" (T11). Sam is 5 foot 9 inches tall. He should definitely be concerned about letting two hundred pounds "creep up" on him.

Quotes

Other immigrants report similar weight gain. Some of them were asked to think why this has happened. Many pointed out the size of restaurant portions. Over and over, they talked about the size of meals served in American restaurants. One woman commented on a huge salad and an enormous dish of pasta that she was served for dinner. She noted that even her 6-foot 5-inch boyfriend couldn't have eaten it all. Yet the meal is a typical size for a dinner in an American restaurant.

Structure: Body

Structure: Body

The amount that Americans eat is only part of the problem. Another problem is the kind of food eaten. In China, a meal might consist of a low-calorie clear soup containing several vegetables. This would satisfy a person's hunger because of the high fiber and water content. But compare this meal with the all-too-common American dinner consisting of a cheeseburger, French fries, and a soft drink. A large portion of each would total about an 1800-calorie meal. Yet, fast food restaurants now account for about 40 percent of the average American family's food budget.

Besides eating large, unhealthy portions, Americans also like to snack, and it's no surprise that many of these popular snacks are high in fat and calories. For example, a 4-ounce bag of cheese puffs or potato chips contains about 640 calories, and a piece of cheesecake has about 470 calories. By contrast, an apple or a pear has fewer than 90 calories.

Another important part of the American weight problem is Americans' lack of exercise. In 1991, nearly half of our schools had daily physical education classes. By 1997, this number decreased to 27 percent. Also, many students watch TV or play video games after school instead of participating in afterschool sports. In a recent study by the Centers for Disease Control, only 28 percent of overweight adults who tried to exercise actually did so enough to make a difference. And many overweight adults do not exercise at all.

Paraphrased Information

So what can we do? Well, here's one good piece of advice: Get a better understanding of what is an appropriate portion. In spite of what restaurants serve, the average eater doesn't need a serving-bowl portion of pasta. Nor should he or she return from the salad bar carrying a plate of nachos in addition to (or in place of) a real salad. Some researchers consider portion control the biggest help in losing weight.

Structure: Body

Also, if you are going to snack, snack sensibly. Read the labels on snack-food packages to see how many calories are in each serving, and beware of packages that don't give this information. Also, remember that unpackaged foods such as fruits and vegetables are the healthiest snacks of all.

Finally, exercise should be an important part of any plan to lose weight. The typical overweight adult should exercise 30 minutes a day, 5 days a week. However, if this schedule is impossible to keep, try to exercise at least three days a week instead.

Obesity is a serious problem in America, and it's not going to disappear anytime soon. However, people can make real progress by following the advice in this report. After all, slimming down and becoming more fit are healthier, happier life choices.

Structure: Conclusion

Works Consulted

Bowser, Betty Ann. "Obese Children." *PBS* 1 May 2001, accessed October 20, 2012, http://www.pbs.org/newshour/bb/health/jan-june01/obesekids_05-01.html.

Goff, Karen Goldberg. "Big, Bigger, SUPERBIG." *Insight on the News* 25 Sept. 2000: 22.

Jibrin, Janis. *The Unofficial Guide to Dieting Safely.* New York: Macmillan, 1998.

Lindner, Lawrence. "It's a Big Country: When People Move to the U.S., They Get Fat. What Does This Tell Us About How We Eat?" *The Washington Post* 27 Mar. 2001: T11.

What Is Obesity? 2 May 2005. American Obesity Association, accessed October 20, 2012, http://www.obesity.org.

Structure: Sources Listed

Rubric

Use this 6-point rubric to score and evaluate a research report.

	6	5	4
Ideas	The topic is clearly defined. Relevant facts and concrete details from reliable sources enhance the ideas.	The topic is clear. Support from reliable sources is accurate and relevant.	The topic is clear. More concrete, relevant information would enhance the writing.
Organization	A strong introduction presents the topic, the body organizes information, and the concluding section (conclusion) supports the information presented.	An introduction, body, and conclusion are present and well defined.	The introduction and conclusion are adequate, and the reader can follow the organization of the body.
Voice	Quotations and information from experts help make the voice sound knowledgeable and credible.	The writer's voice is informed and believable. Several quotations enhance the writer's credibility.	The writer's voice is sometimes weak. A few quotations by experts are used.
Word Choice	Borrowed ideas are accurately paraphrased. The writer's words are distinct from the ideas of others.	Borrowed ideas are paraphrased. Ideas from other sources are clearly defined.	Borrowed ideas are sometimes paraphrased incorrectly or are not distinguished from the writer's words.
Sentence Fluency	A variety of sentence structures gives the writing rhythm and flow.	Sufficiently varied sentence structures give the writing rhythm and flow.	Several sentences could be combined, lengthened, or shortened to improve rhythm and flow.
Conventions	Capitalization is used correctly throughout the report.	Minor errors in capitalization are easily overlooked.	Noticeable errors in capitalization do not get in the way of the message.
+Presentation	Each page of the report is clearly labeled.		

3	2	1	
The topic can be identified. General details fill the writing, and facts are lacking.	The writer's topic is not clear. Few facts are provided, and the sources may not be reliable.	Topic is missing from the writing. No facts are provided.	Ideas
The body is poorly organized in places. The introduction and conclusion are present but both need work.	The report is not organized. The introduction or conclusion may be missing.	The writing is a random list of facts. There is no introduction or conclusion.	Organization
The writer's voice is inconsistent and lacks confidence. Quotations are few or they are unrelated to the topic.	The voice is weak or absent. Quotations, if used, are unrelated to the topic and do not build credibility.	The voice is difficult to identify. No quotations are used.	Voice
Several paraphrases are inaccurate or quote the original too closely. The writer's ideas are hard to tell from those of others.	Paraphrases are not correct or direct quotes from the original. They are not distinguished from the writer's ideas.	The writer does not attempt to paraphrase borrowed ideas.	Word Choice
Most sentences share the same structure. The rhythm is predictable.	Sentences are not varied. Several are very long and hard to follow (or very short and choppy).	Many sentences are incomplete. Ideas are hard to grasp.	Sentence Fluency
Several noticeable errors in capitalization confuse the reader.	Frequent errors in capitalization get in the way of the message.	Many serious errors in capitalization make the writing difficult to read.	Conventions

See Appendix B for 4-, 5-, and 6-point informative/explanatory rubrics.

Using the Research Report Rubric to Study the Model

Did you notice that the model on pages 159–161 points out some key elements of a research report? As she wrote "The Weight Problem in America," Isabel Sandoval used these elements to help her inform her readers. She also used the 6-point rubric on pages 162–163 to plan, draft, revise, and edit the writing. A rubric is a great tool to evaluate writing during the writing process.

Now let's use the same rubric to score the model. To do this, we'll focus on each trait separately, starting with Ideas. We'll use the top descriptor for each trait (column 6), along with examples from the model, to help us understand how the traits work together. How would you score Isabel on each trait?

Ideas

- **The topic is clearly defined.**
- **Relevant facts and concrete details from reliable sources enhance the ideas.**

By clearly stating the topic early on, Isabel helped me focus as I read her report. I learned so much from the many concrete facts she includes. I never knew weight was such a problem here in the United States.

[from the writing model]

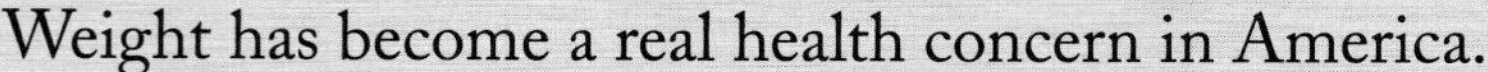

Weight has become a real health concern in America.

[from the writing model]

More than 97 million Americans are overweight. According to the American Obesity Association, about 39 million of these are obese, which means they are more than 30 pounds overweight.

- **A strong introduction presents the topic, the body organizes information, and the concluding section (conclusion) supports the information presented.**

Isabel's report is so well organized. I moved easily from the introduction, through the body, and to the strong ending. I like how she explained, in her opening paragraph, the different areas to be discussed in the report. I think I'll do the same in mine.

[from the writing model]

This paper will present several facts and discuss some of the causes of overweight Americans. It will also suggest possible ways to overcome this epidemic.

- **Quotations and information from experts help make the voice sound knowledgeable and credible.**

I learned so much from Isabel's report! She included many solid, interesting facts, and she used expert sources to back up her claims. Without those facts and sources her paper would read more like an opinion, and much of the impact would have been lost.

[from the writing model]

In a recent study by the Centers for Disease Control, only 28 percent of overweight adults who tried to exercise actually did so enough to make a difference. And many overweight adults do not exercise at all.

- **Borrowed ideas are accurately paraphrased.**
- **The writer's words are distinct from the ideas of others.**

Even though Isabel gathered her information from the American Obesity Association's website, she does a great job reworking that information into her own words. But she's careful to properly document where she gathered her facts.

[from the writing model]

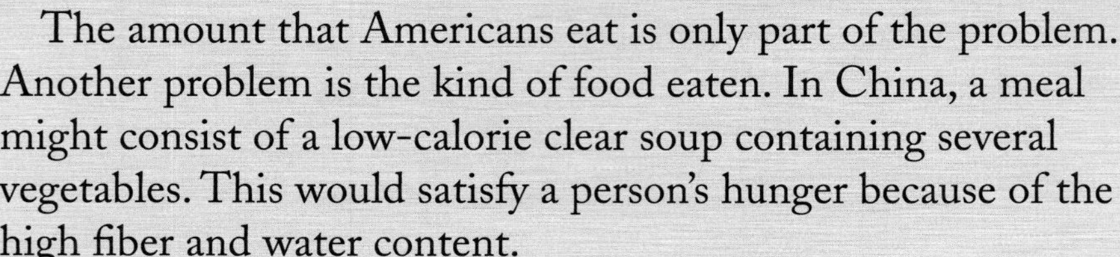
The amount that Americans eat is only part of the problem. Another problem is the kind of food eaten. In China, a meal might consist of a low-calorie clear soup containing several vegetables. This would satisfy a person's hunger because of the high fiber and water content.

- **A variety of sentence structures gives the writing rhythm and flow.**

Isabel's writing is energetic and flows well. She uses a mixture of sentence lengths and types to keep things lively and easy to read.

[from the writing model]

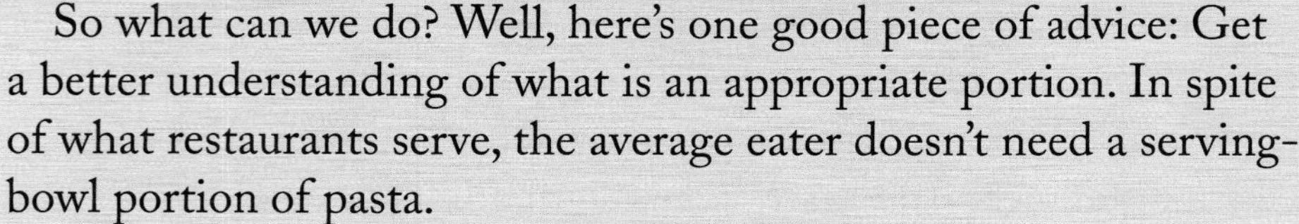
So what can we do? Well, here's one good piece of advice: Get a better understanding of what is an appropriate portion. In spite of what restaurants serve, the average eater doesn't need a serving-bowl portion of pasta.

- **Capitalization is used correctly throughout the report.**

I checked Isabel's spelling, grammar, punctuation, and capitalization, and it looks like she didn't make any mistakes in her writing. She does a really good job with capitalizing proper nouns, proper adjectives, abbreviations, and initials. Take a look at the example here.

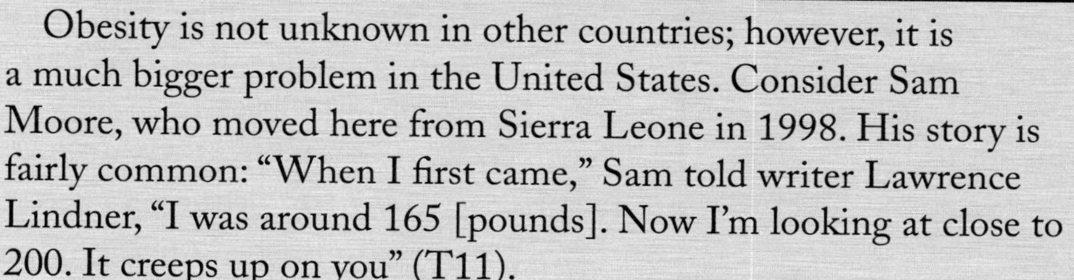

[from the writing model]

Obesity is not unknown in other countries; however, it is a much bigger problem in the United States. Consider Sam Moore, who moved here from Sierra Leone in 1998. His story is fairly common: "When I first came," Sam told writer Lawrence Lindner, "I was around 165 [pounds]. Now I'm looking at close to 200. It creeps up on you" (T11).

+Presentation Each page of the report is clearly labeled.

My Turn!

I'm going to write my own research report. Follow along to see how I use the rubric to help me practice good writing strategies. Wish me luck!

Prewrite

Focus on **Ideas**

The Rubric Says The topic is clearly defined.

Writing Strategy Choose a topic and make a K-W-S Chart to gather research. Then make note cards.

Writer's Term

K-W-S Chart

A **K-W-S Chart** organizes the things you already know, the things you want to know, and the sources you used to answer your research questions.

I like to hike in the woods with my dad, so I'm pretty familiar with plants that grow in the wild. But I've always wondered what kinds of medicines come from these plants. So when my teacher said I'd be writing a research report, I already had my topic chosen. Then I made a K-W-S Chart.

K-W-S Chart

What I Know	What I Want to Know	Sources to Answer My Questions
Many medicines are derived from plants.	How many?	Bierer, Carlson, King article
Quinine and digitalis are well-known medicines from plants.	How were these discovered? What are they used for?	Sumner book
Old tribal remedies are sometimes sources of medicines.	What are some examples?	Cox article
Tropical rain forests are home to many medicinal plants.	Why do so many grow there?	Bierer, Carlson, King article

Writer's Term

Note Cards

A **note card** is a place to put information about a topic. It should contain the following:

- a question from your K-W-S Chart that you would like to get answered
- information relating to the topic (either summarized or directly quoted)
- the source of the information

Use one note card for each source of information.

I found three useful sources. As I went through each one, I made note cards to record the information I found. Here is one of the cards I made. I put the information in quotation marks because it is a direct quote.

Why do so many medicinal plants grow in the rain forest?

"Plants living in tropical forest habitats have had to develop and survive under intense competition for resources and nutrients. They have also had to develop an extraordinary array of defenses, most of them chemical, to protect themselves from viral diseases, fungal pathogens, insects and mammalian predators."

Bierer, Donald E, Thomas J Carlson, and Steven R King. "Shaman Pharmaceuticals: Integrating Indigenous Knowledge, Tropical Medicinal Plants, Medicine, Modern Science and Reciprocity into a Novel Drug Discovery Approach." NetSci May 1996, accessed November 15, 2012, http://www.netsci.org/Science/Special/feature11.html.

Reflect

It seems Emily's K-W-S Chart helped her focus her research. Did she include enough information on each note card?

Apply

Choose a topic and make a K-W-S Chart. Then make note cards to help you keep track of your sources.

Prewrite

Focus on Organization

The Rubric Says A strong introduction presents the topic, the body organizes information, and the concluding section (conclusion) supports the information presented.

Writing Strategy Make an Outline to organize the information from the note cards.

By the time I finished my research, I had a lot of note cards. I had to get my information organized, but I also wanted to do it in a way that would help me structure the introduction, body, and conclusion of my report. So I used a Topic Outline.

Most of the information that I gathered came directly from my research, but I also had some opinions of my own. I marked them on my Outline so that I wouldn't confuse them for facts when I was ready to start drafting.

Writer's Term

Outline

An **Outline** shows the main points and the supporting details of the paragraphs in an essay or report. A **Topic Outline** contains words and phrases to help a writer organize information. A **Sentence Outline** contains complete sentences. Use the same form for both Outlines:

- Use Roman numerals (I, II, III, IV) to indicate major sections or topics.
- Use capital letters (A, B, C, D) to indicate major paragraphs.
- Use Arabic numerals (1, 2, 3, 4) to indicate supporting details within each paragraph.
- Use lowercase letters (a, b, c, d) to indicate less important details in a paragraph.
- Use a period after each symbol.

Outline

I. Some plant-based medicines around for many years
   A. Quinine
      1. derived from bark of cinchona tree
      2. known about at least since 1600s
      3. treatment for malaria
   B. Digitalis
      1. derived from leaves of foxglove plant
      2. treatment for heart ailments (slows down pulse, regulates heartbeats)
   C. More than 120 plant-based medicines in use now

II. Some plant-based medicines found through new research
   A. Research with native peoples
      1. interview with woman in western Samoa
      2. information on more than 100 traditional remedies
      3. one remedy became basis for prostratin (used with AIDS patients)

III. Rain forest problems must be overcome [OPINION]
   A. Fertile source of medicinal plants
      1. 25 percent of medicines come from there
      2. plants strong and effective because they compete to survive
   B. Ethical problems to overcome
      1. much information comes from native people
      2. need to pay these people [OPINION]
      3. long-term and short-term ways to pay
   C. Problem of disappearing rain forests
      1. about 150 acres per minute lost to development
      2. need to work out compromise with developing countries [OPINION]
         a. pay people for information
         b. pay people to help with research

Reflect

How will Emily's Outline help her draft her report?

Apply

Make an Outline to organize your research information.

Draft

Focus on Organization

The Rubric Says A strong introduction presents the topic, the body organizes information, and the concluding section (conclusion) supports the information presented.

Writing Strategy Include a strong introduction, body, and conclusion that will guide the reader through the report.

According to the rubric, I need a strong introduction, body, and conclusion to guide my reader successfully through my report. My outline contains great information to get me started, but first I want to think things through.

I know a good introduction clearly states the topic and prepares the reader for the areas of discussion covered throughout the report. The body must consist of several strong paragraphs that are full of relevant and accurate facts. Everything in the body must relate back to the topic, and the information must be organized in such a way that the reader can follow along easily. The conclusion should be brief, yet strong, and support the information I presented in the report. I definitely should not introduce any new ideas in the conclusion.

Writing my draft will take a while, so I won't worry too much about spelling or capitalization right now. I know I'll go back and fix any mistakes later on.

Proofreading Marks

Indent	Take out something
Make uppercase	Add a period
Make lowercase	New paragraph
Add something	Spelling error

[DRAFT]

Modern Medicines From Ancient Plants

[introduction]

Most Americans know that many of our foods come from plants. It is not so well known, though, that a great number of medicines also come from plants. This paper will give some examples of plant-based medicines. It will also talk about how they are discovered and how scientists learn about them.

Here is a number that might surprise you. More than 30 percent of our medicines. They include treatments for such things as malaria, heart problems, and Parkinson's disease.

One of the best-known plant-based medicines is quinine. It is a standard treatment for malaria. Quinine comes from the bark of the cincho tree. Indians in south America have used the bark for centuries. It was brought to europe in the 1600s. Before that, there was no effective malaria treatment there. As quinine became more commonly used, malaria was all but wiped out in many areas of the world.

Another widely used medicine is digitalis. Digitalis is derived from the leaves of the Foxglove Plant. Some say that it was used as long ago as 1500 B.C. In earlier times, it was used to treat swelling and wounds.

[body]

Now it is used most often as a treatment for heart ailments. It slows down the pulse and regulates the heartbeat.

By talking to native people in remote areas, scientists are constantly learning about more mecidinal plants. For example, Paul Alan Cox is Director of the national tropical botanical gardens in Hawaii and Florida. He interviewed an elderly woman in western Samoa, an island in the pacific. Over several weeks, she gave him instructions on how to prepare more than 100 remedies. These were derived from ferns and flowering plants. The National cancer Institute tested one of her preperations. It became the basis for a new antiviral drug called prostatrin. This drug has been used in treating AIDS.

The tropical rain forests are a fertile source of medicinal plants. About 25 percent of medicines now on the market come from them. Many scientists think the rain forests are home to even more medicinal plants. What is the reason that so many of these plants might be in the rain forests. The answer is simple. Rain forest plants have had to find ways of defending themselves from diseases, funguses, animals, and insects. In doing so, theyve become stronger.

There are at least two problems associated with rain forest research. One is an ethical one. Many plant remedies found in rain forests come from native peoples such as the western Samoan woman. By rights, such people should be payed for sharing their knowledge. It is not always easy to do this, however. Some native medicines may not be proven truly effective for years. Some may never be proven

[body]

[body]

effective. In the meantime, though, people could be payed in other ways. For example, they might recieve health care, educational faculties, or help starting rain-forest-friendly businesses.

The other problem is that the rain forests themselves are disappearing, by, according to some estimates, about 150 acres of rain forest each minute. The reason is development by corporations that clear the forests for timber, grazing lands, mining operations, and roadways. As a result, valuable plants are destroyed. And once a plant species disappears, it is gone forever.

It would be wonderful if a compromise could be worked out. Rain forests are much more valuable than grazing lands or roadways. Maybe local governments could invite more researchers and limit developers. Maybe local people could be paid for pointing out medicinal plants. They could be hired to work with scientists to help discover and study plants.

According to some researchers, less than one percent of plant speecies have been thoroughly examined for mecidinal value. By saving as many of these as we can, who knows what remarkable cures we might find.

[conclusion]

Reflect

How did Emily do? Is her topic clear? Does her writing guide you from one point to the next?

Apply

When you draft your report, make sure to include a strong introduction, body, and conclusion.

Revise

Focus on **Voice**

The Rubric Says Quotations and information from experts help make the voice sound knowledgeable and credible.

Writing Strategy Add quotes and information from experts.

The rubric says adding quotations and information from experts will add credibility to my voice. When I use quotes, I have to blend the words into my own writing, and, most importantly, I have to make sure they're accurate. I must use the exact words from my source, and I must name my source correctly. Doing this helps me avoid plagiarism, which is a serious offense. *Plagiarism* means stealing someone else's quotations or ideas. I just found the perfect place to insert a great quotation.

[DRAFT]

[added a quote]

According to several research chemists, "over 120 pharmaceutical products currently in use are plant-derived" (Bierer, Carlson, and King). This is

Here is a number that might surprise you. More than 30 percent of our medicines. They include treatments for such things as malaria, heart problems, and Parkinson's disease.

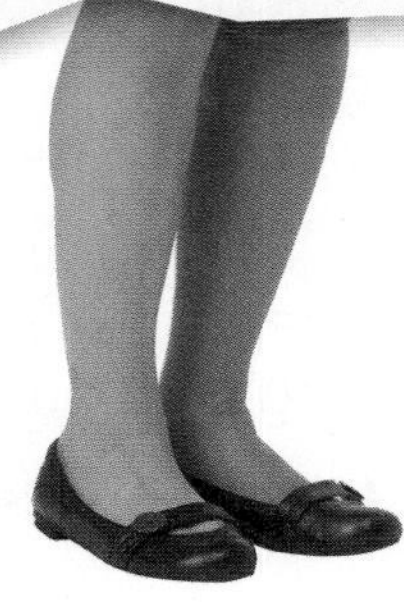

Because I included quotes and other information, I needed to cite my sources in a list of Works Consulted at the end of my report. I used the following examples to help me format my list.

Writer's Term

Citing Sources: Works Consulted

When **citing sources,** list where you found borrowed information. The examples below show how to present this information in a list of **Works Consulted.** Place the list at the end of your paper, and include each source used, regardless of whether direct quotes were pulled from that source. Pay special attention to the order of the information and the use of punctuation. Entries in a list of Works Consulted are arranged alphabetically according to authors' last names. When there is no author, use the first word in the title. In addition, use the styles shown here.

To cite an article in an online periodical:

Author's last name, author's first name. "Article title." *Online periodical title* Date of publication, date of access, web address (URL).

Example:

Bierer, Donald E., Thomas J. Carlson, and Steven R. King. "Shaman Pharmaceuticals: Integrating Indigenous Knowledge, Tropical Medicinal Plants, Medicine, Modern Science and Reciprocity into a Novel Drug Discovery Approach." *NetSci* May 1996, accessed November 15, 2012, http://www.netsci.org/Science/Special/feature11.html.

To cite a magazine or newspaper article:

Author's last name, author's first name. "Article title." *Magazine/newspaper title* Date of publication: page number(s).

Example:

Cox, Paul Alan. "Will Tribal Knowledge Survive the Millennium?" *Science* 7 Jan. 2000: 44.

To cite a book:

Author's last name, author's first name. *Book title.* City of publication: Publisher, date of publication.

Example:

Sumner, Judith. *The Natural History of Medicinal Plants.* Portland: Timber Press, 2000.

Apply

Add quotes and information from experts to the body of your report. Then include a list of Works Consulted at the end.

Revise

Focus on **Word Choice**

The Rubric Says Borrowed ideas are accurately paraphrased. The writer's words are distinct from the ideas of others.

Writing Strategy Make sure that borrowed information is accurately paraphrased.

After I added my expert quote, I looked at the rubric again to see if I was missing anything else. It reminded me to make sure that I had accurately paraphrased borrowed information. So I reread my report, looking for places where I had used someone else's words or ideas. I know it's OK to borrow information, but if I don't explain where it comes from, that's not borrowing; that's stealing!

I quickly realized that I had included several of my own opinions in one of my paragraphs. But there was one opinion that was someone else's—and it was mixed in with my own. I wanted to make sure the reader would understand the difference, so I revised the paragraph, adding the true source of the information.

Writer's Term

Paraphrase/Plagiarize

To **paraphrase** is to restate the meaning of a particular passage in your own words. Don't **plagiarize**! To plagiarize means to present another person's ideas as your own.

[DRAFT]

It would be wonderful if a compromise could be worked out. Rain forests are much more valuable than grazing lands or roadways. Maybe local governments could invite more researchers and limit developers. Maybe, as Dr. Bierer suggests, local people could be paid for pointing out medicinal plants. They could be hired to work with scientists to help discover and study plants.

[accurately paraphrased]

Reflect

What do you think of Emily's revisions? How have they made her writing clearer?

Apply

Make sure borrowed information is paraphrased, not plagiarized.

Revise

Focus on 

The Rubric Says A variety of sentence structures gives the writing rhythm and flow.

Writing Strategy Create sentence variety by breaking up long, wordy sentences.

Before I finished revising my draft, I looked at the rubric one more time. I was reminded to vary my sentence length throughout my report. When I reread my draft, I noticed a place where I had a bunch of long, wordy sentences. I broke them up into smaller sentences to make the writing flow in a much more lively way.

[DRAFT]

[created sentence variety]

The other problem is that the rain forests themselves are disappearing. ~~by,~~ According to some estimates, about 150 acres of rain forest are lost each minute. The reason is development. ~~by~~ Corporations ~~that~~ clear the forests for timber, grazing lands, mining operations, and roadways. As a result, valuable plants are destroyed. And once a plant species disappears, it is gone forever.

Apply

Break up long, wordy sentences in your report. Your readers will thank you!

Edit

Focus on Conventions

The Rubric Says

Capitalization is used correctly throughout the report.

Writing Strategy

Check the capitalization and punctuation of proper nouns, proper adjectives, abbreviations, and initials.

Writer's Term

Proper Nouns/Adjectives, Abbreviations, and Initials

Proper nouns and **proper adjectives** are always capitalized. **Initials** and **abbreviations** that are part of names are capitalized and followed by periods.

It's time to correct spelling and grammar errors. I'll also be sure proper nouns and adjectives, abbreviations, initials, and titles are all capitalized accurately. I caught a few errors in my Works Consulted list, so I went ahead and corrected them.

[DRAFT]

[added correct punctuation]

Bierer, Donald E., Thomas J. Carlson, and Steven R. King. "Shaman Pharmaceuticals: Integrating Indigenous Knowledge, Tropical Medicinal Plants, Medicine, Modern Science and Reciprocity into a Novel Drug Discovery Approach." NetSci May 1996, accessed November 15, 2012, http://www.netsci.org/Science/Special/feature11.html.

Reflect

What do you think? Can you find any capitalization or punctuation errors that Emily missed?

Conventions

Edit for spelling grammar, punctuation, and capitalization. Be sure your title is written properly, too.

For more practice with punctuation and capitalization of proper nouns/adjectives, abbreviations, and initials, use the exercises on the next two pages.

Proper Nouns/Adjectives, Abbreviations, and Initials

Know the Rule

Proper nouns name particular persons, places, and things. All important words in proper nouns are capitalized. **Initials** and **abbreviations** that are part of names are capitalized and followed by periods.

Examples: Dr. Luz T. Lopez, M.D.
The Call of the Wild (book title)
Fell Company

Proper adjectives are formed from proper nouns, and they are always capitalized.

Examples: Danish cheese
Latin music

Practice the Rule

Rewrite the sentences with correct capitalization and punctuation on a separate sheet of paper.

1. Dr Frieda Nannigan, of New york University, has done a number of studies.
2. She was assisted by Louis Franz jr. and other scientists.
3. One of her research papers was called "your health depends on what you eat."
4. Studies have been done by European and canadian researchers as well.
5. A dutch study showed that eating apples might prevent heart attacks.
6. Our science teacher, Mr nakamura, asked us to read some of the studies on food and health.
7. He says that, here in california, we have access to lots of fresh fruits and vegetables.
8. In fact, california supplies fruits and vegetables to stores across the United states.
9. My doctor, dr Nameed, told me I should try to eat more fresh vegetables.
10. Here in the city of los angeles, there are lots of places to buy freshly picked vegetables.

Titles

Know the Rule

Underline the titles of long works, such as **books, magazines, newspapers,** and **movies.** However, these are written in italics in printed text.

Example: Hatchet by Gary Paulsen (a book)

Use quotation marks around the titles of shorter works, such as **songs, stories,** and **poems.**

Example: "Jimmy Jet and His TV Set" by Shel Silverstein (a poem)

Capitalize the first word and the last word in titles. Capitalize all other words except articles, short prepositions, and coordinating conjunctions. Remember to capitalize short verbs, such as *is* and *are*.

Example: "Fire and Rain" (a song)

Practice the Rule

Rewrite each sentence correctly on a separate sheet of paper.

1. I'm halfway through Pride and Prejudice, and I just can't put the book down!
2. Hurry up! We don't want to be late for the 6:00 showing of How to train your dragon.
3. Every day, Nick would race to the mailbox to see if the next issue of Highlights had arrived.
4. Have you ever read Lewis Carroll's poem Jabberwocky out loud? I never knew how fun saying silly words out loud could be.
5. You should stand and place your right hand over your heart every time you sing The Star-Spangled Banner.
6. My grandpa was listening to an old song called where is the love.
7. The New York Times is my mom's favorite newspaper; she reads it every day.
8. We read Paul Revere's ride for our poetry unit last year.
9. When I was little, I thought Charlotte's web was great both as a book and a movie.
10. My Uncle Ted likes to look for recipe ideas in a magazine called Cuisine.

Publish

+Presentation

Publishing Strategy Present the report as part of a multimedia presentation.

Presentation Strategy Label each page.

My class is working hard to combine our reports as one multimedia presentation. My report will be a great addition to the project, and I have the perfect video clip to include with my text. To make sure there's no confusion, though, I'll label each page with both my name and the page number. Creating a header or footer with a computer is easy. But first, I'll use my final checklist to make sure my paper's ready for publication.

My Final Checklist

Did I—

- ✔ capitalize all proper nouns and adjectives, abbreviations, and initials?
- ✔ capitalize and punctuate all titles of books, magazines, websites, and newspapers cited in my report?
- ✔ label each page with my name and the page number?

Apply

Make a checklist to check your research report. Then make a final copy to publish.

Modern Medicines From Ancient Plants

by Emily

Most Americans know that many of our foods come from plants. It is not so well known, though, that a great number of medicines also come from plants. This paper will give some examples of plant-based medicines. It will talk about how they are discovered and how scientists learn about them. It will also explain why we need to be careful about how we treat areas where such plants grow.

Here is a number that might surprise you. According to several research chemists, "over 120 pharmaceutical products currently in use are plant-derived" (Bierer, Carlson, and King). This is more than 30 percent of our medicines. They include treatments for such things as malaria, heart problems, and Parkinson's disease.

One of the best-known plant-based medicines is quinine. It is a standard treatment for malaria. Quinine comes from the bark of the cinchona tree. Indians in South America have used the bark for centuries. It was taken to Europe in the 1600s. Before that, there was no effective malaria treatment there. As quinine became more commonly used, malaria was all but wiped out in many areas of the world.

Another widely used medicine is digitalis. Digitalis is derived from the leaves of the foxglove plant. Some say that it was used as long ago as 1500 B.C. In earlier times, it was used to treat swelling and wounds. Now it is used most often as a treatment for heart ailments. It slows down the pulse and regulates the heartbeat.

By talking to native people in remote areas, scientists are constantly learning about more medicinal plants. For example, Paul Alan Cox is director of the National Tropical Botanical Gardens in

Emily, Page 1

Hawaii and Florida. He interviewed an elderly woman in western Samoa, an island in the Pacific. Over several weeks, she gave him instructions on how to prepare more than 100 remedies. These were derived from ferns and flowering plants. The National Cancer Institute tested one of her preparations. It became the basis for a new antiviral drug called prostratin. This drug has been used in treating AIDS.

The tropical rain forests are a fertile source of medicinal plants. About 25 percent of medicines now on the market come from them. Many scientists think the rain forests are home to even more medicinal plants. What is the reason that so many of these plants might be in the rain forests? The answer is simple. Rain forest plants have had to find ways of defending themselves from diseases, funguses, animals, and insects. In doing so, they've become stronger.

There are at least two problems associated with rain forest research. One is an ethical one. Many plant remedies found in rain forests come from native peoples such as the western Samoan woman. By rights, such people should be paid for sharing their knowledge. It is not always easy to do this, however. Some native medicines may not be truly effective for years. Some may never be proven effective. In the meantime, though, people could be paid in other ways. For example, they might receive health care, educational facilities, or help starting rain-forest-friendly businesses.

The other problem is that the rain forests themselves are disappearing. According to some estimates, about 150 acres of rain forest are lost each minute. The reason is development. Corporations clear the forests for timber, grazing lands, mining operations, and roadways. As a result, valuable plants are destroyed. And once a plant species disappears, it is gone forever.

Emily, Page 2

It'd be wonderful if a compromise could be worked out. Rain forests are much more valuable than grazing lands or roadways. Maybe local governments could invite more researchers and limit developers. Maybe, as Dr. Bierer suggests, local people could be paid for pointing out medicinal plants. They could be hired to work with scientists to help discover and study plants. In western Samoa, the government was promised half the income from prostratin. Perhaps this method could be used in other countries to keep rain forests from disappearing.

According to some researchers, less than one percent of plant species have been thoroughly examined for medicinal value. By saving as many of these as we can, who knows what remarkable cures we might find.

Works Consulted

Bierer, Donald E., Thomas J. Carlson, and Steven R. King. "Shaman Pharmaceuticals: Integrating Indigenous Knowledge, Tropical Medicinal Plants, Medicine, Modern Science and Reciprocity into a Novel Drug Discovery Approach." *NetSci* May 1996, accessed November 15, 2012, http://www.netsci.org/Science/Special/index.html.

Cox, Paul Alan. "Will Tribal Knowledge Survive the Millennium?" *Science* 7 Jan. 2000: 44.

Sumner, Judith. *The Natural History of Medicinal Plants.* Portland: Timber Press, 2000.

Reflect

Did Emily use all the traits of a good research report? Check her paper against the rubric, and don't forget to use the rubric to check your own work, too.

Emily, Page 3

What's a Summary?

It's a short piece of writing that sums up, or tells the main points of, another piece of writing. It's a way to offer my audience a brief retelling of a piece of writing that they might be interested in reading for themselves.

What's in a Summary?

Focus
A summary focuses on one piece of writing. The author reads an article, book, or other piece and then sums up its main points in writing.

Short Length
A summary is brief. It explains the main ideas of a piece of writing, but not in an overly detailed way.

Relevant Details
Every word in a summary should be necessary, or relevant. It's not the time to get creative or use long descriptions. Give just enough relevant details to help other people decide if the summarized piece of writing would be interesting or useful to them.

Direct Style
A summary has a direct, formal style. The author uses declarative sentences and active voice to present information in a small amount of space without getting too casual.

Why write a Summary?

There are a bunch of reasons for writing a summary. I'm still thinking about why I want to write, so I'll list some reasons here.

Share With Others
If I read something good that I want to share with someone else, I can summarize the piece so that others can decide whether they want to read it.

Save Space
I don't have room to keep copies of everything I read. But I have plenty of space to keep summaries. Also, if the material I'm reading belongs to the library, I can summarize it instead of checking it out.

Practice
Summarizing a piece of writing gives me good practice. The skills I use during reading, writing, and summarizing are some of the same skills I'll need in other classes at school.

Research
Summarizing will help me do research. I can skim through sources and summarize the information as I go. Then I can use my summaries to remind me of the most helpful resources.

Linking Informative/Explanatory Traits to a Summary

In this chapter, you will write a brief account of an article you have read. This type of informative/explanatory writing is called a summary. Emily will guide you through the stages of the writing process: Prewrite, Draft, Revise, Edit, and Publish. In each stage, Emily will show you important writing strategies that are linked to the Informative/Explanatory Writing Traits below.

Informative/Explanatory Writing Traits

- a clear, focused thesis
- relevant facts and concrete details that support and develop the thesis

- a strong introduction, body, and conclusion
- paragraphs that have a topic sentence and supporting details
- appropriate and varied transitions that connect ideas and show relationships

- appropriate voice and tone for the purpose and audience

- precise language
- domain-specific vocabulary that is used correctly and explained as necessary

- clear sentences whose structure supports the purpose

- no or few errors in grammar, usage, mechanics, and spelling

Before you write, read Lidia Peretsky's summary of an article. Then use the summary rubric on pages 194–195 to decide how well she did. (You might want to look back at What's in a Summary? on page 188, too!)

Summary Model

"The Structure That Never Sleeps"

by Kim Williams
Summary by Lidia Peretsky

Focus

Relevant Details

Short Length

The Romans did not invent the arch. However, they were the first people who really knew how to build it, and they influenced people who came after them. Before the Romans, people built square rather than curved openings.

The Romans often built freestanding arches to celebrate great victories. Such arches were huge and visible from great distances. "Triumphal" arches of this type have been built in many places around the world.

Today, you will find arches in all kinds of modern buildings and structures. They are built with a variety of materials and in a variety of shapes and sizes. Besides being useful to us, arches also capture our imaginations.

Direct Style

Arc de Triomphe in Paris, France

The Structure That Never Sleeps

by Kim Williams

As tributes to especially important victories or as tributes to the greatness of the emperors themselves, special monumental arches called triumphal arches were erected in Rome. The Arch of Titus was built in A.D. 81 to celebrate Emperor Titus's capture of Jerusalem in A.D. 70, and the Arch of Constantine was built in A.D. 312 and 315 to celebrate Emperor Constantine's victory over his rival and brother-in-law, Emperor Maxentius. These were freestanding arches. That is, they stood alone, without being part of a wall, and were placed in prominent positions so that they could be seen from very far away.

Why did the Romans choose the arch as a symbol of triumph? It may be because the arch represented the triumph of Roman engineering over the most difficult structural problems.

The architects of ancient Egypt and Greece knew about the arch, but their architecture was mostly trabeated, based on vertical columns spanned by horizontal, flat beams. The Romans didn't invent the arch; they adopted the form from the architecture of the Etruscans, the people who ruled Italy before the beginning of the Roman Republic in the sixth century B.C. But to their credit, the Romans perfected the techniques of arch construction, making Roman architecture different from anything that came before it. It was because they understood the techniques of arch construction that Roman architects would later be able to develop even more complicated structures, such as the vault and the dome.

Even though the Roman Empire eventually collapsed in the fifth century A.D., its architecture continued to have a huge influence in later centuries. Triumphal arches were built long after there were no more Roman emperors. Perhaps the most famous triumphal arch of all is the Arc de Triomphe in Paris, commissioned by Napoleon Bonaparte in 1806 to honor the Grand Army and completed in 1836.

In the United States, the Washington Arch was built in New

York City's Washington Square to celebrate the one-hundred-year anniversary of the inauguration of George Washington as President of the United States. Actually, there were two Washington arches. The first one, built in 1889, was a temporary arch made of wood and plaster, and was intended to be taken down when the celebration ended. New Yorkers, however, liked the arch so much that it was soon decided to build a permanent one in marble. This one was dedicated in 1895.

Today arches are found everywhere. Small arches can be used as doors, and large ones as bridges. Arches can be built of brick, stone, concrete, or steel. They don't have to be round, either, but can be made in lots of special shapes. In addition to their usefulness, arches still have the power to capture our imaginations.

One such arch stands on the banks of the Mississippi River in St. Louis, Missouri. The "Gateway to the West" was designed in the late 1940s by architect Eero Saarinen to honor Thomas Jefferson and the expansion of the United States to the west. Topped off in 1965 and dedicated in 1968, the Gateway Arch has the form of a catenary curve. (If you hold each end of a chain and let it droop between your hands, you have created a catenary curve.) As high as a sixty-three-story building, the carbon-steel arch is covered in gleaming stainless steel. A special kind of tram carries visitors to the top.

Of all the ways that architects have invented of going from "here" to "there," the sweeping curves of the arch may be the most beautiful. Now that you know about arches, look around you. You're sure to find these lovely shapes in your town or city, too.

Gateway Arch in St. Louis, Missouri

Rubric

Use this 6-point rubric to plan and evaluate a summary.

	6	5	4
Ideas	The summary contains important main ideas from the source. Details are relevant and important.	The summary contains main ideas from the source. Most details are relevant and important.	The summary may miss one main idea from the source. Some irrelevant or minor details are included.
Organization	Paragraphs have a strong topic sentence and supporting details.	Paragraphs have a topic sentence and supporting details.	The topic sentence in some paragraphs may be hard to find. A few more supporting details would be helpful.
Voice	The writer establishes and maintains a formal style.	The writer establishes a formal style and maintains it throughout most of the summary.	The writer sets a formal style at the start, but it becomes more casual as the summary progresses.
Word Choice	The writing, which uses precise language and domain-specific vocabulary, is concise and economical.	The writing is concise and uses some domain-specific vocabulary. There are few unnecessary words.	The writing is concise most of the time. Some vague or unnecessary words are used, but the message is clear.
Sentence Fluency	Well-written, declarative sentences effectively communicate meaning to the reader.	Declarative sentences effectively communicate meaning to the reader.	Some declarative sentences are poorly written and hard to follow.
Conventions	Pronouns are used correctly and have clear antecedents. The summary is easy to read and understand.	Most pronouns are used correctly and have clear antecedents. The errors do not interfere with meaning.	A few pronouns are used incorrectly and do not have clear antecedents. The errors are noticeable but not distracting.

+Presentation Visuals are labeled and thoughtfully integrated with the text.

3	2	1	
The summary is missing more than one main idea from the source. Several details are irrelevant.	The summary lacks sufficient ideas. The details seem randomly chosen.	The summary lacks a purpose and reads like a random list of thoughts.	Ideas
A few paragraphs lack a topic sentence or supporting details.	Most paragraphs lack a topic sentence or supporting details.	The paragraphs contain no structure. They read like a list of random thoughts.	Organization
The writer's style wavers between formal and casual throughout the summary.	The writer's style is difficult to find.	There is no style in the writing. Words were just put on paper.	Voice
Some of the writing is too wordy, and few domain-specific words are used. Vague language muddies the message.	Wordy, imprecise writing takes away from the meaning. The writer uses domain-specific words incorrectly.	Words are vague and unrelated, and the message is unclear.	Word Choice
Several awkward declarative sentences make the summary hard to read aloud.	Many declarative sentences are awkward or incorrect, making the meaning hard to find.	Sentences are incomplete or incorrect. The reader cannot understand the meaning.	Sentence Fluency
Noticeable, distracting errors with pronouns and antecedents sometimes confuse the reader.	Basic errors with pronouns and antecedents get in the way of the meaning.	Many serious errors with pronouns and antecedents make the writing difficult to understand.	Conventions

See Appendix B for 4-, 5-, and 6-point informative/explanatory rubrics.

Using the Summary Rubric to Study the Model

Did you notice that the model on page 191 points out some key elements of a summary? As she wrote her summary, Lidia Peretsky used these elements to help her summarize an article. She also used the 6-point rubric on pages 194–195 to plan, draft, revise, and edit the writing. A rubric is a great tool to evaluate writing during the writing process.

Now let's use the same rubric to score the model. To do this, we'll focus on each trait separately, starting with Ideas. We'll use the top descriptor for each trait (column 6), along with examples from the model, to help us understand how the traits work together. How would you score Lidia on each trait?

- **The summary contains important main ideas from the source.**
- **Details are relevant and important.**

I like how Lidia's summary gets right to the point. She immediately introduces the main ideas from the article and then provides plenty of relevant, supporting details.

[from the writing model]

The Romans did not invent the arch. However, they were the first people who really knew how to build it, and they influenced people who came after them. Before the Romans, people built square rather than curved openings.

- **Paragraphs have a strong topic sentence and supporting details.**

Lidia's paragraphs are clear and well written. Each has a strong topic sentence, letting me know what the paragraph is about, and several informative supporting sentences.

[from the writing model]

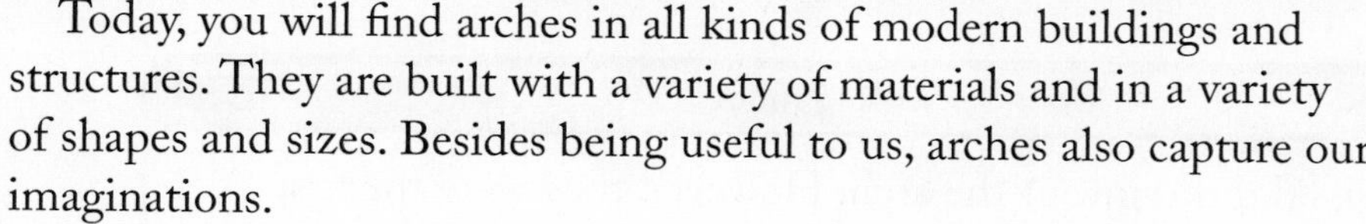

Today, you will find arches in all kinds of modern buildings and structures. They are built with a variety of materials and in a variety of shapes and sizes. Besides being useful to us, arches also capture our imaginations.

- **The writer establishes and maintains a formal style.**

Lidia's purpose is to summarize an informative article, and she uses an appropriately formal style to do it. She gets straight to the point and doesn't use up precious space with personal or casual comments. Her matter-of-fact style is efficient and effective.

[from the writing model]

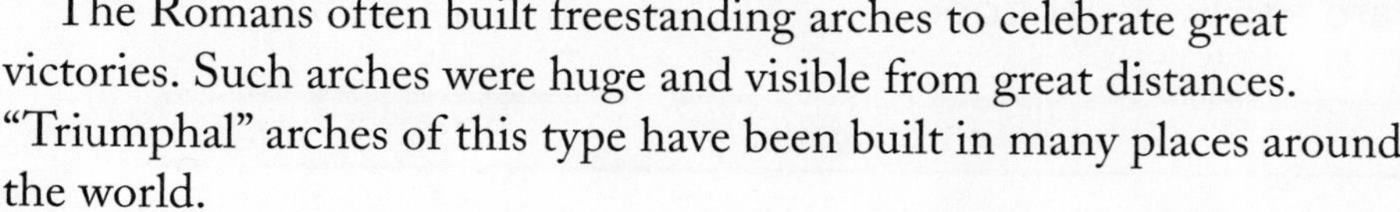

The Romans often built freestanding arches to celebrate great victories. Such arches were huge and visible from great distances. "Triumphal" arches of this type have been built in many places around the world.

- **The writing, which uses precise language and domain-specific vocabulary, is concise and economical.**

Not only does Lidia get right to the point of her summary, but she also uses her "space" wisely. Each word serves a specific purpose. Her language is precise and efficient. She doesn't ramble or repeat herself. She also uses domain-specific words—words that relate to the topic—correctly. Notice how she makes it clear what an arch is.

[from the writing model]

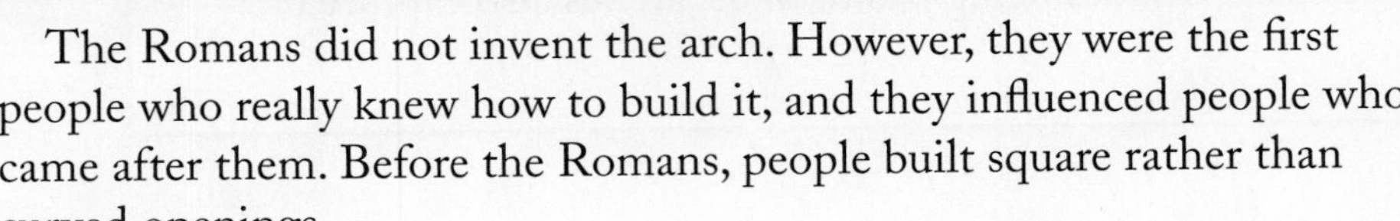
The Romans did not invent the arch. However, they were the first people who really knew how to build it, and they influenced people who came after them. Before the Romans, people built square rather than curved openings.

- **Well-written, declarative sentences effectively communicate meaning to the reader.**

Lidia's summary consists of well-written, declarative sentences. She doesn't confuse the reader with questions or waste space with exclamations. The reader understands her purpose is to inform, and the facts are easily understood.

[from the writing model]

The Romans often built freestanding arches to celebrate great victories. Such arches were huge and visible from great distances. "Triumphal" arches of this type have been built in many places around the world.

- **Pronouns are used correctly and have clear antecedents. The summary is easy to read and understand.**

There are no spelling, capitalization, or punctuation mistakes in Lidia's summary. Also, every pronoun refers back to its antecedent. In this example, it's easy to tell that *They* refers to *arches.*

[from the writing model]

Today, you will find arches in all kinds of modern buildings and structures. They are built with a variety of materials and in a variety of shapes and sizes.

+Presentation Visuals are labeled and thoughtfully integrated with the text.

My Turn!

I'm excited to write a summary of my own. I already have an article in mind. I'm glad I have the rubric to help me with good writing strategies. Follow along as I get started.

Prewrite

Focus on **Ideas**

The Rubric Says The summary contains important main ideas from the source.

Writing Strategy Read an article. Jot down the 5 W's from the article.

When my teacher said to write a summary of an informational article, I got pretty excited. I had just read a really interesting article about spicy food, and I knew I could write a good summary of it. Here is the article I read.

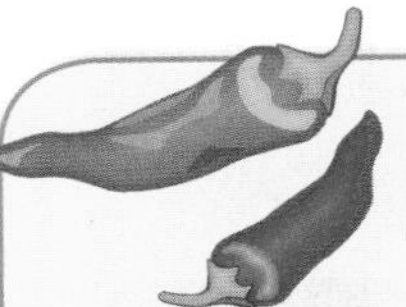

What's So Hot About Spices?

by Gail Jarrow and Paul Sherman

Sour pork curry from India. Spicy shrimp from Vietnam. Hot tamales from Mexico. Spicy foods seem to come from countries with a tropical climate.

Two scientists, Jennifer Billing and Dr. Paul Sherman, wondered why. They thought that healthy eating habits probably helped people survive. But how could eating spicy foods in hot climates make diners healthier?

Spices come from plant parts: leaves, flowers, fruits, seeds, or roots. (Salt isn't a true spice since it doesn't come from a plant.) Chemicals in spice plants have aromas and tastes that people like.

The desire for spices was so great that it affected the course of history. The Arabs, Phoenicians, and Europeans explored the world in search of shortcuts to tropical regions of Asia, where many of the popular spices grew. Christopher Columbus was looking for such a shortcut when he bumped into America.

Without refrigeration, foods spoil quickly and can cause illness. Since ancient times, people have used spices to keep food from spoiling—to preserve it. The Romans used red cumin and coriander. Pirates preserved wild game for sea travel by smoking it and rubbing it with allspice. The Egyptians also knew that spices could prevent decay. They even used them in mummification.

Strong Chemicals

Hundreds of years ago people didn't know how certain spices preserved foods. Since then, scientists have discovered that spices contain powerful chemicals. These chemicals protect the spice plants from bacteria, insects, fungi, and hungry animals. When we use spices, the same chemicals prevent the growth of bacteria that spoil our food and can sometimes make us sick.

Scientists have tested thirty spices on dozens of food-spoiling bacteria. Every spice affected at least one type of bacterium. The super bacteria killers were allspice, garlic, onion, and oregano. These spices killed or slowed the growth of all bacteria on which they were tested.

Some spices aren't so appealing—at least until you get used to them. You probably wouldn't cover yourself with the scent of garlic or onion if you were trying to impress your friends. Eating fresh hot peppers and chilies can blister your mouth.

Then why did people start eating foods seasoned with these red-hot spices? Ms. Billings and Dr. Sherman had a clue. The two scientists guessed that people who added the spices to their food would have been healthier than those who didn't.

If that guess was right, recipes from tropical climates (where foods spoil faster and the risk of food poisoning is higher) should contain more bacteria-killing spices than those from cool climates. To test their idea, the scientists studied recipes in nearly one hundred cookbooks from all over the world.

First they picked traditional dishes that used meat, since meat spoils quickly. They chose older recipes that were first used before refrigeration. Collecting more than 4,500 recipes from thirty-six countries, they listed all the spices used.

The bacteria killers were the big winners! Seven of the world's ten most commonly used spices have strong antibacterial power: onion, garlic, hot peppers, bay leaf, cinnamon, cloves, and thyme.

Another finding puzzled the scientists. Pepper and lemon/lime juice ranked second and fifth in the Top Ten. This was surprising because these two spices aren't great at wiping out bacteria. But it turns out that they boost the bacteria-killing power of other spices used with them.

The Spiciest Dishes

What about climate? Did warmer countries have spicier dishes? The scientists compared the average temperature of each country to the number of spices used. They found that dishes from cooler countries had few spices. (In Scandinavia many recipes have no spices at all.)

Foods get spicier as the climate gets hotter. Dishes from tropical countries like Ethiopia, India, and Indonesia used the most spices in the world. They had an average of more than six spices per recipe.

Recipes from hot climates also won the prize for including the most bacteria-killing spices. For example, key ingredients in curry dishes popular in India are cumin, cinnamon, and cloves, all good at killing bacteria or slowing their growth. In the United States, garlic, onion, and hot peppers are used more in the South than they are in the North.

Spices in our food make it more tasty. But as scientists discovered, spices often do an even more important job. People living in hot climates had good reason to get used to strong-tasting spices. These bacteria killers helped preserve foods and kept people healthy.

Today we have other ways to preserve our food, such as refrigerating it and freezing it. But that tasty chili powder might still make your taco a healthier lunch.

Prewrite

Focus on **Ideas**

The Rubric Says The summary contains important main ideas from the source.

Writing Strategy Read an article. Jot down the 5 W's from the article.

Before writing, I recorded the facts in the article that answer the 5 W's. These are always the most important facts, and I want to be sure to include them in my summary.

The 5 W's for "What's So Hot About Spices?"

What: the value and use of spices

Who: two scientists studying the use of spices

Why: spices important in food preparation and preservation

When: starting in early times and continuing to the present

Where: the hotter the climate, the more spices used

Apply

Find an article that interests you. Then write down the 5 W's from the article.

Prewrite

Focus on **Organization**

The Rubric Says Paragraphs have a strong topic sentence and supporting details.

Writing Strategy Make a Main-Idea Table to organize main ideas and details.

After answering the 5 W's, I used a Main-Idea Table to organize my information. I soon realized I had two main ideas, each with several supporting details. Now I can use my Main-Idea Table to help me write complete, strong paragraphs.

Writer's Term

Main-Idea Table

A **Main-Idea Table** can help you organize the main idea and supporting details for a piece of writing. Write your main ideas in each of the main blocks. Then fill in the "legs" with supporting facts, details, and examples.

Main-Idea Table

Main Idea
People have always known that spices are important in food preservation.

Detail	Detail	Detail	Detail
Early people traveled to find spices.	Spices keep food from spoiling.	Early people didn't know how spices worked.	Scientists found that chemicals keep bacteria from growing.

Main Idea
Scientists wondered if eating spicy food in hot climates made people healthier.

Detail	Detail	Detail	Detail
Scientists compared climates and number of spices used.	They found that people in hot climates used more spices.	Most bacteria-killing spices were also used in hot climates.	People use spices and stay healthy.

Reflect

How will the Main-Idea Table help Emily stay focused as she writes?

Apply

Make your own Main-Idea Table to help organize your thoughts.

Draft

Focus on 

The Rubric Says The writer establishes and maintains a formal style.

Writing Strategy Maintain consistency in style and tone.

The rubric reminds me that I should write with a formal style right from the start and use that style consistently throughout my summary. My purpose is to convey the main points of the article clearly and directly. A casual, chatty style would not be appropriate for this goal. It's easy to lapse into using informal language even after I've started out with a formal style, so I'll need to pay attention and keep my style consistent as I write.

My Main-Idea Table will help me write the topic sentences for each paragraph. I'll look back at the article to make sure I only use information found there. I'll do my best with spelling and grammar, but I know I can fix any mistakes later. Now to get writing!

Writer's Term

Formal Style

Style is made up of the choices you make as you write. The words and phrases you select create your style. When you use a **formal style,** you write as though you are addressing a teacher or other adult whom you want to take your work seriously. You don't have to use long or difficult words to create a formal style. However, you do have to use complete sentences with good grammar and avoid casual or slang expressions.

Proofreading Marks

⊐ Indent	ℓ Take out something
≡ Make uppercase	⊙ Add a period
/ Make lowercase	¶ New paragraph
∧ Add something	(sp) Spelling error

[DRAFT]

"What's So Hot About Spices?"

by Gail Jarrow and Paul Sherman

Summary by Emily

[short summary]

People have always known that spices are important in food preservation. Many early explorers actually were looking for routes to Asia, where they could find the spices they wanted. The Phoenicians and Arabs and even Christopher Columbus went in search of spices, but did they know how spices worked? Now we know that chemicles in it keep all kinds of living bacteria from growing in food, spoiling it, and making us humans sick.

[formal style]

They studied recipes that were used in different climates before refrigeration. They looked at curry recipes and recipes for meat dishes. Two sciencists tried to figure out if eating spicy food in hot countries made early people healthier. The scientists also listed each recipe's ingreedients. We found that people in hot climates—where foods spoil more quickly—used more spices. They also used the most bacteria-killing spices: onion, garlic, hot peppers, and cloves. For both early people and us, spices could really make us a lot healthier.

Reflect

How does using a formal style strengthen Emily's writing?

Apply

As you write your draft, use a formal style throughout.

Revise

Focus on **Ideas**

The Rubric Says Details are relevant and important.

Writing Strategy Delete information that is not relevant or important.

After I wrote my draft, I checked it against the rubric. I thought I stayed on topic very well, but there was one place that contained information that was too detailed for a summary. I want all my details to be relevant, so I deleted the extra information.

[DRAFT]

[deleted irrelevant details]

They studied recipes that were used in different climates before refrigeration. ~~They looked at curry recipes and recipes for meat dishes.~~ Two sciencntists tried to figure out if eating spicy food in hot countries made early people healthier. The scientists also listed each recipe's ingreedients. We found that people in hot

Apply

Delete irrelevant or overly detailed information from your draft.

Revise

Focus on **Word Choice**

The Rubric Says The writing, which uses precise language and domain-specific vocabulary, is concise and economical.

Writing Strategy Recognize and eliminate wordiness and redundancy.

Summaries are meant to be brief. The rubric says my writing should be concise and economical—meaning that every word I use is important and I shouldn't waste space with unnecessary words. I need to mention only the most important ideas from the article and use only the necessary words to do so. I'll reread my draft now and either delete unnecessary words or add precise words where more information is required.

[DRAFT]

[deleted unnecessary words]

The Phoenicians and Arabs and even Christopher Columbus went in search of spices, but did they know how spices worked? Now we know that chemicles in it keep ~~all kinds of living~~ bacteria from growing in food~~, spoiling it, and making us humans sick~~.

Reflect

What do you think? How have Emily's revisions helped make her summary stronger and more precise?

Apply

Delete any unnecessary words, and use only informative and precise words in your summary.

Revise

Focus on 

The Rubric Says Well-written, declarative sentences effectively communicate meaning to the reader.

Writing Strategy Choose punctuation for effect.

The rubric says to use well-written, declarative sentences in my summary. I can see how questions and exclamations don't work well when the purpose is to give information to the reader. My essay should not be littered with distracting question marks and exclamations. Declarative sentences state facts, and that's exactly what I want to do. As I reread my draft, I found a sentence that needs some revision.

[DRAFT]

The Phoenicians and Arabs and even Christopher Columbus went in search of spices, but ~~did they~~ early people didn't know how spices worked~~?~~. Now we know that chemicles in it keep ~~all kinds of living~~ bacteria from growing in food. ~~spoiling it, and making us humans sick~~

[formed a declarative sentence]

Apply

Use declarative sentences to present the facts of your summary.

Edit

Focus on **Conventions**

The Rubric Says Pronouns are used correctly and have clear antecedents. The summary is easy to read and understand.

Writing Strategy Recognize and correct inappropriate shifts in pronoun number and person.

Writer's Term

Pronouns and Antecedents

A **pronoun** is a word that takes the place of a noun. Examples include *I, you, them, it, he, she, our, we,* and *they*. Pronouns must have clear antecedents. An **antecedent** is the word that a pronoun refers to or replaces.

It's time to check for mistakes and misspelled words, but according to the rubric, I should also check my use of pronouns.

[DRAFT]

[corrected pronoun]

~~at curry recipes and recipes for meat dishes~~. Two ~~scienctists~~ scientists tried to figure out if eating spicy food in hot countries made early people healthier. The scientists also listed each recipe's ~~ingreedients~~ ingredients. ~~We~~ They found that people in hot climates—where foods spoil more quickly—used more spices. ~~They~~ Those people also used the most bacteria-killing spices: onion, garlic, hot peppers, and cloves. For both early people and us, spices could

[corrected an unclear antecedent]

Reflect

How did Emily's edits help make her summary easier to understand? Are all her pronouns correct and antecedents clear?

Apply

Conventions

Check your draft for spelling, punctuation, and capitalization, making sure pronouns and antecedents are also used correctly.

For more practice with pronouns and antecedents, use the exercises on the next two pages.

Pronouns and Antecedents

Know the Rule

The pronouns *I, we, you, he, she, it,* and *they* are **subject pronouns**. Use them as subjects of sentences.

Subject of sentence: Irv and **I** like spicy food.

The pronouns *me, us, you, him, her, it,* and *them* are **object pronouns**. Use them as objects following verbs and as objects of prepositions.

Object of verb: A researcher informed Irv and **me**.

Object of preposition: He said, "Take some for **you** and **him**."

The pronouns *my, mine, our, ours, your, yours, his, hers, its, their,* and *theirs* are **possessive pronouns**. Use them to show possession. Do not use an apostrophe in a possessive pronoun.

Possession: Those samples are **mine.**

A pronoun should have a clear **antecedent,** or noun that it refers to. A pronoun must agree with its antecedent in number and gender.

Example: Irv took **his** samples because **he** liked **them**.

Practice the Rule

Read the sentences, looking for pronoun and antecedent errors. Then write each sentence correctly on a separate sheet of paper.

1. Frankie began to get very red after their first taste of Tepin peppers.
2. The peppers spread its heat through 300 gallons of salsa.
3. It should never be consumed in a concentrated form.
4. The next thing Denzel offered to we was a pepper soup.
5. Frankie and Jill were afraid to swallow any of our soup.
6. Them knew it would be too hot to handle.
7. The trick is to slice a pepper lengthwise and remove only a few of his seeds.
8. Frankie prefers a milder flavor, so him removes all of the seeds.
9. Me told Denzel that very spicy foods don't agree with me.
10. Because Denzel didn't want to make me uncomfortable, they made a mild dish.

Pronouns in Pairs

Know the Rule

Use a **subject pronoun** in a compound subject. Use an **object pronoun** in a compound direct object, a compound indirect object, or a compound object of a preposition.

Examples: My **brother and I** both love to hike. (compound subject)
Dad took **my brother and me** hiking. (compound direct object)

Practice the Rule

On a separate sheet of paper, write each sentence with the correct pronoun.

1. Every year, my parents and (I, me) camp for a week in New Hampshire's White Mountains.
2. This year, Dad invited his uncle to come along with my family and (I, me).
3. Before dawn, Dad woke Uncle Gerard and (I, me).
4. Uncle Gerard and (I, me) sat in the back with the family dog, Skipper.
5. Skipper took up so much space that (he, him) and Uncle Gerard had to squeeze over to one side of the car.
6. Soon we stopped for breakfast, which was good because Uncle Gerard and (I, me) were hungry!
7. Dad ordered eggs for (he, himself) and Mom, but Uncle Gerard and (I, me) had pancakes.
8. Mom said the campground looked the same as when (she, her) and her sister went there as children.
9. Dad set up two tents, one for Uncle Gerard and (I, me) and another for (he, him) and Mom.
10. At the end of the week, Dad, Mom, Uncle Gerard, Skipper, and (I, me) packed up our tents and went home.

Publish

+Presentation

Publishing Strategy Publish my summary in a class news magazine.

Presentation Strategy Use visuals that enhance the text. Label the visuals.

Now I'm ready to publish my summary! But how, exactly, should I do this? I could read it to my friend Simone, or I could hang it on my science class's display board. It is about cooking ingredients, after all! But I'd really like to include it in the news magazine my class has been working on all year. I'll include some related, labeled visuals to enliven and enhance my summary. Then I'll read it through one last time to make sure I've done everything on my final checklist.

My Final Checklist

Did I—

- ✔ use all pronouns correctly?
- ✔ make sure each pronoun agreed with the number and gender of its antecedent?
- ✔ use appropriate visuals that enhance my summary?
- ✔ thoughtfully integrate my visuals with the text?
- ✔ label my visuals accurately?

Apply

Make a checklist to check your summary. Then make a final copy to publish.

"What's So Hot About Spices?"

by Gail Jarrow and Paul Sherman

Summary by Emily

People have always known that spices are important in food preservation. Many early explorers actually were looking for routes to Asia, where they could find the spices they wanted. The Phoenicians and Arabs and even Christopher Columbus went in search of spices, but early people didn't know how spices worked. Now we know that chemicals in them keep bacteria from growing in food.

Two scientists tried to figure out if eating spicy food in hot countries made early people healthier. They studied recipes that were used in different climates before refrigeration. The scientists also listed each recipe's ingredients. They found that people in hot climates—where foods spoil more quickly—used more spices. Those people also used the most bacteria-killing spices: onion, garlic, hot peppers, and cloves. For both early people and us, spices could add to better health.

Hot red peppers

Garlic

Reflect

How did Emily do? Did she use all the traits of a good summary? Don't forget to use the rubric to check your own summary.

What's a Problem-Solution Essay?

A problem-solution essay sets out a problem and offers one or more solutions to the problem. Solving problems can be fun, and I would like to learn how to put problem-solving steps into writing.

What's in a Problem-Solution Essay?

Introduction
The introduction of a problem-solution essay states a problem and explains why the reader should care about it. The introduction should get the reader engaged and ready to follow along.

Body
The body of a problem-solution essay develops at least one solution thoroughly. The writer may describe more than one possible solution, explaining why one solution is better than the others.

Conclusion
The conclusion says something decisive about a solution or a combination of solutions. A good conclusion closes the essay in a way the reader will remember.

Style
The style of a problem-solution essay should not be too light or casual. The writer wants the reader to take the problem and proposed solutions seriously. The style should be fairly formal. At the same time, though, it should not be stiff or boring.

Why write a Problem-Solution Essay?

I'm thinking about why I might write a problem-solution essay. I am not ready to choose a topic yet, but here are some reasons I would want to write this kind of essay.

Understanding

If I want to solve a problem, I need to understand it first. Researching the problem and developing possible solutions would really help me expand my understanding.

Information

By the time I'm ready to write, I should have quite a bit of information I want to share. I will want to inform readers so that they'll understand the problem and solutions in my essay.

Explanation

In my essay, I need to explain not only the facts about my topic but how my topic connects to the wider world. I want readers to understand why the problem matters and why I have chosen a certain solution.

Linking Informative/Explanatory Writing Traits to a Problem-Solution Essay

In this chapter, you will write an essay that explains a problem and proposes one or more solutions. This type of informative/explanatory writing is called a problem-solution essay. Emily will guide you through the stages of the writing process: Prewrite, Draft, Revise, Edit, and Publish. In each stage, Emily will show you important writing strategies that are linked to the Informative/Explanatory Writing Traits below.

Informative/Explanatory Writing Traits

- a clear, focused thesis
- relevant facts and concrete details that support and develop the thesis

- a strong introduction, body, and conclusion
- paragraphs that have a topic sentence and supporting details
- appropriate and varied transitions that connect ideas and show relationships

- appropriate voice and tone for the purpose and audience

- precise language
- domain-specific vocabulary that is used correctly and explained as necessary

- clear sentences whose structure supports the purpose

- no or few errors in grammar, usage, mechanics, and spelling

Before you write, read Alan Wong's problem-solution essay on the next three pages. Then use the problem-solution rubric on pages 220–221 to decide how well he did.

Problem-Solution Essay Model

The Best Way To Go

by Alan Wong

Introduction

Our cities have been struggling with pollution and traffic for many years. Cars fill the highways and city streets, drivers complain about spending hours trapped in bottlenecks during rush hour, and everyone hates breathing the fumes from all those cars idling as they're stuck in traffic. What's the solution? How do we make the traffic flow more quickly and help clean up the air in the cities? More people should try these three ways to get around: carpooling, riding the bus, and biking.

Formal Style

Let's look at the pros and cons of each solution, starting with carpooling. When people carpool, they share a car to reach the same destination. For example, people who work in the same office building would drive to and from work together every day, instead of going in separate cars. The members of the carpool might take turns driving the others, or one person might be the driver and the others would contribute some money toward the cost of the gas used for the trip.

Carpooling has three obvious advantages: flexibility, companionship, and economy. Since carpools usually consist of just three or four people, members of the carpool have some control over what time they leave in the morning or return in the evening. If their work hours permit some flexibility, the group can decide to drive earlier or later to avoid the worst of rush hour. Carpool members can also enjoy each other's company as they travel in a quiet, comfortable car. And as members share the cost of gas, driving into town is cheaper for everyone.

Each advantage is mirrored by a disadvantage, however. The flexibility of a carpool only reaches so far. If one member needs to stay late at work, it's not fair to make everyone wait for that person. Each carpool member needs to have a back-up form of transportation for days when he or she can't ride with the rest of the group. When it comes to companionship, some people may find it hard to carpool with a person whose company they do not enjoy. And while it's true that carpoolers use less gas than if they traveled separately, the cars do still burn fuel—which means expense and pollution.

Body

Body

Riding the bus has similar advantages to those of a carpool. Bus riders can be flexible: you can catch a bus at different times of day, and usually buses run more frequently at rush hour. Riding the bus can be a more sociable experience than driving alone in a car, too. You may not chat with your fellow riders, but you can watch people of all sorts getting on and off the bus. Lastly, when it comes to fuel, the bus is even more economical than a carpool. One bus filled with thirty passengers burns a lot less gas than thirty separate cars driving the same distance.

What's the negative side to riding the bus? As with a carpool, the flexibility only extends so far. Buses stop only at certain points along their routes. You may have to transfer from one bus to another to get where you are going. Most likely, too, you'll have to walk a little distance from your bus stop to your home or workplace. On the social side, you have no control over who shares your space in a bus. In a carpool, you have some choice in your fellow riders; on a bus, if your fellow riders are loud and unpleasant, you're stuck with them until you reach your stop. In terms of fuel economy, the same comment applies to a bus as to a carpool: the bus does burn gas and create pollution, although riding a bus is a much more economical solution than driving a car.

Biking offers a non-motorized way to travel from point A to point B. Biking is probably the best solution in terms of flexibility, companionship, and economy. Bike riders have complete flexibility to decide what time they leave for work and what time they return. They are not limited by bus routes but can ride from their front door all the way to the office. Cyclists who live or work near each other can decide to ride together for companionship or ride alone when their schedules for the day do not match those of their friends. Best of all, it's the rider who provides the energy to make the bike go forward; no fuel is burned. In addition, biking is wonderful exercise and great for your health.

It's true, however, that even biking is not a perfect solution. In bad weather or icy conditions, a bike rider might decide to take a different means of transportation. In addition, it can be hard to carry a large load on a bicycle. Bike shops do sell saddlebags and offer other solutions for

Body

carrying all sorts of cargo, but a cyclist may still need to give some thought to what he or she will choose to bring to work each day. A bicycle is also a slower means of transportation than a car or bus. On the other hand, when you are biking, you are also getting your day's exercise, which might save you a trip to the gym. And on days when cars and buses are stalled in heavy traffic, a bike might just turn out to be the fastest way to move!

Knowing that there are three good alternatives to driving individual cars to work, how do we encourage people to try them? A solid program of education for riders, drivers, and all citizens of every community in the country would be a great start. Both the government and private organizations could work together to create signs and advertising campaigns to inform people about alternative choices in transportation. Since traffic and pollution are issues that concern everyone, it is appropriate to involve all areas of society.

Several cities have special carpool lanes on their highways to encourage people to share rides. More cities could adopt this helpful policy and make sure everyone knows that carpooling will allow them to get to their destinations faster. To encourage people to use buses, cities could make sure the buses are clean and pleasant to ride. Some cities are using technology to make bus riding easier, too. Riders can check online to see what time the next bus will arrive at their stop. City governments should also make sure information about routes and schedules is easy to get whether riders have access to the Internet or not.

To encourage biking, cities and private organizations could take several steps. Establishing special bike lanes along major streets would make biking much safer and easier in cities. City governments could also set up bike racks in convenient locations throughout the community so that cyclists could lock up their bikes. Private cycling organizations could launch education campaigns to teach drivers to look out for bikers and bikers to ride safely in city traffic. With just a little cooperation from governments, private organizations, and citizens, we can transform our cities into clean, low-traffic spaces!

Conclusion

Rubric

Use this 6-point rubric to plan and score a problem-solution essay.

	6	5	4
Ideas	A clear thesis statement states the problem, its importance, and a recommended solution. One or more solutions are fully developed with relevant facts and concrete details.	A thesis statement states the problem and a recommended solution. At least one solution is fully developed with some relevant facts and concrete details.	A thesis statement states the problem and a solution. One solution is partially developed with facts and details.
Organization	Ideas are organized logically in a strong introduction, body, and conclusion. Appropriate, effective transitions clarify relationships among ideas.	Ideas are organized logically in an introduction, body, and conclusion. Transitions link and clarify ideas.	Ideas are organized but the introduction, body, and/or conclusion could be stronger. Transitions are used.
Voice	The voice sounds knowledgeable and engages the reader. A formal tone is maintained consistently.	The voice informs and engages the reader most of the time. The tone may be overly formal (textbook-like).	The voice informs and engages the reader some of the time. The tone is informative in parts.
Word Choice	Domain-specific content vocabulary is used effectively and defined clearly.	Domain-specific content vocabulary is used correctly. One definition could be clearer.	Domain-specific content vocabulary is used correctly. Several definitions need clarification.
Sentence Fluency	Sentences are clear, including parallel structures that emphasize a relationship.	Sentences are clear most of the time, but one or two parallel structures are inconsistent.	Sentences are clear. Parallel structures are attempted.
Conventions	The writing has been carefully edited. All verbs are used correctly.	Minor errors are present but do not interfere with meaning. Verbs are used correctly.	A few errors cause confusion. Irregular verbs may be used incorrectly.

+Presentation The format helps readers access the information.

3	2	1	
A thesis statement states the problem but not a solution. The solution is not well developed and details are lacking.	A thesis statement is present, but the problem and solution are not clear. No solution is fully developed.	No thesis statement is present. The ideas are incomplete.	Ideas
Ideas are presented but are not well organized. More or better transitions are needed to link ideas.	There is no clear introduction, body, or conclusion. Transitions are confusing or are used incorrectly.	The ideas are not organized. Transitions are not used.	Organization
The voice informs in the beginning then fades. An informative tone is not maintained.	The voice is weak or distant. The tone is too informal or casual to be informative.	The voice is absent. The tone is not established.	Voice
Domain-specific content vocabulary is used, but none are defined.	Some words are ordinary or overused. Domain-specific content vocabulary is not used.	Limited vocabulary and repetition dulls meaning. Some words are used incorrectly.	Word Choice
Sentences are clear some of the time. Parallel structures, if present, are not correct.	Many sentences are unclear. Parallel structures are not used.	Sentences are awkward to read or they are incomplete.	Sentence Fluency
Many errors are repeated and cause confusion. Irregular verbs may be used incorrectly.	Serious errors interfere with meaning. Verbs are used incorrectly.	The writing has not been edited.	Conventions

See Appendix B for 4-, 5-, and 6-point informative/explanatory rubrics.

Problem-Solution Essay Using the Rubric to Study the Model

Did you notice that the model on pages 217–219 points out some key elements of a problem-solution essay? As he wrote "The Best Way to Go," Alan Wong used these elements to help him explain a problem and present solutions. He also used the 6-point rubric on pages 220–221 to plan, draft, revise, and edit the writing. A rubric is a great tool to evaluate writing during the writing process.

Now let's use the same rubric to score the model. To do this, we'll focus on each trait separately, starting with Ideas. We'll use the top descriptor for each trait (column 6), along with examples from the model, to help us understand how the traits work together. How would you score Alan on each trait?

- **A clear thesis statement states the problem, its importance, and a recommended solution.**
- **One or more solutions are fully developed with relevant facts and concrete details.**

Alan's introduction leads up to a crystal clear thesis statement. I know exactly what problem he plans to discuss and how he thinks it can be solved. Once he's set out his thesis, he goes on to explore each of his solutions using concrete details and relevant facts.

[from the writing model]

How do we make the traffic flow more quickly and help clean up the air in the cities? More people should try these three ways to get around: carpooling, riding the bus, and biking.

Let's look at the pros and cons of each solution, starting with carpooling.

- **Ideas are organized logically in a strong introduction, body, and conclusion.**
- **Appropriate, effective transitions clarify relationships among ideas.**

I like the way this essay is organized. The introduction states the problem and solution, the body develops each solution in detail, and the conclusion proposes ways the solutions could be implemented. In addition, Alan uses transitions at key points throughout the essay to show the reader how his ideas connect. In this paragraph, he uses *however* to show that he's about to offer a contrast and *in addition* to show that he's moving on to a new, connected thought.

[from the writing model]

It's true, however, that even biking is not a perfect solution. In bad weather or icy conditions, a bike rider might decide to take a different means of transportation. In addition, it can be hard to carry a large load on a bicycle.

- **The voice sounds knowledgeable and engages the reader.**
- **A formal tone is maintained consistently.**

Since Alan wants his reader to take his ideas seriously, he uses a formal tone and makes sure he sounds knowledgeable. That doesn't mean he sounds stiff or boring, though. Here, he keeps his tone formal, shows his knowledge of his topic, and uses *you* to add a personal note and engage the reader.

[from the writing model]

Riding the bus has similar advantages to those of a carpool. Bus riders can be flexible: you can catch a bus at different times of day, and usually buses run more frequently at rush hour. Riding the bus can be a more sociable experience than driving alone in a car, too. You may not chat with your fellow riders, but you can watch people of all sorts getting on and off the bus.

- **Domain-specific content vocabulary is used effectively and defined clearly.**

Carpooling is a key concept and a domain-specific term in Alan's essay, and he takes care to define the word for his readers. It's important to make sure your readers understand your terms. Otherwise, your solutions won't make sense to them!

[from the writing model]

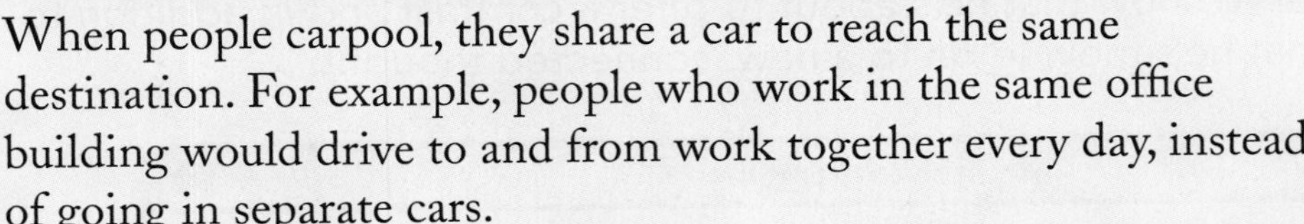
When people carpool, they share a car to reach the same destination. For example, people who work in the same office building would drive to and from work together every day, instead of going in separate cars.

- **Sentences are clear, including parallel structures that emphasize a relationship.**

Alan obviously took great care in composing his sentences. Each one conveys his meaning clearly. When he's discussing the pros and cons of bus riding and carpooling, for example, he introduces the cons in a similar way. That makes it easy for me to see the relationship between the ideas he is explaining.

[from the writing model]

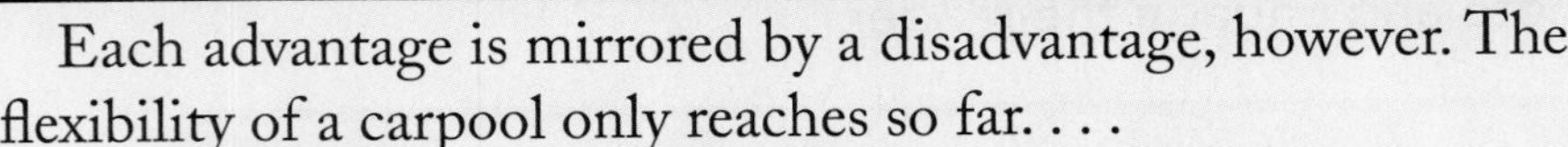
Each advantage is mirrored by a disadvantage, however. The flexibility of a carpool only reaches so far. . . .

What's the negative side to riding the bus? As with a carpool, the flexibility only extends so far.

- **The writing has been carefully edited.**
- **All verbs are used correctly.**

Alan must have checked punctuation, spelling, and capitalization very carefully: I don't see any errors. He uses verbs correctly throughout the essay. Notice the sentences in this example, where he uses the verbs *would* and *could* to help explain an idea he proposes as a solution.

[from the writing model]

A solid program of education for riders, drivers, and all citizens of every community in the country would be a great start. Both the government and private organizations could work together to create signs and advertising campaigns to inform people about alternative choices in transportation.

+Presentation The format helps readers access the information.

My Turn!

Now it's my turn to write a problem-solution essay. I'll use the rubric and good writing strategies to help me. Read on to see how I do it.

Prewrite

Focus on **Ideas**

The Rubric Says A clear thesis statement states the problem, its importance, and a recommended solution.

Writing Strategy Choose and narrow a topic that can be explained in an essay. Take notes.

In social studies each week we discuss current events. That's how I learned that our state senate had voted not to renew the license of a nuclear power plant. I was concerned about the problems that came up in the discussion, but didn't have a clear understanding of how government and energy are related. I wanted to understand that idea better, and that's one reason I decided on the topic for my essay. It took me a while to state the problem clearly. Then I began to list solutions. I put stars beside the solutions I think are best, but I need to do more research to clarify my ideas.

Notes for Essay

Problem

What can people of Vermont do to replace energy that came from their only nuclear power plant?

Solutions

repair the nuclear plant and change management; vote to renew license

build a new power plant

buy more energy from Canada or other states

* explore alternatives to nuclear energy

* support safe, clean, green energy projects

Apply

Think about a problem and how to state it in your essay. List some solutions to research and consider.

Prewrite

Focus on **Organization**

The Rubric Says Ideas are organized logically in a strong introduction, body, and conclusion.

Writing Strategy Make a Problem-Solution Frame to organize the notes.

I can also use a Problem-Solution Frame to help me structure the paragraphs of my essay. The text in the Problem box will contain the information for my introduction and conclusion. The information in the Solution boxes will go into the body of my essay.

Problem-Solution Frame

Problem Box

What is the problem? *what to do when Vermont Yankee nuclear power plant shuts down*
Why is it a problem? *power plant supplies more than 1/3 of state's electricity*

Solution Box

Solution 1:	Solution 2:
Build or connect to new nuclear power plant	*Develop more renewable energy resources in state*

Pros	Cons	Pros	Cons
• *new power plants have better technology* • *federal government helps fund because cleaner than oil or coal*	• *nuclear waste still a problem* • *new technology might not work*	• *state has renewable resources—wind, solar, water, trees, and 'bio fuels'* • *businesses in state try for clean, green ways to use*	• *still only small portion of total energy resources for state* • *need time, money, and plans to develop more*

Reflect

What do you notice about the way Emily filled in the Problem-Solution Frame? How will this organizer help with her draft?

Apply

Use a Problem-Solution Frame or another organizer to prepare to write your essay.

Draft

Focus on **Word Choice**

The Rubric Says Domain-specific content vocabulary is used effectively and defined clearly.

Writing Strategy Define words that are unfamiliar to the audience.

From the rubric I know that I should be aware of domain-specific content terms and defining the ones that readers might not understand. Domain-specific terms are words that relate to an area of knowledge that includes my topic. This essay will contain several words related to energy that my readers may not fully comprehend. I'll need to be careful and make sure I define my terms. If necessary, I'll check the definitions in a dictionary or other reliable source, but I'll use my own words to define them for my readers.

The Problem-Solution Frame helped me get started. Notice how the problem and solution boxes helped me phrase my thesis statement in the second paragraph. I'll check my draft against it to make sure I have included key points.

While writing the draft, I'll keep in mind that I will come back a few more times to revise and edit, so I won't try to fix everything at once.

Proofreading Marks

- Indent
- Make uppercase
- Make lowercase
- Add something
- Take out something
- Add a period
- New paragraph
- Spelling error

[DRAFT]

State Power over Nuclear Power

Recently lawmakers in Vermont's State Senate voted not to renew the contract of Vermont Yankee, a nuclear power plant that has supplied a big portion of the state's electricity for almost forty years. Like other nuclear power plants, it generates and regulates high heat using nuclear fuel that comes from uranium, a radioactive element.

[defined domain-specific word]

The decision of Vermont's Senate was based on difficulties at the plant, such as, broken equipment, fire hazards, security issues, communication failures, and possible leaks of radioactive materials. The lawmakers' vote against the nuclear power plant expressed the concerns of citizens throughout the state. However, the decision raised another problem: how to replace this major source of electricity for the state. Two possible solutions should be explored. The state could build a new, better nuclear power plant, or it could develop renewable energy sources.

[effective use of domain-specific words]

[thesis statement]

Reflect

How does Emily's use of domain-specific content words help you understand her essay?

Apply

When you draft your essay, make sure to define any domain-specific content words.

Revise

Focus on Ideas

The Rubric Says One or more solutions are fully developed with relevant facts and concrete details.

Writing Strategy Use details that are concrete and credible.

The rubric reminds me to develop one or more solutions. In my draft I tried to develop two solutions, but I want to add more concrete and relevant details to support my ideas. I did more research about nuclear and other kinds of energy. I mentioned the source for one very specific fact I found so that the reader will know my information is reliable. I think my revisions make my solution seem more complete and believable. Do you agree?

[DRAFT]

[added credible details]

These companies also are finding ways to use wood, crops, and animal waste products without polluting the air or harming the environment.

Vermont, like many other states, has a variety of renewable energy resources. It also has companies that have already developed clean and effective ways to use rivers, wind, and sunlight. ^ Until now, Vermont's renewal resources have been only ~~a small part~~ 8% of the state's energy ^, according to a recent official report (Page 2010, 2).

[added factual detail]

[reliable source]

Apply

Make sure to include concrete and relevant facts from reliable sources to support your ideas.

Revise

Focus on Organization

The Rubric Says Appropriate, effective transitions clarify relationships among ideas.

Writing Strategy Use transition words or phrases to connect sentences and paragraphs.

The rubric reminds me to guide my readers with appropriate transition words between sentences and paragraphs. I found a paragraph that needed transitions to lead the reader from one idea to the next. I was careful to choose transition words that would show clearly how my ideas are connected. What do you think? Do my ideas flow more smoothly with transitions?

Writer's Term

Transitions

Transitions are words that guide the reader from one thought or paragraph to the next. Transitions that indicate results include *as a result*, *because*, *since*, and *therefore*. Transitions that indicate additional information include *in addition*, *moreover*, *furthermore*, and *similarly*.

[DRAFT]

[added transitions]

Laws and funds that support the promising efforts of clean energy companies in Vermont would generate new businesses, new jobs, and a greater supply of energy from within the state. In addition, a broader view of energy efficiency and available energy resources would save costs for customers. Furthermore, improved technology with renewable energy resources in Vermont could lead the way for other states, the country, and the planet. As a result, a small state like Vermont could have a big impact.

Reflect

How do the added transition words make a difference in your reading of this part of the draft?

Apply

Read through your draft and find places to add appropriate, effective transition words.

Revise

Focus on Sentence Fluency

The Rubric Says Sentences are clear, including parallel structures that emphasize a relationship.

Writing Strategy Use parallel sentence structures.

I know from the rubric that I should check for parallel structures in my sentences. Used thoughtfully, parallel structure can help show that certain ideas are related. I shouldn't repeat too many similar structures, but just enough to make a stronger connection for the reader. Here is one of my revisions, to strengthen the comparison of two types of energy.

[DRAFT] [revised for parallel structure]

Nuclear energy has been called a clean, green energy. ~~When they are burned in power plants,~~ The processes of burning coal, oil, or natural gas all release carbon dioxide, a gas that harmfully raises temperatures around on Earth. The processes of a nuclear power plant create heat and steam without releasing carbon dioxide.

Apply

Look for places where you can make a point by using sentences with parallel structure.

Edit

Focus on **Conventions**

The Rubric Says The writing has been carefully edited. All verbs are used correctly.

Writing Strategy Recognize and correct inappropriate shifts in verb tense.

Writer's Term

Auxiliary Verbs

Auxiliary verbs, or helping verbs, are used with a main verb to show tense, for negatives and questions, and to convey possibilities. *Will, might*, and *could* are some auxiliary verbs that convey how likely an event is to happen.

I'm making corrections and paying special attention to verbs, as the rubric says. I want to use correct tenses and forms so my meaning is clear to the reader. I also made a proof mark to start a new paragraph.

[DRAFT]

[corrected auxiliary verbs]

To encourage this change, the federal government has begun to help fund construction of new nuclear power plants. Recent technology ~~made~~ could make them more safe and efficient than the early ones. ¶ However, the newest technologies ~~will not be~~ have not been tested over time. They might cost more or work less well than expected.

[corrected verb tense]

Reflect

Notice the edits. What changes did Emily make? How did they improve her draft?

Apply

Conventions

Edit your draft for spelling, grammar, punctuation, and capitalization. Look carefully at verb tenses.

For more practice in correctly using irregular verbs and auxiliary verbs, do the exercises on the next two pages.

Auxiliary Verbs

Know the Rule

An **auxiliary verb**, or helping verb, works with a main verb. Auxiliary verbs have different purposes.

- to show tense
  Example: We **are** learning about Mayan societies.
- to form negatives
  Example: People today **do** not know about the Maya.
- to form a question
  Example: **Have** you ever studied the Maya?
- to refer to a possible action or tell how likely it is that something will happen
  Example: I **might** like to visit Belize or Guatemala some day.

Practice the Rule

Number a separate sheet of paper 1–10. For each sentence, write the auxiliary verb followed by the main verb. Then use the following letters to note the purpose of the auxiliary verb: **T** = show tense, **N** = form negatives, **Q** = form a question, **P** = refer to a possible action or how likely an action will be.

1. Throughout history, people have used renewable energy sources.
2. Until two hundred years ago, many societies had relied on wood, a renewable resource.
3. Do you think of hydro-power as something new?
4. Do not forget that mills and other early industry depended on dammed rivers, a form of hydro-power.
5. Before the nineteenth century, industry had not relied on coal, a nonrenewable resource.
6. The use of oil, another nonrenewable resource, has grown along with the major forms of transportation on the road today.
7. Patterns of using renewable and nonrenewable energy might change in the near future.
8. Many people would prefer a greater development of renewable energy resources that don't harm the environment.
9. Some new research projects will focus on renewable energy sources called *biomass*.
10. Did you know that biomass includes wood, animal waste, and fuels from vegetable crops?

Irregular Verbs

Know the Rule

Many verbs are **irregular**; they do not add *-ed* in the past tense. Here are some of the verbs, in three tenses:

Present	Past	Past Participle
break	broke	broken
bring	brought	brought
build	built	built
come	came	come
pay	paid	paid
speak	spoke	spoken
stand	stood	stood
take	took	taken
tell	told	told
write	wrote	written

Practice the Rule

Number a separate sheet of paper 1–10. Write each sentence with the underlined verb corrected for the tense given.

1. Do you know where you <u>stood</u> on every issue about our environment? (*present*)
2. If you have not <u>took</u> a close look at some key issue, try writing an essay about it. (*past participle*)
3. Studying an issue has <u>brung</u> out new ideas and perspectives for me. (*past participle*)
4. I researched several news articles before I <u>write</u> my draft. (*past*)
5. I don't usually <u>spoke</u> with friends and family about an issue unless I have to write about it. (*present*)
6. My parents <u>tell</u> me some points that they thought were important. (*past*)
7. The company that <u>build</u> the power plant is not the company that runs it now. (*past*)
8. For many years the management has <u>came</u> from outside our state. (*past participle*)
9. This company has not <u>pay</u> attention to the concerns of people in our state. (*past participle*)
10. Now I know where I <u>have stood</u> on this particular issue, and I am ready to publish my essay. (*present*)

Publish

+Presentation

Publishing Strategy Publish my problem-solution essay in a class magazine.

Presentation Strategy Use text features and illustrations.

Our essays will be published in a class magazine, so parents, classmates, and students in other grades will get to read them. My topic is pretty complicated, so I should pay special attention to organizing the presentation of my essay. I'll use text features such as spacing and bold font to help readers identify parts of my essay. I also plan to include a photo of a nuclear power plant and a photo of at least one kind of renewable energy. I might include a pie chart that shows the different kinds of energy used in Vermont. I'll ask my teacher if I need help inserting illustrations with my word processing program. I'll use my checklist as I prepare to publish.

My Final Checklist

Did I—

- ✔ correct all punctuation, capitalization, and spelling?
- ✔ correct grammar, including use of auxiliary and irregular verbs?
- ✔ use clear spacing, bold headings, and readable fonts to group topics?
- ✔ choose appealing visuals that bring out my ideas?
- ✔ place visuals to fit with the text?

Apply

Make a checklist to check your problem-solution essay. Then make a final copy to publish.

State Power over Nuclear Power

by Emily

Recently lawmakers in Vermont's State Senate voted not to renew the contract of Vermont Yankee, a nuclear power plant that has supplied a big portion of the state's electricity for almost forty years. Like other nuclear power plants, it generates and regulates high heat using nuclear fuel that comes from uranium, a radioactive element.

The decision of Vermont's Senate was based on difficulties at the plant, such as broken equipment, fire hazards, security issues, communication failures, and possible leaks of radioactive materials. The lawmakers' vote against the nuclear power plant expressed the concerns of citizens throughout the state. However, the decision raised another problem: how to replace this major source of electricity for the state. Two possible solutions should be explored. The state could build a new, better nuclear power plant, or it could develop renewable energy sources.

Change to new improved nuclear power. Nuclear energy has been called a clean, green energy. The processes of burning coal, oil, or natural gas all release carbon dioxide, a gas that harmfully raises temperatures on Earth. The processes of a nuclear power plant create heat and steam without releasing carbon dioxide. Using more nuclear energy would help the United States meet world standards for a cleaner, greener environment. To encourage this change, the federal government has begun to help fund

construction of new nuclear power plants. Recent technology could make them more safe and efficient than the early ones.

However, the newest technologies have not been tested over time. They might cost more or work less well than expected. Also, any nuclear power plant creates nuclear waste. Unfortunately the nation has not yet worked out how to deal with hazards from transport and storage of nuclear waste. These are all good reasons to question any plans for a new nuclear power plant in Vermont.

Change to develop more renewable energy resources. The sun, wind, and water can be sources of renewable energy. Renewable energy resources are resources that can be replaced in a relatively short period of time. Developing renewable resources has become a promising alternative to the increasing difficulties of drilling for oil or mining coal and uranium.

Vermont, like many other states, has a variety of renewable energy resources. It also has companies that have already developed clean and effective ways to use rivers, wind, and sunlight. These companies also are finding ways to use wood, crops, and animal waste products without polluting the air or harming the environment. Until now, Vermont's renewable resources have been only 8% of the state's energy, according to a recent official report (Page 2, 2010).

Laws and funds that support the promising efforts of clean energy companies in Vermont would generate new businesses, new jobs, and a greater supply of energy from within the state. In addition, a broader view of energy efficiency and available energy resources would save costs for customers. Furthermore, improved technology with renewable energy resources in Vermont could lead the way for other states, the country, and the planet. As a result, a small state like Vermont could have a big impact.

Compare the choices. To summarize, a plan that focuses on developing renewable resources within the state has more promise than any plan that depends mainly on nuclear energy. Changing toward safer, cleaner, renewable energy is a better choice than changing to an improved method of getting energy from uranium, coal, or oil. The people of Vermont, including lawmakers, can make good decisions to solve problems that matter to people everywhere.

Works Consulted

"Definition of a Nuclear Power Plant," eHow, accessed October 6, 2012, http://www.ehow.com/nuclear-power-plants.

"Energy Sources," Central Vermont Public Service, accessed October 8, 2012, http://www.cvps.com/ProgramsServices/EnergySources.aspx.

"Energy Sources," U.S. Energy Information Agency, Department of Energy, accessed October 6, 2012, http://www.eia.doe.gov/kids/energy.cfm?page=2.

Page, Guy. May 2010. "Renewable Energy Sources in Vermont, A Status Report, May 2010." Montpelier, VT: Vermont Energy Partnership.

Reflect

Read the essay and check it against the rubric. Which traits do you think are the strongest? When your own essay is complete, remember to check it against the rubric also.

Informative/ Explanatory test writing

Read the Writing Prompt

When you take a writing test, you will be given a writing prompt. Most writing prompts have three parts:

Setup This part of the writing prompt gives you the background information you need to get ready to write.

Task This part of the writing prompt tells you exactly what you are supposed to write: a cause-and-effect report.

Scoring Guide This section tells how your writing will be scored. To do well on the test, you should include everything on the list.

Remember the rubrics you've been using? When you take a writing test, you don't always have all of the information that's on a rubric. But a scoring guide is a lot like a rubric. It lists everything you need to think about to write a good paper. Like the rubrics you've used, many scoring guides are based on the six traits of writing:

Are you a spender or a saver? Think about how spending or saving your money affects your behavior.

Write a cause-and-effect report on the effects of your spending/saving habits.

Be sure your writing

- has a clear thesis statement and accurate, concrete supporting details.
- is well organized and uses appropriate transition words to clarify the relationship between causes and effects.
- uses a voice that matches the purpose and audience.
- is concise, not too wordy.
- has sentences that support the purpose.
- contains correct grammar, punctuation, capitalization, and spelling.

Writing Traits in the Scoring Guide

The scoring guide in the prompt on page 241 has been made into this chart. Does it remind you of the rubrics you've used? Not all prompts include all of the writing traits, but this one does. Use them to do your best writing. Remember to work neatly and put your name on the test.

- Be sure your writing has a clear thesis statement and accurate, concrete supporting details.

- Be sure your writing is well organized and uses appropriate transition words to clarify the relationship between causes and effects.

- Be sure your writing uses a voice that matches the purpose and audience.

- Be sure your writing is concise, not too wordy.

- Be sure your writing has sentences that support the purpose.

- Be sure your writing contains correct grammar, punctuation, capitalization, and spelling.

Look at Reginald James's cause-and-effect report on the next page. Did he follow the scoring guide?

Saving for Bigger Things

by Reginald James

Have you ever heard the saying "A penny saved is a penny earned"? Well, I live by that statement! I put most of my allowance in my savings account and keep only what I really need. Although saving money means that I haven't been able to buy everything I want, it has taught me some important lessons.

Saving money has helped me understand the difference between what I want and what I need. For instance, I have a lot of friends who have big collections of DVDs and video games. While there are some cool DVDs and games that I would love to have, I don't really need them. Unless it's something that I feel is really necessary, I generally just don't buy it.

Another effect of saving money is that I have learned how to budget. I set aside $10 per week to use on the things I need, such as snacks and drinks after basketball practice. If I know I am going to need a little more one week for something like a new pair of shoes, then I try to save my spending money so that I won't have to dip into my savings.

Probably the best outcome of all my savings, though, is the fact that I am going to have enough money to buy something I've wanted for a long time. I love to go biking, and I know that if I want a new mountain bike, I'm going to have to pay for it myself. So I began saving money earlier this year, hoping to have enough saved up by next summer. Now, my savings account is quite large. I will have enough money to pay for a brand new bike as soon as spring arrives.

Sure, saving may not be as much fun as spending, but in the end, it teaches you important lessons while giving you the freedom to buy the things you really want.

Using the Scoring Guide to Study the Model

Now let's use the scoring guide to check Reginald's writing test, "Saving for Bigger Things." Let's see how well his essay meets each of the six writing traits.

- **The thesis statement is clear.**
- **The writing includes several accurate, concrete supporting details.**

Reginald immediately introduced his thesis statement in a clear and easy-to-understand way. Then he provided several solid examples of what he actually learned from saving his money.

> Although saving money means that I haven't been able to buy everything I want, it has taught me some important lessons.
>
> Saving money has helped me understand the difference between what I want and what I need.

- **The writing is well organized and uses appropriate transition words to clarify the relationship between causes and effects.**

Reginald guides the reader from one supporting example to the next with transition words such as *for instance* and *another effect.* These words signaled to me that although a new example was being given, all were related.

> Another effect of saving money is that I have learned how to budget. I set aside $10 per week to use on the things I need, such as snacks and drinks after basketball practice.

- **The voice matches the purpose and audience.**

It's clear that Reginald understands both his purpose and his audience. His voice is casual, which helps the reader connect with his writing, yet still informative.

Sure, saving may not be as much fun as spending, but in the end, it teaches you important lessons while giving you the freedom to buy the things you really want.

- **The writing is concise and not too wordy.**

I like how Reginald uses only the words necessary to get his point across. He never repeats himself. This made it so much easier to read, connect with, and understand his report.

Probably the best outcome of all my savings, though, is the fact that I am going to have enough money to buy something I've wanted for a long time.

Using the Scoring Guide to Study the Model

- **The writing consists of sentences that support the purpose.**

Reginald uses mostly declarative sentences, which makes sense as his purpose is to inform. I'll keep this in mind as I write my own cause-and-effect report.

I love to go biking, and I know that if I want a new mountain bike, I'm going to have to pay for it myself. So I began saving money earlier this year, hoping to have enough saved up by next summer.

- **The writing contains correct grammar, punctuation, capitalization, and spelling.**

Using correct grammar and mechanics in a writing test is important, and I can tell that Reginald paid attention to this. I didn't see any errors in his grammar, punctuation, capitalization, or spelling. I'll be sure to check my test for errors, too!

Planning My Time

Before giving us a writing prompt, my teacher always tells us how much time we'll have to complete the test. Since I already know the steps of the writing process, I like to break up the total amount of time into each step. This way, I know I'll have enough time to do everything I need to do. If the test takes an hour, here's how I can organize my time. Planning your time will help you, too!

Prewrite

Focus on **Ideas**

Writing Strategy Study the writing prompt to find out what to do.

When I take a writing test, I always study my writing prompt before I begin. A writing prompt usually has three parts (the setup, the task, and the scoring guide), but the parts aren't always labeled. Look for these sections on your writing prompt. Then label each one, like I did below. Also circle key words in the setup and the task that tell what kind of writing you will be doing and who your audience will be. I circled my topic in red. I also used blue to circle the kind of writing I'll be doing (a cause-and-effect report). My writing prompt doesn't say who my audience will be, so I'll write for my teacher.

My Writing Test Prompt

Setup — Have you ever overslept on a school day? This can cause a lot of problems for everyone involved.

Task — Write a cause-and-effect report on what happens when you get up late for school.

Scoring Guide — Be sure your writing

- has a clear thesis statement and accurate, concrete supporting details.
- is well organized and uses appropriate transition words to clarify the relationship between causes and effects.
- uses a voice that matches the purpose and audience.
- is concise, not too wordy.
- has sentences that support the purpose.
- contains correct grammar, punctuation, capitalization, and spelling.

Think about how the scoring guide relates to the six traits of good writing you've studied in the rubrics. Not all of the traits are included in every scoring guide, but you'll still want to remember them to write a good report.

Ideas

- **Be sure your writing has a clear thesis statement and accurate, concrete supporting details.**

I'll clearly introduce my thesis statement and support it with concrete details and accurate facts.

Organization

- **Be sure your writing is well organized and uses appropriate transition words to clarify the relationship between causes and effects.**

I'll be sure to use carefully chosen transition words to guide my reader from point to point.

Voice

- **Be sure your writing uses a voice that matches the purpose and audience.**

As I write, I'll keep in mind both my purpose and my audience, and adjust my voice appropriately.

Word Choice

- **Be sure your writing is concise, not too wordy.**

I'll take the time to choose strong and accurate words.

Sentence Fluency

- **Be sure your writing has sentences that support the purpose.**

Before I start writing, I'll decide which sentence types are most appropriate for my purpose.

Conventions

- **Be sure your writing contains correct grammar, punctuation, capitalization, and spelling.**

This is important, so I'll make sure to check for mistakes in grammar and mechanics.

Prewrite

Focus on Ideas

Writing Strategy **Respond to the task.**

I've learned that good writers gather information before they begin writing, so that's what I'll do. I can gather a lot of information from the writing prompt. Let's take another look at the task, since that's the part of the writing prompt that explains what I'm supposed to write. When you write for a test, you don't have a lot of time, so you need to think about how you're going to respond before you start writing.

I'm supposed to write a cause-and-effect report on the problems caused by getting up late for school. I'll think about a time when I overslept. Then I'll jot down some notes.

Task — Write a cause-and-effect report on what happens when you get up late for school.

Notes

- ✔ I overslept.
- ✔ I missed the bus.
- ✔ My sister was late.
- ✔ I got my first tardy mark.

Apply

Since you won't have much time during a test, first think about how you'll respond to the task. Then jot down notes to help you gather information.

Prewrite

Focus on **Organization**

Writing Strategy Choose a graphic organizer.

The next step is to arrange the details of my report. I'll choose a graphic organizer to help me do this quickly and efficiently. Since I'm writing a cause-and-effect report, I'll use a Cause-and-Effect Chain to show how one cause led to a chain reaction of events.

First I'll fill in the primary cause (oversleeping); then I'll list the effects. Next I'll fill in the three resulting causes of those effects, which in turn, led to three more final effects.

Primary Cause	Effect/Cause	Effect/Cause	Effect
I kept hitting the snooze button on my alarm.	I woke up 45 minutes late.	I had no time to get ready.	I couldn't do my hair, plan my outfit, or eat breakfast.
	I had to take my sister to school later than usual.	Her school had already started.	My sister was late for school.
	I missed the bus.	I had to run to school, and I got there late.	I got a tardy mark.

Reflect

Has Emily included enough information in her Cause-and-Effect Chain to help her begin writing?

Apply

Choose a graphic organizer that will show the relationship between your primary cause and all of its effects.

Prewrite

Focus on Organization

Writing Strategy Check my graphic organizer against the scoring guide.

Without much time to revise during a test, prewriting is really important. Before I begin drafting, I'll check my Cause-and-Effect Chain against the scoring guide in the writing prompt.

Primary Cause
I kept hitting the snooze button on my alarm.

Effect/Cause	Effect/Cause	Effect
I woke up 45 minutes late. →	I had no time to get ready. →	I couldn't do my hair, plan my outfit, or eat breakfast.
I had to take my sister to school later than usual. →	Her school had already started. →	My sister was late for school.
I missed the bus. →	I had to run to school, and I got there late. →	I got a tardy mark.

Ideas

- **Be sure your writing has a clear thesis statement and accurate, concrete supporting details.**

Based on what I've written in my graphic organizer, I'm sure it'll be easy to write a good thesis statement and include concrete, factual supporting details.

Organization

- **Be sure your writing is well organized and uses appropriate transition words to clarify the relationship between causes and effects.**

To help readers follow the chain of causes and effects I'm explaining, I'll use clear and appropriate transitions.

Voice

- **Be sure your writing uses a voice that matches the purpose and audience.**

Since I'm telling an amusing story, my voice should be casual and entertaining. I'll also use first-person point of view.

Word Choice

- **Be sure your writing is concise, not too wordy.**

I'll be sure not to ramble or repeat myself. I'll use only accurate and descriptive words.

Sentence Fluency

- **Be sure your writing has sentences that support the purpose.**

I'll use mostly declarative sentences, as my purpose is to present facts.

Conventions

- **Be sure your writing contains correct grammar, punctuation, capitalization, and spelling.**

I'll check for proper grammar and mechanics when I edit my report.

Reflect

Emily's Cause-and-Effect Chain seems pretty complete. Can you think of anything that she might be missing?

Apply

Compare your graphic organizer with the scoring guide before you start to write. This way, you'll know what to do when you begin drafting.

Draft

Focus on **Ideas**

Writing Strategy Write a clear, concise thesis statement.

The scoring guide says that I should have a clear thesis statement. Making my Cause-and-Effect Chain reminded me of how many problems were caused by oversleeping on a school day. Using this information, it will be easy to come up with a clear and concise thesis statement.

[DRAFT]

Cause for Alarm

by Emily

Having to get up early for school can be a real bummer. But I learned the hard way that a few extra minutes of sleep, while pleasant at the time, can result in total chaos. So take it from me—don't use the snooze button in the morning. ← **[concise thesis statement]**

I remember one Thursday morning when a few extra minutes of sleep disrupted my entire morning routine. Normally, my alarm goes off at 6:45 A.M., allowing me plenty of time to get ready for school. But on this perticular morning, I was so tired that I kept hitting the snooze button until 7:30—just ten minutes before I was supposed to catch the bus! I jumped out of bed and threw on an outfit that didn't even match. I didn't have time to take a shower, so I quickly brushed

Proofreading Marks

- ⊐ Indent
- ≡ Make uppercase
- / Make lowercase
- ∧ Add something
- ℓ Take out something
- ⊙ Add a period
- ¶ New paragraph
- (SP) Spelling error

my teeth and threw my hair up into a ponytale. Even though I was starved, there was no time to eat breakfast. I usually eat a bowl of cereal.

My parents leave early for work. I am responsable for walking my younger sister, Paige, to school before I catch the bus. She was already up and ready to go. I knew her teacher wasn't happy.

I feared the worst consaquence of all: getting my first tardy mark. With school starting right at 8:00 A.M., I ran as fast as I could. Even though I hurried, I arrived at 8:25 A.M. I was exhausted, hungry, and out of breath. When I walked into the classroom, my teacher gave me a stern look and said, Emily, you're late. Unless you have a good excuse, I have to give you a tardy mark."

There was no excuse for missing the morning lesson, but a lesson was learned that day Do not use the snooze button. It's only cause for alarm!

Reflect

What do you think? Is Emily's thesis statement clear and concise?

Apply

Include a clear and concise thesis statement in your cause-and-effect report.

Revise

Focus on **Organization**

Writing Strategy Use appropriate transition words to show cause and effect.

Using transition words is a great way to keep my writing organized. Some transition words, such as *first, now*, and *after dinner*, help show the order of events. Other transition words, such as *so, because*, and *therefore,* show cause and effect. As I reread my draft, I found a place that could use some clarification, so I'll add some transition words now.

[used cause-effect transition word]

My parents leave early for work, so I am responsable for walking my younger sister, Paige, to school before I catch the bus. She was already up and ready to go. I knew her teacher wasn't happy. Now I feared the worst consaquence of all: getting my first tardy mark.

[used time-order transition word]

Apply

Use transition words to show the order of events and to connect causes and effects.

Revise

Focus on **Voice**

Writing Strategy Connect with the readers.

To truly connect with my reader, I have to use a voice that is appropriate for both my purpose and my audience. Since I'm telling a personal story, I'll keep my voice casual and engaging, and I'll use first-person point of view. I found a place where first person was needed. What do you think of my revisions?

[DRAFT]

I didn't have an ← **[used first person]** → I did learn

~~There was no~~ excuse for missing the morning lesson, but a lesson

of my own

~~was learned~~ that day. Do not use the snooze button. It's only cause for alarm!

Reflect

How do Emily's revisions help you better connect with the ending of her cause-and-effect paper?

Apply

To connect with your reader, use a voice that's appropriate for both your purpose and your audience.

Revise

Focus on **Word Choice**

Writing Strategy Choose language that expresses ideas precisely and concisely, recognizing and eliminating wordiness and redundancy.

The scoring guide says my writing should be concise and not too wordy. I know that when I repeat information or include unnecessary details, I weaken my writing and confuse my reader. I'll take a moment to reread my draft and delete any unnecessary words.

[DRAFT]

I didn't have time to take a shower, so I quickly brushed my teeth and threw my hair up into a ponytale. Even though I was starved, there was no time to eat breakfast. ~~I usually eat a bowl of cereal~~.

[deleted unnecessary words]

Reflect

What do you think? Does the deletion of repeated or unnecessary information strengthen Emily's writing?

Apply

To keep your writing clear and strong, use only necessary words and details.

Edit

Focus on Conventions

Writing Strategy **Check my grammar, punctuation, capitalization, and spelling.**

I never turn in a paper without checking it for mistakes in grammar and mechanics. Editing my work after it is completed helps me find and correct mistakes that I made while drafting. I'll read through my report one last time, correcting mistakes as I read.

Cause for Alarm

by Emily

Having to get up early for school can be a real bummer. But I learned the hard way that a few extra minutes of sleep, while pleasant at the time, can result in total chaos. So take it from me—don't use the snooze button in the morning.

I remember one Thursday morning when a few extra minutes of sleep disrupted my entire morning routine. Normally, my alarm goes off at 6:45 A.M., allowing me plenty of time to get ready for school. But on this ~~perticular~~ particular morning, I was so tired that I kept hitting the snooze button until 7:30—just ten minutes before I was supposed to catch the bus! I jumped out of bed and threw on an outfit that didn't even match. I didn't have time to take a shower, so I quickly brushed my

Apply

Check your grammar, punctuation, capitalization, and spelling every time you write for a test.

But because I had overslept, she had to wait for me. We had to run to her school, but by the time we got there, all the students were already inside!

ponytail
teeth and threw my hair up into a ~~ponytale~~. Even though I was starved, there was no time to eat breakfast. ~~I usually eat a bowl of cereal~~.

, so responsible
My parents leave early for work, I am ~~responsable~~ for walking my younger sister, Paige, to school before I catch the bus. She was already up and ready to go. I knew her teacher wasn't happy.

Now consequence
I feared the worst ~~consaquence~~ of all: getting my first tardy

School always starts so
mark. ~~With school starting right~~ at 8:00 A.M., I ran as fast as I could. Even though I hurried, I arrived at 8:25 A.M. I was exhausted, hungry, and out of breath. When I walked into the classroom, my teacher gave

"
me a stern look and said, Emily, you're late. Unless you have a good excuse, I have to give you a tardy mark."

I didn't have an I did learn
~~There was no~~ excuse for missing the morning lesson, but a lesson

of my own :
~~was learned~~ that day Do not use the snooze button. It's only cause for alarm!

The distance from home to school is only a five-minute bus ride, but as it turns out, it's a fifteen-minute run.

Reflect

Is Emily missing anything? Check her report against the scoring guide, and remember to check your work against your writing prompt's scoring guide, too.

Well now, that wasn't so bad! Just remember to use the writing process when you take a writing test. The process is just a little different for a test, but if you remember these important tips, I'm sure you'll do just fine!

TEST TIPS

1. **Study the writing prompt before you start to write.** Most writing prompts have three parts: the setup, the task, and the scoring guide. The parts probably won't be labeled. You'll have to figure them out for yourself!
2. **Make sure you understand the task before you start to write.**
   - Read all three parts of the writing prompt carefully.
   - Circle key words in the task part of the writing prompt that tell what kind of writing you need to do. The task might also identify your audience.
   - Make sure you know how you'll be graded.
   - Say the assignment in your own words to yourself.
3. **Keep an eye on the clock.** Decide how much time you will spend on each part of the writing process and try to stick to your schedule. Don't spend so much time on prewriting that you don't have enough time left to write.
4. **Reread your writing. Compare it to the scoring guide at least twice.** Remember the rubrics you've used? A scoring guide on a writing test is like a rubric. It can help you keep what's important in mind.
5. **Plan, plan, plan!** You don't get much time to revise during a test, so planning is more important than ever.
6. **Write neatly.** Remember: If the people who score your test can't read your writing, it doesn't matter how good your essay is!

Argument writing convinces the reader of something.

Hi, there! I'm Tyler. Right now, my class is learning about argument writing, and I can't wait to try it. I have a lot of opinions, so it will be fun to try to convince people to agree with me.

IN THIS UNIT

- Editorial
- Business Letter
- Website Review
- LITERATURE CONNECTION Response to Literature
- Writing for a Test

Name: Tyler
Home: Georgia
Hobbies: reading, hiking, working with animals
Favorite Book: *Holes* by Louis Sachar

What's an Editorial?

It's writing that expresses the author's opinion. The writer of a problem-solution editorial states a problem and offers one or more solutions, hoping to convince readers to agree with the proposed solutions.

What's in an Editorial?

Three Parts
An editorial has an introduction that states a problem (or claim), a body that presents one or more solutions, and a conclusion that has a call to action.

Supporting Evidence
Facts and statistics can be used as supporting details in an editorial. You can cite statistics from a scientific study, or you can present facts from other sources. The goal is to support your argument with credible information.

Clear Rationale
A rationale is the thought process behind an opinion. All facts and details included in an editorial should support the writer's rationale. It's also important to acknowledge alternate or opposing claims to show that both sides of the story are understood.

Why write an Editorial?

I can think of a bunch of reasons to write an editorial. I have as many reasons as I have opinions! I listed some purposes for writing here.

Solve a Problem

A good reason to write an editorial is to help solve a real-world problem. I can suggest a solution and try to convince other people to support it.

Logical Thinking

I can practice logical thinking while writing my editorial. If I am able to present a good, logical argument, my readers will be more likely to agree with my claims.

Information

Presenting information is another good reason to write. If I present a lot of relevant and accurate information in my editorial, people will be well informed about the issue I'm describing.

Organization

I can learn organizational skills while writing an editorial. I'll have to choose a problem, explain why it's a problem, and then offer at least one solution. I'll have to decide which points to make first and which to make last.

Linking Argument Writing Traits to an **Editorial**

In this chapter, you will express your opinion about an important issue to a news source. This type of argument writing is called an editorial. Tyler will guide you through the stages of the writing process: Prewrite, Draft, Revise, Edit, and Publish. In each stage, Tyler will show you important writing strategies that are linked to the Argument Writing Traits below.

Argument Writing Traits

- clearly stated claims, often balanced by alternate or opposing claims
- supporting evidence from accurate and credible sources

- a strong introduction that presents the writer's position
- reasons and evidence that are organized logically
- a conclusion that follows and supports the argument
- transitions that clarify the relationships between the claim(s), the supporting evidence, and any counterclaims

- a voice that supports the writer's purpose

- language that is compelling

- sentences that vary in length and begin in different ways

- no or few errors in grammar, usage, mechanics, and spelling

Before you write, read the editorial on the next page. Then use the editorial rubric on pages 268–269 to evaluate the editorial. (You might want to look back at What's in an Editorial? on page 264, too!)

Editorial Model

Turn It Off!

by the editors of
The Springfield Middle School Gazette

Part I: Introduction

Supporting Evidence

When was the last time you read a good book? How long ago was it that you went camping or took a weekend hike in the woods? There was a time when people were likely to get involved in pastimes like these. Now, though, the most common activity in many people's lives is watching television, but this isn't much of an "activity" at all. According to recent research compiled by RealVision, a program that states facts about television, the average teenager watches television more than twenty hours per week. He or she might even be bombarded with as many as 20,000 commercials per year. By the age of eighteen, that teenager will have seen more than 200,000 violent acts and more than 16,000 murders. At the same time, due to lack of any real activity, that teenager's likelihood of becoming seriously overweight rises steadily. Clearly, something is wrong here.

Clear Rationale

Part II: Body

As a school, we can take steps to do something about excessive television watching and the problems it causes. Our suggestion is that we participate in the national TV-Turnoff Week next April. More than 3,000 groups, many of them schools, were part of this event last year. Most students who were involved thought it was great. They found that they had time to do many more things. Some listened to music. Others read or exercised. Still others cooked, made scrapbooks, and played board games. For a small fee, the TV-Turnoff Network, a not-for-profit organization that encourages less television watching, can provide our school with planning booklets to get us started. It can also supply posters and T-shirts to keep us motivated. Teachers can hold classroom discussions about activities to replace television. Once enough students become interested, it shouldn't be hard to get the whole school to participate.

But will one week away from staring at screens change our lives? It's hard to know. Many students who joined TV-Turnoff Week in the past said it really made a difference. It provided a springboard for breaking old viewing habits. With luck, the program can do the same for us.

Part III: Conclusion

Rubric

Use this 6-point rubric to plan and score an editorial.

	6	5	4
Ideas	The claim (problem), solution, and relevant evidence are clear. Logical reasoning and quality evidence support the claim.	The claim (problem), solution, and relevant evidence are clear. The reasoning and evidence support the claim most of the time.	Either the claim (problem) or solution is not stated clearly. Some evidence is weak or not relevant.
Organization	The introduction states the claim (problem), the body offers solutions, and the concluding section (conclusion) has a call to action.	The introduction states the claim (problem) and the body offers a solution. The call to action may be weak or missing.	The introduction states the claim (problem) and the writing is easy to follow. The solution is somewhat unclear and the call to action is weak or missing.
Voice	The writer consistently maintains a confident voice and a formal style.	The writer uses a formal style throughout most of the writing.	The writer's voice often fades in and out. The voice starts out formal but lapses into casual language.
Word Choice	Specific words are used effectively. Unfamiliar words are explained for the reader.	Specific words make the writing clear. Unfamiliar words are explained.	Most words are specific and communicate the meaning. Most unfamiliar words are explained.
Sentence Fluency	Striking variety in sentence beginnings gives the text flow and rhythm and clarifies ideas.	Noticeable variety in sentence beginnings makes the text flow.	Most sentences have varied beginnings. The writing is choppy in a few places.
Conventions	Appositives are punctuated correctly. Indefinite pronouns are clear. The writing is easy to understand.	Most appositives are punctuated correctly, and most indefinite pronouns are clear. The writing is not hard to read.	A few errors with appositives and indefinite pronouns don't interfere with the meaning.
+Presentation	The editorial is prepared neatly and legibly.		

3	2	1	
The problem and solution are identifiable but not clearly stated. Some evidence is weak or unrelated.	The problem or solution cannot be identified. Much of the evidence is weak or invented.	No problem or solution can be identified. Evidence is lacking.	Ideas
The introduction or conclusion needs work. The body is poorly organized, and the reader struggles to follow the writing.	Both the introduction and conclusion need work. Information is out of order and the reader feels lost.	There is no obvious introduction or conclusion. Details are listed but not organized.	Organization
The writer's voice is weak and does not connect with the audience. It wavers frequently between formal and informal.	The writer isn't interested in the topic. The voice isn't appropriate for the topic or audience.	The writing has no voice. The writer's lack of knowledge about the topic is obvious.	Voice
Words are often unclear and not explained, muddying the writer's meaning.	Many words are overused or used incorrectly. Unfamiliar words are not explained.	Words are vague and the text is often wordy. Reading takes work.	Word Choice
Some of the sentences are choppy, and beginnings are repetitious.	Many sentences begin the same way. Many parts of the writing are hard to read.	Sentences are incorrect or incomplete. The writing is hard to read out loud.	Sentence Fluency
Noticeable errors with appositives and indefinite pronouns slow down the reader.	Many errors with appositives and indefinite pronouns get in the way of reading.	Frequent serious errors with appositives and indefinite pronouns make the writing hard to understand.	Conventions

See Appendix B for 4-, 5-, and 6-point argument rubrics.

Using the Editorial Rubric to Study the Model

Did you notice that the model on page 267 points out some key elements of an editorial? As they wrote "Turn It Off!" the editors of the Springfield Middle School Gazette used these elements to help explain their claims. They also used the 6-point rubric on pages 268–269 to plan, draft, revise, and edit the writing. A rubric is a great tool to evaluate writing during the writing process.

Now let's use the same rubric to score the model. To do this, we'll focus on each trait separately, starting with Ideas. We'll use the top descriptor for each trait (column 6), along with examples from the model, to help us understand how the traits work together. How would you score the editors on each trait?

- **The claim (problem), solution, and relevant evidence are clear.**
- **Logical reasoning and quality evidence support the claim.**

The authors clearly state the problem early on, as well as provide clearly outlined solutions to the issue at hand. They also provide so many relevant, accurate facts, it was easy to understand and agree with their point of view. It's clear they know what they're talking about!

[from the writing model]

Now, though, the most common activity in many people's lives is watching television, but this isn't much of an "activity" at all.

[from the writing model]

By the age of eighteen, that teenager will have seen more than 200,000 violent acts and more than 16,000 murders.

- **The introduction states the claim (problem), the body offers solutions, and the concluding section (conclusion) has a call to action.**

The authors not only clearly define the problem and suggest a solution, but they also really inspire me to give their idea a try. The last paragraph's call to action is strong and clear—I know taking a break from television was the right thing to do.

[from the writing model]

But will one week away from staring at screens change our lives? It's hard to know. Many students who joined TV-Turnoff Week in the past said it really made a difference. It provided a springboard for breaking old viewing habits. With luck, the program can do the same for us.

- **The writer consistently maintains a confident voice and a formal style.**

It's clear that the authors have done their research and that they believe it themselves. Their voice is confident and informative, and the language, although formal, is still easy to connect with. The authors seem to truly want to help their readers get healthy and get moving.

[from the writing model]

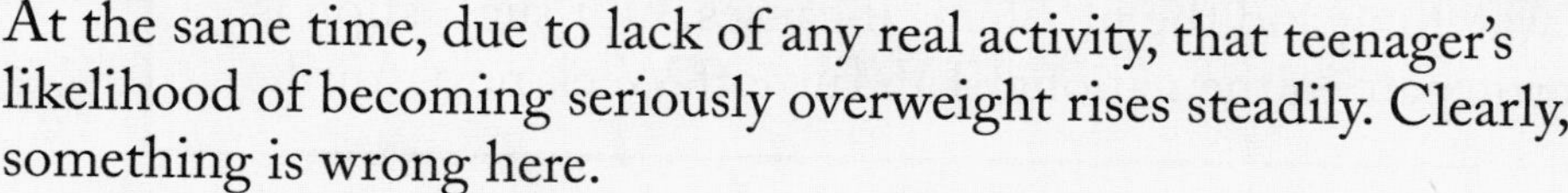
At the same time, due to lack of any real activity, that teenager's likelihood of becoming seriously overweight rises steadily. Clearly, something is wrong here.

- **Specific words are used effectively.**
- **Unfamiliar words are explained for the reader.**

Strong and specific words help me get the most from this editorial. *Discussions* is more descriptive than *talks*. *Participate* is more accurate than *join in*. There were no difficult words left undefined. It's easier to respond to the authors' call to action when the writing is strong, specific, and fully understood.

[from the writing model]

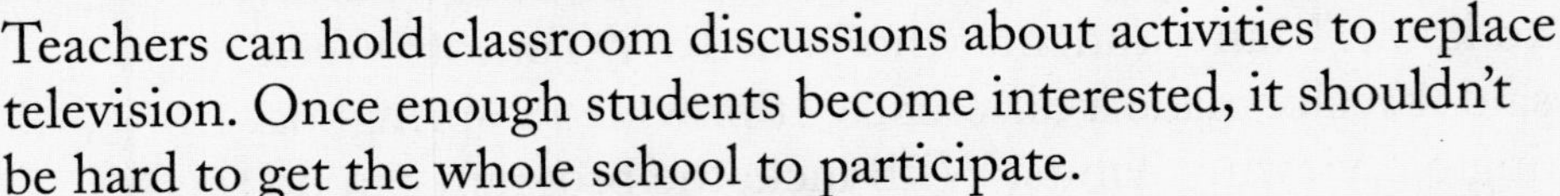
Teachers can hold classroom discussions about activities to replace television. Once enough students become interested, it shouldn't be hard to get the whole school to participate.

- **Striking variety in sentence beginnings makes the text flow, gives it rhythm, and clarifies ideas.**

I like how the authors use a variety of sentence structures throughout their editorial. Mixing up how sentences begin keeps me interested, helps me understand the information, and makes the text smooth and enjoyable to read.

[from the writing model]

As a school, we can take steps to do something about excessive television watching and the problems it causes. Our suggestion is that we participate in the national TV-Turnoff Week next April.

- **Appositives are punctuated correctly.**
- **Indefinite pronouns are clear.**
- **The writing is easy to understand.**

Wow! I can't find any spelling or grammatical errors at all in this editorial. Also, all appositives are correctly punctuated, and each indefinite pronoun is clear. I want my editorial to be perfect, too.

[from the writing model]

For a small fee, the TV-Turnoff Network, a not-for-profit organization that encourages less television watching, can provide our school with planning booklets to get us started.

+Presentation The editorial is prepared neatly and legibly.

My Turn!

Follow along to see how I use good writing strategies to write an editorial of my own. I'll use the rubric as a guide.

Prewrite

Focus on **Ideas**

The Rubric Says The claim (problem), solution, and relevant evidence are clear.

Writing Strategy Brainstorm to choose a problem, or claim, for which there is a solution.

When our teacher told us we were going to be writing editorials, our class brainstormed some writing ideas. We came up with all kinds of potential topics: our cafeteria is dirty, our library needs to be open before school, there's too much bullying going on in the hallways, and activity period should be longer.

But I decided to write about bullying because I have some ideas on how to solve the problem. My claim will be that bullying is a problem that must be solved. I brainstormed by myself for more ideas. Then I wrote them down.

The Problem: Bullying

- happens in hallways, bathrooms
- could happen to anyone
- cause of violence in some schools (need examples)
- everyone afraid to rat on others
- some kids get hurt
- some kids are scared

We need:

- "no tolerance" policy
- help from teachers
- tables-turned activities
- more student involvement
- schoolwide campaign

Apply

Brainstorm to find a problem for which you can propose a solution. Then jot down some notes to get your thoughts together.

Prewrite

Focus on Organization

The Rubric Says The introduction states the claim (problem), the body offers solutions, and the concluding section (conclusion) has a call to action.

Writing Strategy Make a Problem-Solution Frame to organize the ideas.

Writer's Term

Problem-Solution Frame
Use a **Problem-Solution Frame** to define a problem and organize the information that solves it.

I know from the rubric that it's important to organize my information. A Problem-Solution Frame will help me do this. I'll use the notes I gathered while brainstorming to help me think of possible results.

Problem-Solution Frame

Problem Box

What is the problem?

- bullying

Why is it a problem?

- some kids are scared
- some kids have been hurt
- cause of violence in some schools (need examples)
- everyone afraid to rat on others

Who has the problem?

- our school—in the hallways and in the bathrooms

Solution Box

Solutions

- schoolwide campaign
- "no tolerance" policy
- help from teachers
- tables-turned activities
- more student involvement

Results

- will make everyone more aware of the problem
- everyone will know rules and what will happen if they're broken
- will supervise bathrooms and little-used hallways to keep things from happening
- will show bullies what it feels like
- can show disapproval by recommending ways to change things

End Result Box

- might not totally solve the problem, but will be a great start toward stopping it

Reflect

How will Tyler's Problem-Solution Frame help him focus his writing?

Apply

Make a Problem-Solution Frame to organize your ideas.

Draft

Focus on **Ideas**

The Rubric Says Logical reasoning and quality evidence support the claim.

Writing Strategy Research the subject and gather accurate and relevant facts or statistics.

Writer's Term

Credible Websites

How do you know a website can be trusted? Ask yourself these questions:

- Who wrote the website?
- What is the purpose of the website?
- Does the information match up with at least two other sources?
- Does the website look professionally designed?

Bullying is a big problem in my school and in schools all around the country. The rubric says I should include quality evidence and logical reasoning to support my claim. If I use reference sources in the library and search credible websites on the Internet, finding plenty of solid facts should not be difficult.

First, I'll focus on the bullying that's happening in my school and what could happen if we ignore the problem. Then, I'll follow my Problem-Solution Frame to develop the body, which will focus on the solution. This is where quality evidence and logical reasoning will really help convince my reader. Finally, my conclusion will summarize what could happen as a result of my proposed solutions.

Right now, I'll just focus on getting my ideas down. I'll worry about fixing any spelling or grammar mistakes later.

Proofreading Marks

- Indent
- Make uppercase
- Make lowercase
- Add something
- Take out something
- Add a period
- New paragraph
- Spelling error

[DRAFT]

[introduction]

Stop the Bullying!

Yesterday, a sixth grader was found hiding near the janitor's closet. Someone finally got him to admit, "XXX is after me." (XXX, an eighth grader has a reputation for bullying other students.) Last week, another sixth grader went to class with his shirt ripped and a scrach on his face. Though he wouldn't say what had happened, a lot of kids knew that he had had a run-in with YYY another bully. Allmost any student in our School could give more examples like these. Bullying the act of one kid terrorizing another, is happening all the time in our hallways and bathrooms. Some parents have even removed their children from school because the bullying has gotten so bad.

[claim/problem]

Reflect

What do you think of Tyler's introduction? In what ways does it grab your interest?

Apply

Write a draft that holds the reader's interest throughout. Remember to use quality evidence and logical reasoning. And don't forget a clear call to action!

Revise

Focus on Organization

The Rubric Says The introduction states the claim (problem), the body offers solutions, and the concluding section (conclusion) has a call to action.

Writing Strategy Strengthen the conclusion.

I just read over my draft, and I'm really happy with the way I've presented both the problem, or claim, and the solution. But my conclusion is a bit weak. I want to do more than just inform my readers—I want to get them thinking and get them involved. Using a question-answer pattern will both engage the reader and make my conclusion stronger and more realistic. What do you think of my revision?

[DRAFT]

[strengthened the conclusion]

Can we get rid of bullying overnight? Probably not.

^Bullying has been going on around here for a long time. But if we start some new policies and make sure everyone follows up on them, we can make a real start on solving the problem.

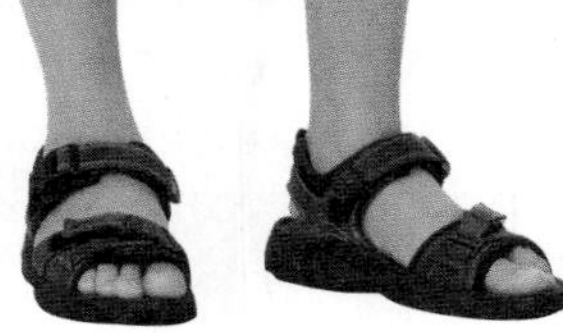

Apply

Strengthen your conclusion by engaging your reader.

Revise

Focus on **Voice**

The Rubric Says

The writer consistently maintains a confident voice and a formal style.

Writing Strategy

Use a blend of first-person and third-person points of view.

I know that an opinion needs to be expressed in an impartial way. If I get too personally involved in the writing, I'll drive my reader away. I also need to sound confident and use a formal style to be taken seriously. That means using third-person point of view will work best in my editorial. However, this *is* a subject I feel strongly about, and occasionally using first person will help me directly connect with the reader. If I establish a connection with my readers, they will feel more motivated to read and understand my argument.

[DRAFT]

[used first-person point of view]

So how can ~~this problem be solved~~ we solve this problem? The best solution is a schoolwide campaign against bullying. Everyone can play a part.

Reflect

How have Tyler's revisions helped? How has using the word *we* affected his writing?

Apply

Use a confident and formal voice as you write. Use a limited amount of first person to connect effectively with your reader.

Revise

Focus on **Word Choice**

The Rubric Says Specific words are used effectively. Unfamiliar words are explained for the reader.

Writing Strategy Replace vague words with specific ones.

As I reread my draft, I looked for vague words I could replace with strong, specific words. I also made sure I explained any words that needed defining for my reader. For example, I explained both *bullying* and *no tolerance*. I found some vague words that need replacing. *Witness* is more accurate than *see*, and *disapprove* is stronger than *don't approve*. I'll make these changes now to strengthen my writing.

[DRAFT]

[used specific words]

Students and teachers, the people most likely to ~~see~~ witness bullying, must play an active part. Students must learn to show that they ~~don't approve~~ disapprove of bullying, and they must understand that there is nothing wrong with reporting it to an authority figure.

Apply

Fully explain all unfamiliar terms and use strong, specific words to strengthen your editorial.

Edit

Focus on Conventions

The Rubric Says

Appositives are punctuated correctly. Indefinite pronouns are clear. The writing is easy to understand.

Writing Strategy

Check the use of appositives and indefinite pronouns.

Writer's Term

Appositives

An **appositive** is a word or a phrase that identifies a noun. An appositive usually follows the noun it identifies, and it is usually separated from the rest of the sentence by one or more commas.

The rubric says all appositives should be accurately punctuated and all indefinite pronouns should be clear. I'll find and fix any errors now.

[DRAFT]

[corrected appositive punctuation]

scratch
~~scrach~~ on his face. Though he wouldn't say what had happened, a lot of kids knew that he had had a run-in with YYY, another bully. Almost ~~Allmost~~

Reflect

What do you think? How have Tyler's choice of words and edits improved his writing?

Apply

Conventions

Edit your draft for grammar and mechanics, making sure that appositives are set off with commas and indefinite pronouns are clear.

For more practice with appositives and indefinite pronouns, use the exercises on the next two pages.

Appositives

Know the Rule

An **appositive** is a word or a phrase that identifies a noun. An appositive usually follows the noun it identifies, and it's separated from the rest of the sentence by commas.

Examples: We volunteer one day each month at The Shelter**, a local nonprofit organization.**

Volunteers**, people who work for no money,** are important to nonprofit organizations.

Practice the Rule

Rewrite each sentence with correct punctuation on a separate sheet of paper.

1. Nonprofit organizations groups that work for a cause without expecting to make a profit can do a lot of good.
2. There are more than one million "recognized" organizations groups with official names and regular employees in the United States.
3. Some of these nonprofit organizations focus on social issues problems that affect many people across society.
4. Free legal representation a real issue for people unjustly accused of crimes is the focus of some groups.
5. A nonprofit organization that influences many people's lives is public television a source of excellent programming.
6. Donations gifts of money given freely by other groups or individuals are what help nonprofits survive.
7. After learning about nonprofit organizations, I was inspired to join Meals Door-to-Door a group that hand-delivers hot meals to the elderly during the winter months.
8. Nonprofit organizations are exempt from taxes money paid to the city based on the value of the property owned by the business.
9. Citizens people living in a community profit greatly when several nonprofits join together to help a cause.
10. Sometimes, the directors people who work full-time for the nonprofit groups get paid to compensate them for their time.

Indefinite Pronouns

Know the Rule

Indefinite pronouns refer to persons or things that are not identified as individuals. Indefinite pronouns include *all, anybody, anyone, both, either, anything, everyone, few, many, most, one, several, nobody,* and *someone.*

Example: Out of the twenty students in gym class, **most** signed up for the student-teacher basketball game.

Practice the Rule

Copy each sentence onto a separate sheet of paper. Circle the indefinite pronouns in each sentence.

1. All are invited to our Holiday Open-House celebration—the bigger the crowd, the better!
2. Ten of my friends are coming, and some are bringing their parents.
3. I think I've invited everyone I know—it should be a great party!
4. I invited two of my uncles from out of town, but neither could come.
5. Mom and I couldn't decide whether to serve pizza or tacos, so we're going to serve both.
6. Four of my friends asked if they could bring something to the party.
7. Anna makes amazing brownies, so I asked her to bring some.
8. I don't know what type of salad dressing all my friends like, so I bought several.
9. We asked the neighbors if we could borrow their card tables for the party because we have none.
10. We'll all be tired the next day, but everybody will be pleased they came to the party!

Publish +Presentation

Publishing Strategy Submit the editorial for publication in the school newspaper.

Presentation Strategy Prepare the editorial on a computer.

The writing is done! I think this editorial's topic is so important that it should be in the school's newspaper. My submission should be typed on the computer so the editors can format it to fit the paper, but it's still my job to have everything neat and accurate before submitting it. I'll check it against my final checklist now to make sure I didn't miss anything.

My Final Checklist

Did I—

- ✔ punctuate all appositives properly?
- ✔ make sure all indefinite pronouns are accurate and clear?
- ✔ type my editorial neatly on a word processor?
- ✔ indent each new paragraph and include my name on the page?

Apply

Make a checklist to check your editorial. Then make a final draft to publish.

STOP THE BULLYING!

by Tyler

Yesterday, a sixth grader was found hiding near the janitor's closet. Someone finally got him to admit, "XXX is after me." (XXX, an eighth grader, has a reputation for bullying other students.) Last week, another sixth grader went to class with his shirt ripped and a scratch on his face. What had happened? Although he wouldn't say, a lot of kids knew that he had had a run-in with YYY, another bully. Almost any student in our school could give more examples like these. Bullying, the act of one kid terrorizing another, is happening all the time in our hallways and bathrooms. When the World Health Organization sponsored a recent survey of more than 15,000 students, it found that more than 10 percent of the students were bullied "sometimes" or "weekly." Some parents have even removed their children from school because the bullying has gotten so bad.

Bullying is a problem that must be solved. So how can we solve this problem? The best solution is a schoolwide campaign against bullying. Everyone can play a part. First, the administration should make it clear that they don't approve of bullying. Then, they should announce a "No Tolerance" policy. This would mean that every time a bully is caught, he or she would be punished.

Students and teachers, the people most likely to witness bullying, must play an active part. Students must learn to show that they disapprove of bullying, and they must understand that there is nothing wrong with reporting it to an authority figure. But they should also know that their names would be kept confidential. Teachers should patrol hallways and bathrooms, the places where bullying goes on the most, and they should make it clear that bullies will be punished. They should also use homeroom periods to give individual guidance.

Can we get rid of bullying overnight? Probably not. Bullying has been going on around here for a long time. But if we start some new policies and make sure everyone follows up on them, we can make a real start on solving the problem.

Reflect

How did Tyler do? Did you notice how he used the rubric as he wrote? Don't forget to use the rubric to check your own editorial, too!

What's a Business Letter?

It's a formal letter written to a person or a company. The writer of an argument-based business letter tries to convince the receiver to take action about a specific issue.

What's in a Business Letter?

Letter Form
A good business letter has six parts: heading, inside address, greeting, body, closing, and signature. The letter form makes it easy for the receiver to respond to the letter.

Important Issue
A business letter should always have a direct focus; otherwise, it's not worth writing. I'll use my business letter to explain an important issue to the recipient.

Call to Action
When a business letter is written to present an argument, it should have a clear call to action. The call to action explains what the writer wants the recipient to think, say, or do.

Evidence
The writer of a business letter will want to include enough details so that the recipient will understand the issue and possibly act upon a solution.

Why write a Business Letter?

I can think of many reasons for writing a business letter. Here are some examples.

Make Something Happen
A business letter often contains the writer's request to the recipient to make something happen. Stating my case to the right person can result in the change that I am seeking.

Organize
Writing a business letter forces me to organize my ideas. I have to present everything in a logical, convincing form. This is a skill that will be helpful for years to come.

Get Help
Sometimes I can't solve problems on my own. But if I write a letter to the right person, I might be able to get the help that I need.

Inform
I can use a business letter to inform someone about an issue. I can educate the reader while explaining my solution to a problem.

Linking Argument Writing Traits to a Business Letter

In this chapter, you will write to an organization to convince them to act in some way. This type of argument writing is called a business letter. Tyler will guide you through the stages of the writing process: Prewrite, Draft, Revise, Edit, and Publish. In each stage, Tyler will show you important writing strategies that are linked to the Argument Writing Traits below.

Argument Writing Traits

- clearly stated claims, often balanced by alternate or opposing claims
- supporting evidence from accurate and credible sources

- a strong introduction that presents the writer's position
- reasons and evidence that are organized logically
- a conclusion that follows and supports the argument
- transitions that clarify the relationships between the claim(s), the supporting evidence, and any counterclaims

- a voice that supports the writer's purpose

- language that is compelling

- sentences that vary in length and begin in different ways

- no or few errors in grammar, usage, mechanics, and spelling

Before you write, read Susan Bernini's letter on the next page. Then use the business letter rubric on pages 290–291 to decide how well she did. (You might want to look back at What's in a Business Letter? on page 286, too!)

Business Letter Model

38 Oak Lane
Ridge Park, IL 60100
November 12, 2012

Letter Form: Heading

Director of Children's Services
Municipal Services of Ridge Park
455 Laurel Road
Ridge Park, IL 60100

Letter Form: Inside Address

Dear Sir or Madam: Letter Form: Greeting

Important Issue

A group of families from Nigeria has recently moved into our area. About twenty students from these families are enrolled at my school, Trout Junior High. These students need special services to help them adapt to living here—help that your agency could provide. The following are some of the reasons I think you should assist them. Call to Action

Letter Form: Body

To begin with, these students are in dire need of translators or other language helpers. Our school has special classes for English-language learners. However, the teachers know little about these students' native languages. If translators could work with these students in their regular classes, it would really help them. Right now, these students just sit quietly and shake their heads when a teacher calls on them. Even after two months of school, they can barely communicate with us.

Evidence

Another thing the students need help with is proper clothing for the winter. You might help them just by providing some warm hand-me-downs. However, it would be even better if you could get them some new, in-style clothing.

As you can see, there are many ways you could help our new students.

Yours truly, Letter Form: Closing

Susan Bernini Letter Form: Signature

Susan Bernini

Rubric

Use this 6-point rubric to plan and score a business letter.

	6	5	4
Ideas	The claim is clear and balanced with an opposing claim. Accurate facts and examples are relevant and support the claim.	The claim is clear and an opposing claim is mentioned. Accurate facts, examples, and explanations support the claim.	The claim is clear, but there is no clear opposing claim. Some accurate and relevant information is included.
Organization	The letter is organized around a claim that inspires a call to action. Each body paragraph contains a strong and complete topic sentence.	The letter contains a call to action. Each body paragraph contains a topic sentence and supporting details.	Some parts of the letter are not related to the call to action. Some topic sentences may be hard to identify.
Voice	The writer's voice is convincing. The formal style is ideal for the topic and audience.	The writer's voice is convincing. The style is appropriate most of the time.	The writer's voice sounds convincing most of the time. The style, or tone, may be informal or inappropriate some of the time.
Word Choice	The language is striking. All words, including frequently confused words and homophones, are used correctly.	Words and phrases are clear. Frequently confused words and homophones are used correctly.	The language is clear, and most words are used correctly.
Sentence Fluency	Sentences are varied, interesting, and stand apart from other writing. The writing is smooth when read out loud.	Sentences are varied and interesting. The writing is easy to read.	There is some variety in sentence beginnings and lengths. Occasionally, the writing is choppy.
Conventions	Sentences are clear and correct: there are no double negatives, and infinitive phrases are effective.	A few double negatives or errors with infinitive phrases don't interfere with the meaning.	Some noticeable errors with infinitive phrases and double negatives do not interfere with reading.
+Presentation	The letter and envelope are neat and in the correct format.		

3	2	1	
The claim is somewhat clear. No opposing claim is mentioned. Some information is lacking or not relevant.	The claim is not clear. Little relevant information is included. Details are missing or inaccurate.	No claim is stated. No details are provided. The writer knows little about the topic.	Ideas
Several parts of the letter are not related to the call to action. Some paragraphs lack a topic sentence or supporting details.	The call to action is hard to identify. Several paragraphs lack a topic sentence and/or supporting details.	There is no call to action or organization to the writing. The writing is not organized into paragraphs.	Organization
The writer's voice sounds unconvincing. The tone may be uninterested, informal, or inappropriate.	The writer's voice is weak and not convincing. The tone may be rude, informal, or uninformed.	The voice is flat or absent. The writer does not connect with the audience.	Voice
Some vague words make the writing unclear. Several words are used incorrectly.	Much of the language is unclear, and many words are used incorrectly.	The language is vague. Words simply fill the page. Many words are used incorrectly.	Word Choice
Sentence beginnings are alike, and there is little variety in length.	Incomplete, choppy sentences are found throughout, making it hard to read.	Most sentences are incomplete or choppy. The writing is a challenge to read.	Sentence Fluency
Errors with infinitive phrases and double negatives are noticeable and interfere with reading out loud.	Many errors with infinitive phrases and double negatives interfere with meaning.	Frequent serious errors with infinitive phrases and double negatives make the writing hard to understand.	Conventions

See Appendix B for 4-, 5-, and 6-point argument rubrics.

Using the Business Letter Rubric to Study the Model

Did you notice that the model on page 289 points out some key elements of a business letter? As she wrote her letter, Susan Bernini used these elements to help her explain why she wanted help for the new Nigerian students. She also used the 6-point rubric on pages 290–291 to plan, draft, revise, and edit the writing. A rubric is a great tool to evaluate writing during the writing process.

Now let's use the same rubric to score the model. To do this, we'll focus on each trait separately, starting with Ideas. We'll use the top descriptor for each trait (column 6), along with examples from the model, to help us understand how the traits work together. How would you score Susan on each trait?

- **The claim is clear and balanced with an opposing claim.**
- **Accurate facts and examples are relevant and support the claim.**

I like how Susan clearly presents her concern right at the start of the letter. She explains the issue in a logical and direct way and provides solid, relevant examples and facts to support her requests.

[from the writing model]

A group of families from Nigeria has recently moved into our area. About twenty students from these families are enrolled at my school, Trout Junior High. These students need special services to help them adapt to living here—help that your agency could provide.

- **The letter is organized around a claim that inspires a call to action.**
- **Each body paragraph contains a strong and complete topic sentence.**

What a strong letter! Every body paragraph relates back to Susan's call to action, which is clearly stated right at the beginning. Each point is made in a topic sentence, and then several supporting sentences provide all the information needed to fully understand her point of view.

[from the writing model]

To begin with, these students are in dire need of translators or other language helpers. Our school has special classes for English-language learners. However, the teachers know little about these students' native languages.

- **The writer's voice is convincing.**
- **The formal style is ideal for the topic and audience.**

Susan understands her audience—an adult who is the Director of Children's Services. Her voice is strong and convincing, and her style remains appropriate and courteous throughout the letter.

[from the writing model]

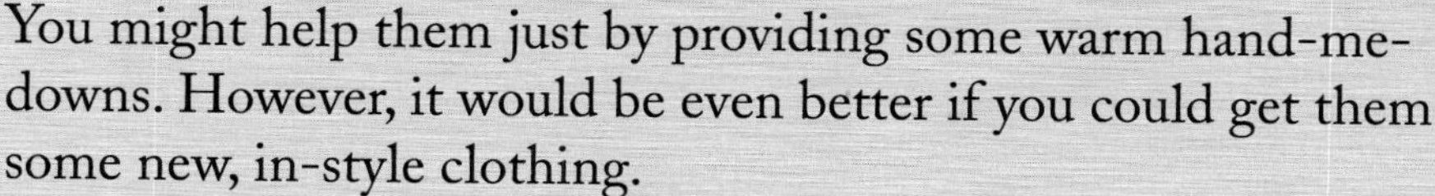
You might help them just by providing some warm hand-me-downs. However, it would be even better if you could get them some new, in-style clothing.

- The language is striking.
- All words, including frequently confused words and homophones, are used correctly.

Susan uses all words correctly—even tricky homophones and other easily confused words. In this example, she uses *here* (not *hear*) when discussing a place and *your* (not *you're*) when referring to the Director's agency. I'll work hard to use words accurately, too.

[from the writing model]

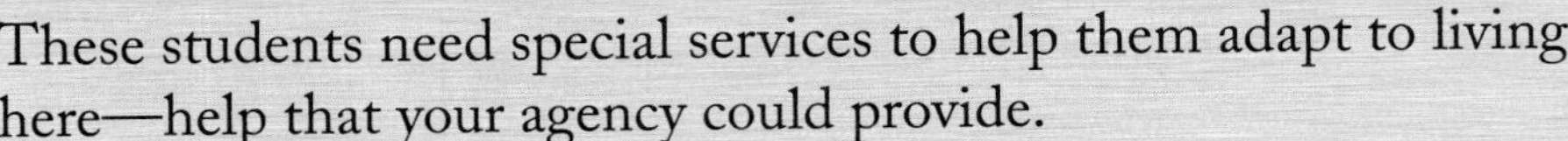

These students need special services to help them adapt to living here—help that your agency could provide.

- Sentences are varied, interesting, and stand apart from other writing.
- The writing is smooth when read out loud.

I especially like how Susan varies her sentence structures. Using a variety of sentences is more effective and helps the writing sound natural. It's hard to pay attention to the same sentence type used over and over again. Susan's writing would sound smooth if it were read out loud.

[from the writing model]

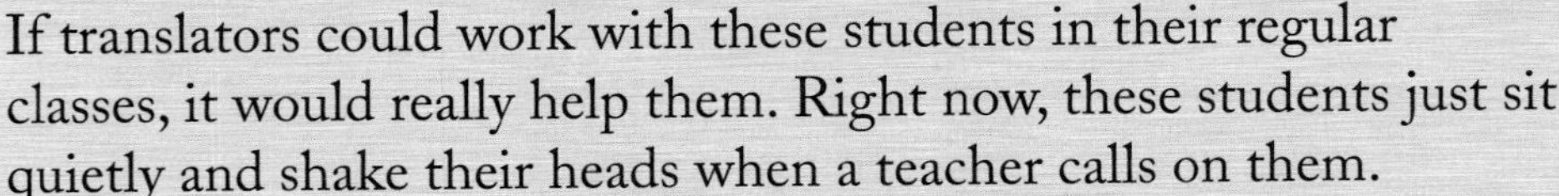

If translators could work with these students in their regular classes, it would really help them. Right now, these students just sit quietly and shake their heads when a teacher calls on them.

- **Sentences are clear and correct: there are no double negatives, and infinitive phrases are effective.**

I couldn't find a single mistake in Susan's letter! She even avoided using double negatives, a mistake that many people make. In the sentence below, she correctly uses *can barely* instead of *can't barely*.

[from the writing model]

Even after two months of school, they can barely communicate with us.

+Presentation The letter and envelope are neat and in the correct format.

My Turn!

I'm going to write a business letter about something that concerns me. I'll follow the rubric and use good writing strategies. Read on to see how I do it!

Prewrite

Focus on Ideas

The Rubric Says The claim is clear and balanced with an opposing claim. Accurate facts and examples are relevant and support the claim.

Writing Strategy Choose an issue that you have a strong opinion about. List explanations, facts, and examples to support your opinion.

I had no trouble coming up with a topic for my business letter. The school board is planning to stop buying new books for our school library, and I am opposed to this. I decided to address my letter to the school board president, Ms. Williams. Then I listed explanations, facts, and examples that would support my opinion. I also thought about an opposing claim I want to mention, to show that I've really thought the issue through from all sides.

Opinion: Don't stop buying new books.

Explanations:

- need accurate, up-to-date information
- need recent books students can understand

Opposing Claim:

- students can find info they need on the Internet

Facts/Examples:

- a lot of research projects
- info about human genome project: library books really out of date
- Internet articles sometimes too difficult to help
- a lot of current nonfiction books written for students our age

Choose an important issue about which you have a strong opinion. Then list several reasons, facts, and examples to support your opinion.

Prewrite

Focus on **Organization**

The Rubric Says The letter is organized around a claim that inspires a call to action.

Writing Strategy Make an Argument Map to show how the reasons, facts, and examples support the call to action.

My next step was to organize my ideas. Since I'd be using my letter to persuade Ms. Williams, I thought an Argument Map would be the best choice of a graphic organizer. I listed my call to action first, followed by my reasons. Then I filled in facts and examples wherever they fit best.

Writer's Term

Argument Map/Call to Action
An **Argument Map** organizes reasons, examples, and facts that support your **call to action**. A call to action is a direct invitation to the audience to do something.

Argument Map

Call to Action
Convince board members to change their minds.

Reason 1
Students need accurate, up-to-date information.

Example
Our library has outdated information (human genome project).

Reason 2
Students need information they can understand.

Fact
Internet information is often too hard to read.

Example
There are many nonfiction books written for students our age.

Reflect

Do you think Tyler's Argument Map and notes are helpful? Has he included enough convincing information?

Apply

Use an Argument Map to organize your ideas.

Draft

Focus on **Organization**

The Rubric Says The letter is organized around a claim that inspires a call to action. Each body paragraph contains a strong and complete topic sentence.

Writing Strategy Write well-organized paragraphs that support the call to action.

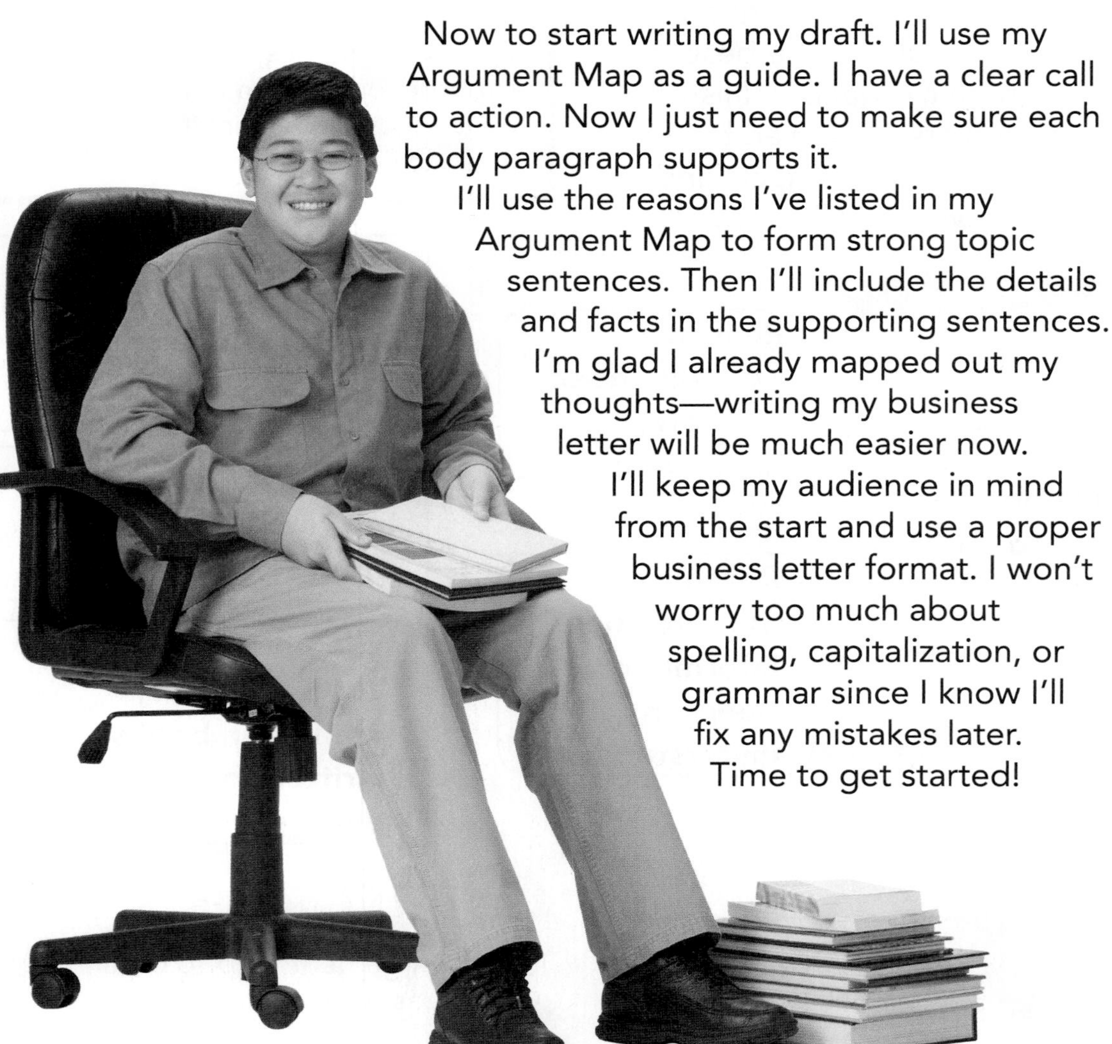

Now to start writing my draft. I'll use my Argument Map as a guide. I have a clear call to action. Now I just need to make sure each body paragraph supports it.

I'll use the reasons I've listed in my Argument Map to form strong topic sentences. Then I'll include the details and facts in the supporting sentences. I'm glad I already mapped out my thoughts—writing my business letter will be much easier now.

I'll keep my audience in mind from the start and use a proper business letter format. I won't worry too much about spelling, capitalization, or grammar since I know I'll fix any mistakes later. Time to get started!

Proofreading Marks

- ⊐ Indent
- ≡ Make uppercase
- / Make lowercase
- ∧ Add something
- Take out something
- ⊙ Add a period
- ¶ New paragraph
- (sp) Spelling error

[DRAFT]

42 Georgia Pine Way
Atlanta, GA 30303
April 23, 2012

[heading]

Ms. Corrine Williams
School Board President
Consolidated District 2
456 South Peachtree Street
Atlanta, GA 30303

[inside address]

Dear Ms. Williams: ← [greeting]

I heard on the local news that the school board is having budget problems. One perposed solution is to stop buying new books for our school libraries. I am a student at Thompson Middle School, and I think that's really foolish and I'm really upset! Here are the reasons for my opinion.

[strong topic sentence]

Students need accurite, up-to-date information on scientific and political events. For example, I was recently asked to do a class report on the human genome project. The book in our school library said that all human genes would be identified "in the next ten years." My mother told me, though, that the identification was already completed. None of our library books weren't current enough to have this information. Students can't hardly do accurite research in books like these.

Reflect

How do you think Ms. Williams will respond to Tyler's opening paragraphs?

Apply

Write a draft, making sure to use the correct letter form and strong topic sentences.

Revise

Focus on 

The Rubric Says The writer's voice is convincing. The formal style is ideal for the topic and audience.

Writing Strategy Use a respectful and courteous tone.

The rubric says my voice should be convincing and my writing style should be appropriate for both my topic and audience. I am asking Ms. Williams to do something for me, and, if I want her to take my thoughts seriously, my letter should be formal, respectful, and polite. I want her to happily agree with me and not feel bullied in any way. As I reread my draft, I found a place that sounded too pushy. I'll fix it now.

[DRAFT]

problems. One perposed solution is to stop buying new books for our school libraries. I am a student at Thompson Middle School, and I think that this is a big mistake. ~~that's really foolish and I'm really upset!~~ Here are the reasons for my opinion.

[used courteous tone]

Apply

Keep your voice convincing, yet respectful and courteous.

Revise

Focus on **Word Choice**

The Rubric Says All words, including frequently confused words and homophones, are used correctly.

Writing Strategy Check the use of all homophones and other frequently confused words.

Writer's Term

Frequently Confused Words

Frequently confused words include **homophones** and words with similar sounds and/or meanings like **sit** and **set** or **lie** and **lay**. A homophone is a word that sounds the same as another word but has a different meaning and spelling like **they're, their,** and **there**.

The rubric tells me to check my use of words. I know that homophones and other words that sound similar can be tricky. I found a passage where I had made several errors by using the wrong words, so I went back and made some changes.

[DRAFT]

[corrected homophone errors]

we can get all the information we need on the Internet. The Internet, though, isn't hardly always ~~to~~ too helpful. I tried to find information on the human genome project ~~their~~ there. All I could find were papers written by scientists for other scientists. We need more ~~then~~ than that. We need

[corrected a frequently confused word]

Reflect

How have Tyler's revisions regarding voice and word accuracy strengthened his business letter?

Apply

Check your draft for errors in the use of homophones and other frequently confused words.

Revise

Focus on **Sentence Fluency**

The Rubric Says Sentences are varied, interesting, and stand apart from other writing. The writing is smooth when read out loud.

Writing Strategy Use different sentence structures, such as conditional sentences.

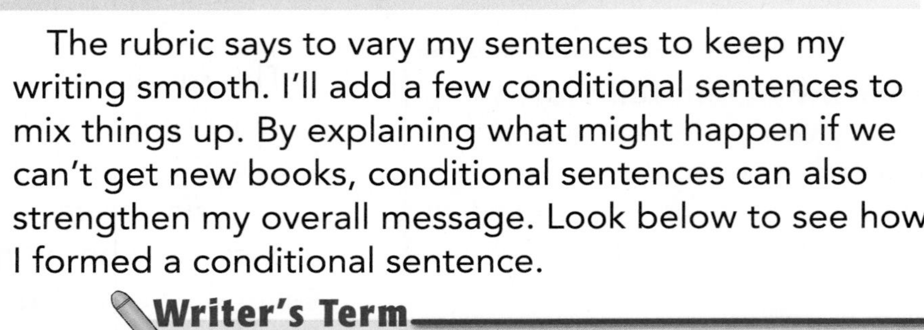

The rubric says to vary my sentences to keep my writing smooth. I'll add a few conditional sentences to mix things up. By explaining what might happen if we can't get new books, conditional sentences can also strengthen my overall message. Look below to see how I formed a conditional sentence.

Writer's Term

Conditional Sentences

A **conditional sentence** often contains **if, unless, provided, as long as,** or **would** to show that one thing depends on another. Conditional sentences also tell about situations that might happen.

[DRAFT]

The Internet, though, isn't hardly always ~~to~~ too helpful. I tried to find information on the human genome project ~~their~~ there. All I could find were papers written by scientists for other scientists. We need more ~~then~~ than that. We need nonfiction books by people who write just for students if we're going to do a good job on our research.

[formed a conditional sentence]

Apply

Where can you add conditional sentences?

Edit

Focus on **Conventions**

The Rubric Says Sentences are clear and correct: there are no double negatives, and infinitive phrases are effective.

Writing Strategy Make sure that there are no double negatives and that infinitives are correct.

Writer's Term

Double Negatives

Negative words are words like **no, not, nothing, nobody, never, nowhere, neither, none, hardly, barely, scarcely, without,** and any contraction ending in **n't**. Using two negative words together creates the error called a **double negative**.

When rereading my draft, I found a few double negatives. I'll go and correct them now. While I'm at it, I'll also make sure all infinitive phrases are used effectively.

[DRAFT]

[corrected a double negative]

told me, though, that the indentification was already completed. None of our library books ~~weren't~~ were current enough to have this information. Students can't ~~hardly~~ do ~~accurite~~ accurate research in books like these. Here is another, even worse example. The world atlas in our library shows Germany divided into two separate countries, but it was reunited in 1990!

[deleted a double negative]

Reflect

How do Tyler's revisions help his sentences to flow? In what ways have Tyler's edits helped his writing?

Apply

Conventions

Edit for spelling, punctuation, and capitalization. Be sure infinitives are correct and that there are no double negatives.

For more practice with infinitives and avoiding double negatives, complete the next two pages.

Double Negatives

Know the Rule

Negative words are words like *no, not, nothing, nobody, never, nowhere, neither, none, hardly, barely, scarcely, without,* and any contraction ending in *n't*. A **double negative** occurs when more than one negative word is used to express a negative idea. Double negatives confuse the reader and confuse the writer's meaning. Avoid them whenever possible.

Double Negative: The school board doe**sn't** have **no** money.
Corrected: The school board doesn't have any money.

Practice the Rule

Rewrite each sentence below on a separate sheet of paper, correcting the double negative used in each one.

1. It wasn't hardly lunchtime, and Kellie was already hungry.
2. She couldn't ask her teacher no questions about the menu.
3. So she distracted herself by sharpening a pencil that didn't have no point.
4. She scarcely never had a pencil with a point.
5. While she was sharpening her pencil, she couldn't barely wait to eat.
6. Kellie returned to her work, only to realize she didn't have no time to finish.
7. When the bell sounded, she couldn't hardly run fast enough to the cafeteria.
8. Kellie waited and waited, but her friends weren't nowhere to be seen.
9. She got in line for a sandwich or salad, but the lunch lady said that neither wasn't left.
10. Hungry and disappointed, Kellie decided to buy a yogurt, but her pocket didn't hold no money!

Infinitive Phrases

Know the Rule

An **infinitive** is a phrase made up of the word *to* followed by the present form of a verb (*to discover*). Infinitives may act as adjectives, adverbs, or nouns. An **infinitive phrase** is made up of an infinitive and any other words that complete its meaning.

Example: My dream is **to learn how to walk on a tightrope.**

Practice the Rule

Copy the sentences onto a separate sheet of paper. Circle the infinitive phrases in each sentence.

1. Last night, Dad wanted us to have dinner early so that we could go out for ice cream afterward.
2. I was able to get home from school in time to help him make dinner.
3. Unfortunately, my brother had forgotten to mention that he had baseball practice after school.
4. Mom likes to take the bus home from work, and traffic was terrible.
5. She tried to call and let us know she was running late, but the battery in her cell phone died.
6. Of course, Dad and I didn't realize the rest of the family was going to be late for dinner.
7. We started to chop the vegetables and get everything ready.
8. As you can imagine, there was only one way for this story to turn out.
9. By the time Mom and my brother got home, dinner was far too burned to eat.
10. It's not very often that we go out to eat on a weeknight.

Publish

+Presentation

Publishing Strategy Mail the letter to the appropriate person.

Presentation Strategy Make sure the letter has all six parts.

Now to mail my letter! I'll use the proper business letter format, so that the person who receives the letter will take it seriously. And I'll accurately address the envelope. The United States Postal Service won't be able to deliver my letter if I leave out vital information. In fact, I can check how to properly address my envelope by checking www.usps.com. But first I'll check it against my final checklist.

My Final Checklist

Did I—

- ✔ avoid using double negatives?
- ✔ include effective infinitive phrases?
- ✔ handwrite or type both my letter and envelope neatly?
- ✔ include all six parts in my letter?

Apply

Check your business letter against your checklist. Then make a final copy to publish.

42 Georgia Pine Way
Atlanta, GA 30303
April 23, 2012

Ms. Corrine Williams
School Board President
Consolidated District 2
456 South Peachtree Street
Atlanta, GA 30303

Dear Ms. Williams:

I heard on the local news that the school board is having budget problems. One proposed solution is to stop buying new books for our school libraries. I am a student at Thompson Middle School, and I think that this is a big mistake. Here are the reasons for my opinion.

Students need accurate, up-to-date information on recent scientific and political events. For example, I was recently asked to do a class report on the Human Genome Project. The book in our school library said that all human genes would be identified "in the next ten years." My mother told me, though, that the identification was already completed. None of our library books were current enough to have this information. Here is another, even worse example. The world atlas in our library shows Germany divided into two separate countries, but it was reunited in 1990! Students can't do accurate research in books like these.

Another reason to continue buying library books is that we, the students, need information we can understand. You might think that we can get all the information we need on the Internet. The Internet, though, isn't always too helpful. I tried to find information on the Human Genome Project there. All I could find were papers written by scientists for other scientists. We need more than that. We need nonfiction books by people who write just for students if we're going to do a good job on our research.

I hope my letter has convinced you how important it is to keep buying new library books. Please try to convince the other school board members to change their minds on this issue.

Yours truly,

Tyler Lee

Tyler Lee

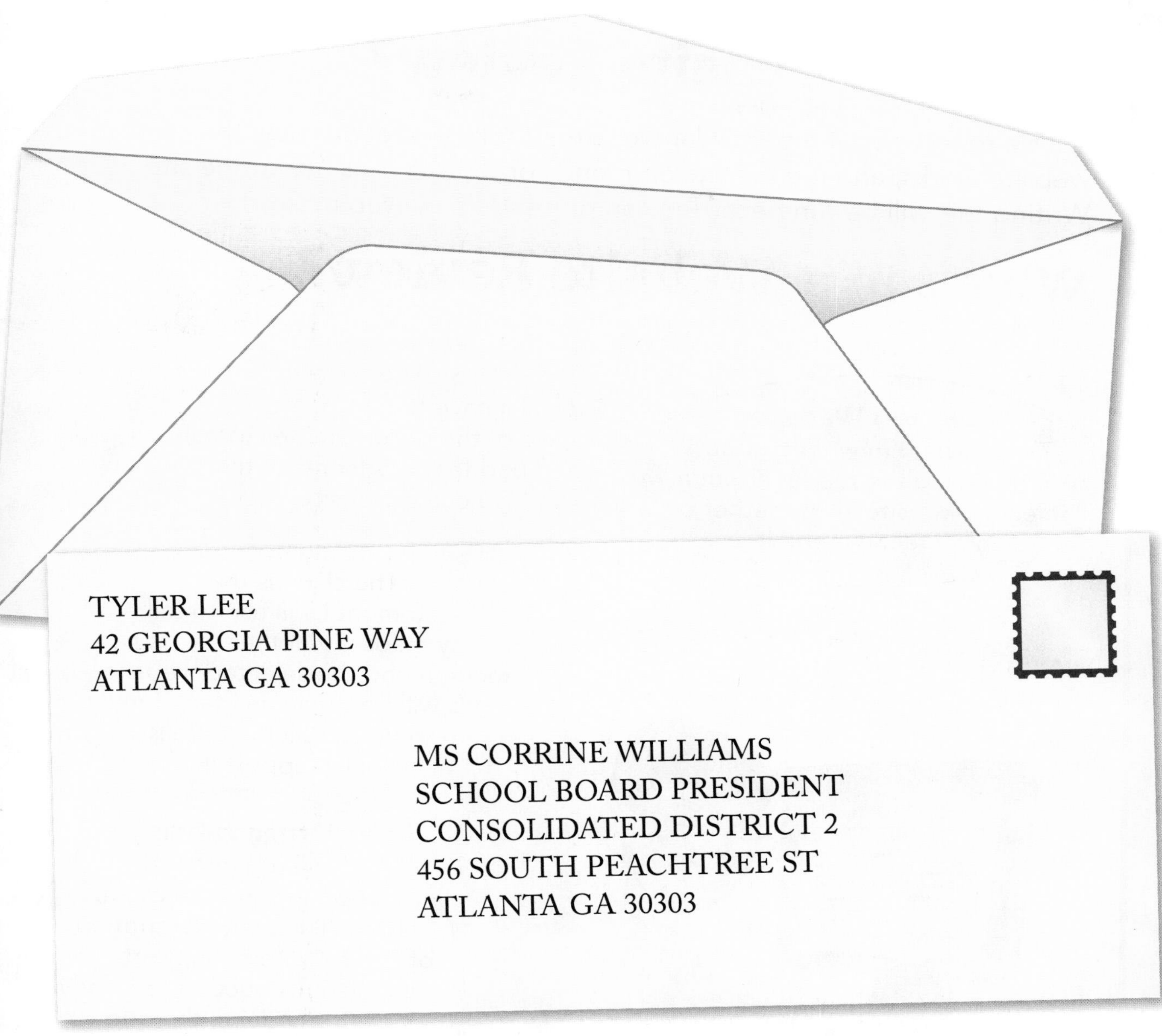

Reflect

How did Tyler do? Did he use all the traits of a good business letter in his writing? Check it against the rubric. Then use the rubric to check your own business letter.

What's a Website Review?

It's a report about a particular website. It tells the reader how the website works, and it either recommends or discourages use of the site. Writing this will be fun because I can pretend I'm a Web master!

What's in a Website Review?

Selected Website
This is what I'm writing about. I'll be telling the reader about a selected website and whether or not I recommend it.

Pros and Cons
I'll have to inform my readers of the good features (pros) and bad features (cons) of the selected website.

Claim
The claim is the statement I will use to tell my readers whether or not I recommend the selected website. This will be the main idea of my review, and all the details should support it.

Organization
I will organize my report around the claim. Then I'll use my description of the website as support. I can use the introduction to clearly present my claim, the body to present supporting facts, and the conclusion to summarize my review and restate my claim.

Why write a Website Review?

What are some reasons for writing a website review? I listed some here, since I'm still thinking about why I want to write.

Entertain

A website review can be entertaining. I can write with a lively style and include information that interests my readers. It's always good for the reader to be pleased and entertained.

Convince

I can form my own opinion about a website and then, using details to support my opinion, write a review to try to convince others to agree with me.

Inform

Some websites are extremely useful. A website review can inform readers about a particular site. Then they can decide if the site would be useful to them.

Summarize

Sometimes websites are complicated and hard to navigate. Information is often hidden or lost because of flashy pictures, advertisements, or large titles. That's when it's important to summarize the details the reader really needs to know.

Linking Argument Writing Traits to a **Website Review**

In this chapter, you will evaluate a website. This type of argument writing is called a website review. Tyler will guide you through the stages of the writing process: Prewrite, Draft, Revise, Edit, and Publish. In each stage, Tyler will show you important writing strategies that are linked to the Argument Writing Traits below.

Argument Writing Traits

- clearly stated claims, often balanced by alternate or opposing claims
- supporting evidence from accurate and credible sources

- a strong introduction that presents the writer's position
- reasons and evidence that are organized logically
- a conclusion that follows and supports the argument
- transitions that clarify the relationships between the claim(s), the supporting evidence, and any counterclaims

- a voice that supports the writer's purpose

- language that is compelling

- sentences that vary in length and begin in different ways

- no or few errors in grammar, usage, mechanics, and spelling

Before you write, read Marie Tokonada's website review on the next three pages. Then use the website review rubric on pages 316–317 to decide how well she did. (You might want to look back at What's in a Website Review? on page 310, too!)

Website Review Model

Space Camp Anyone?

by Marie Tokonada

Selected Website

Organization: Introduction

We all run across bad websites every now and then. Sometimes information is hard to retrieve because a site is too complex, or worse yet, the information is inaccurate or out of date. That's when we continue to search for a good site that loads quickly and contains just the information we're looking for. That's when we hope to run across a site like www.spacecamp.com. This site is easy to use, full of information, reliable, and up to date.

Claim

When I enter the Space Camp Web address in my computer's address bar, I am almost instantly taken to the site; I do not have to wait for images to load or for links to become functional. However, the opening screen is a bit cluttered. Menus run across the top, sides, and bottom of a box in the center of the page. The box shows alternating images of, and captions about, Space Camp, but the sequence sometimes moves so quickly that it is a little hard to follow.

Pros

Cons

Organization: Body

Organization: Body

Pros The many menus offer multiple ways to find information; however, I found it difficult to decide which buttons would give me the best facts. Cons For example, to find a schedule of Space Camp dates, you can click on "Space Camp" under Programs, "Dates & Rates" under Information, "Space Camp" on the bars running across the top of the page, or "Register Now" on one of the stamps running down the right side of the central screen. This kind of accessibility does have a positive side, however. I'd rather find the same information in several different places, than not find the information at all!

Cons Although the multiple buttons can be a bit confusing, they do work very well. Pros Anything I clicked on loaded quickly. In this way, I could rapidly access any of the subpages on the site. It was easy to find the forms needed to make a reservation for a particular week or year. I could even name friends and siblings with whom I wanted to camp. Further, I could type in my name as I wanted it to appear on my Space Camp patch. I thought that was a fantastic feature!

Pros But what about the application form for Space Camp? Well, it was also easy to find. However, I was a bit let down at first because the form could not be completed online. Cons But then I realized why: The application is long. I will have to write essays and get letters of recommendation. I will also have to list science projects with which I've been involved. It's good to know that this information is accessible and accurate, especially since the application process is so involved.

Pros The information on www.spacecamp.com is also very up to date; the home page shows a copyright date of this year. Not to mention, the simple click of a button allows you to check the availability of camps for the next year. Even the photographs were recent, showing people with up-to-date clothing and haircuts. All of this leads me to believe the site is credible and trustworthy.

Organization: Body

Pros Finally, the site is very functional, which is excellent for a place that teaches about state-of-the-art technology. The site's interactive features also clearly state the security measures that were taken to protect my personal information, and contact information is clearly given on the home page as well as the "Contact Us" section.

In conclusion, I would strongly recommend www.spacecamp.com to anyone who is interested in learning about Space Camp. Even though it is a bit overdesigned, it is fast, reliable, and informative. So if you want to go to Space Camp, you should get online and download your application today!

Organization: Conclusion

Rubric

Use this 6-point rubric to plan and evaluate a website review.

	6	5	4
Ideas	The claim is clearly stated. The review clearly presents both pros and cons about the website.	The claim is stated. The review presents pros and cons.	The claim is stated. Some pros and cons are presented.
Organization	The structure of the writing organizes the evidence logically and is perfect for the topic. The conclusion follows and supports the argument presented.	The structure of the writing is logically organized. The conclusion supports the argument.	The structure of the writing often works. The conclusion works.
Voice	The writer uses a confident, formal style. The voice is well suited for the audience and purpose.	The writer uses a strong voice. The style is suited for the audience and purpose.	The writer's voice is strong, and the style is appropriate most of the time.
Word Choice	The words support the author's purpose and help convince the reader. Site-specific terms are clearly defined.	The words are purposeful and convincing. Most site-specific terms are defined.	Most of the words are to the point and convincing. Most site-specific terms are defined.
Sentence Fluency	Transitions connect sentences, create variety, and clarify relationships among ideas.	Transitions connect sentences and create some variety.	Some sentences lack transitions, disrupting the flow of reading.
Conventions	Semicolons and colons are used correctly and effectively. The writing is easy to understand.	A few minor errors with semicolons and colons are present but do not interfere with meaning.	Some errors with semicolons and colons are noticeable but do not interfere with meaning.
+Presentation	All paragraphs are indented.		

3	2	1	
The claim can be identified but is not clearly stated. Pros and cons are presented but not balanced.	The claim is hard to identify. Only pros or cons are stated, but not both.	The review lacks a claim. No pros or cons can be identified.	Ideas
The writing often isn't focused on the topic. The conclusion is present but may need work.	Information is out of order and creates confusion for the reader. The conclusion is vague or may be missing.	The writing is confusing and lacks any writing structure. No conclusion is present.	Organization
The writer's voice does not sound confident. The style may not be appropriate.	The writer's voice sounds weak and not convincing. The style doesn't work for the audience and purpose.	The voice is flat or absent from the writing. The writing lacks information about the topic.	Voice
Several words are weak or unrelated to the purpose. Some site-specific terms are not defined.	Many of the words are incorrect or are too general to be convincing. Site-specific terms, if used, are not defined.	The words don't make sense and are vague. Site-specific words are not used.	Word Choice
Sentences are too similar in sections. Transitions would help create variety and help clarify how ideas are related.	Sentences are choppy throughout the review. Transitions are missing. It's unclear how ideas are related.	Incomplete sentences run together. No transitions are used.	Sentence Fluency
Noticeable errors with semicolons and colons might slow down the reader.	Many obvious errors with semicolons and colons get in the way of reading the writing.	Errors with semicolons and colons are frequent and make reading difficult.	Conventions

See Appendix B for 4-, 5-, and 6-point argument rubrics.

Using the Website Review Rubric to Study the Model

Did you notice that the model on pages 313–315 points out some key elements of a website review? As she wrote "Space Camp Anyone?" Marie Tokonada used these elements to help her review a website. She also used the 6-point rubric on pages 316–317 to plan, draft, revise, and edit the writing. A rubric is a great tool to evaluate writing during the writing process.

Now let's use the same rubric to score the model. To do this, we'll focus on each trait separately, starting with Ideas. We'll use the top descriptor for each trait (column 6), along with examples from the model, to help us understand how the traits work together. How would you score Marie on each trait?

- **The claim is clearly stated.**
- **The review clearly presents both pros and cons about the website.**

Marie clearly states her claim early on. She then mentions several things she likes and doesn't like about the website. Her balanced comments gave credibility and weight to her opinion.

[from the writing model]

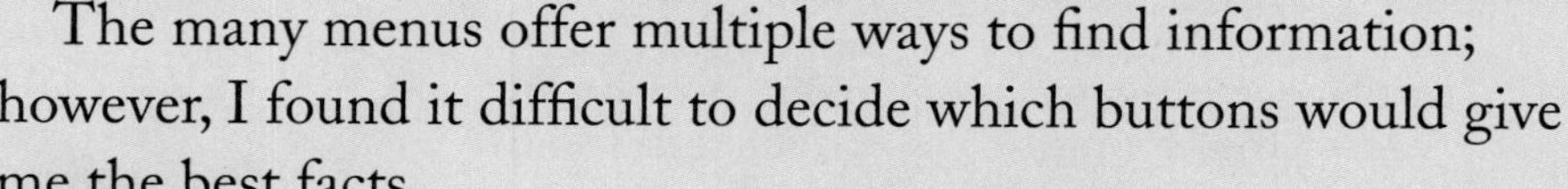

The many menus offer multiple ways to find information; however, I found it difficult to decide which buttons would give me the best facts.

- The structure of the writing organizes the evidence logically and is perfect for the topic.
- The conclusion follows and supports the argument presented.

By organizing each observation into a separate paragraph, Marie makes it easy to follow her review, point by point. The concluding section reflects back to her opening claim, which helps me better understand her overall message.

[from the writing model]

In conclusion, I would strongly recommend www.spacecamp.com to anyone who is interested in learning about Space Camp. Even though it is a bit overdesigned, it is fast, reliable, and informative.

- The writer uses a confident, formal style.
- The voice is well suited for the audience and purpose.

Marie uses a style and language that show me she understands what I may have experienced when surfing the Internet. Even though she's relating directly to the reader in this paragraph, she doesn't make the mistake of letting her language become too casual. This makes it easy to trust her opinion and connect with her purpose.

[from the writing model]

We all run across bad websites every now and then. Sometimes information is hard to retrieve because a site is too complex, or worse yet, the information is inaccurate or out of date. That's when we continue to search for a good site that loads quickly and contains just the information we're looking for.

Website Review

- **The words support the author's purpose and help convince the reader.**
- **Site-specific terms are clearly defined.**

Marie effectively uses strong, descriptive words like *credible* and *trustworthy* when describing the website. These words help shape my view of the site, too, even though I've never visited it. She's also careful to define any words used on the website that her reader might not understand.

[from the writing model]

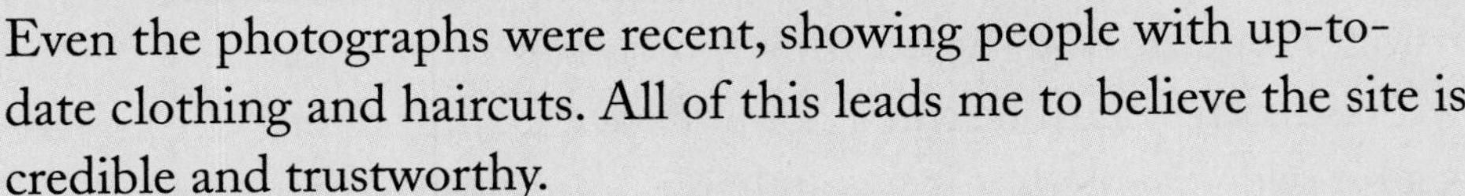
Even the photographs were recent, showing people with up-to-date clothing and haircuts. All of this leads me to believe the site is credible and trustworthy.

- **Transitions connect sentences, create variety, and clarify relationships among ideas.**

Marie is very good at using transition words, like *further*, to show how ideas are related. At the same time, she keeps her writing interesting and lively by using all kinds of sentence structures. Transitions provide variety in sentence patterns and length.

[from the writing model]

I could even name friends and siblings with whom I wanted to camp. Further, I could type in my name as I wanted it to appear on my Space Camp patch. I thought that was a fantastic feature!

- **Semicolons and colons are used correctly and effectively. The writing is easy to understand.**

Marie's review doesn't contain any spelling or capitalization errors. In addition, she uses colons and semicolons correctly.

[from the writing model]

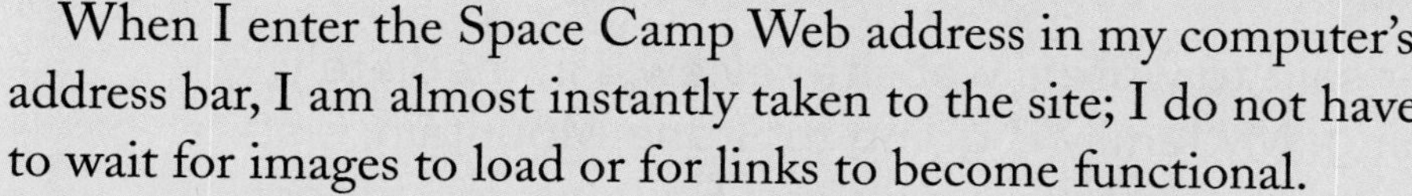

When I enter the Space Camp Web address in my computer's address bar, I am almost instantly taken to the site; I do not have to wait for images to load or for links to become functional.

Here, Marie uses a colon to show that the second sentence further explains the first.

[from the writing model]

But then I realized why: The application is long.

+Presentation All paragraphs are indented.

My Turn!

I can't wait to start my own website review. I'll use the rubric and good writing strategies. Read on to see how I do it!

Prewrite

Focus on **Ideas**

The Rubric Says The claim is clearly stated. The review clearly presents both pros and cons about the website.

Writing Strategy Find a website about a topic of interest and list responses to it.

When my teacher said to write a website review, I immediately thought of something: My family is going to Stone Mountain, a state park here in Georgia, for a weekend getaway. So I entered *Stone Mountain* in my search engine, and, out of several choices, I selected www.stonemountainpark.com, the official website for the park. Then I took notes on the site to see if it is reliable, valid, and easy to use. I also wanted to see if the site would help me plan our trip.

My Notes

- ✔ "Contact Us" and "FAQ" pages helpful for park information
- ✔ Too much information on "Contact Us" page
- ✔ Logical categories and links
- ✔ Cool trip planner
- ✔ Helpful "Maps & Directions" page
- ✔ No special-needs section
- ✔ Some pages a bit cluttered
- ✔ Attractive and easy to use

Apply

Do some online research, and select a website to review. Take good notes. You'll need them when you write.

Prewrite

Focus on **Organization**

The Rubric Says The structure of the writing organizes the evidence logically and is perfect for the topic.

Writing Strategy Make a Pro-and-Con Chart to organize the responses.

Writer's Term

Pro-and-Con Chart

A **Pro-and-Con Chart** can help you organize your opinions and evaluate opposing claims. By presenting a website's **pros** (positive points) and **cons** (negative points) in order of importance, you can summarize the site and explain why you liked and/or disliked it.

Since I am building an argument about whether a website should be recommended, I will use a Pro-and-Con Chart to organize my comments. Then I can decide whether to separate the pros and cons or mix them when I talk about a single feature.

Pro-and-Con Chart

Pros	Cons
"Contact Us" and "FAQ" pages helpful for park information	Too much information on "Contact Us" page
Logical categories and links	No special-needs section
Cool trip planner	Some pages a bit cluttered
Helpful "Maps & Directions" page	
Attractive and easy to use	

Reflect

How will Tyler's Pro-and-Con Chart help him organize his writing into paragraphs?

Apply

Use a Pro-and-Con Chart to organize your responses.

Draft

Focus on **Voice**

The Rubric Says The writer uses a confident, formal style. The voice is well suited for the audience and purpose.

Writing Strategy Use credible sources of information and fair language.

Writer's Term

Credible Website

A **credible website** is an online source that contains accurate, trustworthy, up-to-date information. An example of a credible website is www.britannica.com. Information on this site comes from the same people who write the **Encyclopaedia Britannica,** a current and respected source.

Now that my Pro-and-Con Chart is done, I need to decide whether I want to recommend www.stonemountainpark.com to others. I *did* list more pros than cons, and I *did* find the site both useful and fun, so I'll definitely recommend this site.

The rubric says to use a confident voice and formal style. Also, my teacher reminded me to use a credible source. Now that I think about it, the site I choose to review will affect my ability to use a confident voice. If I write about a website that lacks credibility and lists false information, my voice will reflect that. The site I've selected is sound, so I'm good there.

Of course, the words I use also create voice. I'll use fair and balanced language so my reader can trust my information. I'll keep my style fun but formal so I'll be taken seriously. Now to get writing!

Proofreading Marks

- ⊐ Indent
- ≡ Make uppercase
- / Make lowercase
- ∧ Add something
- Take out something
- ⊙ Add a period
- ¶ New paragraph
- (sp) Spelling error

[DRAFT]

When Are You Going to Stone Mountain?

A Website Review by Tyler

How do you find out about places you've never been? How would you find information about the grand canyon or Mexico city? You can find a reliable website. Credible websites have uptodate information, good contact information, and are easy to use. My family is going on a weekend getaway to Stone Mountain, a popular vacation spot for people in Georgia. It is a large park containing a huge, bare rock that you can see from far away. But when is the park open? What can you do there? I found a great website to help me plan my trip: www.stonemountainpark.com. It is a credible, attractive, and easy-to-use website that contains full information on the events and sights of Stone Mountain.

[interesting and formal voice]

[formal, balanced language]

Reflect

How would you describe the language Tyler uses in the beginning of his review?

Apply

Be sure to use fair and balanced language when discussing your chosen website. Keep your voice interesting and formal.

Revise

Focus on Ideas

The Rubric Says The claim is clearly stated. The review clearly presents both pros and cons about the website.

Writing Strategy State a clear claim and include at least one con.

My claim is clear and supported by plenty of relevant information. But I need to include both pros *and* cons about the site. When I include a comment that's the opposite of my overall opinion, my reader is more likely to believe my claim, because I'm being fair to both sides.

[DRAFT]

There were even links embedded in the answer to almost every question. ^ Although, I must say, there was so much information listed here that it did seem a bit overwhelming.

[added a con]

Apply

Include both pros and cons in your website review for credibility.

Revise

Focus on **Word Choice**

The Rubric Says The words support the author's purpose and help convince the reader. Site-specific terms are clearly defined.

Writing Strategy Use words with the right connotation.

The rubric says I should use words that support my purpose. I think www.stonemountainpark.com is an excellent site, and I want my reader to agree. One way I can convince the reader is to use words with positive connotations, that is, words that have positive ideas or images associated with them. As I reread my draft, I came across some descriptive words that could be stronger. By using words with a positive connotation, like *top-notch*, I'll strengthen my writing and message.

[DRAFT]

You can edit your trip planner at any time so that it shows only the things you want to do. I printed out my trip planner so that I could go over it with Mom and Dad. This tool is ~~great~~ top-notch; it really helped me.

[used strong positive word]

Reflect

How have Tyler's revisions affected your opinion of his review?

Apply

Use words with appropriate associations to describe your website.

Revise

Focus on **Sentence Fluency**

The Rubric Says Transitions connect sentences, create variety, and clarify relationships among ideas.

Writing Strategy Vary sentences by using transition words.

The rubric says to use transitions to connect sentences and ideas and add variety. Transitions make the flow of the sentences and the ideas smooth. A paper with smooth sentences is enjoyable to read and holds the reader's attention. Here's a paragraph that could use some transitions. I'll add them now.

Writer's Term

Transition Words

Transition words tie ideas together and move writing from one idea to the next. **Compare-and-contrast transition words** include **similarly, likewise, although, however, yet,** and **but**. **Time-order transition words** include **before, after, during, first, second, third, next, soon, later, finally,** and **then**.

[DRAFT]

[added transition words]

Although the website is excellent in most areas, one area is weak, what about accesability for special-needs patrons? My father will go with us to Stone Mountain and he uses a wheelchair. I couldn't find a section on the site that discusses acomodations for people with special needs. Other websites I've looked at have sections that explain special parking ramps, and general accesability of attractions; however, I had to search through the information on each sub page of this site just to find one or two sentences on accesability.

Apply

Use transition words to write smooth and interesting sentences.

Edit

Focus on **Conventions**

The Rubric Says Semicolons and colons are used correctly and effectively. The writing is easy to understand.

Writing Strategy Choose punctuation for effect.

Writer's Term

Colons and Semicolons

A **colon** is used after the greeting in a business letter, between the city of publication and the publisher in a bibliographic entry, to introduce a list or series, and to separate two clauses when the second clause further explains the first. A **semicolon** is used in place of a comma and a conjunction when combining two related independent clauses.

Before I'm done, I need to check my spelling, punctuation, and capitalization. The rubric also says to make sure I used colons and semicolons correctly, so I'll check that now.

[DRAFT]

[correct use of a semicolon]

The Stone Mountain website also has a great tool called a trip planner; it helps people plan their trips. It works a bit like an online shopping cart. There is an "Add to My Trip Plan" link at the top of most of the park's events and activities pages. If you click on the link, the activity will immediately be added to your planner: a description of the event will then show up in your trip planner.

[corrected a colon error]

Reflect

Did Tyler catch all his errors? How have his edits improved his writing? What effect does punctuation have on the writer's message?

Apply

Conventions

Edit your draft for spelling and grammar, making sure to use colons and semicolons correctly.

For more practice with colons and semicolons, use the exercises on the next two pages.

Semicolons

Know the Rule

A **semicolon** is used in place of a comma and a conjunction when combining two related independent clauses to make a compound sentence. Note that a semicolon goes outside quotation marks.

Example: Bicycles used to be much harder to ride; they didn't come with multiple speeds.

Semicolons are often misused in writing. Understanding the function of semicolons will help you use them properly when you write.

Practice the Rule

Write each sentence with correct punctuation on a separate sheet of paper.

1. Last year's dance was horrible it rained so heavily, the school roof leaked.
2. Buckets were placed all over the gym floor to catch the water dripping from the roof people kept tripping over them.
3. Students were soaked by the heavy downpour when they arrived many joked that they should have worn bathing suits!
4. The funny thing is that bathing suits would have been appropriate the theme of the dance was "Let's Have a Beach Party."
5. Happily, the students were good sports about it all everyone had fun in spite of the water.
6. The rain cleared up during the dance by the time we left the sky was clear and dry.
7. This year things should be better the roof has been repaired.
8. The theme for the dance is "Desert Moon" maybe the weather will be hot and dry to match!
9. I'm the chair of the dance committee I'm really hoping everything goes right this year.
10. I'll do my best to make sure the refreshments, music, and decorations are great there's nothing I can do about the weather, though.

Colons

Know the Rule

Use a **colon**

- to introduce a list or a series at the end of a complete sentence.
  Example: The art kit included the following: paint, brushes, and crayons.
- after the greeting in a business letter.
  Example: Dear Madam:
- between the city of publication and the publisher in a bibliographic entry.
  Example: Columbus: Zaner-Bloser
- to separate two clauses when the second clause is a direct result of the first.
  Example: The cupboards were bare: We went shopping.

Colons, like semicolons, are often misused. Understanding the function of colons will help you use them correctly in your own writing.

Practice the Rule

Write each sentence or word group with correct punctuation on a separate sheet of paper.

1. A good first-aid kit contains the following items antibiotic cream, cotton gauze, and bandages.
2. Dad forgot to set his alarm last night he missed the train this morning.
3. Chicago Fun Books, Inc.
4. Uncle Joel's package contained several things two books, six packs of gum, and a feather.
5. Watch for these birds on our hike chickadees, cardinals, and doves.
6. Dear Mr. Puglia
7. Boston Beacon Press
8. Adam didn't know the answer he grabbed a dictionary and looked it up.
9. Dear Principal O'Toole
10. Here's what I like on my tacos lettuce, tomato, avocado, and cheese.

Publish + Presentation

Publishing Strategy Submit the review to the appropriate website.

Presentation Strategy Indent or add space between the paragraphs.

I'm done! Since the concern I had about the information on accessibility was pretty serious, I've decided to submit my website review to the park's director. Hopefully, my report can help bring about actual change! Before I send it though, I need to make sure I indent each paragraph, or, if I use block-style paragraphs, I'll leave space between them to help the reader visually. Then I'll read my review one last time to make sure I've done everything on my final checklist.

My Final Checklist

Did I—

- ✔ fix any spelling, grammar, and punctuation errors?
- ✔ use semicolons correctly in my writing?
- ✔ use colons properly and effectively?
- ✔ indent or leave space between paragraphs?

Apply

Make a checklist to check your work. Then make a final copy to publish.

When Are You Going to Stone Mountain?

A Website Review by Tyler

How do you find out about places you've never been? How would you find information about the Grand Canyon or Mexico City? You can find a reliable website. Credible websites have up-to-date information, good contact information, and are easy to use. My family is going on a weekend getaway to Stone Mountain, a popular vacation spot for people in Georgia. It is a large park containing a huge, bare rock that you can see from far away. But when is the park open? What can you do there? I found a great website to help me plan my trip: www.stonemountainpark.com. It is a credible, attractive, and easy-to-use website that contains full information on the events and sights of Stone Mountain.

Several features of www.stonemountainpark.com show that it is credible. A main feature is the many ways to contact the park for information. First, the "Contact Us" button leads to a well-organized subpage that contains several links such as "Directions to the Park," "Operating Schedule," and "Tickets/Prices." Here, you can also find 24-hour local and nationwide park phone numbers, along with the option to fill in some personal information so that park employees can electronically answer your questions and send you an e-newsletter. Second, the "FAQ" button leads to yet another subpage that contains categorized answers to frequently asked questions. This page was very helpful since many of my own questions were the same as some of the FAQs. There were even links embedded in the answer to almost every question. Although, I must say, there was so much information listed here that it did seem a bit overwhelming.

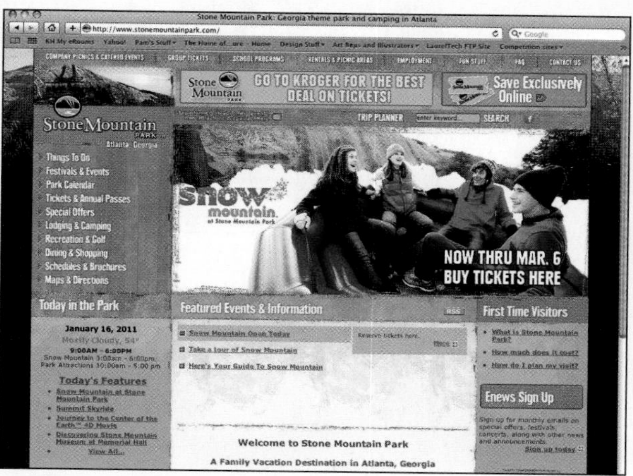

The Stone Mountain website also has a great tool called a trip planner; it helps people plan their trips. It works a bit like an online shopping cart. There is an "Add to My Trip Plan" link at the top of most of the park's events and activities pages. If you click on the link, the activity will immediately be added to your planner: A description of the event will then show up in your trip planner. You can edit your trip planner at any time so that it shows only the things you want to do. I printed out my trip planner so that I could go over it with Mom and Dad. This tool is top-notch; it really helped me.

In addition, the maps on www.stonemountainpark.com are a great feature; they can be accessed from the homepage by clicking on the "Maps & Directions" button. Grid patterns overlay the park map. When you click on one square in the grid, that segment pops up larger and more detailed. When you click on the "Written Driving Directions" link, you are given a written description of driving directions to the park, from any one of nine different regions. This is great because some people aren't very good at reading maps!

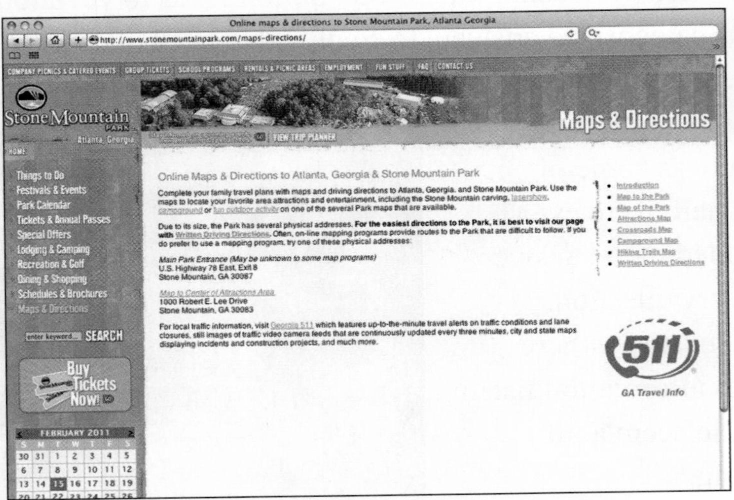

Although the website is excellent in most areas, one area is weak: What about accessibility for special-needs patrons? My father will go with us to Stone Mountain, and he uses a wheelchair. I couldn't find a section on the site that discusses accommodations for people with special needs. Other websites I've looked at have sections that explain special parking, ramps, and general accessibility of attractions; however, I had to search through the information on each subpage of this site just to find one or two sentences on accessibility.

Other than that one complaint, though, I found this website to be very attractive and easy to use. It loads almost instantly, as do all of the features. Although some of the pages are a bit cluttered, most of the pages are spacious and easy to read. Not to mention, I could easily navigate the site, moving back to the previous page when I was done reading, and moving ahead to an entirely new page when I wanted to read more.

Because of its reliability, credibility, ease-of-use, and cool features like the trip planner, I highly recommend www.stonemountainpark.com for anyone who wants to visit Stone Mountain. My family is currently working on a trip planner for our upcoming visit. What about you? When are you going to Stone Mountain?

Reflect

How did Tyler do using all the traits of a website review? Check his writing against the rubric, and don't forget to use the rubric to check your own work, too.

What's a **Response to Literature?**

It's an essay I write to share my ideas about something I've read. I just read a great story, and I will be writing a literary analysis that I hope will convince people to accept my interpretation of the story.

What's in a **Response to Literature?**

Summary
A response to literature starts out with a summary of what the writer read. The summary of a story should give a brief description of the main ideas of the plot and important characters.

Claim
The claim is the heart of the response to literature. It states the writer's opinion of the story.

Supporting Evidence
These are details that support the claim and build the argument. Supporting evidence can include quotations from the story, paraphrases (restating text or passages in the writer's own words), details from the story, and the writer's own knowledge.

Analysis
In a literary analysis, the writer offers an interpretation of the literature. For example, a writer could examine the theme and then discuss what it means or how the characters get the theme across to the readers.

Why write a Response to Literature?

Here are some reasons I can think of to respond to literature.

Argument
When I get excited about a story, or have ideas about what I've read, I like to share them and try to convince others to agree with my opinion. That way they might decide to read the story themselves!

Information
Responding to literature is a way to let other readers know about a story they might enjoy. Or it might be a way to let readers know that this is a story that would not interest them.

Understanding
As I write, I can learn a lot about how I think or feel about something I've read. Sometimes I surprise myself!

Linking Argument Writing Traits to a Response to Literature

In this chapter, you will try to convince your reader to believe your claim about a piece of literature. This type of argument writing is called a response to literature. Tyler will guide you through the stages of the writing process: Prewrite, Draft, Revise, Edit, and Publish. In each stage, Tyler will show you important writing strategies that are linked to the Argument Writing Traits below.

Argument Writing Traits

- clearly stated claims, often balanced by alternate or opposing claims
- supporting evidence from accurate and credible sources

- a strong introduction that presents the writer's position
- reasons and evidence that are organized logically
- a conclusion that follows and supports the argument
- transitions that clarify the relationships between the claim(s), the supporting evidence, and any counterclaims

- a voice that supports the writer's purpose

- language that is compelling

- sentences that vary in length and begin in different ways

- no or few errors in grammar, usage, mechanics, and spelling

Before you write, read Lucinda Juarez's response to literature on the next page. Then use the response to literature rubric on pages 340–341 to decide how well she did. (You might want to look back at What's in a Response to Literature? on page 336, too!)

Response to Literature Model

Tables Turned

by Lucinda Juarez

I just read a story that really made me laugh, "The Ransom of Red Chief," by O. Henry. The characters were funny, the story just did not let up, and the plot has a surprise twist that I guarantee you have never come across before in any of your reading. It was over the top, strange, and hilarious. ← Claim

Summary → The three main characters are two kidnappers, Sam and Bill, and their victim, if you can call him that. Actually, it is the kidnappers who become the victims. But let me backtrack a bit. The two kidnappers are con men who need some extra money to pull off a fraudulent land scheme. They decide that the most brilliant way to get their needed funds is to kidnap the son of the richest man in town and make the father pay a steep ransom. They accomplish this and take him to a cave. What the kidnappers didn't count on was that, instead of feeling kidnapped, the boy is thrilled to be out. "I've never had so much fun in all my life," he tells them. The kid imagines himself to be an Indian chief (the "Red Chief" in the story's title). His boundless imagination comes up with various, relentless activities.

As Sam tries to work out the setup and details of collecting the kidnap money, Bill's job is to try to keep the kid amused. "Red Chief" finds endless ways to torture Bill, including trying to scalp him, putting a red-hot boiled potato down his back, and riding him like a horse. As the kidnappers' unexpected ordeal continues, Sam and Bill actually lower the ransom they had in mind. In the end, they go one step further—they actually pay the father money in order to get rid of him! That's a very original plot and turn of events.

← Supporting Evidence

The author, O. Henry, is a fantastic storyteller. He really knows how to give life to his characters. I thoroughly enjoyed myself, and at times had to laugh out loud, too. The tale is outrageously ironic, to be sure, and it makes you think about how the tables can turn regardless of how well and cleverly you think you have planned! The kidnappers certainly did not plan on having to pay a ransom to be able to return "Red Chief" to his father.

Analysis

Work Cited

Henry, O. "The Ransom of Red Chief." *The Literature Network.* Jalic, n.d. Web. 21 April 2011.

Rubric

Use this 6-point rubric to plan and score a response to literature.

	6	5	4
Ideas	The writing shows an in-depth understanding of the literature. Quotations support the writer's claim and are accurately referenced.	The writing shows an understanding of the literature. Quotations support the writer's claim.	The writing shows a partial understanding of the literature. Quotations do not fully support the writer's claim.
Organization	The introduction is engaging and states the claim, the body organizes the reasons in a compelling way, and the concluding section is strong.	The introduction states the claim, the body organizes the reasons, and the concluding section refers back to the claim.	The introduction introduces the literature and the body provides reasons, but the concluding section is weak.
Voice	A consistent formal style and personal voice engage the reader and support the writer's claim.	A formal style and personal voice engage the reader and support the writer's claim most of the time.	The reader catches glimpses of the writer's style and voice, but they are inconsistent.
Word Choice	Precise language conveys the message to the reader.	Precise language is used most of the time.	Precise language is used occasionally but not consistently.
Sentence Fluency	A variety of sentence structures contributes to the rhythm and flow. The writer's ideas are easy to follow.	Most of the sentence structures are varied. Most of the writer's ideas are easy to follow.	Several sentences in a row share the same structure. They slow the flow of ideas.
Conventions	The writing has been carefully edited. Homophones, if used, are correct.	Minor errors are present but do not interfere with meaning. Homophones are correct.	A few errors may cause confusion. One or two homophones may be used incorrectly.

+Presentation The literary analysis is neat and legible.

3	2	1	
The writing shows only a basic understanding of the literature. Quotations do not support the writer's claim.	The writer's ideas need development and support. Quotations are not used.	The writing reflects a lack of understanding of the literature.	Ideas
There is an introduction, a body, and a conclusion.	There is no introduction or conclusion. The writing has little organization or direction.	The writing is not organized as a response.	Organization
Some style and voice come through in the beginning then fade.	The voice sounds distant or tentative. A personal style is not established.	The voice is absent. The reader does not have a sense of who the writer is.	Voice
The language is mostly clear. Some vague words could cause misunderstanding.	Some of the writing is unclear or too general. It lacks precision.	Vague or wrong word choice takes away from the writing. The writing doesn't make sense.	Word Choice
Many sentences in a row share the same structure. They dull the flow of ideas.	Most sentences are very short. The writing sounds choppy, especially when read aloud.	The writing contains fragments and run-on sentences. The ideas are incomplete or hard to follow.	Sentence Fluency
Many errors are repeated and cause confusion. Homophones may be used incorrectly.	Serious errors interfere with meaning. Homophones are not used correctly.	The writing has not been edited.	Conventions

See Appendix B for 4-, 5-, and 6-point argument rubrics.

Using the Response to Literature Rubric to Study the Model

Did you notice that the model on page 339 points out some key elements of a response to literature? As she wrote "Tables Turned," Lucinda Juarez used these elements to help her respond to the short story "The Ransom of Red Chief." She also used the 6-point rubric on pages 340–341 to plan, draft, revise, and edit the writing. A rubric is a great tool to evaluate writing during the writing process.

Now let's use the same rubric to score the model. To do this, we'll focus on each trait separately, starting with Ideas. We'll use the top descriptor for each trait (column 6), along with examples from the model, to help us understand how the traits work together. How would you score Lucinda on each trait?

- **The writing shows an in-depth understanding of the literature.**
- **Quotations support the writer's claim and are accurately referenced.**

Lucinda seems to really understand and appreciate the story and what the author's intentions were. To show how tables are turned in the story, she uses a striking quote. Note that Lucinda found the story online and provided information about it at the bottom of her essay.

[from the writing model]

What the kidnappers didn't count on was that, instead of feeling kidnapped, the boy is thrilled to be out. "I've never had so much fun in all my life," he tells them.

- **The introduction is engaging and states the claim, the body organizes the reasons in a compelling way, and the concluding section is strong.**

Right off the bat, Lucinda tells the reader her response to the story and gives us a glimpse into her reasoning. After reading the introduction, I was eager to know more. Lucinda follows up with a body that gives solid reasons for her reactions and a conclusion that makes me want to read "The Ransom of Red Chief" myself.

[from the writing model]

I just read a story that really made me laugh, "The Ransom of Red Chief," by O. Henry. The characters were funny, the story just did not let up, and the plot has a surprise twist that I guarantee you have never come across before in any of your reading. It was over the top, strange, and hilarious.

- **A consistent formal style and personal voice engage the reader and support the writer's claim.**

Lucinda's writing is very lively and not stiff. She is comfortable with her readers and connects with them using a style that is warm but not too casual. Her writing has a sense of humor that seems to reflect the amusement she felt while reading "The Ransom of Red Chief." Look how she gives a hint about who is really the victim in this story, and then how she brings the reader back to the beginning of the plot.

[from the writing model]

The three main characters are two kidnappers, Sam and Bill, and their victim, if you can call him that. Actually, it is the kidnappers who become the victims. But let me backtrack a bit. The two kidnappers are con men who need some extra money to pull off a fraudulent land scheme.

- **Precise language conveys the message to the reader.**

Lucinda's writing is very descriptive and precise. She is precise when referring to parts of the story, using words such as *characters, plot, twist, story's title*, and *author*. She is also not afraid to use a literary term. Look at how she used the word *ironic* when describing the twist at the end.

[from the writing model]

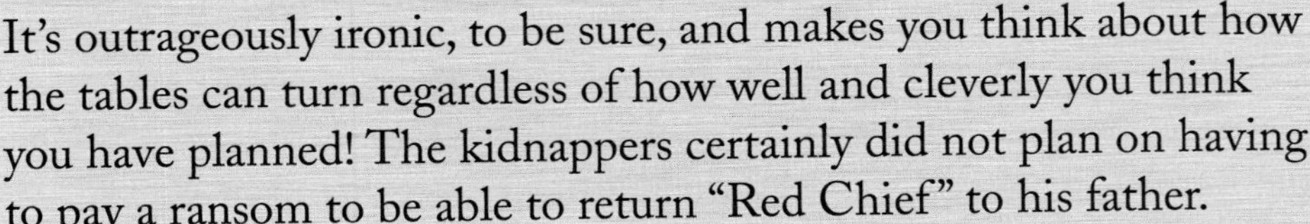
It's outrageously ironic, to be sure, and makes you think about how the tables can turn regardless of how well and cleverly you think you have planned! The kidnappers certainly did not plan on having to pay a ransom to be able to return "Red Chief" to his father.

- **A variety of sentence structures contributes to the rhythm and flow.**
- **The writer's ideas are easy to follow.**

It was easy to follow Lucinda's ideas. Her response never gets boring, because her writing has a fluid rhythm. A variety of sentence structures keeps things interesting throughout the essay. Look at how she describes the way Red Chief makes life miserable for the kidnappers.

[from the writing model]

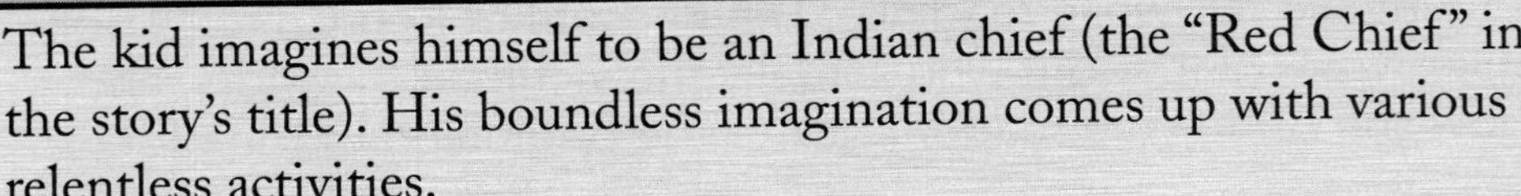
The kid imagines himself to be an Indian chief (the "Red Chief" in the story's title). His boundless imagination comes up with various relentless activities.

As Sam tries to work out the setup and details of collecting the kidnap money, Bill's job is to try to keep the kid amused. "Red Chief" finds endless ways to torture Bill, including trying to scalp him, putting a red-hot boiled potato down his back, and riding him like a horse.

- **The writing has been carefully edited.**
- **Homophones, if used, are correct.**

Lucinda's analysis has been carefully edited. I do not see any errors in spelling, grammar, or punctuation. I also see that she uses homophones correctly. For example, the words *to*, *two*, and *too* are homophones—they sound the same, but they are spelled differently and have different meanings. Look at how Lucinda uses these homophones correctly.

[from the writing model]

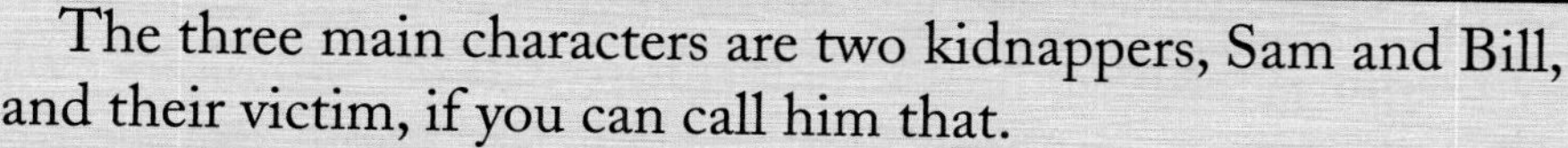

The three main characters are two kidnappers, Sam and Bill, and their victim, if you can call him that.

[from the writing model]

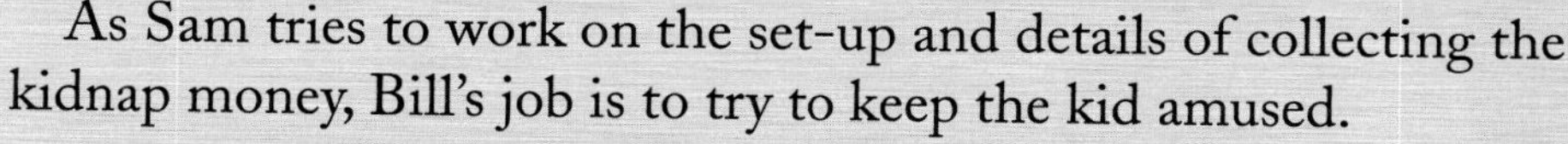

As Sam tries to work on the set-up and details of collecting the kidnap money, Bill's job is to try to keep the kid amused.

[from the writing model]

I thoroughly enjoyed myself, and at times had to laugh out loud, too.

+Presentation The literary analysis is neat and legible.

My Turn!

Now it's my turn to respond to literature. I'll use the rubric and good writing strategies to help me. Read on to see how I do it.

Prewrite

Focus on Ideas

The Rubric Says The writing shows an in-depth understanding of the literature.

Writing Strategy List the theme and reactions to the literature.

We've read several short stories in class this year. Our teacher has asked us to write a literary analysis of our favorite one. I know which story was my favorite: "The Tell-Tale Heart" by Edgar Allan Poe. I'm looking forward to explaining why that story speaks to me. I made a list of some details from the story and thoughts I have about it.

My List

Story
"The Tell-Tale Heart" by Edgar Allan Poe

Summary
The narrator of the story tells about murdering another man. He goes crazy, even though he keeps saying he's not. He keeps hearing a heartbeat—the heartbeat of the man he murdered, he thinks. The murderer confesses at the end.

My Claim
You can't commit a crime and get away with it. Your conscience will get you in the end.

Supporting Evidence
The narrator murdered a man and was able to hide all the evidence. Even though he could have gotten away with the murder, his heartbeat drives him to confess to the murder.

Apply

Choose your favorite story. Then make a list of some details from the story and thoughts you have about it.

Prewrite

Focus on **Organization**

The Rubric Says The introduction is engaging and states the claim, the body organizes the reasons in a compelling way, and the concluding section is strong.

Writing Strategy Use a Paragraph Organizer to plan the writing.

My next step is to plan my literary analysis. I'll use a Paragraph Organizer to plan each of the sections. In the **introduction,** I'll draft my claim. In the **body,** I'll include a summary, support for the claim, and personal observations. In the **conclusion**, I'll wrap it all up.

Writer's Term

Paragraph Organizer
A **Paragraph Organizer** organizes information that will go in the **introduction, body,** and **conclusion** of your writing.

Paragraph Organizer

Introduction
- You can't get away with murder. You can get rid of evidence, but you can't get rid of your conscience.

Body
- The narrator of the story is a murderer. He is trying to convince the reader that he is not crazy. Then he tells how he killed an old man. The heartbeat enters the story as he is about to kill the man. The narrator thinks the heartbeat belongs to the old man, but the heartbeat remains even after the man is dead. The police don't suspect the murderer because he's done such a good job of covering up the crime. But the heartbeat the murderer keeps hearing finally drives him to confess to the police.

Conclusion
- The heartbeat is the murderer's conscience. The murderer confesses to the police, but this may not bring him relief. He'll have to live with his conscience for as long as his tell-tale heart keeps beating.

Reflect

How will the Paragraph Organizer help Tyler plan out his writing?

Apply

Use a Paragraph Organizer to plan the introduction, body, and conclusion of your response.

Draft

Focus on **Word Choice**

The Rubric Says Precise language conveys the message to the reader.

Writing Strategy Use exact words.

All the planning I did should make writing my draft go pretty smoothly. The paragraph organizer really helped me to get my ideas on paper, especially my claim.

As I write, I'll try to remember to use exact words. Using exact words will help capture the reader's interest in the writing and will help the reader understand and appreciate the story and my claim. Examples of exact words to use when describing parts of the story include *plot, character, conflict, resolution,* and *theme*. Literary terms include *irony, simile, personification,* and *foreshadowing.*

As I draft my literary analysis, I'll try to avoid mistakes in grammar and spelling, but I know I can fix my mistakes later.

You can read the beginning of my draft on the next page. What do you think?

Proofreading Marks

- Indent
- Make uppercase
- Make lowercase
- Add something
- Take out something
- Add a period
- New paragraph
- Spelling error

[DRAFT]

You Can't Get Away with Murder

by Tyler

[claim]

Even if you commit a perfect crime and have gotten rid of all the evidence, there is one piece of evidence you can never get rid of—your conscience. That's the message I got from reading Edgar Allan Poe's "The Tell-Tale Heart." This short, intense story is the scariest and most disturbing I've ever read. It's a horror story of a murder told by a psychologically disturbed narrator who also happens too be the murderer. In the end, even after he has successfully covered up his crime, he does not get away with what he has done because his own guilty conscience gives him away What sets off his guilty conscience is the steady heartbeat that he keeps hearing.

[precise words]

Reflect

What do you think about the writing process so far? How have the prewriting activities helped?

Apply

Use your Paragraph Organizer to respond to a favorite story that you've read.

Revise

Focus on **Ideas**

The Rubric Says Quotations support the writer's claim and are accurately referenced.

Writing Strategy Choose quotations that support the claim.

I know that an opinion, or claim, has to be backed up with details and other kinds of information. When writing about literature, it is common to use quotations to support the claim. After I finished my draft, I read it silently to myself and checked to see whether I backed up my claim with details. I found a place to add a quote that perfectly illustrates my point that the narrator is not sane.

Writer's Term

Plagiarism

Plagiarism is using someone else's words and ideas without giving credit. Avoid plagiarizing by using quotation marks around exact words from the story and by including full references.

[DRAFT]

You get a sense that something is terribly wrong, but you don't know what it is. Also, you don't have any idea if you can really trust the point of view and judgment of the narrator. He then reveals that he has taken the life of the man he lives with. This was not a crime of passion or one done for money. Actually, he says he loved the man. He did it because of the man's eye! "He had the eye of a vulture—a pale blue eye, with a film over it." (p. 228)

[added quotation]

Apply

Make sure that you use quotations that support your claim.

Revise

Focus on **Organization**

The Rubric Says The introduction is engaging and states the claim, the body organizes the reasons in a compelling way, and the concluding section is strong.

Writing Strategy Strengthen the conclusion.

I've reread my draft, and I'm really happy with most of it. The introduction engages the reader and clearly states my claim, and the body presents well-organized supporting reasons. But the essay just ends. I need to strengthen my conclusion and make it meaningful. The conclusion should refer to the claim, summarize some of the reasons, and include a personal insight. Look at how I revised my conclusion. Do you think it works better now?

[referred to claim]

The beating heart the killer heard was not the heartbeat of his victim. It was his own heartbeat.

No crime can ever be perfect, because the criminal must live with his own conscience. Throughout the story, he deceived himself into

A heartbeat is very powerful. Hearts beat faster when we are anxious—the more anxious, the faster.

thinking that all was fine with him, that he wasn't crazy. But he was. The heartbeat of the murderer was a relentless, steady reminder of the heartbeat he took away. In the end, he sought relief from it by confessing.

But we do not know if even the confession will bring him relief, as he will have to live with the knowledge of what he has done for the rest of his life, for as long as his tell-tale heart keeps beating.

[added personal insights]

Reflect

How did Tyler's revisions help to make his essay stronger?

Apply

Check your draft and make sure your conclusion is strong.

Revise

Focus on **Sentence Fluency**

The Rubric Says A variety of sentence structures contributes to the rhythm and flow. The writer's ideas are easy to follow.

Writing Strategy Write different kinds of sentences.

The rubric says that a variety of sentences will help the flow of my writing. When the sentences all sound the same, the writing can sound choppy, causing the reader to get bored and lose interest. Smooth, flowing writing is much more enjoyable for the reader.

To get an idea about how my writing sounded, I read my draft out loud to myself. I listened for places where I needed some variety. I can add phrases or clauses to lengthen some sentences. I can also break apart rambling sentences. Here's what I did to combine some short, choppy sentences. Now I've got two longer, flowing sentences followed by a short, punchy quote.

The police came shortly thereafter~~. They were~~, checking up because ~~A~~ a neighbor had reported hearing a cry~~. It was~~, the only sound the victim had made when he was about to be killed. The killer~~ was~~, confident that ~~H~~he had erased all signs of the crime~~. He~~, let them in. "I smiled—for what had I to fear?" (p. 232)

[combined short, choppy sentences]

Apply

Read your draft aloud to yourself and listen for places where you may want to vary your sentences.

Edit

Focus on **Conventions**

The Rubric Says The writing has been carefully edited. Homophones, if used, are correct.

Writing Strategy Make sure to always use the right word.

Writer's Term

Homophones

Homophones are words that sound alike but that have different meanings. A few examples of homophones are **to/two/too, ate/eight, be/bee,** and **right/write**.

Now it's time to check my draft for spelling, punctuation, grammar, and capitalization. While checking my draft, I found an incorrectly used homophone. It's easy to confuse homophones, and the computer spell checker will not find those errors. I'm going to correct it now. I'll also correct any other errors I see.

[DRAFT]

[changed to correct homophone]

It's a horror story of a murder told by a psychologically disturbed narrator who also happens ~~too~~ to be the murderer. In the end, even after he has successfully covered up his crime, he does not get away with what he has done because his own guilty conscience gives him away.

[corrected punctuation]

Reflect

What do you think of Tyler's edits? How do they make the literary analysis easier to read and understand?

Apply

Conventions

Edit for spelling, punctuation, and capitalization. Also make sure that you haven't used any incorrect homophones.

For practice with homophones and frequently confused words, see the exercises on the next two pages.

Homophones

Know the Rule

Homophones are words that sound the same but that are spelled differently and have different meanings.

Examples: **pair, pear,** and **pare**
toe and **tow**

Practice the Rule

Complete each sentence with the correct homophone on a separate sheet of paper. Write your own sentence for the unused homophone.

1. The climbers wanted to reach the ______ of the mountain and see the spectacular view of the valley below. (peek/peak)
2. A giant cone dropped down from the ancient ______ tree. (fir/fur)
3. The cyclists felt hot and tired and decided to ______ in the shade for a drink of water. (paws/pause)
4. The divers were ecstatic to catch a glimpse of the huge, rarely ______ oarfish. (seen/scene)
5. The ______ had to make an emergency landing when the pilot detected problems with one of the engines. (plain/plane)
6. Let's take a ______ in the class to see how many students can speak a second language. (pole/poll)
7. The last thing you would want to come across while hiking in the jungle is a wild ______ charging at you. (bore/boar)
8. It was a difficult ______ to finish first in the marathon. (feat/feet)
9. The speaker was ______ from talking so long to the group. (horse/hoarse)
10. Make sure you don't drop that vase and ______ it! (brake/break)

Frequently Confused Words

Know the Rule

People often confuse **words that look or sound similar**. If a writer uses the wrong word, the reader may not understand the intended message. Be sure to check the words carefully when you compose on the computer because the spell checker will not catch this kind of error!

Example: A **desert** is a very dry place that gets little rainfall.
A **dessert** is a sweet treat eaten after a meal.

Practice the Rule

Write each sentence with the correct word or words on a separate sheet of paper.

1. Please _____ my apology for being so late. (except/accept)
2. Everyone _____ Millie was at the soccer game this afternoon. (except/accept)
3. Martine donated dresses, coats, and other _____ to the clothing drive. (clothes/cloths)
4. For the car wash, we'll need a box full of _____ to use for drying cars. (clothes/cloths)
5. On the _____ of July, this country celebrates its independence. (Fourth, Forth)
6. The explorers went _____ around the globe and brought back many riches from faraway lands. (fourth/forth)
7. Be careful not to _____ your keys. (loose/lose)
8. You are not allowed to let your dog run _____ in the park. (loose/lose)
9. Hank _____ a cake at the bakery and _____ it to the birthday party. (brought/bought)
10. Sometimes when you _____ , it's good to take a deep _____. (breathe/breath)

Publish

+Presentation

Publishing Strategy **Present the literary analysis as part of a class-published book.**

Presentation Strategy **Use neat handwriting or word processing.**

My writing will be in a class-published book that will be on display in the library. I'll use my best handwriting, or, even better, I'll use the computer to make sure my analysis is neat and readable. I can use the word-processing features to make good margins, put a heading at the top of my essay, and choose clear, readable fonts. I might be able to find a picture of the author on the Internet to use in my response. I may even consider making a short video of my favorite scene from the story to share with the class. First, though, I'll make a final checklist.

My Checklist

Did I—

- ✔ check for correct capitalization, punctuation, grammar, and spelling?
- ✔ make sure all homophones and frequently confused words are used correctly?
- ✔ use a computer or good handwriting to make sure my essay is neat and readable?
- ✔ look for a picture of the author to include with my response?

Apply

Check your literary analysis against your final checklist. Then make a final copy to publish.

YOU CAN'T GET AWAY WITH MURDER

by Tyler

Even if you commit a perfect crime and have gotten rid of all the evidence, there is one piece of evidence you can never get rid of—your conscience. That's the message I got from reading Edgar Allan Poe's "The Tell-Tale Heart." This short, intense story is the scariest and most disturbing I've ever read. It's a horror story of a murder told by a psychologically disturbed narrator who also happens to be the murderer. And, in the end, even after he has successfully covered up his crime, he does not get away with what he has done because his own guilty conscience gives him away. What sets off his guilty conscience is the steady heartbeat that he keeps hearing.

Right at the start, the reader knows that there is something wrong with the narrator. He begins the story trying to convince the reader, and probably himself, that though he's "very, very, dreadfully nervous," (p. 228) he's not crazy. You get a sense that something is terribly wrong, but you don't know what it is. Also, you don't have any idea if you can really trust the point of view and judgment of the narrator. He then reveals that he has taken the life of the man he lives with. This was not a crime of passion or one done for money. Actually, he says he loved the man. He did it because of the man's eye! "He had the eye of a vulture—a pale blue eye, with a film over it." (p. 228)

As the story unfolds, the narrator describes the creepy way he went about preparing to murder the man, all the while saying that he is not a madman. Every night at midnight for a week, he thrust his head into the old man's bedroom and watched him sleep. Then, one night, he accidentally made a noise that woke the old man up. This was the part of the story that was the scariest, and saddest, to me. The old man sat up and was terrified that something was wrong. The killer waited for the old man to lie back down again, which he finally did. The killer then opened his lantern a tiny bit, to get some light, and saw the man's open eye, the eye that he hated so much. At that moment, he also started hearing "a low, dull quick sound." (p. 230) He recognized the sound as the beating of the old man's terrified heart.

The sound became louder and louder, until the killer was afraid that the neighbors would hear it. In an instant, he jumped into the room and killed the old man. To cover his crime, he dismembered the old man's body, cutting "off the head and the arms and the legs." (p. 231) He then hid the body parts under the flooring of the room, so that no evidence of his crime could be seen. All this he did very quickly, and, he thought, cleverly to conceal his gruesome crime.

The police came shortly thereafter, checking up because a neighbor had reported hearing a shriek, the only sound the victim had made when he was about to be murdered. The killer, confident that he had erased all signs of the crime, welcomed them in. "I smiled—for what had I to fear?" (p. 232)

The killer could have gotten away with his crime. The police were satisfied that everything was fine. But he started to hear the steady noise again, the beating heart. "—much such a sound as a watch makes when enveloped in cotton. I gasped for breath—and yet the officers heard it not." (p. 232)

The sound grew louder and louder to the killer. The policemen continued as if all was fine. But the murderer became convinced that the policemen knew, that they heard the sound, too. How could they not? It was becoming louder and louder and louder. Finally he could not take it any longer, and he confessed. "I admit the deed!—tear up the planks! here, here!—it is the beating of his hideous heart." (p. 233)

No crime can ever be perfect, because the criminal must live with his own conscience. The beating heart the killer heard was not the heartbeat of his victim; it was his own heartbeat. Throughout the story, he deceived himself into thinking that all was fine with him, that he wasn't crazy. But he was. A heartbeat is very powerful. Hearts beat faster when we are anxious—the more anxious, the faster. The heartbeat of the murderer was a relentless, steady reminder of the heartbeat he took away. In the end, he sought relief from it by confessing. But we do not know if even the confession will bring him relief, as he will have to live with the knowledge of what he has done for the rest of his life, for as long as his tell-tale heart keeps beating.

Work Cited

Poe, Edgar Allan. "The Tell-Tale Heart." *The Fall of the House of Usher and Other Writings*. Ed. David Galloway. London: Penguin, 2003. 228–233. Print.

Reflect

How did Tyler do? Did he include all the traits of a response to literature? Check it against the rubric. Then use the rubric to check your own literary analysis.

Argument
test writing

Read the Writing Prompt

When you take a writing test, you will be given a writing prompt. Most writing prompts have three parts:

Setup This part of the writing prompt gives you the background information you need to get ready to write.

Task This part of the writing prompt tells you exactly what you are supposed to write: an argument essay.

Scoring Guide This section tells how your writing will be scored. To do well on the test, you should include everything on the list.

Remember the rubrics you've used in writing class? When you take a writing test, you don't always have all of the information that's on a rubric. But a scoring guide is a lot like a rubric. It lists everything you need to think about to write a good paper. Like the rubrics you've used, many scoring guides are based on the six traits of writing:

The parent-teacher group at your school has proposed a Turn-Off-the-TV Week for students in your school.

Write an argument essay for your teacher telling why you support or oppose this plan.

Be sure your writing

- clearly states your claim and provides relevant evidence.
- is well organized. State your claim, give a new reason in each paragraph, and restate your claim at the end.
- uses a voice that sounds convincing.
- uses words that support your purpose.
- has varied sentences.
- has correct grammar, punctuation, capitalization, and spelling.

Writing Traits in the Scoring Guide

The scoring guide in the prompt on page 361 has been made into this chart. Does it remind you of the rubrics you've used? Not all prompts include all of the writing traits, but this one does. Use them to do your best writing. Remember to work neatly and put your name on each page.

- **Be sure your writing clearly states your claim and provides relevant evidence.**

- **Be sure your writing is well organized. State your claim, give a new reason in each paragraph, and restate your claim at the end.**

- **Be sure your writing uses a voice that sounds convincing.**

- **Be sure your writing uses words that support your purpose.**

- **Be sure your writing has varied sentences.**

- **Be sure your writing has correct grammar, punctuation, capitalization, and spelling.**

Look at Leah Alexander's argument essay on the next page. Did she follow the scoring guide?

Turn It Off? No Way!

by Leah Alexander

If my school planned to have a Turn-Off-the-TV Week, I would be the first to protest. There are several reasons why I feel this way.

First of all, television is an excellent way of discovering what is going on in the world. Others might disagree and say that you can always read a news magazine or the newspaper instead, but sometimes there is important news that changes from minute to minute. For example, in the 2000 presidential election, people did not know which candidate had gotten more votes. For several weeks, TV was the best source of up-to-date information. Besides, a picture is worth a thousand words. You just can't get the same kind of visual experience from other media.

Another reason for watching TV is that sometimes we kids need a break. After spending an hour on the school bus, six hours in school, and a couple of hours doing homework (not to mention an hour or two of sports and afterschool clubs), we need some time off! I can't think of anything more relaxing than a good sitcom. That doesn't mean I want to watch TV all night. I'm the first one to pick up a good book in my free time. I just think that it's important not to work so hard all the time.

There is a third reason I don't support a week without television. I want to be an actress when I grow up. I think it's really helpful to watch both good and bad actors to see how—or how not—to act. Some people might say I should just go to the movies, but they are too expensive. Since television is usually free, you don't waste your money if the show isn't good.

I can see skipping a night of TV now and then. I do it myself, especially if I have to study for a big test. But a whole week without television seems like overkill.

I have no doubt that there are many reasons why people support the idea of a week of no television for kids. But for responsible students like me, the reasons *not* to turn off the TV outweigh them.

Using the Scoring Guide to Study the Model

Now let's use the scoring guide to check Leah's writing test, "Turn It Off? No Way!" Let's see how well her essay meets each of the six writing traits.

- **The claim is clearly stated.**
- **Relevant evidence is included.**

I like how Leah gets right to the point and gives the reader her opinion, or claim, in the very first sentence. There's no questioning the way she feels about the topic.

If my school planned to have a Turn-Off-the-TV Week, I would be the first to protest.

Throughout her essay, Leah provides plenty of relevant supporting evidence to back up her point of view.

First of all, television is an excellent way of discovering what is going on in the world. Others might disagree and say that you can always read a news magazine or the newspaper instead, but sometimes there is important news that changes from minute to minute.

- **The writing is well organized.**
- **The claim is stated, a new reason is given in each body paragraph, and the claim is restated at the end.**

Leah's writing is so well organized, I had no trouble understanding, and even agreeing with, her argument. She even restates her opinion in the conclusion, just to be sure her point is completely clear.

I have no doubt that there are many reasons why people support the idea of a week of no television for kids. But for responsible students like me, the reasons *not* to turn off the TV outweigh them.

- **The writer's voice sounds convincing.**

Leah's voice is so confident, and her arguments are so solid, that I found it easy to agree with her point of view. She's clearly thought her opinion through.

That doesn't mean I want to watch TV all night. I'm the first one to pick up a good book in my free time. I just think that it's important not to work so hard all the time.

- **The writer uses words that support the purpose.**

Leah was clever to use words like *best source of up-to-date information, visual experience,* and *media*. These words are appropriate for the topic, and give her writing strength and credibility.

For several weeks, TV was the best source of up-to-date information. Besides, a picture is worth a thousand words. You just can't get the same kind of visual experience from other media.

Using the Scoring Guide to Study the Model

- **The writing contains a variety of sentences.**

Reading Leah's writing is enjoyable and it really got me thinking. She uses a variety of sentence structures to keep the writing smooth and lively. I especially like her use of parentheses in the example below.

After spending an hour on the school bus, six hours in school, and a couple of hours doing homework (not to mention an hour or two of sports and afterschool clubs), we need some time off! I can't think of anything more relaxing than a good sitcom.

- **The writing contains correct grammar, punctuation, capitalization, and spelling.**

As far as I can see, Leah did not make any serious mistakes in capitalization, punctuation, sentence structure, or spelling. But don't forget to check for mistakes in your own work. For example, if you know you often misspell words, you should make sure to pay close attention to spelling. Editing for grammar and mechanics at every step of the writing process will help you avoid errors on your writing test.

Planning My Time

Before giving us a writing prompt, my teacher always tells us how much time we'll have to complete the test. Since I'm familiar with the steps of the writing process, I can think about how much time I need for each one. If I break up the total amount of time into small sections to complete each step, I'll be sure to have enough time to do everything I need. If the test takes an hour, here's how I can organize my time. Planning your time will help you, too!

Prewrite

Focus on **Ideas**

Writing Strategy Study the writing prompt to find out what to do.

I always study my writing prompt before I take a test. A writing prompt usually has three parts (the setup, task, and scoring guide), but they're not always labeled. When you study your writing prompt, look for these sections and label each one, just like I did below. Then circle key words in the setup and the task that tell what kind of writing you will be doing and who your audience will be. I circled my topic in purple. I also used red to circle what kind of writing I'll be doing (an argument essay) and who my audience is (others). I'll assume that my classmates are the "others."

My Writing Test Prompt

Setup

You believe that a special holiday should be created to honor a particular person or event. Think about a person or event that is important enough to you to be honored in this way.

Task

Write an essay to convince others that this person or event should be honored.

Scoring Guide

Be sure your writing

- clearly states your claim and provides relevant evidence.
- is well organized. State your claim, give a new reason in each paragraph, and restate your claim at the end.
- uses a voice that sounds convincing.
- uses words that support your purpose.
- has varied sentences.
- has correct grammar, punctuation, capitalization, and spelling.

Think about how the scoring guide relates to the six traits of good writing you've studied in the rubrics. Not every trait will be included in every scoring guide, but you'll still want to remember them all in order to write a good essay.

Ideas

- **Be sure your writing clearly states your claim and provides relevant evidence.**

I'll begin my essay with my claim, or opinion, so it's clear early on. Then, I'll include lots of relevant evidence in the body paragraphs.

Organization

- **Be sure your writing is well organized. State your claim, give a new reason in each paragraph, and restate your claim at the end.**

I'll be sure to give a new supporting reason in each paragraph and then clearly repeat my claim in the conclusion.

Voice

- **Be sure your writing uses a voice that sounds convincing.**

Strong yet friendly language will help me connect with the reader and persuade my audience to agree with my opinion.

Word Choice

- **Be sure your writing uses words that support your purpose.**

Word choice is so important. I'll work hard to use words appropriate for both my subject and audience.

Sentence Fluency

- **Be sure your writing has varied sentences.**

To keep my writing smooth and energetic, I'll use a variety of sentence structures.

Conventions

- **Be sure your writing has correct grammar, punctuation, capitalization, and spelling.**

I don't want to have any mistakes in my essay, so I'll be sure to leave enough time for editing.

Prewrite

Focus on **Ideas**

Writing Strategy Respond to the task.

Before you start writing for a test, you should collect information. The first place to look for information is the writing prompt. Although I don't have a whole lot of time to complete my test, I know that prewriting is important because it will help me get my ideas together before I begin drafting.

My writing prompt instructs me to write an argument essay to convince others that a holiday should be created to honor a person or an event. First I have to think of someone or something that should be honored. My dog, Cato, was sick not too long ago, and our vet, Dr. Lamb, saved his life. I remember how happy I was when I found out that Cato would be OK, so I think I'll honor Dr. Lamb with this essay. I'll begin by quickly writing down some notes.

Task — Write an essay to convince others that this person or event should be honored.

Notes

- ✔ Dr. Lamb saved my dog's life.
- ✔ She cares for pets whose owners can't pay her.
- ✔ Everyone likes her because she really cares about pets and people.

Apply

Think about how you'll respond to the task before you begin writing. Then jot down notes to help you gather information.

Prewrite

Focus on **Organization**

Writing Strategy

Choose a graphic organizer.

Now that I've decided on a topic, it's time to start organizing my ideas. Since I'm writing an argument essay, I'll use an Argument Map. I'll use the information from the setup and task sections of the writing prompt as my call to action, and I'll fill in the rest of my Argument Map with the notes I took earlier, as well as other ideas.

Call to Action
Honor Dr. Lamb with a holiday.

Reason 1
Dr. Lamb saved my dog's life.

Facts/Examples
- She performed surgery after he ate a necktie.
- She gave up her evening out.

Reason 2
She cares for pets whose owners can't pay her.

- She flies to Central America to offer free pet services.
- She runs a pet clinic in her neighborhood.
- She charges only $5.00 for a visit.

Reason 3
Everyone likes her because she really cares about pets and people.

- She came to Career Day at school.
- People send her cards and thank-you notes.

Reflect

Has Tyler included enough information in his Argument Map?

Apply

Choose a graphic organizer that will suit your purpose for writing.

Prewrite

Focus on **Organization**

Writing Strategy **Check the graphic organizer against the scoring guide.**

You don't always get much time to revise during a writing test. So prewriting is more important than ever. Before I write, I'll check the information on my Argument Map against the scoring guide in the writing prompt.

Call to Action
Honor Dr. Lamb with a holiday.

Reason 1
Dr. Lamb saved my dog's life.

Facts/Examples
- She performed surgery after he ate a necktie.
- She gave up her evening out.

Reason 2
She cares for pets whose owners can't pay her.

- She flies to Central America to offer free pet services.
- She runs a pet clinic in her neighborhood.
- She charges only $5.00 for a visit.

Reason 3
Everyone likes her because she really cares about pets and people.

- She came to Career Day at school.
- People send her cards and thank-you notes.

Proofreading Marks

⊐	Indent	ℓ	Take out something
≡	Make uppercase	⊙	Add a period
/	Make lowercase	¶	New paragraph
∧	Add something	(sp)	Spelling error

[DRAFT]

The second reason I think Dr. Lamb should be recognized is because of the volunteer work that she do. Every year, she flies to Central America with a group of other vets. There they care for the pets of people who don't have enough money for proper pet care. Even at home, Dr. Lamb helps people and their pets. Once a month, she runs a pet clinic here in town where you can have your pet examined for just five dollars.

Dr. Lamb came to our school on Career Day to tell about the work she does. If you ever visit her office. You will be amazed at all the cards and letters on her bulletin board. These are all thank-you notes from pet owners that she has helped.

I am so happy with Dr. Lamb that I would like to become a veterinarian when I grow up. I think a great way to recognize her would be to hold a pet parade on the street in front of her office. Maybe she could even wear a crown that says Top Dog! Although there are many other heroes who might deserve a holiday of their won, Dr. Lamb definitely gets my vote!

Reflect

Do you think Tyler's claim is clear?

Apply

You may not get a chance to recopy your paper in a writing test, so try to be neat when you write.

Revise

Focus on Organization

Writing Strategy **Organize the ideas into an introduction, body, and conclusion.**

My Argument Map was so helpful when writing my draft. I put my call to action in the first paragraph and supporting details in the body. Then I restated my claim in the conclusion. But there's one paragraph where it's not clear that I'm mentioning a new reason, and it's confusing. I'll strengthen my organization by adding a line to let my reader know a new point is being made.

[DRAFT]

The last reason I think Dr. Lamb is a hero is because of the way she treats both animals and people.

She

~~Dr. Lamb~~ came to our school on Career Day to tell about the work she does. If you ever visit her office. You will be amazed at all the cards and letters on her bulletin board.

[organized writing]

Apply

Make sure your ideas are organized logically and clearly.

Revise

Focus on 

Writing Strategy Sound convincing.

As with any writing assignment, my voice should match my purpose and audience. My purpose in this paper is to convince others that Dr. Lamb deserves her own holiday. I need to sound confident, include strong and relevant reasons to back up my opinion, and use balanced, positive language. Mostly I did a great job, but there's one line where I don't sound too sure of myself. I'll rewrite that line now to sound more confident.

[DRAFT]

[used convincing tone]

Since ~~it looks like~~ she ~~kind of~~ saved my dog's life, the first reason is personal. Cato likes to chew on things. Once he even chewed up the tire on my bicycle! The time he really got into trouble, however, was when he swallowed one of my dad's neckties.

Reflect

How have Tyler's organization and voice revisions affected his writing?

Apply

Use strong, relevant reasons and positive language to sound convincing.

Revise

Writing Strategy Use words with the right connotation.

I know from the scoring guide that I should choose words that support my purpose. My goal is to convince my reader to agree with my point of view. The words I choose will directly affect how my reader responds to my claim. I need to use words that are associated with positive emotions or reactions—words with positive connotations. As I reread my draft, I found some words I could replace with others that have stronger positive connotations. I'll change them now.

[DRAFT]

[used strong positive words]

I am so ~~happy with~~ impressed by Dr. Lamb that I would like to become a veterinarian when I grow up. I think a great way to ~~recognize~~ honor her would be to hold a pet parade on the street in front of her office.

Apply

Make your point with words that have the right connotations.

Edit

Focus on **Conventions**

Writing Strategy **Check the grammar, punctuation, capitalization, and spelling.**

It's always a good idea to check your writing test one last time before turning it in. The scoring guide says to use correct grammar, punctuation, capitalization, and spelling. I always leave plenty of time to correct errors in these important areas.

FINAL DRAFT

Dr. Kitty Lamb Day

by Tyler

The person I nominate to be honored with a special holiday is Dr. Kitty Lamb, our veterinarian. (Believe it or not, that's her real name.) Dr. Lamb has been my ~~dogs~~ dog's doctor since he was a pup. There are several reasons why I think she is a hero.

Since she saved my dog's life, the first reason is personal. Cato likes to chew on things. Once he even chewed up the tire on my bicycle! The time he really got into trouble, however, was when he swallowed one of my dad's neckties. We didn't know he had done anything wrong until he stopped eating and started whining a lot. That's when we called Dr. Lamb. She said to bring Cato right over. When we got there, she was all dressed up because ~~her~~ she and her husband were on ~~there~~ their way to a party. She had to perform surgery for five ~~ours~~ hours to save that silly dog's life. After a few weeks, Cato completely recovered.

FINAL DRAFT

The second reason I think Dr. Lamb should be recognized is because of the volunteer work that she ~~do~~ does. Every year, she flies to Central America with a group of other vets. There, they care for the pets of people who don't have enough money for proper pet care. The doctors don't get paid for the work they do there, and they even pay for their own plane tickets. Even at home, Dr. Lamb helps people and their pets. Once a month, she runs a pet clinic here in town where you can have your pet examined for just five dollars.

The last reason I think Dr. Lamb is a hero is because of the way she treats both animals and people. ~~Dr. Lamb~~ She came to our school on Career Day to tell about the work she does. If you ever visit her office, ~~Y~~you will be amazed at all the cards and letters on her bulletin board. These are all thank-you notes from pet owners that she has helped.

I am so ~~happy with~~ impressed by Dr. Lamb that I would like to become a veterinarian when I grow up. I think a great way to ~~recognize~~ honor her would be to hold a pet parade on the street in front of her office. Maybe she could even wear a crown that says Top Dog! Although there are many other heroes who might deserve a holiday of their ~~won~~ own, Dr. Lamb definitely gets my vote!

Reflect

Before Tyler turns in his test, he should check it against the scoring guide one last time. Remember to use your writing prompt's scoring guide to check your writing whenever you take a test.

Apply

Don't turn in a test paper until you've done a final edit to check for grammar and spelling mistakes.

I'm done! That was easy! When you take a writing test, remember to use the writing process. The process is just a little different for a test, but if you keep in mind these important tips, you'll do just fine.

TEST TIPS

1. **Study the writing prompt before you start to write.** Most writing prompts have three parts: the setup, the task, and the scoring guide. The parts probably won't be labeled. You'll have to figure them out for yourself!
2. **Make sure you understand the task before you start to write.**
   - Read all three parts of the writing prompt carefully.
   - Circle key words in the task part of the writing prompt that tell what kind of writing you need to do. The task might also identify your audience.
   - Make sure you know how you'll be graded.
   - Say the assignment in your own words to yourself.
3. **Keep an eye on the clock.** Decide how much time you will spend on each part of the writing process and try to stick to your schedule. Don't spend so much time on prewriting that you don't have enough time left to write.
4. **Reread your writing. Compare it to the scoring guide at least twice.** Remember the rubrics you've used? A scoring guide on a writing test is like a rubric. It can help you keep what's important in mind.
5. **Plan, plan, plan!** You don't get much time to revise during a test, so planning is more important than ever.
6. **Write neatly.** Remember: If the people who score your test can't read your writing, it doesn't matter how good your story or essay is!

Descriptive writing brings clear word pictures to the reader.

Hi, there! My name is Andre. Welcome to the world of descriptive writing. Descriptive writing sounds like fun. I'll get to paint pictures with words as I describe objects, people, places, and events. Living in Alaska gives me a lot of stuff to describe, and I can't wait to get started!

IN THIS UNIT

- Biographic Sketch
- Observation Report
- Geographic Description
- MATH CONNECTION ▶ Poem
- Writing for a Test

Name: Andre
Home: Alaska
Hobbies: snowboarding, camping, hiking, astronomy
Favorite Book: *Water Sky* by Jean Craighead George
Favorite Food: hamburgers

What's a Biographic Sketch?

It's a true account of a period of a real person's life. I think I'll like writing one because I like finding out about people.

What's in a Biographic Sketch?

Subject
That's the person I'm going to write about. I'll need to do some research and maybe interview the subject of my biographic sketch. It's my job to tell his or her story.

The Senses
I'll need to use my senses to write good details. I'll include details that appeal to whichever senses are appropriate for my subject. I'll use these to paint a picture for my audience.

Quotations
I'll use quotations to bring my subject to life. I'll listen carefully for sayings or quotes my subject uses. The quotations will say a lot about my subject.

Why write a Biographic Sketch?

I'm going to think about reasons to write a biographic sketch. Maybe that will help me figure out whose life I want to write about.

Entertainment
I have met people who are funny, exciting, or influential. I want to share these people with an audience. Entertaining the reader is one good reason to write a biographic sketch.

Personal Reflection
Writing helps me reflect, or make sense out of the things I see. A biographic sketch can help me understand how I've been affected by someone I've met.

Honoring
There are some people who make a big difference in the world. A biographic sketch is a way to honor them. I could even use my sketch to nominate someone for an award.

Linking Descriptive Writing Traits to a Biographic Sketch

In this chapter, you will write about a real person. This type of descriptive writing is called a biographic sketch. Andre will guide you through the stages of the writing process: Prewrite, Draft, Revise, Edit, and Publish. In each stage, Andre will show you important writing strategies that are linked to the Descriptive Writing Traits below.

Descriptive Writing Traits

- a clear topic that is developed by relevant supporting details
- descriptive details that are well chosen for the topic

- well-organized paragraphs that logically follow the order of the description, whether by time, location, or another order
- varied and appropriate transitions that show the relationship between ideas and concepts

- a voice that is appropriate for the purpose and audience

- precise words and phrases, possibly including figurative language, that create an accurate picture for the reader

- sentences that vary in length and type to add flow to the writing

- no or few errors in grammar, usage, mechanics, and spelling

Before you write, read Elaine Dixon's biographic sketch on the next page. Then use the biographic sketch rubric on pages 388–389 to decide how well she did. (You might want to look back at What's in a Biographic Sketch? on page 384, too!)

Biographic Sketch Model

Jane Ellis: Teacher, Alaskan

by Elaine Dixon

Who is the oldest person you know? For the students at Nell Scott Middle School, it is a math teacher, Mrs. Jane Ellis. Mrs. Ellis was born in 1923 in San Francisco, California. This was 30 years before the school principal was even born and 70 years before the building she now teaches in was built! Subject

In 1944, Mrs. Ellis started teaching in Modesto, California. Then the U.S. Army sent her and her husband to Alaska in 1948. The cold, crisp landscape was beautiful to Mrs. Ellis. She got a teaching job right away at a government school and taught all grades and all subjects. "Those children taught me to be a teacher," Mrs. Ellis explains. "When I got it right, they learned like kittens lapping up milk. If they weren't learning, I had only one place to look—in the mirror!" Quotation

Mrs. Ellis is a special teacher! But she's special not just because she's been teaching for a long time. She's special because she loves a good joke, remembers the name of each student she ever taught, and makes students think math is fun and important. She does this with her creative teaching methods. For instance, after ringing a shiny brass bell on her desk, she likes to call out in a strong voice, "Time for a lightning drill." Soon the room is filled with shouting as students call out the times tables for their assigned number. When she's satisfied, Mrs. Ellis rings the bell again and says, "Class, what have you achieved?" And the class shouts back: "The times tables!"

Sensory details

Besides being a good teacher, Mrs. Ellis is simply hard to forget. Tall and thin, she wears a flowery perfume that trails behind her. She often wears purple slacks with a purple sweater and fur-lined boots. "I always want to be ready for anything!" she says. Her hair is silver and tightly curled. And her eyes sparkle on a face that is covered with wrinkles. "These aren't wrinkles," Mrs. Ellis says. "They're wisdom lines!" She has a quip or a quote for everything!

When is Mrs. Ellis going to retire? Not any time soon! As she likes to say, "My students still have a lot to teach me!"

Rubric

Use this 6-point rubric to plan and evaluate a biographic sketch.

	6	5	4
Ideas	Relevant descriptive details, including sensory details, capture the subject.	Relevant details, including sensory details, describe the subject.	Several sensory details describe the subject, but some details are not relevant.
Organization	The beginning introduces the character and draws the reader in. Details are organized logically.	The beginning is interesting and introduces the character. Most details are organized logically.	The beginning introduces the character. Most details are organized logically.
Voice	Quotations are effective and give voice to the character.	Quotations are used to help the reader understand the character.	Some quotations are used, but not all of them help the reader understand the character.
Word Choice	Vivid, descriptive language gives the reader a clear picture of the subject.	Clear language helps the reader understand the subject.	Some vague or dull language sometimes muddies the picture of the subject.
Sentence Fluency	Well-placed prepositional phrases add flow and information to sentences.	Prepositional phrases are used and enhance sentence flow in several places.	Prepositional phrases are used but not consistently.
Conventions	Phrases are clear and enhance the meaning of sentences.	Phrases are clear and add meaning to sentences.	Some phrases are used and don't interfere with the meaning.

+Presentation The biographic sketch is neat and legible.

3	2	1	
Few sensory details are included, and the subject is hard to picture.	Very few sensory details are used. Most details are irrelevant. The subject is not described.	Few or no details describe the subject. No sensory details are used.	Ideas
The character is not clearly introduced. The organization can be followed, but several details are out of place.	It is hard to tell who is the subject of the writing. The details are poorly organized and hard to follow.	The writing has no clear subject. The details are not organized at all.	Organization
Quotations are poorly used; they do not give voice to the character.	Few quotations are included, and their meaning is confusing.	No quotations are used; the character does not have a voice.	Voice
Vague or dull language is used in several places. The reader does not have a clear picture of the subject.	Most of the language is vague or dull. It is easy to lose interest in the subject.	The language is hard to follow. The writer has not tried to describe the subject.	Word Choice
Some prepositional phrases are used, but not all of them are correct.	Prepositional phrases are placed incorrectly and interfere with meaning.	Prepositional phrases are missing from the writing.	Sentence Fluency
Some phrases are placed incorrectly in sentences. They may interfere with meaning.	Phrases are placed incorrectly and interfere with meaning.	Phrases are missing from the writing.	Conventions

See Appendix B for 4-, 5-, and 6-point descriptive rubrics.

Using the Biographic Sketch Rubric to Study the Model

Did you notice that the model on page 387 points out some key elements of a biographic sketch? As she wrote "Jane Ellis: Teacher, Alaskan," Elaine Dixon used these elements to help describe her subject. She also used the 6-point rubric on pages 388–389 to plan, draft, revise, and edit the writing. A rubric is a great tool to evaluate writing during the writing process.

Now let's use the same rubric to score the model. To do this, we'll focus on each trait separately, starting with Ideas. We'll use the top descriptor for each trait (column 6), along with examples from the model, to help us understand how the traits work together. How would you score Elaine on each trait?

- **Relevant descriptive details, including sensory details, capture the subject.**

I like the way Elaine describes not only how Mrs. Ellis looks, but also how she smells. The picture of Mrs. Ellis in my mind is vivid and alive, and this makes the writing stronger and more interesting.

[from the writing model]

Besides being a good teacher, Mrs. Ellis is simply hard to forget. Tall and thin, she wears a flowery perfume that trails behind her. She often wears purple slacks with a purple sweater and fur-lined boots.

- The beginning introduces the character and draws the reader in.
- Details are organized logically.

I like how Elaine opens her sketch with a question. I automatically felt connected to the topic and couldn't wait to read more. Elaine's details are well-organized and give me a complete picture of Mrs. Ellis.

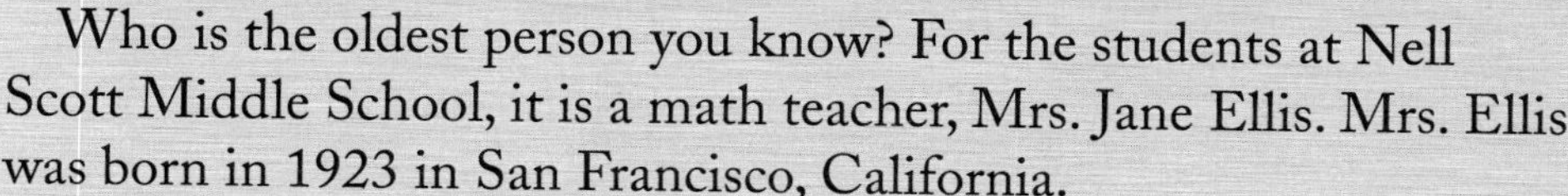

Who is the oldest person you know? For the students at Nell Scott Middle School, it is a math teacher, Mrs. Jane Ellis. Mrs. Ellis was born in 1923 in San Francisco, California.

- Quotations are effective and give voice to the character.

Elaine does a great job of choosing quotations that make an impression and really show me Mrs. Ellis's personality—funny, smart, and witty. Now I can envision the whole person, not just what she looks like on the outside.

"These aren't wrinkles," Mrs. Ellis says. "They're wisdom lines!" She has a quip or a quote for everything!

- Vivid, descriptive language gives the reader a clear picture of the subject.

Elaine has really inspired me to work hard at describing the subject of my own sketch. Her descriptions are so strong and creative—I want my reader to have the same reaction to my writing.

Her hair is silver and tightly curled. And her eyes sparkle on a face that is covered with wrinkles.

- Well-placed prepositional phrases add flow and information to sentences.

Elaine uses lots of prepositional phrases to add variety to her sentences. These phrases mix things up and made reading her work easier and more enjoyable. They also contain interesting facts!

[from the writing model] 

In 1944, Mrs. Ellis started teaching in Modesto, California. Then the U.S. Army sent her and her husband to Alaska in 1948.

- **Phrases are clear and enhance the meaning of sentences.**

Elaine has very good spelling and punctuation. I couldn't find any errors in her work. I read her sketch another time to see if she has any dangling modifiers. She does not!

[from the writing model]

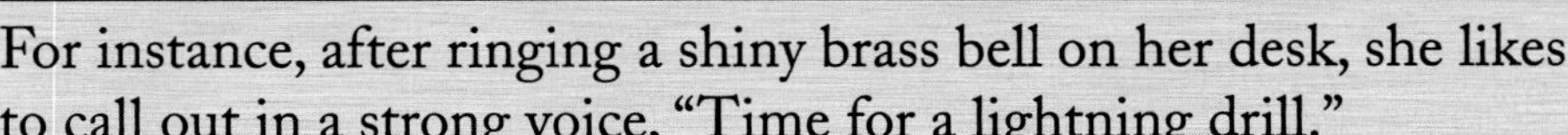

For instance, after ringing a shiny brass bell on her desk, she likes to call out in a strong voice, "Time for a lightning drill."

+Presentation The biographic sketch is neat and legible.

My Turn!

I'm going to write a biographic sketch about someone in my school. I'm glad to have the rubric and good writing strategies to use as a guide. Keep reading to see how I do!

Prewrite

Focus on **Ideas**

The Rubric Says Relevant descriptive details, including sensory details, capture the subject.

Writing Strategy Describe someone at school (a teacher, a classmate, or other close friend) in a biographic sketch.

My big question is: who should be the subject of my sketch? There are plenty of interesting people here in Alaska. I've thought about some of my Aleut friends and about an old man I know who still digs for gold. But I think I'll write about my best friend, Seth. He and his family raise dogs that pull sleds in races like the Iditarod. He's quite a character! I'll start by listing details about Seth, and then choose the most interesting details to include in my sketch.

Description of Seth

- tall, skinny, won't play basketball
- loves dogs more than anything
- feeding dogs is daily chore
- knows how to hook up the dog sled and drive the dogs
- almost always wears jeans, parka, boots, Seawolves cap
- lets the dogs lick him on the face (gross!)
- sled dogs are part of his family
- funny sense of humor

Apply

Choose a person you think is interesting. Jot down some descriptions of that person.

Prewrite

Focus on **Organization**

The Rubric Says Details are organized logically.

Writing Strategy Make a Character Chart.

Writer's Term

Character Chart
A **Character Chart** is a table in which a writer can list details about a character according to looks, personality, and actions.

OK, the rubric tells me to organize my details logically. That makes sense. I will describe Seth in a way that won't confuse my reader. I think a Character Chart will help me organize my details and keep track of them.

CHARACTER CHART

Character: My friend Seth

Looks	Personality	Actions
• red hair • tall and skinny • grew 3 inches in one summer • changes clothes after school • jeans, parka, rubber boots, Seawolves cap	• steady and easy-going • knows his mind • loves dogs more than anything else • knows what he wants in life (to raise dogs)	• feeds the sled dogs every night • dogs lick him (yuck!) • can hitch up the sled • can drive the sled

Reflect

How does Andre's chart look? Does he have enough information to write his sketch?

Apply

Use your notes to make a Character Chart about your subject.

Draft

Focus on **Ideas**

The Rubric Says Relevant descriptive details, including sensory details, capture the subject.

Writing Strategy Draft a biographic sketch. Use plenty of sensory details to provide a clear mental picture for the reader.

Writer's Term

Sensory Details

Sensory details appeal directly to one of the five senses (seeing, feeling, smelling, tasting, and hearing).

It's time to start writing my draft. I've picked out the person I want to write about—my friend Seth. Then I organized what I want to say about him. I want to show my readers a side of Seth that they don't see at school. I want them to feel as if they are right beside him as he feeds his dogs and takes them out for a ride.

The rubric tells me to use sensory details. Sensory details will help me help my readers to see, feel, smell, and hear a part of Seth's life. I don't think any tasting is involved—except for the dog kibbles!

I think I'll start my biographic sketch by telling the audience some facts about Seth. Then I'll give them a word picture of Seth at home. When he's working with the dogs, he's really in his zone. I'm just going to get started. I won't worry about grammar and spelling mistakes yet. I know I'll be fixing them later.

Proofreading Marks

⊐ Indent	ℓ Take out something
≡ Make uppercase	⊙ Add a period
/ Make lowercase	¶ New paragraph
∧ Add something	(sp) Spelling error

[DRAFT]

My Friend, Sled Dog Seth

Seth is a seventh grader at Nell Scott Middle School. At school, Seth is just like anybody else. But after school, most often, you see Seth dressed in blue jeans, an unzipped parka, and shiny green rubber boots, carrying a bucket of smelly brown kibbles. A steel scoop sticks out the top. He is heading out to feed the sled dogs.

His boots make a squishing sound in the spongey ground. Nearing the dog pens, the squishing sound is drowned out by barking. The dogs' metal food pans go skitering as the dogs run up to the fence. Seth rubs their soft fur and lets each dog like his face. He is kind and affectionut as he feeds the dogs.

[sensory details]

Reflect

How does Andre's draft sound to you? How do his sensory details bring the subject of his biographic sketch alive?

Apply

Use your Character Chart to write a draft of your biographic sketch. Make sure to put in some sensory details to help your readers get a clear mental picture.

Revise

Focus on 

The Rubric Says The beginning introduces the character and draws the reader in.

Writing Strategy Introduce the character right away.

So now it's time to revise my draft. The rubric says I should introduce my character right away and in a way that grabs my reader's attention. I did introduce Seth in the beginning, but not in a very exciting way. I want my reader to be interested in finding out more about him. I will revise the first paragraph now to really draw the reader in.

[DRAFT]

[used exciting introduction]

Meet Sled Dog Seth!
^Seth is a seventh grader at Nell Scott Middle School. At school, Seth is just like anybody else. But after school, most often, you see Seth dressed in blue jeans, an unzipped parka, and shiny green rubber boots, carrying a bucket of smelly brown kibbles.

Introduce your character in the beginning in an attention-grabbing way.

Revise

Focus on **Voice**

The Rubric Says **Quotations are effective and give voice to the character.**

Writing Strategy **Add several sayings or quotes that the subject frequently uses.**

The rubric says that I should use quotations in my biographic sketch. Using my subject's own words will help bring him to life for the reader. I want my readers to really hear Seth's unique voice! I will mix some of Seth's quotes throughout my writing. This will liven up the sketch and help the writing flow. I already found a place where a quote would fit in perfectly.

[DRAFT]

[added quotes]

"I love my dogs," Seth always says. "They are a part of my family, just like my mom and dad and my sister, Katie."

What do you think? Does Andre's introduction grab your attention? How do his details and quotes bring his subject to life?

Add some quotes or sayings to bring your character to life for your audience.

Revise

Focus on 

The Rubric Says Vivid, descriptive language gives the reader a clear picture of the subject.

Writing Strategy Use a thesaurus to replace vague words with vivid, descriptive ones.

Writer's Term

Thesaurus

A **thesaurus** is a book of words and their synonyms (words with a similar meaning) and antonyms (words with an opposite meaning). You can use either a print or an online thesaurus.

The rubric says to use vivid and descriptive language to describe Seth. Thinking of creative and different words is sometimes difficult, so I will use a thesaurus to help me out. It's fun using unique words to describe things. What do you think of my choices?

[DRAFT]

[replaced vague word]

silky

up to the fence. Seth rubs their ~~soft~~ fur and lets each dog like his face. He is kind and affectionut as he feeds the dogs.

[vivid details]

right up to the roots of his carrot-colored hair

With a crunch, the scoop hits the kibbles. With a clatter, the kibbles hit the pans.

Apply

Use a thesaurus to find and use vivid and descriptive words to describe your subject.

Edit

Focus on **Conventions**

The Rubric Says Phrases are clear and enhance the meaning of sentences.

Writing Strategy Check prepositional phrases and avoid misplaced participial phrases (dangling modifiers).

Writer's Term

Dangling Modifier

A modifier describes, clarifies, or gives more detail about a concept. A **dangling modifier** is a word or phrase that modifies a word not clearly stated in the sentence.

Different kinds of phrases add meaning to my writing. However, I have to be careful how I place them in my sentences. For example, a participial phrase that doesn't clearly relate to the subject will mislead my readers.

[DRAFT]

[corrected dangling modifier]

His boots make a squishing sound in the ~~spongey~~ spongy ground. ~~Nearing~~ As he nears the dog pens, the squishing sound is drowned out by barking. The dogs' metal food pans go ~~skitering~~ skittering as the dogs run up to the fence.

Reflect

Andre used lots of vivid, descriptive words. He also worked hard to fix any dangling modifiers and ensure correct use of phrases. Can you find any mistakes he might have missed?

Apply

Conventions

Edit your draft for spelling, punctuation, and capitalization. Be sure to use all phrases correctly.

For more practice fixing dangling modifiers and using prepositional phrases, use the exercises on the next two pages.

Dangling Modifiers

Know the Rule

Dangling modifiers most frequently occur at the beginning of sentences as introductory participial phrases.

Incorrect: After reading the original study, the article remains unconvincing.

The article—the subject of the main clause—did not read the original study. Who did? When you figure that out, you can fix the sentence.

Correct: After reading the original study, I found the article unconvincing.

Practice the Rule

Read each sentence below. Find the dangling modifiers. Write each sentence correctly on a separate sheet of paper.

1. Looking for a certain breed, sled dogs are often not purebreds.
2. After examining them, the dogs are ready to be identified.
3. Using a syringe, a microchip gives each dog a code.
4. After doing a blood test, the dogs can be hitched to the sled.
5. While waiting to start, the crowd is restless.
6. Wearing dog booties, the jagged ice won't hurt their paws.
7. Panting and barking eagerly, the drivers ready the dog sleds.
8. When fired, the dogs leap forward at the sound of the starting gun.
9. Riding on the back of the sled, the dogs respond to the commands of the drivers.
10. After winning the race, a prize is awarded to the lead dog team.

Prepositional Phrases

Know the Rule

A **prepositional phrase** can tell how, what kind, when, how much, or where. A prepositional phrase begins with a **preposition**, such as *in, over, of, to,* or *by*. It ends with a noun or pronoun that is the **object of the preposition**. The words between the preposition and its object are part of the prepositional phrase. A prepositional phrase can be anywhere in a sentence.

Example: Please place this book **on the second shelf of the bookcase** that is **in the corner of my office.**

Practice the Rule

Find the prepositional phrases in each sentence. Write them on a separate sheet of paper.

1. In the morning, we are driving out of town and across the state toward our favorite amusement park.
2. It's a long ride to the park, but we entertain ourselves by reading books and listening to music in the car.
3. When we arrive, we will pass through the gates and head to the roller coaster.
4. We're told by our parents that we should meet near the park entrance before lunchtime.
5. After a picnic lunch, I hope to sit beside my brother and sail above the treetops on the relaxing gondola ride.
6. There are hundreds of games in the arcade located in the southeast corner of the park.
7. After sundown, all the lights turn on and transform the park into a magical world of light and sound and fun.
8. During the ride home, I fall asleep with my head on my big sister's shoulder and dream about my wonderful day.
9. When we arrived home, I stumbled up the steps and into the house.
10. Minutes later, my head was on my pillow and I was dreaming again.

Publish

+Presentation

Publishing Strategy Display the biographic sketch on a "Who Am I?" bulletin board in the school hallway.

Presentation Strategy Use clear, readable fonts or neat handwriting.

Done! Now it's time for the fun part—publishing my work. I've decided to display my sketch on a "Who Am I?" board in the school hallway. I know my work must be legible for display. That means I should use a word processor to type my work in a clear, readable font. If I write my sketch by hand, I should use my best handwriting. I'll use the spell checker, but I'll also be sure to check my spelling myself, because the computer won't catch errors such as typing *to* when I should use *too*. First I need to check my paper one last time against my checklist.

My Final Checklist

Did I—

- ✔ fix any dangling modifiers?
- ✔ correctly and effectively use all prepositional phrases?
- ✔ correct any spelling, grammar, or punctuation errors?
- ✔ neatly handwrite or type out my biographic sketch?

Apply

Make a final checklist to check your own biographic sketch. Then make a final copy to publish.

SLED DOG SETH

by Andre

Meet Sled Dog Seth! Seth is a seventh grader at Nell Scott Middle School. At school, Seth is just like anybody else. But after school, most often, you see Seth dressed in blue jeans, an unzipped parka, and shiny green rubber boots, carrying a bucket of smelly brown kibbles. A steel scoop sticks out the top. He is heading out to feed the sled dogs.

"I love my dogs!" Seth always says. "They are a part of my family, just like my mom and dad and my sister, Katie." His boots make a squishing sound in the spongy ground. As he nears the dog pens, the squishing sound is drowned out by barking. The dogs' metal food pans go skittering as the dogs run up to the fence. Seth rubs their silky fur and lets each dog lick his face right up to the roots of his carrot-colored hair. He is kind and affectionate as he feeds the dogs. With a crunch, the scoop hits the kibbles. With a clatter, the kibbles hit the pans.

After the dogs' dinner, Seth hitches them up to a sled. He checks each dog's paws and adjusts reins and harnesses. He pulls up his hood and zips up the parka. Then he yells, "Mush!" and off he goes! Snowflakes hit his face like a thousand needles. The cold wind turns his nose bright red.

Seth is growing fast. He grew three inches taller over the summer, making him the tallest, skinniest boy in his class! He always gets invited to play on the school's basketball team, but he always shakes his head no. "I don't have time. After school, I work with the dogs," he says. That's his life. His parents have cared for sled dogs all their lives, and so will Seth!

Reflect

Check Andre's biographic sketch against the rubric. Did he do a good job? Use the rubric and your checklist to check your own biographic sketch.

What's an Observation Report?

It's a report that describes an object, person, event, or process that the writer has seen. It's my chance to describe something amazing.

What's in an Observation Report?

Information
An observation report is about facts. It presents a lot of information by using descriptive language to help the reader "see" the subject.

Concrete Details
Sometimes I read things that make no sense to me because there are no concrete details to support the ideas. I'll include plenty of concrete details to help my readers grasp exactly what I'm describing. I'll include some pictures, too.

Personal Experiences
Writing lets me tell about things that have happened to me or things that I have experienced. In Alaska, there are so many things that other people don't often see. I can bring those things to life for people who have never been to the North.

Organization
Ideas can't be all jumbled up or just presented in an unconnected list! I'll need to group my observations into paragraphs and lead the reader through them with logical transitions.

Why write an Observation Report?

There are plenty of reasons for writing an observation report. I listed some here.

Entertainment

Some things that I see are so strange, beautiful, or mysterious that I just want to share them with someone else. Entertaining the reader is one good reason to write an observation report.

Personal Reflection

Writing about something I've seen will help me to understand it better because I have to think it through in order to put my thoughts in words.

Information

Some observations can inform the reader. My story can bring experiences from Alaska down to the mainland.

Contribution to Science

Most science involves observation. Astronomers observe the stars. Biologists watch and observe animals and plants. Their observations build understanding and knowledge. I can contribute, too! Sharpening my observation skills will be important to my success in science.

Linking Descriptive Writing Traits to an Observation Report

In this chapter, you will describe an object, person, event, or process. This type of descriptive writing is called an observation report. Andre will guide you through the stages of the writing process: Prewrite, Draft, Revise, Edit, and Publish. In each stage, Andre will show you important writing strategies that are linked to the Descriptive Writing Traits below.

Descriptive Writing Traits

- a clear topic that is developed by relevant supporting details
- descriptive details that are well chosen for the topic

- well-organized paragraphs that logically follow the order of the description, whether by time, location, or another order
- varied and appropriate transitions that show the relationship between ideas and concepts

- a voice that is appropriate for the purpose and audience

- precise words and phrases, possibly including figurative language, that create an accurate picture for the reader

- sentences that vary in length and type to add flow to the writing

- no or few errors in grammar, usage, mechanics, and spelling

Before you write, read Naomi Greenberg's observation report on the next page. Then use the observation report rubric on pages 410–411 to decide how well she did. (You might want to look back at What's in an Observation Report? on page 406, too!)

Observation Report Model

Observations of a Bird Watcher

by Naomi Greenberg

An outdoor bird feeder can be fun to observe any time of the year. Watching the one in my backyard for just a few months gave me a real education in bird behavior.

Factual information

Personal experience

Cardinals, for example, are not only beautiful, they are also very clever. The all-red, crested male approaches the feeder on his own and checks out the territory. When he has made sure no enemies (that is, cats) are nearby, he leaves, and then the female, more brown than red, arrives to feed at her leisure. Mr. Cardinal still keeps watch, though, from a nearby branch. Later, he and his mate may perch together in an out-of-the-way spot, with the male transferring tasty tidbits from his beak to hers. At such moments the two may "cheep" softly to each other. At other times, though, their call may be loud, almost strident.

Concrete details

Other loud birds around the feeder are the blue jays. These crested fellows are good-looking, but they have very poor manners, pushing smaller birds away in their eagerness to eat. Only recently did I realize that some of the jay's noisiness has a purpose. Listening to the bird's loud, repeated "jay, jay" call one day, it occurred to me that it sounded like a warning siren. I looked out at the feeder, and sure enough, a cat was stalking nearby.

Organized with logical transitions

Besides the beautiful cardinals and jays, several more ordinary-looking birds often crowd around the feeder. Flocks of gray-brown sparrows usually arrive in groups but politely wait their turn, perching on the telephone wire just above the feeder. House finches, sparrow-like birds with a reddish forehead and breast, show the same good manners, chattering to each other as they sit and wait. Mourning doves often pick at seeds that have fallen from the feeder.

During spring migration, new species arrive. Tiny, bright yellow goldfinches dropped by one day late last April. But the biggest thrill was the visit of the gorgeous grosbeaks. One or two of the black, white, and gold-colored males came first, in early May, followed the next day by at least ten companions. After a day or two of feeding, the birds lost their bedraggled look and moved on, perhaps to other bird feeders.

Rubric

Use this 6-point rubric to plan and evaluate an observation report.

	6	5	4
Ideas	Concrete details support each topic sentence. Visuals support the text.	Concrete details support most topic sentences. Visuals support the text.	Some details are vague and do not support the topic sentences. Visuals are included.
Organization	Varied, appropriate transitions create cohesion and make the paragraphs easy to follow.	Appropriate transitions create cohesion and help the paragraphs flow.	Transitions are appropriate and helpful most of the time but lack variety.
Voice	The writer's voice is informative and enthusiastic. It draws the reader into the text.	The writer's voice is informative and enthusiastic.	The writer's voice loses energy as the report progresses. More knowledge of the topic would help.
Word Choice	Precise words and phrases capture the experience and bring it to life for the reader.	Precise words and phrases describe the experience clearly.	In some places, imprecise words and phrases create a fuzzy picture for the reader.
Sentence Fluency	Varied sentence lengths and patterns make the report enjoyable to read.	Varied sentence lengths and patterns are noticeable.	There is some variety in sentence lengths and beginnings.
Conventions	Subjects and verbs agree. The meaning is clear.	A few minor errors in subject-verb agreement are present, but they do not interfere with the meaning.	A few problems with subject-verb agreement may confuse the reader.
+Presentation	Paragraphs are indented.		

3	2	1	
Several topic sentences lack supporting details. Visuals are included but do not relate to the text.	Few or no concrete details are included. Topic sentences are missing or unsupported. Visuals are missing or unrelated.	The writer has included neither topic sentences nor concrete details. No visuals are used.	Ideas
Transitions are lacking in some places. Transitions that are included may be inappropriate or lack variety.	Transitions are lacking, dull, and/or incorrectly used.	The writer has included no transitions.	Organization
The writer's voice is flat and poorly informed in places.	The writer's voice is sometimes difficult to identify.	The writer's voice is missing.	Voice
Words and phrases are vague in several places; the reader has to work to understand the experience.	The descriptions are very hard to follow because the words and phrases are too broad or vague.	The description is impossible to understand because the language is too vague.	Word Choice
Sentence beginnings and lengths tend to be the same.	Many sentences are too short or too similar. The report is choppy to read.	Some sentences are incomplete or incorrect.	Sentence Fluency
Many problems with subject-verb agreement interfere with meaning.	Many problems with subject-verb agreement are present, and they constantly interfere with meaning.	Frequent, serious errors with subject-verb agreement make the writing very hard to understand.	Conventions

See Appendix B for 4-, 5-, and 6-point descriptive rubrics.

Using the Observation Report Rubric to Study the Model

Did you notice that the model on page 409 points out some key elements of an observation report? As she wrote "Observations of a Bird Watcher," Naomi Greenberg used these elements to help her describe her experience. She also used the 6-point rubric on pages 410–411 to plan, draft, revise, and edit the writing. A rubric is a great tool to evaluate writing during the writing process.

Now let's use the same rubric to score the model. To do this, we'll focus on each trait separately, starting with Ideas. We'll use the top descriptor for each trait (column 6), along with examples from the model, to help us understand how the traits work together. How would you score Naomi on each trait?

- **Concrete details support each topic sentence.**
- **Visuals support the text.**

Naomi uses many concrete details to support her ideas. Look how she follows her topic sentence about cardinals with solid information that explains just why she thinks cardinals are clever. The picture she uses adds to my understanding by providing a great visual of these interesting birds.

[from the writing model]

Cardinals, for example, are not only beautiful, they are also very clever. The all-red, crested male approaches the feeder on his own and checks out the territory. When he has made sure no enemies (that is, cats) are nearby, he leaves, and then the female, more brown than red, arrives to feed at her leisure.

- **Varied, appropriate transitions create cohesion and make the paragraphs easy to follow.**

Writing that has cohesion is writing that fits together well. All parts are logically connected and flow together smoothly. Naomi uses transitions to connect ideas and paragraphs, so it is easy to follow along. Here, she uses the phrase *Other loud birds* to make a graceful transition to discussing blue jays.

[from the writing model]

Other loud birds around the feeder are the blue jays. These crested fellows are good-looking, but they have very poor manners, pushing smaller birds away in their eagerness to eat.

- **The writer's voice is informative and enthusiastic.**
- **It draws the reader into the text.**

Naomi definitely knows what she's talking about. Her voice is energetic and respectful of these tiny creatures. Bird watching sounds like fun!

[from the writing model]

Listening to the bird's loud, repeated "jay, jay" call one day, it occurred to me that it sounded like a warning siren. I looked out at the feeder, and sure enough, a cat was stalking nearby.

- **Precise words and phrases capture the experience and bring it to life for the reader.**

Naomi uses words that accurately and clearly describe what she sees. Precise words such as *perch* and *tasty tidbits* create a stronger image than general words such as *sit* and *food.*

[from the writing model]

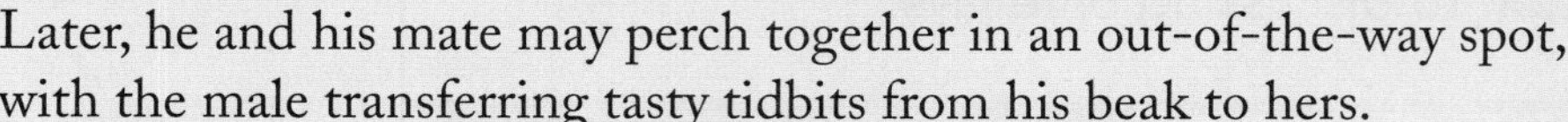

Later, he and his mate may perch together in an out-of-the-way spot, with the male transferring tasty tidbits from his beak to hers.

- **Varied sentence lengths and patterns make the report enjoyable to read.**

Naomi has a nice mix of short and long sentences, and there is variety in their structure. Here are some examples. The first example starts with a dependent clause; the second example starts with a prepositional phrase.

[from the writing model]

When he has made sure no enemies (that is, cats) are nearby, he leaves. . .

[from the writing model]

During spring migration, new species arrive.

- **Subjects and verbs agree.**
- **The meaning is clear.**

I didn't notice any problems with Naomi's subject-verb agreement in the report. The following sentences show you how carefully she avoids this error.

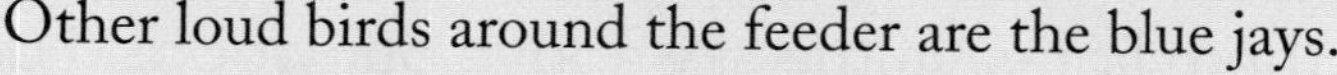

[from the writing model]

Other loud birds around the feeder are the blue jays.

[from the writing model]

House finches, sparrow-like birds with a reddish forehead and breast, show the same good manners . . .

Presentation Paragraphs are indented.

My Turn!

Now it's my turn to write! I'm going to write an observation report of my own. Watch to see how I use the rubric to practice good writing strategies.

Prewrite

Focus on Ideas

The Rubric Says Concrete details support each topic sentence.

Writing Strategy Choose an aspect of nature to observe. Make notes (with sketches) about the observations.

Last week Mom and I saw the aurora borealis, or northern lights, in the sky above our woods. I decided the lights would be a perfect topic for my observation report.

Last night the northern lights were back, and the show was amazing! To plan my report, I made notes and drew sketches of what I saw. I'll use both to add lots of concrete details to my report. I want my reader to understand exactly what I experienced.

My Notes on the Aurora Borealis

- ✔ cold night, crisp breezes, smell of fresh pine
- ✔ one arc of light spreads across the sky, followed by several more (white, with red and purple at edges)
- ✔ rays of light form "drapes" across the sky, seem to blow softly in the wind (light up whole sky)
- ✔ hissing noises as sky lights up
- ✔ drapes disappear and reappear as new rays shoot down from space (white with purple in between)
- ✔ after 10–15 minutes drapes start to spread wider, color starts to fade
- ✔ lights blink on and off, then disappear

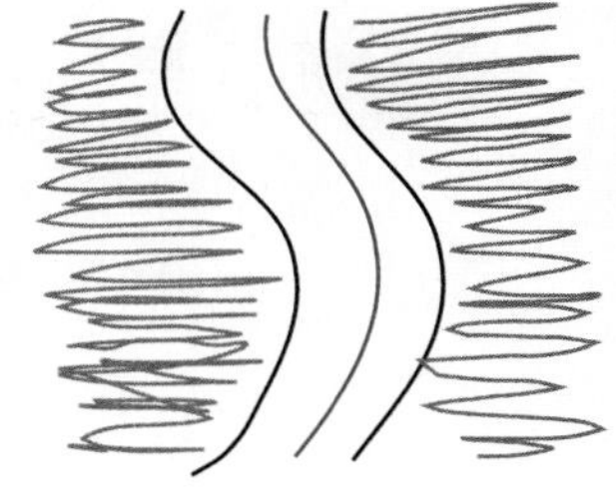

Apply

Think about things you have seen. Choose one to write about and gather information by making notes on what you saw.

Prewrite

Focus on **Organization**

The Rubric Says Varied, appropriate transitions create cohesion and make the paragraphs easy to follow.

Writing Strategy Make an Observation Chart to organize the notes around the five senses.

Writer's Term

Observation Chart

An **Observation Chart** organizes information that has been gathered by using sight, sound, touch, taste, and smell. Appealing to as many senses as possible is a good way to get the reader involved in the experience.

So I thought it would be helpful to organize my notes into an Observation Chart. Organizing my notes will also help me write strong, well-focused paragraphs. Once I have my observations organized by senses, it will be easy to think about a variety of transitions between paragraphs.

OBSERVATION CHART

TOPIC: aurora borealis

SIGHT	SOUND	TOUCH	TASTE	SMELL
• arcs of white light spread across the sky (red and purple at edges) • rays of light form "drapes" that seem to sway in the wind • drapes disappear, then reappear (mostly white; purple in between) • lights spread thinner, blink on and off, fade out	• hissing noises at height of light show	• crisp evening breezes		• sweet smell of pine trees in the air

Reflect

How will organizing details according to the senses help Andre write a logical report?

Apply

Use an Observation Chart to organize your ideas around the five senses.

Draft

Focus on **Organization**

The Rubric Says Varied, appropriate transitions create cohesion and make the paragraphs easy to follow.

Writing Strategy Use transitions to connect ideas.

Once I collected all my information, I was ready to draft my report. I decided to describe the light show in the order in which things happened. This wasn't too difficult because I had listed the sights on my observation chart in chronological, or time, order.

The rubric reminds me that transitions are important. Well-chosen transitions will guide my reader through my paragraphs. They'll also connect my ideas in a logical way. That's what *cohesion* means—it's what happens when the ideas in an essay are clearly and strongly linked. Since I'm writing my essay in chronological order, I'll think about including time-order transitions in logical places.

When I drafted my report, I worried mainly about getting my ideas down. I figured I could check for errors later.

Writer's Term

Transitions

Transitions are words or phrases that link ideas between or within paragraphs. Some time-order transition words are *first, while,* and *then.*

Proofreading Marks

- Indent
- Make uppercase
- Make lowercase
- Add something
- Take out something
- Add a period
- New paragraph
- Spelling error

[DRAFT]

Observing the Aurora Borealis, or Northern Lights

Sometimes I'm really happy that we live so far north. This is the reason. If you are lucky, on certin nights you may see the aurora borealis, or northern lights.

[transition within paragraph]

[time-order transition]

It is a perfect night for a light show. The air feels crisp and cold as a gentle breeze touches my skin. I can smell the fresh pine trees growing in the nearby woods. Stars are twinkeling.

While I watch the sky, a great white arc of light begin to appear. It stretches larger and larger. Several more follow it. They expand. They become red and purple, especially at the edges.

Then the formation changes. Green and white rays of light seems to drop straight down from above. The rays flow and form themselves into drapes that spred across the entire sky. The drapes are mostly white, but with some purple in between. A hissing noise begins as the drapes slowly disappear and then reppear in new forms.

Reflect

How did Andre do? How did his transitions help link his ideas together?

Apply

Write a draft using observations from your Observation Chart and including a variety of appropriate transitions.

Revise

Focus on 

The Rubric Says The writer's voice is informative and enthusiastic. It draws the reader into the text.

Writing Strategy Show that I know and care a lot about the subject.

Writer's Term

Personal Reaction
A **personal reaction** tells how an observation made you feel and what it made you think about.

I like what I've written so far. I think my reader will picture the aurora borealis vividly. But my voice seems a little flat and boring. I think I need to add my personal reactions to my observations to liven things up. Watching the lights was thrilling, and I want my audience to feel my excitement as they read.

[DRAFT]

[added personal reaction] → Inside, my heart is beating faster. Seeing the northern lights is exciting!

It is a perfect night for a light show. The air feels crisp and cold as a gentle breeze touches my skin. I can smell the fresh pine trees growing in the nearby woods. Stars are twinkeling.

While I watch the sky, a great white arc of light begin to appear. It stretches larger and larger. Several more follow it.

Apply

How did your observation make you feel? Add some personal reactions to your writing.

Revise

Focus on Word Choice

The Rubric Says Precise words and phrases capture the experience and bring it to life for the reader.

Writing Strategy Replace ordinary, vague words with specific words.

The rubric says I should use specific words to bring my experience to life for my reader. As I reread my draft, I notice some of my words are vague and overused. It only makes sense that the more creative and specific my words are, the easier it will be for the reader to share my experience with the aurora borealis. I'll replace the vague words with stronger, more specific words now. What do you think of my revisions?

[DRAFT]

After ten or fifteen minutes, the aurora borealis starts to ~~go~~ fade away. The formation of drapes get wider and wider but becomes less and less ~~there~~ distinct.

[replaced vague words]

Reflect

Now that Andre has replaced vague words with specific words, can you better envision the lights?

Apply

Replace overused, vague words with colorful, specific words in your report.

Revise

Focus on 

The Rubric Says Varied sentence lengths and patterns make the report enjoyable to read.

Writing Strategy Vary sentence patterns for meaning, reader interest, and style.

Writer's Term

Sentence Pattern

A **sentence pattern** is the order in which the parts of a sentence are arranged. Sentence patterns include subject-verb (*The dog ate*) and subject-verb-object (*The dog ate her dinner*). Using the same sentence pattern over and over makes your writing boring.

Now to check for sentence fluency. The rubric tells me I should vary my sentence lengths and patterns to keep things interesting. I found one paragraph that needed work, so I revised it to add variety. I think the meaning comes through more clearly in my revised sentences, too.

[DRAFT]

[combined sentences]

It stretches larger and larger, and soon several more follow it. ~~They expand~~ as they expand. They become red and purple, especially at the edges.

Do your sentence beginnings all sound the same? If so, replace some of them with a descriptive clause or phrase.

Edit

Focus on 

The Rubric Says Subjects and verbs agree. The meaning is clear.

Writing Strategy Check to see that the subject and verb in each sentence agree.

Writer's Term

Subject-Verb Agreement

Singular subjects name only one thing and must be used with singular verbs. Singular verbs usually end in *-s* or *-es*. Plural subjects name more than one thing and must be used with plural verbs. The pronoun *you* also uses a plural verb. Compound subjects joined with *and* are generally plural.

Now I have to look for errors. I always check for grammar mistakes and misspelled words. According to the rubric, I should also make sure subjects agree with verbs.

[DRAFT]

[corrected subject-verb agreement error]

Then the formation changes. Green and white rays of light seems to drop straight down from above.

Reflect

Check over Andre's writing. Has he fixed all subject-verb agreement errors? Can you find any other mistakes?

Apply Conventions

Edit your draft for spelling, punctuation, and capitalization. Check for and fix subject-verb agreement errors.

For more practice fixing errors with subject-verb agreement, use the exercises on the next two pages.

Subject-Verb Agreement

Know the Rule

Use **singular subjects** with **singular verbs**. Use **plural subjects** and the pronoun *you* with **plural verbs.**

Example: Singular: The **dog runs** fast. Plural: The **dogs run** fast.

Compound subjects joined with *and* are nearly always plural. In compound subjects joined with *or* or *nor,* the verb agrees with the last item in the subject.

Example: The **dog and the cat like** to play in the snow. The **dog or the cat likes** to play in the snow.

Be sure that the verb agrees with the subject and not with the object of a preposition that comes before the verb.

Example: **One** of the dogs **is** hungry.

To make sure the subject and verb agree in a question, reword the sentence as an answer to the question in subject-verb order.

Example: Question: Where **are** the **collars** for the dogs?
Reworded: The **collars** for the dogs **are** in the basement.

Practice the Rule

Write each sentence correctly on a separate sheet of paper.

1. An aurora borealis (is/are) not the only unusual sight in the night sky.
2. The region above storm clouds also (contain/contains) remarkable lights.
3. Sprites, elves, and blue jets (is/are) the names given to these light forms.
4. (Has/Have) you ever heard of these formations before?
5. The flashes of light given off by a sprite (creates/create) a curtain-like effect above thunderstorm clouds.
6. The core of a storm's clouds (is/are) the source of a blue jet.
7. Elves (is/are) disk-shaped and (last/lasts) only thousandths of a second.
8. Pictures of blue jets (has/have) been taken from airplanes.
9. Scientists (is/are) still learning about these light forms.
10. I (am/are) lucky to have seen these light forms.

More Subject-Verb Agreement

Know the Rule

A **collective noun**—such as *collection, group, team, country,* or *family*—names more than one person or object acting together as one group. These nouns are almost always considered singular.

Example: My whole **family is** moving to Iowa.

Most **indefinite pronouns**, including *everyone, nobody, nothing, something,* and *anything*, are considered singular.

Example: I know **someone** who **likes** broccoli on pizza.

A few indefinite pronouns, such as *many* and *several*, are considered plural.

Example: I know **many** who **like** plain cheese pizza.

Practice the Rule

Choose the correct verb in each sentence below. Then write the complete sentences on a separate sheet of paper.

1. Everyone (has/have) a favorite seasonal tradition.
2. Several (is/are) specific to just one family.
3. For example, every summer around the Fourth of July, my whole family (gathers/gather) at my grandparents' lake house.
4. Everyone (knows/know) to take a nap in the afternoon because we'll be up late.
5. In the afternoon, a group of us (goes/go) for a swim in the cold lake.
6. Later, nothing (beats/beat) a bonfire by the lake with all my relatives gathered together to watch it.
7. Someone always (brings/bring) marshmallows we can roast.
8. We play charades by the light of the fire, and my team always (wins/win).
9. Some of us, especially the younger ones, (goes/go) to bed after charades.
10. Many (stays/stay) up until midnight talking quietly and enjoying the night.

Publish +Presentation

Publishing Strategy Add the report to the class's science journal.

Presentation Strategy Indent every paragraph.

I think I'm done now! My report is about the aurora borealis, something that doesn't happen very often and that many people have never seen. I'm sure readers will find it interesting, so that's why I'm excited to include my report in my science class's journal. To make my text more readable, I need to indent each new paragraph. Indenting makes it easy for readers to tell when a new paragraph—and a new idea—is starting. Last I'll check my work one more time against my final checklist. I want my report to be perfect!

My Final Checklist

Did I—

- ✔ make sure all subjects and verbs agree?
- ✔ indent each new paragraph?
- ✔ use proper grammar, spelling, and punctuation?

Apply

Make your own final checklist to check your observation report. Then make a final copy to publish.

Observing the Aurora Borealis, or Northern Lights

by Andre J.

Sometimes I'm really happy that we live so far north. This is the reason. If you are lucky, on certain nights you may see the aurora borealis, or northern lights. Here is my observation from a night last week when the lights appeared.

It is a perfect night for a light show. The air feels crisp and cold as a gentle breeze touches my skin. I can smell the fresh pine trees growing in the nearby woods. Stars are twinkling. Inside, my heart is beating faster. Seeing the northern lights is exciting!

While I watch the sky, a great white arc of light begins to appear. It stretches, larger and larger, and soon several more follow it. They become red and purple, especially at the edges, as they expand.

Then the formation changes. Green and white rays of light seem to drop straight down from above. The rays flow and form themselves into drapes that spread across the entire sky. The drapes are mostly white, but I see some purple in between. A hissing noise begins as the drapes slowly disappear and then reappear in new forms.

After ten or fifteen minutes, the aurora borealis starts to fade away. The formation of drapes gets wider and wider but becomes less and less distinct. The lights seem to blink on and off. Finally, they disappear altogether.

Reflect

What do you think? Did Andre use all the traits of a good observation report? Check it against the rubric. Then use the rubric to check your own report.

What's a Geographic Description?

It's a detailed report about a particular place. I think this kind of writing will be interesting because I get to do some research.

What's in a Geographic Description?

Point of View
My description can be from either first-person or third-person point of view. If I write about a place I've actually been to, then I'll use first-person point of view. Otherwise, it makes more sense to write from the third-person point of view.

Real-Place Focus
The report is focused on one real place. This means that my report must be true. And the facts must come from a good source. I'll need to use reference books such as an atlas and reliable websites.

Descriptive Details
I want my readers to really know what it's like to be at this place, so I'll bring it to life with lots of accurate details and make sure I include only facts that are relevant to my description.

Organization
I'll organize my description with an introduction, body, and conclusion. The body is where I'll give most of the details about the place. Further, I'll organize the information into categories that make sense to the reader.

Why write a Geographic Description?

There are all kinds of reasons to write a geographic description. Here are some of them. I'll have to think about them to help me decide what to write about.

Entertainment

I've read about many interesting places. I can entertain readers with my own description of a place. Entertainment is a good reason to write a geographic description.

Virtual Travel

I can travel all over the world and even to worlds that have never existed by reading about them. Now I'll help other people to travel virtually with my own geographic description.

Share Information

Writing a geographic description is a great way to share information about a place. I can write a description to educate, instruct, or inform my reader.

Understanding

Sometimes reading about places can feel like fact overload. Deciding which details to use in a piece of writing, however, helps me think through how they are important.

Linking Descriptive Traits to a Geographic Description

In this chapter, you will describe a place. This type of descriptive writing is called a geographic description. Andre will guide you through the stages of the writing process: Prewrite, Draft, Revise, Edit, and Publish. In each stage, Andre will show you important writing strategies that are linked to the Descriptive Writing Traits below.

Descriptive Writing Traits

- a clear topic that is developed by relevant supporting details
- descriptive details that are well chosen for the topic

- well-organized paragraphs that logically follow the order of the description, whether by time, location, or another order
- varied and appropriate transitions that show the relationship between ideas and concepts

- a voice that is appropriate for the purpose and audience

- precise words and phrases, possibly including figurative language, that create an accurate picture for the reader

- sentences that vary in length and type to add flow to the writing

- no or few errors in grammar, usage, mechanics, and spelling

Before you write, read Timothy O'Malley's geographic description on the next page. Then use the geographic description rubric on pages 432–433 to decide how well he did. (You might want to look back at What's in a Geographic Description? on page 428, too!)

Geographic Description Model

A Visit to the Past

by Timothy O'Malley

Third-person point of view

Introduction

In August of A.D. 79, life ended for the Italian city of Pompeii. Mount Vesuvius, a volcano just to the north, exploded with violent force. Most of the city's citizens escaped, but some refused to leave their homes. Everyone who stayed behind was either asphyxiated by poisonous gases or buried alive under pumice, ash, and other materials. Buried in more than 15 feet of volcanic debris, Pompeii remained untouched for centuries. Excavations have now uncovered the remains of a city that was literally stopped dead in its tracks.

In Pompeii today, it is possible to see evidence of the citizens' everyday life and of the sudden, terrible death of many. The remains help to paint a picture of the city as it was when time stood still on that August day.

Relevant facts

The Forum is where major religious and government events took place. Much of it is still standing. Several two-story marble columns that marked off the open meeting area remain. They hover like sentinels standing guard. Nearby are half-destroyed temples and other buildings. East of the city lies the amphitheater. Grass covers much of it now with a soft green blanket. But it is easy to imagine audiences shouting and applauding as they watched gladiators perform here.

Stores and businesses are on many of the streets. These provide a close look at where citizens bought and sold their wares. Baked goods, fine woven cloth, and drinking vessels were just a few of the items that citizens could buy. Some of the stores stood separate from other buildings. Others were tucked into corners of larger homes. Still others were storefronts, with families living behind them.

Accurate details

One fascinating aspect of Pompeii is the large number of private houses. Nowhere else is it possible to see such a wide range of structures from so many time periods. One structure is called the House of the Faun. It fills a full city block. Its walls feature beautiful mosaics and murals. Other large homes feature elaborate, pillared entrances. Most are decorated with floor mosaics worked into detailed patterns. Such houses generally enclose lovely courtyards and gardens.

The excavations of the buildings and streets of Pompeii show a well-off, bustling city. Other remains show just how quickly the volcano did its work. Many human remains were found. Covered with layers of smoothed-down molten ash, the bodies look like sculptures made of soft clay. Many were found in completely natural positions. They probably never knew what hit them.

A site like Pompeii can show us many things. It can show how citizens of ancient Roman cities lived and worked. It can show us their art and culture. It also points out very clearly how overwhelming natural forces can be. There are indeed many lessons to learn from Pompeii.

Body

Conclusion

Rubric

Use this 6-point rubric to plan and evaluate a geographic description.

	6	5	4
Ideas	Relevant facts and accurate details develop the topic. Thoughtful comparisons clarify the writer's ideas.	Many accurate details are used, and most facts are relevant. Comparisons are used effectively.	Some imprecise details and irrelevant facts are used, but the topic is developed. At least one comparison is used effectively.
Organization	Information is logically organized into categories. The introduction, body, and conclusion work well together.	Most information is organized into logical categories. There is a clear introduction, body, and conclusion.	Some information is not in a logical category. Introduction, body, and conclusion are present but may not work well together.
Voice	The writer's voice suits the purpose and draws the reader in.	The writer's voice is strong. It connects consistently with the audience.	The voice comes and goes. It is acceptable for the writer's purpose and audience.
Word Choice	Figurative language is used in ways that are attention-getting and unusual. It enhances the description.	Figurative language is used in clear and original ways and is effective.	Figurative language is often clear and somewhat effective.
Sentence Fluency	Great variety in sentence lengths and beginnings make the writing a pleasure to read.	The writing contains a significant variety in sentence length. It flows well.	Some of the sentences vary in length and are easy to read.
Conventions	Adjectives and adverbs are used correctly and enhance the writing.	A few minor errors in the use of adjectives and adverbs do not distract the reader.	Some noticeable errors in the use of adjectives and adverbs may distract the reader.

+Presentation Visuals are thoughtfully integrated with the text.

3	2	1	
Several imprecise details or irrelevant facts distract the reader. The writer uses comparisons, but they are not clear.	The writing is hard to follow because many details and facts are wrong or irrelevant. No comparisons are used.	Facts and details are vague and not connected to the topic. No comparisons are used.	Ideas
The logic of the categories is hard to follow. The introduction or conclusion is missing.	Information is not organized into categories. The introduction and conclusion are missing.	Information is random and unconnected. There is no sign of introduction, body, or conclusion.	Organization
The writer's voice is sincere. The voice may not be acceptable for the topic.	The voice isn't always identifiable and isn't a good match for the purpose and audience.	This is the wrong voice for this piece of writing. It is not appropriate for the purpose and audience.	Voice
Figurative language is vague and unclear.	Figurative language is misused.	The writing contains no figurative language.	Word Choice
The writing sounds choppy. Many sentences are about the same length.	The writing may contain run-on and choppy or incomplete sentences. There is little variety in length.	Fragments and choppy sentences make the writing difficult to read.	Sentence Fluency
Several errors in the use of adjectives and adverbs make the reader pause.	Many errors in the use of adjectives and adverbs make the writing hard to understand in places.	Many serious errors in the use of adjectives and adverbs make the writing very hard to understand.	Conventions

See Appendix B for 4-, 5-, and 6-point descriptive rubrics.

Using the Geographic Description Rubric to Study the Model

Did you notice that the model on page 431 points out some key elements of a geographic description? As he wrote "A Visit to the Past," Timothy O'Malley used these elements to help him write a geographic description. He also used the 6-point rubric on pages 432–433 to plan, draft, revise, and edit the writing. A rubric is a great tool to evaluate writing during the writing process.

Now let's use the same rubric to score the model. To do this, we'll focus on each trait separately, starting with Ideas. We'll use the top descriptor for each trait (column 6), along with examples from the model, to help us understand how the traits work together. How would you score Timothy on each trait?

- **Relevant facts and accurate details develop the topic.**
- **Thoughtful comparisons clarify the writer's ideas.**

Timothy definitely did some research before writing his geographic description. The way he easily blends accurate facts and creative comparisons keeps me interested and informs me about Pompeii.

[from the writing model]

In August of A.D. 79, life ended for the Italian city of Pompeii. Mount Vesuvius, a volcano just to the north, exploded with violent force.

[from the writing model]

Covered with layers of smoothed-down molten ash, the bodies look like sculptures made of soft clay.

- **Information is logically organized into categories.**
- **The introduction, body, and conclusion work well together.**

Timothy introduces his topic in the introduction. He then logically organizes his information into categories, with each body paragraph describing a different type of building. Finally he neatly wraps up his discussion in a brief conclusion.

[from the writing model]

A site like Pompeii can show us many things. It can show how citizens of ancient Roman cities lived and worked. It can show us their art and culture. It also points out very clearly how overwhelming natural forces can be. There are indeed many lessons to learn from Pompeii.

- **The writer's voice suits the purpose and draws the reader in.**

As I read Timothy's paper, I could feel his respect and awe for Pompeii. His voice reflects that, although something tragic occurred there, Pompeii is beautiful and rich with history. It was easy to share his excitement and want to learn more about it all.

[from the writing model]

One fascinating aspect of Pompeii is the large number of private houses. Nowhere else is it possible to see such a wide range of structures from so many time periods.

- **Figurative language is used in ways that are attention-getting and unusual. It enhances the description.**

Timothy's use of figurative language, such as similes and metaphors, created powerful and vivid images in my mind as I read. Picturing grass as a soft green blanket, spread out across the amphitheater, enlivened the scene and really held my attention.

[from the writing model]

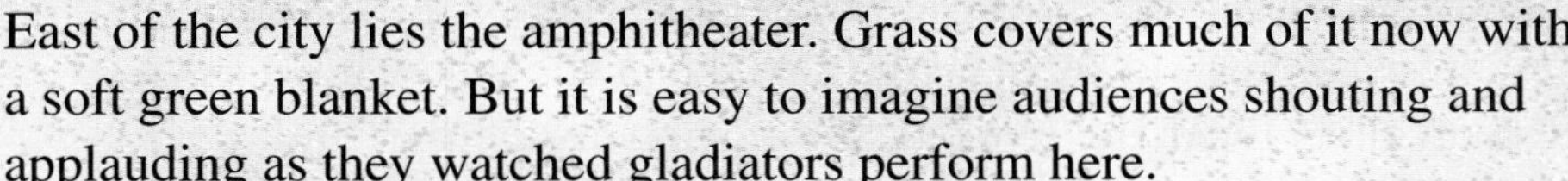
East of the city lies the amphitheater. Grass covers much of it now with a soft green blanket. But it is easy to imagine audiences shouting and applauding as they watched gladiators perform here.

- **Great variety in sentence lengths and beginnings make the writing a pleasure to read.**

Timothy uses both long and short sentences throughout his geographic description. This made reading it easier and more enjoyable. I will follow his lead and mix up my sentence lengths, too.

[from the writing model]

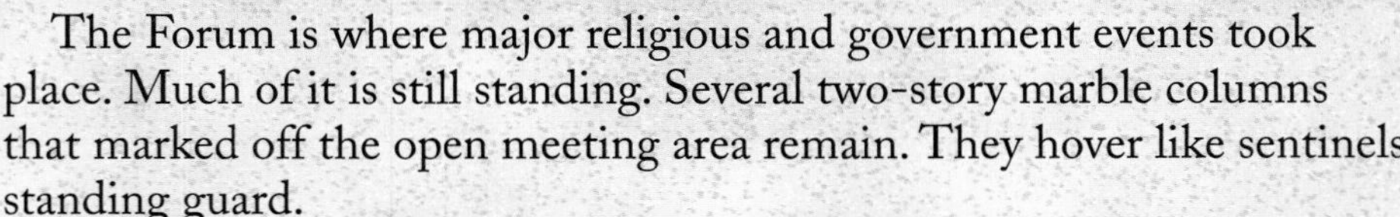
The Forum is where major religious and government events took place. Much of it is still standing. Several two-story marble columns that marked off the open meeting area remain. They hover like sentinels standing guard.

- **Adjectives and adverbs are used correctly and enhance the writing.**

The writer uses adjectives and adverbs correctly. Here are a few examples.

[from the writing model]

The excavations of the buildings and streets of Pompeii show a well-off, bustling city. Other remains show just how quickly the volcano did its work. Many human remains were found. Covered with layers of smoothed-down molten ash, the bodies look like sculptures made of soft clay.

+Presentation Visuals are thoughtfully integrated with the text.

My Turn!

I can't wait to get started on my own geographic description. I can follow the rubric and make sure I use good writing strategies. Read on to see how it turns out!

Prewrite

Focus on **Ideas**

The Rubric Says Relevant facts and accurate details develop the topic.

Writing Strategy Use an atlas to find a place to describe. Then research the place in three other appropriate sources.

Writer's Term

Atlas

An **atlas** is a book that contains maps and geographic information.

I went to the atlas to choose a place for my topic, but I didn't have to look long. I picked a place where it gets even colder than Alaska. I chose Antarctica!

The atlas showed the location of Antarctica and gave information about its terrain. When we talk about places in social studies class, though, we always include topics like climate, animals that live there, the people who live there, and other things. I know my audience will want to read information that will surprise as well as inform. So I'll do my research carefully to ensure my facts are accurate *and* interesting.

I came up with a list of questions I thought my audience would want answers for, so I jotted them down on an index card.

What does Antarctica look like?
What is the weather like in Antarctica?
What plants and animals live in Antarctica?
Do people live in Antarctica?

I followed the strategy and chose three sources, besides the atlas, to use for more information. It was fun to do research online, but I chose my Internet source carefully. Most Internet sites are good, but some are put together sloppily or offer opinions not supported by facts. And, as I said before, accuracy is key!

Writer's Term

Appropriate Source

An **appropriate source** is a place to get information that is suitable, right, or proper for your purpose. Here are some good sources of information about specific places:

- An **encyclopedia** to get a good overview of the place
- An **almanac** to get current facts and figures about things such as government, population, and dimensions of mountains and rivers
- A **travel guidebook** to learn about specific areas and what to see in them
- A **website** to get answers to common questions about the place and to see pictures of it

The three sources I chose were an encyclopedia, a website, and a recent book about Antarctica that I found in the school library. I jotted down notes from each source that would help me answer my questions.

Website:
mostly scientists live in Antarctica
they live in science "stations"
    Amundsen-Scott Station—huge geodesic dome
    McMurdo Station—more than 100 buildings
temperatures as low as –128°F

Encyclopedia:
fierce, biting winds
covered with huge sheet of ice
Emperor and Adélie penguins live there
huge birds called skuas live there

Library Book:
East Antarctica—a high, flat plateau
West Antarctica—mountainous islands
too dry to snow much
lichen and mosses grow

Apply

Choose an interesting place. Gather information by making notes on what you read.

Prewrite

Focus on **Organization**

The Rubric Says Information is logically organized into categories.

Writing Strategy Make a Web to organize the descriptive details.

I got a lot of information from my sources, but I needed to make it all work together. My strategy was to use a Web to organize the most important descriptive details into categories. My main categories came from my list of questions. They are in the green shapes.

Writer's Term

Web

A **Web** organizes details around a central topic.

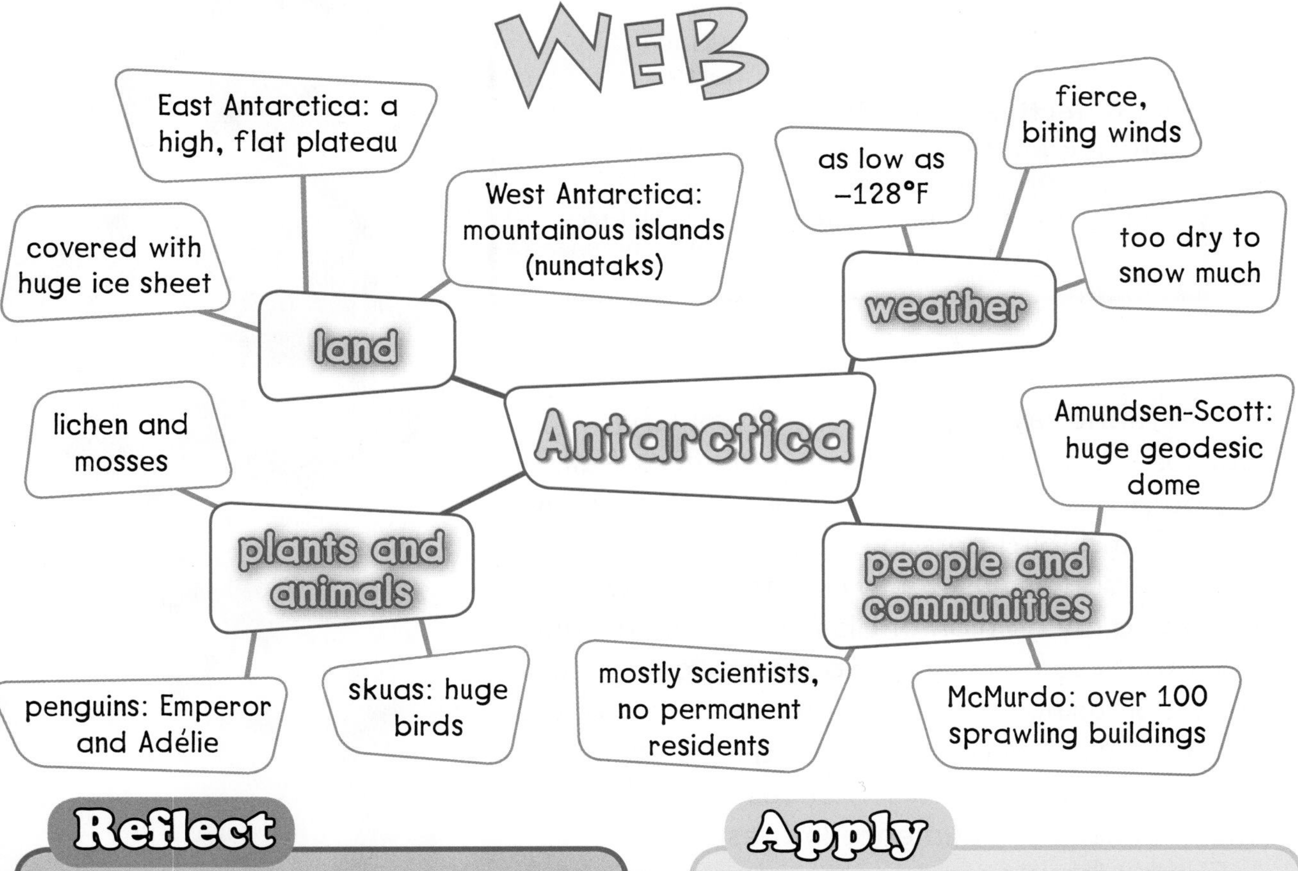

Reflect

How will Andre's Web help him when he writes his report? Did he include all the details he'll need?

Apply

Use a Web to organize the details you found when you researched your geographic description.

Draft

Focus on 

The Rubric Says The writer's voice suits the purpose and draws the reader in.

Writing Strategy Use third-person point of view and an objective tone.

Writer's Term

Objective Tone

Objective means sticking to the facts and avoiding emotions or opinions. When writing about a topic you have not experienced yourself, it's best to use an **objective tone**. This allows you to provide information creatively without sharing personal opinions or biases. Use third-person point of view (*he, she, it*) to support an objective tone.

The rubric says my voice should match my purpose and connect with my audience. Well, my purpose is to inform and my audience is my class. Using third-person point of view is perfect. Third person allows me to give the facts without providing my opinion or bias, while also making clear that I've never been to Antarctica myself. Although using third person takes me out of the writing, I can still give my writing a personality by crafting the words and sentences carefully. That will help keep my audience interested.

First I'll focus on getting my ideas down; I'll find and fix mistakes later. Now to start writing!

Proofreading Marks

Indent	Take out something
Make uppercase	Add a period
Make lowercase	New paragraph
Add something	Spelling error

[third-person point of view]

A White World

[DRAFT]

"Everywhere you look, all you see is white." This is how many travelers to Antarctica explain their reaction to this isolated continent. Antarctica is not a place where most people would want to live. However, to many visitors it appears quite remarkably.

Antarctica is covered almost complete with a huge ice sheet. It extends almost five and a half million square miles, and the thickly part averages about 6,500 feet. The land is divided into sections. East Antarctica is a high, flat plateau. West Antarctica is smallest. It is a series of mountainus islands held together by the ice sheet. Nunataks are mountains buried so deep that only their tips peek through the ice. Between East and West Antarctica are the Transantarctic mountains. They cut the land into two neat chunks. On either side of West Antarctica are big floating ice sheets. One, the Ross Ice Shelf, is as large as France.

[facts about the land]

Writing a Geographic Description

[DRAFT]

[facts about weather]

The weather in Antarctica is real cold. Winter tempertures drop as low as –128 degrees Fahrenheit. The average winter temperature range is from –40 to –94 degrees inland. These tempertures can freeze spit in midair! You have to take them serious. Winds are fierce and biting. Gusts over 100 miles per hour are not uncommon. Even in summer, in warmer coastal areas, +32 degrees is the average temperature. But no snow falls in many parts of Antarctica. Strong winds kick up existing snow, but the air is usually so dry that new snow cannot form. This is why Antarctica is sometimes called *The white Desert.*

Plants and animals are more commonlier in Antarctica than you might expect. There are several hundred species of lichens. They grow good along the rocks. They create colorful colonies of yellow, green, and black. Mosses can also be found. The main animals living in Antarctica are penguins, of which the emperor penguin, about three or four feet tall, scoots around the ice like an industrious headwaiter. The Adélie are slightly smaller and also live in large colonies. The South Polar skua is a huge and powerful flying bird. It has been seen as far inland as the Pole. It has also been seen as far north as the Equator.

[facts about plants and animals]

[facts about people]

[DRAFT]

Surprisingly, people also live in Antarctica. Nearly all of them are scientists. (No one, though, makes this cold continent a permanent home.) Including the United States, 29 countries have research stations. The largest is the American facility called McMurdo Station. It is on Ross Island in the Ross Ice Shelf. This community contains about 100 low, sprawling buildings. There are dormitories, a gymnasium, a science lab, and other structures. About 250 people spend the winter there. In summer, the population rises to 1,000. A smaller facility is the Amundsen-Scott South Pole Station. It is very close to the Pole. The main building is a huge aluminum geodesic dome. It is more than 55 feet high at its highest point. Housing space for 27 people, equipment depots, and various research areas are either within it or connected to it by covered passageways. Glinting in the sun in the empty Antarctic plain, the station looks like the hom of visitors from another planet.

Tourists do visit Antarctica. However, it can cost as much as $40,000 to get all the way to the South Pole. If they have the money and are adventuraous enough to make the trip, they can visit this unique isolated continent.

[conclusion]

Reflect

How did Andre do? Did he organize his details? Does his voice match his purpose and audience?

Apply

It's your turn to write a draft using details from your Web. Don't forget to start generally, then get specific, and go back to general for your conclusion.

Revise

Focus on **Ideas**

The Rubric Says Thoughtful comparisons clarify the writer's ideas.

Writing Strategy Use a comparison to make the description more complete.

The rubric tells me to use thoughtful comparisons to clarify my ideas. I know *I* learn new information best when it is paired up with something I already know. Comparing the new information with familiar knowledge really helps me grasp the idea. So I'll do this for my reader, too.

[DRAFT]

In Alaska, the average winter temperature ranges from 12 to −20 degrees. **[used a comparison]**

The weather in Antarctica is real cold. Winter tempertures drop as low as −128 degrees Fahrenheit. The average winter temperature in Antarctica range is from −40 to −94 degrees inland. These tempertures can freeze spit in midair!

Apply

Include some thoughtful comparisons in your geographic description to make your writing more complete.

Revise

Focus on **Word Choice**

The Rubric Says Figurative language is used in ways that are attention-getting and unusual.

Writing Strategy Add some figurative language, including similes and metaphors.

Writer's Term

Figurative Language

Figurative language is language that goes beyond the normal meaning of the words in it. Figurative language, which includes similes and metaphors, creates a mental picture for the reader. A simile compares two different things by using the words *like* or *as*. A metaphor compares two different things by calling one thing another.

I read my draft to my writing partner, Jill. She liked most of my descriptive details, but she said that my description of the land itself was kind of dull. So I went back and added some figurative language, including some similes and metaphors.

[DRAFT]

thickly part averages about 6,500 feet. The land is divided into sections. East Antarctica is a high, flat plateau —an icy table of land. West Antarctica is smallest. It is a series of mountainus islands held together by the ice sheet. In some areas, nunataks dot the surface like punctuation marks. Nunataks are mountains buried so deep that only their tips peek through the ice. Between East and West Antarctica are the

[added a metaphor]

[added a simile]

Reflect

How did using comparisons and figurative language affect Andre's writing?

Apply

Add some figurative language to your geographic description. Try to include at least one simile and at least one metaphor.

Revise

Focus on 

The Rubric Says Great variety in sentence lengths and beginnings make the writing a pleasure to read.

Writing Strategy Combine short, choppy sentences.

Jill commented on some of my sentences. She mentioned that some were really short and started in similar ways. My description sounded choppy. The way I fixed one of my paragraphs was to combine two or three short sentences that were about the same subject. As a result, I not only created sentences of different lengths, but I also varied the beginnings of the sentences.

[DRAFT]

[combined short sentences]

Plants and animals are more commonlier in Antarctica than you might expect. ~~There are~~ several hundred species of lichens. ~~They~~ grow good along the rocks. They create colorful colonies of yellow, green, and black. Mosses can also be found.

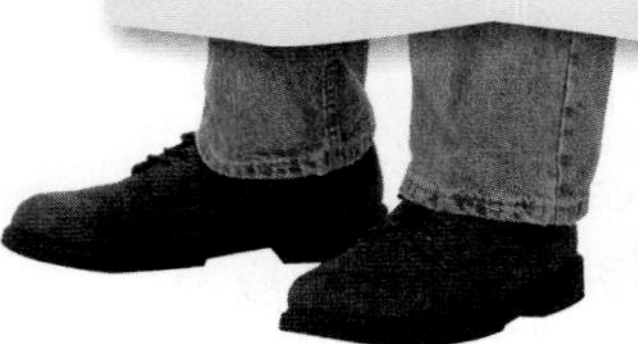

Apply

Check the length of your sentences. Do short, choppy ones need to be combined? Put a couple of them together.

Edit

Focus on 

The Rubric Says Adjectives and adverbs are used correctly and enhance the writing.

Writing Strategy Check to see that adjectives and adverbs are used correctly.

Writer's Term

Adjective and Adverb

An **adjective** is a word that describes a noun or pronoun. An **adverb** is a word that describes a verb, an adjective, or another adverb.

Now I need to proofread my geographic description for errors. I always check for spelling, punctuation, and capitalization errors. The rubric also tells me to check my adjectives and adverbs. I know that sometimes it's easy to get the two mixed up.

[DRAFT]

[corrected adverb] [changed adverb to adjective] [corrected adjective]

Antarctica is covered almost ~~complete~~ completely with a huge ice sheet. It extends almost five and a half million square miles, and the ~~thickly~~ thickest part averages about 6,500 feet. The land is divided into sections. East Antarctica is a high, flat plateau—an icy table of land. West Antarctica is ~~smallest~~ smaller. It is a series of ~~mountainus~~ mountainous islands held together by the ice sheet.

Reflect

What do you think? Can you find any mistakes that Andre has missed? How have his revisions helped his writing?

Apply

Conventions

Edit your draft for spelling, punctuation, and capitalization. Be sure to fix any mistakes in adjectives and adverbs.

For more practice using adjectives and adverbs correctly, use the exercises on the next two pages.

Grammar, Usage & Mechanics

Adjectives and Adverbs

Know the Rule

An **adjective** describes a noun or pronoun. An adjective

- tells which one, what kind, or how many.
  Examples: blue car, **shiny** star, **eight** caterpillars
- may follow a linking verb.
  Examples: The rug feels **soft**.

The articles *a, an,* and *the* are adjectives that indicate the presence of a noun.
Examples: The cat chases **a** mouse.

An **adverb** describes a verb, an adjective, or another adverb. An adverb

- tells how, when, where, or to what extent.
  Examples: The train whistled **loudly**.
- may end in *-ly,* although many common ones do not.
  Examples: deep, deeply; fair, fairly

Practice the Rule

Write each sentence on a separate sheet of paper. Underline the words that are adjectives. Circle the words that are adverbs.

1. The preparations for a long and adventurous trip can be exhausting.
2. Detailed lists must be written carefully to make sure supplies are appropriate.
3. Properly packing your supplies into suitcases and backpacks takes great patience and much practice.
4. Thorough planning will certainly help to make the trip enjoyable.
5. For an efficient departure, you must learn how to quickly eat a nutritious breakfast and dress appropriately for the weather.
6. If you accidentally forget something, you will just have to be very calm.
7. While on your adventure, don't forget to politely ask for directions and leave generous tips to the hard-working hotel staff.
8. When you finally return, you will be amazed at your wonderful accomplishments.
9. Offer your friends and family a complete description of your trip.
10. They will be thoroughly impressed.

Comparative and Superlative Forms

Know the Rule

Use the **comparative form** of an adjective or adverb when comparing two things. Use the **superlative form** when comparing three or more things. Make the comparative form of an adjective or adverb by adding *-er* or using the word *more*. To make the superlative form of an adjective or adverb, add *-est* or use *most*.

Examples: The oak tree is **taller** than the maple tree. The redwood, though, is the **tallest** of the three. (adjectives)

English class starts **earlier** than social studies. Math starts **earliest**. (adverbs)

Practice the Rule

On a separate sheet of paper, write the correct form of the underlined adjective or adverb.

1. Being the first person to reach the Pole was the <u>great</u> goal of many explorers.
2. Of the two poles, the North Pole was reached <u>soonest</u>.
3. Robert Peary, an American explorer, made his <u>earlier</u> of six tries in 1893.
4. On the first trip, Peary's sled dogs <u>quicker</u> became sick or froze to death.
5. Matthew Henson was the <u>better</u> of all of Peary's assistants.
6. On May 8, 1900, Peary and Henson passed a point <u>farthest</u> north than anyone had ever gone.
7. In 1906, President Roosevelt awarded Peary National Geographic's <u>high</u> honor, the Hubbard Medal.
8. Henson was awarded the same medal much <u>latest</u>, in 2000.
9. Some have questioned whether the conquest of the Pole, Peary's <u>greater</u> accomplishment, actually happened.
10. They believe he reached the <u>farther</u> point north for his time but did not reach the North Pole.

Publish +Presentation

Publishing Strategy Submit the description to the school's magazine.

Presentation Strategy Choose visuals that will work with the text.

Guess what? I'm almost done! I can't wait to show my parents and submit my piece to my school's magazine. But I think I need to add one more thing: some great visuals. I'll search the Internet for related photographs, maps, or illustrations that are OK to use. I'll insert them near the text they describe and include captions for my readers to understand what each visual shows. It's easy to do with my word-processing program! Finally, I'll check my writing against this checklist to make sure I did everything right.

My Final Checklist

Did I—

- ✔ use all adjectives and adverbs correctly?
- ✔ use comparative and superlative forms accurately?
- ✔ fix all spelling, grammar, and punctuation mistakes?
- ✔ use effective and appropriate visuals?

Apply

Make a final checklist to check your geographic description. Then publish your final copy.

A WHITE WORLD

by Andre

"Everywhere you look, all you see is white." This is how many travelers to Antarctica explain their reaction to this isolated continent. Antarctica is not a place where most people would want to live. However, to many visitors it appears quite remarkable.

Antarctica is covered almost completely with a huge ice sheet. It extends almost five and a half million square miles, and the thickest part averages about 6,500 feet. The land is divided into sections. East Antarctica is a high, flat plateau—an icy table of land. West Antarctica is smaller. It is a series of mountainous islands held together by the ice sheet. In some areas, nunataks dot the surface like punctuation marks. Nunataks are mountains buried so deep that only their tips peek through the ice. Between East and West Antarctica are the Transantarctic Mountains. They cut the land into two neat chunks. On either side of West Antarctica are huge floating ice sheets that hug the land like armrests on a chair. One, the Ross Ice Shelf, is as large as France.

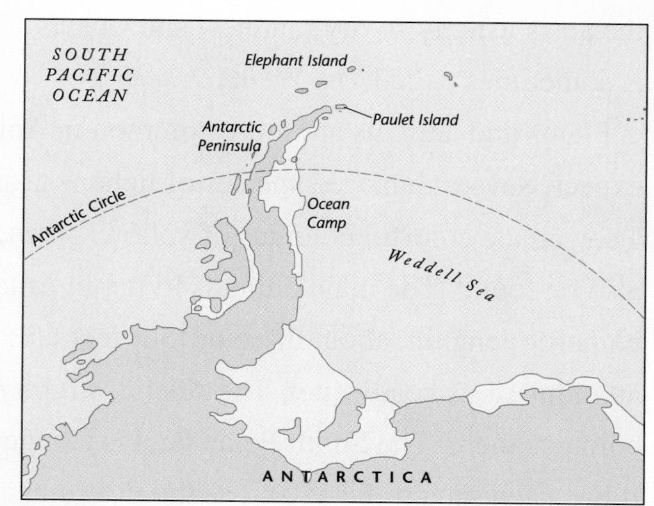

The weather in Antarctica is really cold. Winter temperatures drop as low as –128 degrees Fahrenheit. In Alaska, the average winter temperature ranges from 12 to –20 degrees. The average winter temperature range in Antarctica is from –40 to –94 degrees inland. These temperatures can freeze spit in midair! You have to take them seriously. Winds are fierce and biting. Gusts over 100 miles per hour are not uncommon. Even in summer, in warmer coastal areas, +32 degrees is the average temperature. But no snow falls in many parts of Antarctica. Strong winds kick up existing snow, but the air is usually so dry that new snow cannot form. This is why Antarctica is sometimes called *The White Desert*.

Plants and animals are more common in Antarctica than you might expect. Several hundred species of lichens grow well along the rocks. They create colorful colonies of yellow, green, and black. Mosses can also be found. The main animals living in Antarctica are penguins. The emperor penguin, about three or four feet tall, scoots around the ice like an industrious headwaiter. The Adélie, slightly smaller, also live in large colonies there. The South Polar skua is a huge and powerful flying bird. It has been seen as far inland as the Pole and as far north as the Equator.

Surprisingly, people also live in Antarctica. Nearly all of them are scientists. (No one, though, makes this cold, forbidding region a permanent home.) Including the United States, 29 countries have research stations. The largest is the American facility called McMurdo Station. It is on Ross Island in the Ross Ice Shelf. This community contains about 100 low, sprawling buildings. There are dormitories, a gymnasium, a science lab, and other structures. About 250 people spend the winter there. In summer the population rises to 1,000. A smaller facility is the Amundsen-Scott South Pole Station. It is very close to the Pole. The main building is a huge aluminum geodesic dome. It is more than 55 feet high at its highest point. Housing space for 27 people, equipment depots, and various research areas are either within it or connected to it by covered passageways. Glinting in the sun in the empty Antarctic plain, the station looks like the home of visitors from another planet.

Tourists do visit Antarctica. However, it can cost as much as $40,000 to get all the way to the South Pole. If you have the money and are adventurous enough to make the trip, you can visit this unique isolated continent.

Reflect

How did Andre do? Did he use all the traits of a good geographic description? Would you give him a top score for each item of the rubric? Don't forget to use the rubric to check your geographic description, too.

What's a Poem?

It's a piece of writing that expresses the thoughts or feelings of the writer. A poem can also describe or explain an event, object, or subject. Poems can take many different forms.

What's in a Poem?

Line
A poem is made up of a number of lines, each ending where the writer feels there should be a break, not necessarily at a comma or period. Punctuation rules are not always followed in poems.

Figurative Language
Figurative language such as simile, personification, and metaphor are often found in poetry. Creative use of language can help the reader "see" an everyday event or object in an entirely new way.

Rhythm
Poems are meant to be both read and heard. The writer uses line breaks to control the poem's rhythm or speed. This controlled rhythm adds a whole new dimension to the poem when spoken out loud.

Rhyme
Not every poem rhymes, but many do. Rhyming words can be found on the same line, at the ends of alternating lines, or anywhere else in a poem. Rhyming words help connect ideas within the poem—and they're fun to read and hear.

Why write a Poem?

There are plenty of reasons to write a poem. Here are just a few.

Description

A poem is a great way to describe something—an object, an event, even a feeling—in a completely different way. You can be as creative and experimental as you like when you write a poem. That way, you can offer the reader a totally new way of looking at something.

Personal Reflection

Writing poems is a wonderful way to safely explore our inner thoughts and feelings. Words are powerful. Even if you never share your poem with a reader, the act of writing a poem itself can be a great way to gain personal insights.

Enjoyment

Writing poetry is fun! Experimenting with the sounds of words, figurative language, and poem structure is an exciting form of self-expression. Also, the feeling of satisfaction when the poem is finished can't be beat.

Understanding

Poetry can be used as a different approach when trying to help the reader understand a specific idea or topic. No subject is off limits when it comes to poetry, so why not explain an event in history, current events, science, or even math through a poem?

Linking Descriptive Writing Traits to a Poem

In this chapter, you will describe or explain a math concept in a poem. Andre will guide you through the stages of the writing process: Prewrite, Draft, Revise, Edit, and Publish. In each stage, Andre will show you important writing strategies that are linked to the Descriptive Writing Traits below.

Descriptive Writing Traits

- a clear topic that is developed by relevant supporting details
- descriptive details that are well chosen for the topic

- well-organized paragraphs that logically follow the order of the description, whether by time, location, or another order
- varied and appropriate transitions that show the relationship between ideas and concepts

- a voice that is appropriate for the purpose and audience

- precise words and phrases, possibly including figurative language, that create an accurate picture for the reader

- sentences that vary in length and type to add flow to the writing

- no or few errors in grammar, usage, mechanics, and spelling

Before you write, read Sage Quintley's poem on the next page. Then use the poem rubric on pages 460–461 to decide how well she did. (You might want to look back at What's in a Poem? on page 456, too!)

Poem Model

Pythagoras

by Sage Quintley

Just a man, you say?
No way!
Born on the Isle of Samos
In the year 570 B.C.E.
His mind, it shone like
The crystal waters flowing
Through the Aegean Sea.

Rhyme

Figurative language (simile)

He discovered a secret
About right triangles,
A truth about the lengths of their sides.
So listen up now,
And let me explain.
His genius cannot be denied!

Varied line lengths to control rhythm

Three sides to a right triangle—
Side a, side b, side c.
Side c is the hypotenuse,
Let that be as clear as can be.

Now square the lengths of sides a and b,
Then add them,
And what you'll discover—
Is that *that* number equals
The square of side c.

(Just a man, you say?
No way!)

The Pythagorean Theorem—it's more than just a theory!

Rubric

Use this 6-point rubric to plan and evaluate a poem.

	6	5	4
Ideas	The poem focuses on a single subject. Well-chosen descriptive details create clear images.	The poem focuses on a single subject. Most of the details create clear images.	The poem focuses on a single subject. A few details create clear images.
Organization	The poem is organized for description. Ideas are easy to follow.	The poem is organized for description. Most of the ideas are easy to follow.	The poem is organized. One or two ideas may not be in the best order.
Voice	The poet's voice connects with the audience from beginning to end.	The poet's voice connects with the audience most of the time.	The poet's voice is clear at first but then fades.
Word Choice	Precise vocabulary and figurative language are used purposefully and effectively.	Most words are used purposefully. One comparison could be more effective.	Most of the words are used purposefully. Several comparisons could be more effective.
Sentence Fluency	The lines and line breaks establish an appropriate cadence and rhythm.	Rhythm and flow are maintained most of the time. One or two lines may need improvement.	Rhythm and flow are maintained some of the time. Several lines need improvement.
Conventions	The writing has been carefully edited. Adjective and adverb clauses are used correctly.	Minor errors are present but do not interfere with meaning. Clauses are used correctly.	A few errors cause confusion. Several clauses may be used incorrectly.
+Presentation	The poem is placed attractively and neatly on the page.		

3	2	1	
The focus is somewhat clear. Details are few; some are not clear.	The focus is not clear. Some details may be unrelated.	The writing is not a poem. Details are not clear or are unrelated.	Ideas
Some of the ideas seem to be out of order.	The poem is not organized. The ideas are incomplete or hard to follow.	The writing is not organized. Ideas are difficult or impossible to follow.	Organization
The voice is weak and does not get or hold the audience's attention.	The voice is not clear. The audience does not know who is speaking.	The poet's voice is absent. The audience does not know who is speaking.	Voice
Most of the words are used purposefully. Comparisons may be unclear.	Many words are ordinary or overused. Comparisons are unclear or absent.	Words are very basic and limited. Some words may be used incorrectly.	Word Choice
The rhythm is inconsistent. Some line breaks interrupt the flow.	Rhythm is not established. The lines do not flow.	The lines do not make a poem.	Sentence Fluency
Many errors are repeated and cause confusion. Several clauses are used incorrectly.	Serious errors interfere with meaning. Clauses are used incorrectly.	The writing has not been edited.	Conventions

See Appendix B for 4-, 5-, and 6-point descriptive rubrics.

Using the Poem Rubric to Study the Model

Did you notice that the model on page 459 points out some key elements of a poem? As she wrote "Pythagoras," Sage Quintley used these elements to help her describe a mathematical concept. She also used the 6-point rubric on pages 460–461 to plan, draft, revise, and edit the writing. A rubric is a great tool to evaluate writing during the writing process.

Now let's use the same rubric to score the model. To do this, we'll focus on each trait separately, starting with Ideas. We'll use the top descriptor for each trait (column 6), along with examples from the model, to help us understand how the traits work together. How would you score Sage on each trait?

- **The poem focuses on a single subject.**
- **Well-chosen descriptive details create clear images.**

Sage's poem clearly focuses on one thing: Pythagoras and the Pythagorean Theorem. She includes great details that help me both envision Pythagoras (born on an ancient Greek island) and understand his theorem.

[from the writing model]

Just a man, you say?
  No way!
Born on the Isle of Samos
  In the year 570 BCE.

[from the writing model]

He discovered a secret
  About right triangles,
    A truth about the lengths of their sides.

- **The poem is organized for description.**
- **Ideas are easy to follow.**

Sage's ideas are organized in a clear and logical way. She introduces her subject and then provides supportive, explanatory details. I had no problem understanding her description of Pythagoras's great discovery.

[from the writing model]

Now square the lengths of sides a and b,
Then add them,
And what you'll discover—
Is that *that* number equals
The square of side c.

- **The poet's voice connects with the audience from beginning to end.**

I really enjoyed reading Sage's poem. Her voice is casual and friendly, with a slight hint of humor. I felt like she was speaking directly to me, and this connection helped me stay engaged and better understand the topic.

[from the writing model]

So listen up now,
And let me explain.
His genius cannot be denied!

- **Precise vocabulary and figurative language are used purposefully and effectively.**

Sage uses an effective and clever simile at the beginning of her poem. She describes Pythagoras's mind as being so brilliant, it shines like the "crystal waters" in the Aegean Sea—the sea that just happens to surround Samos. This simile energizes the poem and adds to my vision of Pythagoras.

[from the writing model]

His mind, it shone like
  The crystal waters flowing
Through the Aegean Sea.

- **The lines and line breaks establish an appropriate cadence and rhythm.**

While reading Sage's poem out loud, I noticed a beat or rhythm. She uses line breaks and word repetition in such a way that I can't help but read some sections faster and some slower. This rhythm was fun to read aloud and listen to.

[from the writing model]

Three sides to a right triangle—
  Side a, side b, side c.
Side c is the hypotenuse,
  Let that be as clear as can be.

- **The writing has been carefully edited.**
- **Adjective and adverb clauses are used correctly.**

Even though poems have more flexibility as far as structure and form, conventions are still important. Sage did a nice job of using grammar, capitalization, and punctuation in a way that is not only clear but also effective for her poem. She even used parentheses correctly.

[from the writing model]

(Just a man, you say?
No way!)
The Pythagorean Theorem—it's more than just a theory!

+Presentation The poem is placed attractively and neatly on the page.

My Turn!

Now it's my turn to write a poem. I'll use the rubric and good writing strategies to help me. Follow along to see how I do it.

Prewrite

Focus on **Ideas**

The Rubric Says The poem focuses on a single subject.

Writing Strategy Choose a topic. Make a list of descriptive details.

Well, this is different! My math teacher has asked everyone in class to explain a mathematical concept—*in a poem*. I've never thought to do that, but this assignment sounds like fun. Each student gets to choose a subject, but we have to make it clear through the use of descriptive details that we fully understand the topic. What will I write about? I'm excited to use my creativity and unique point of view. I'll start by taking some notes on the possible topics I could cover. Then I'll decide which to use and take it from there.

Possible Math Poem Topics

— pi and circles—finding the circumference and diameter
— understanding mean, median, mode, and range
— identifying angles—right, acute, obtuse ← *This is the one!*
    —right angle is ninety degrees
        —corner of a room, corner of a street
    —acute angle is less than ninety degrees
        —clothespin, alligator jaws
    —obtuse angle is greater than ninety degrees
        —open magazine, mostly extended arm

Apply

Brainstorm possible topics for your poem. Jot down a few notes about each. Then choose one for your poem's subject.

Prewrite

Focus on **Organization**

The Rubric Says The poem is organized for description.

Writing Strategy Use a Web to plan the poem.

I've decided to focus on different types of angles. I've worked hard this year learning how to differentiate between right, acute, and obtuse angles, and I'd like to share my knowledge with my reader. I'll organize the facts and details in a Web. This graphic organizer will be a huge help when I draft my poem. All the details will be right there in front of me, guiding me as I write.

Web

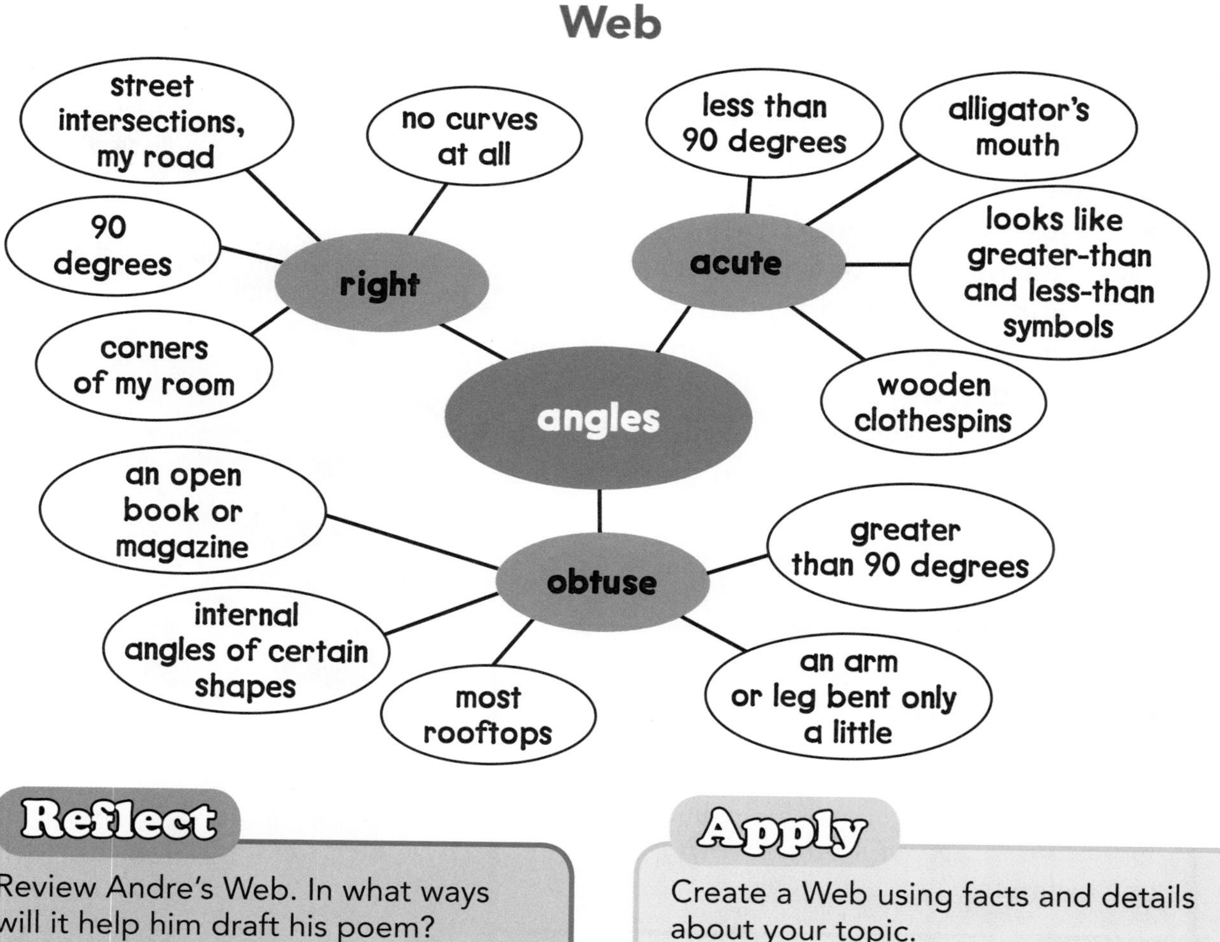

Reflect

Review Andre's Web. In what ways will it help him draft his poem?

Apply

Create a Web using facts and details about your topic.

Draft

Focus on 

The Rubric Says Precise vocabulary and figurative language are used purposefully and effectively.

Writing Strategy Choose words and phrases for effect.

With all of my details organized in a Web, I'm ready to draft my poem. The rubric reminds me to use vocabulary and figurative language purposefully and effectively. There are typically fewer words in poems, so I have to be sure to use only words and phrases that will help me clearly describe my topic—angles.

The more descriptive language I use—such as adjectives, adjective clauses, adverbs, and adverb clauses—the more clearly my reader will "see" each angle I describe. I also used personification—a type of figurative language—to help engage the reader and present my topic in a new and creative way.

As I draft, I won't worry about making mistakes. I just want to get my ideas down on paper first. I'll fix any errors later on.

Writer's Term

Personification

Personification is giving an inanimate object (such as a mountain) or abstract quality (such as honor) human or lifelike qualities (such as thoughts, feelings, or personalities). *The mountain hungered for the morning sun* is one example.

Proofreading Marks

- Indent
- Make uppercase
- Make lowercase
- Add something
- Take out something
- Add a period
- New paragraph
- Spelling error

[DRAFT]

Angles
by Andre

So I decided, to invite some over
And settle it once and for all.
Soon a crowd of angles
Were standing in my front hall.

Angels can be hard
When you don't know them by name.
If you've never met
They all might look the same

Each one introduced itself and a
Pattern was quickly shown.
I wrote it down and now I know
What my math teachers have always known.

[used personification]

Right angles: 90 degrees—
  The corners of my room
  Lines that go up and across,
  At the corner of my street.

Acute angles: less than 90—
  A "less than" or "greater than" sign
  A clothespin, an open alligators mouth
  But no more than 90 degrees by design.

Obtuce angles: greater than 90—
  My father's mostly extended arm
  An open magazine, the library roof
  Each internal angle of a regular octogon.

Now I know each angle's name
Which all depends on the degrees.
but can someone help me figure out
How to serve angles biscits and tea.

Reflect

How did Andre do? In what ways did his Web help him organize his poem?

Apply

Use your Web to draft your poem. Remember to focus on one topic, use precise words, and have fun with figurative language.

Revise

Focus on **Ideas**

The Rubric Says Well-chosen descriptive details create clear images.

Writing Strategy Choose details that bring the topic to life.

After rereading my poem, I realized that some of my details were confusing and ineffective. The details *Lines that go up and across* and *At the corners of my street* don't effectively or vividly "show" a right angle at all. So I revised these details for more accurate and creative images, and I'm happy with my changes. What do you think?

[DRAFT]

Right angles: 90 degrees—
The corners of my room
Intersections, the Red Cross sign
~~Lines that go up and across,~~
But nowhere on a balloon.
~~At the corner of my street.~~

[used well-chosen details]

Apply

Use details that creatively and vividly describe or explain the subject of your poem.

Revise

Focus on **Organization**

The Rubric Says The poem is organized for description. Ideas are easy to follow.

Writing Strategy Check the order of the lines and stanzas.

When I reread the first two stanzas of my poem, even I felt some confusion. As I read the first line, I felt like I had missed something. Then I realized that if I switched the order of the stanzas, everything made more sense. I needed to explain *why* I invited angles to my house *first* for the reader to easily follow along. Then the crowd of angles in my front hall made sense.

[DRAFT]

So I decided, to invite some over
And settle it once and for all.
Soon a crowd of angles
Were standing in my front hall.

~~Angels~~ Angles can be hard
When you don't know them by name.
If you've never met
They all might look the same

[revised stanza order for clarity]

Reflect

What do you think? How has Andre's revision helped clarify the ideas and images in his poem?

Apply

Organize your poem's lines and stanzas effectively, so that the reader can easily follow along.

Revise

Focus on 

The Rubric Says The lines and line breaks establish an appropriate cadence and rhythm.

Writing Strategy Place line breaks where they make sense.

When you work with prose (any writing that is not poetry), using a variety of complete sentences helps the writing flow easily. In poetry, you create rhythm and flow by grouping words together and carefully placing the breaks between lines. A poet needs to read the poem out loud several times to know exactly where to break a line and which words should be spoken together. As I read my poem out loud, I found a spot where the rhythm was off. So I revised the line break for the cadence, or beat, I wanted.

[DRAFT]

[adjusted line break for rhythm]

Each one introduced itself and a
Pattern was quickly shown.
I wrote it down and now I know
What my math teachers have always known.

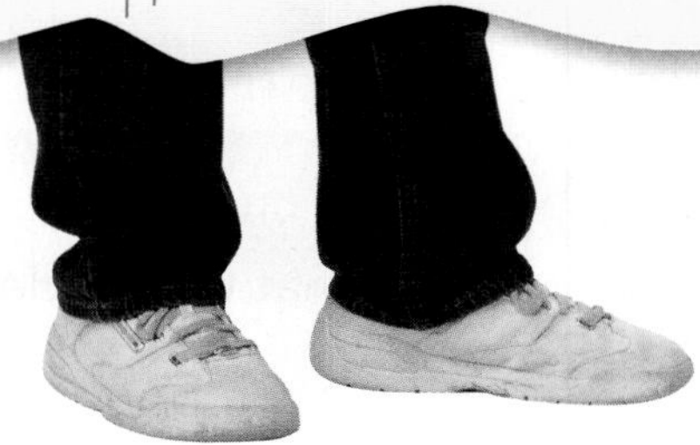

Apply

Read your poem out loud. Use line breaks to give your poem the rhythm you want to achieve.

Edit

Focus on Conventions

The Rubric Says The writing has been carefully edited. Adjective and adverb clauses are used correctly.

Writing Strategy Check the use and punctuation of adjective and adverb clauses.

Writer's Term

Adjective and Adverb Clauses

An **adjective clause** always begins with a relative pronoun and describes a noun. An **adverb clause** always begins with a subordinating conjunction and tells why, where, when, under what circumstances, or to what degree.

Time to fix all spelling, grammar, and punctuation mistakes. I'll also make sure adjective and adverb clauses are used correctly. If a dependent clause begins a sentence, a comma should immediately follow the clause.

[DRAFT]

Now I know each angle's name,
Which all depends on the degrees.
but can someone help me figure out
How to serve angles biscits and tea?

[fixed spelling and punctuation errors]

Reflect

How did Andre do with his editing? Can you find any mistakes he might have missed?

Apply

Conventions

Edit your draft for spelling, punctuation, and capitalization. Check all adjective and adverb clauses.

For more practice identifying adjective and adverb clauses, use the exercises on the next two pages.

Adjective Clauses

Know the Rule

A clause has a subject and a verb. An **adjective clause** is a dependent clause that describes a noun or a pronoun. An adjective clause always follows the word it describes and begins with a relative pronoun such as *who, whom, whose, which,* or *that.*

Example: Ming has math in the room that overlooks the parking lot.

When a clause is essential to the meaning of a sentence, it is restrictive. If the clause can be removed without affecting the meaning of the sentence, it is nonrestrictive. Separate nonrestrictive clauses from the rest of the sentence with commas.

Example: I need my math book, which is on the kitchen table.

Practice the Rule

Read the following sentences. On a separate sheet of paper, write each adjective clause and then indicate whether it is restrictive or nonrestrictive.

1. I'm off for a week's vacation with my aunt, who just happens to be this year's state poet laureate.
2. A poet laureate is a poet whom the state might call upon when a poem needs to be written for an official event.
3. Aunt Grace has written many poems that have been published in literary magazines all over the country.
4. She lives in a small, antique house with my Uncle Gabe, whose real name happens to be Gabriel.
5. Aunt Grace says that the wildflowers in her fields whisper to her, which sounds so magical I wish it were true.
6. My cousin River, who has grown up already and moved to the city, is also an accomplished poet.
7. But River writes musical poems, or songs, that are designed to help injured children heal faster.
8. His music is used as a form of therapy in hospitals whose patients are mostly children.
9. Listening to or singing the songs strengthens the children's immune systems, which is essential for healing to take place.
10. I'm so lucky to have family members who inspire me in so many ways.

Adverb Clauses

Know the Rule

An **adverb clause** is a dependent clause that tells about a verb, an adjective, or an adverb. Adverb clauses tell where, when, why, to what degree, or under what circumstances. They begin with a subordinating conjunction such as *than, although, because, if, as, as if, while, when,* or *whenever*. When an adverb clause begins a sentence, follow it with a comma.

Example: Before I go to the library, I'll call to be sure they are open.

Practice the Rule

Read the following sentences. On a separate sheet of paper, copy each adverb clause that you find. Then circle each subordinating conjunction.

1. I'm nearly jumping out of my skin with excitement because tomorrow I leave for Camp Wahoo!
2. While staying at Camp Wahoo last summer, I made some of the greatest friends, and I can't wait to see them again.
3. Well, I've finally arrived at Camp Wahoo's gates, and it feels as if I never left.
4. Before my parents went back home, they gave me a special gift: a beautiful, handmade journal.
5. Although we hike and swim here, Camp Wahoo is basically a camp for budding poets, like me!
6. If learning to write better poetry is your goal, this camp was designed just for you.
7. After we wake up, we start our day with morning exercise and breakfast, just like other summer camps.
8. When breakfast is over, we break into groups and study the style and writings of several famous poets from around the world.
9. I've been writing poetry in my new journal whenever I have time to myself.
10. I can't wait to show my journal to my teacher after I get home.

Publish

+Presentation

Publishing Strategy Present the poem in a multimedia presentation.

Presentation Strategy Display information clearly.

I did it! I'm so proud of my finished poem. Now to publish it in an exciting way. I think it would be fun to present my poem as a multimedia experience. I can play music and project fun images on a screen behind me as I read "Having Tea With Angles." I'll also neatly print out my poem to make it easy to read. But first I want to use my final checklist to make sure I haven't forgotten anything.

My Final Checklist

Did I—

- ✔ use and punctuate all adjective and adverb clauses correctly?
- ✔ edit for spelling, grammar, and punctuation mistakes?
- ✔ present my poem in a clear and interesting way?
- ✔ remember to put my name beneath the title?

Apply

Make your own final checklist to check your poem. Then write a final copy and publish it.

Having Tea With Angles

by Andre

Angles can be tricky
When you don't know them by name.
If you've never been introduced
They all might look the same.

So I decided to invite them over
And settle it once and for all.
Soon a crowd of various angles
Were standing in my front hall.

Each one introduced itself
And a pattern was quickly shown.
I wrote it down and now I know
What my math teachers have always known.

Right angles: 90 degrees—
    The corners of my room
    Intersections, the Red Cross sign
    But nowhere on a balloon.

Acute angles: less than 90—
    A "less than" or "greater than" sign
    A clothespin, an open alligator's mouth
    But no more than 90 degrees by design.

Obtuse angles: greater than 90—
    My father's mostly extended arm
    An open magazine, the library's roof
    Each internal angle of a regular octagon.

Now I know each angle's name,
Which all depends on the degrees.
But can someone help me figure out
How to serve angles biscuits and tea?

Reflect

What do you think? Did Andre use all the traits of a good poem? Check it against the rubric. Then use the rubric to check your own poem.

Descriptive test writing

Read the Writing Prompt

When you take a writing test, you will be given a writing prompt. Most writing prompts have three parts:

Setup This part of the writing prompt gives you the background information you need to get ready to write.

Task This part of the writing prompt tells you exactly what you are supposed to write: an observation report.

Scoring Guide This section tells how your writing will be scored. To do well on the test, you should include everything on the list.

Remember the rubrics you used earlier in the unit? When you take a writing test, you don't always have all of the information that's on a rubric. However, the scoring guide is a lot like a rubric. It lists everything you need to think about to write a good paper. Like the rubrics you've used in this unit, many scoring guides are based upon these important traits of writing:

Think about a time of extreme or out-of-the-ordinary weather, such as a thunderstorm, hail, or even snow. It can be something you saw in person or that you learned about on the news.

Write an observation report that describes in detail what you saw or experienced.

Be sure your writing

- has sensory details that paint a visual image.
- has details arranged in a natural and logical order.
- uses a voice that suits the audience and purpose.
- uses precise words and phrases to develop the topic.
- uses a variety of sentence lengths and types.
- contains correct grammar, punctuation, capitalization, and spelling.

Writing Traits in the Scoring Guide

The scoring guide in the prompt on page 479 has been made into this chart. Does it remind you of the rubrics you've used? Not all prompts include all the writing traits, but this one does. Use them to do your best writing. Remember to write neatly and put your name on each page.

- Be sure your writing has sensory details that paint a visual image.

- Be sure your writing has details arranged in a natural and logical order.

- Be sure your writing uses a voice that suits the audience and purpose.

- Be sure your writing uses precise words and phrases to develop the topic.

- Be sure your writing uses a variety of sentence lengths and types.

- Be sure your writing contains correct grammar, punctuation, capitalization, and spelling.

Look at Merritt Graves's story on the next page. Did she follow the scoring guide?

The Ice Storm

by Merritt Graves

Snow! Awakening early, I peek outside to glimpse what looks like snow on the ground. I go out to get a closer look and thump! I slip and fall to the ground. This isn't snow; it's something much meaner and more deceiving. It's a North Texas ice storm, and I've fallen right into its frigid, slippery trap.

I push myself up with my bare hands. The ice on the ground is numbing, and my fingers get a chill. I blow on them and see the puffs of white come out of my mouth. The air is cold and damp and feels as though it's going right through my body. Carefully, I navigate my way back inside. I'd rather view the ice storm from the warmth of our house.

Now I take a closer look at what nature has dealt us. The trees are frosted. Their branches look burdened with the weight of the ice pulling them down. The grass has a layer of frost on it, its blades each coated with rain and dampness that's been frozen overnight. The metal on our patio furniture has a glaze to it, and the cushions are coated with a frosty layer.

I let our dog, Muzzles, a small, white Maltese, go outside. Crunch, crunch, crunch, go his little paws on the grass, leaving behind indentations in the ice with each step he takes. I notice Muzzles's footsteps are the only sounds; today, no cars rush by on their morning commute. Muzzles quickly turns around and heads for the door, sliding along the ice-covered patio before making it inside.

The skies still look angry—cloudy and gray and still. It's as though they want to make sure the ice doesn't melt any time soon. I know that until it does melt, much of the town will stay tucked indoors.

Using the Scoring Guide to Study the Model

Now let's use the scoring guide to check Merritt's writing test, "The Ice Storm." Let's see how well her essay meets each of the writing traits.

- **The writing has sensory details that paint a visual image.**

Merritt's description of the North Texas ice storm is so vivid, so complete, that I can almost feel the brutal cold and hear Muzzles walk across the crunchy, frozen grass.

The trees are frosted. Their branches look burdened with the weight of the ice pulling them down. The grass has a layer of frost on it, its blades each coated with rain and dampness that's been frozen overnight.

Crunch, crunch, crunch, go his little paws on the grass, leaving behind indentations in the ice with each step he takes.

- **The details are in a natural and logical order.**

Merritt organizes her details in a natural and logical order. Her goal is to share a sensory experience, so she focuses on one sense at a time. As I read, I could easily and vividly imagine what the cold felt like, as well as how the day looked and sounded.

I let our dog, Muzzles, a small, white Maltese, go outside. Crunch, crunch, crunch, go his little paws on the grass, leaving behind indentations in the ice with each step he takes.

- **The voice suits the audience and purpose.**

Merritt grabbed my attention with the very first word! She definitely knew who she was writing for—other kids her own age. Her voice throughout the story reflects the excitement she felt on the day of the ice storm. As I read, I couldn't help but feel that excitement, too.

Snow! Awakening early, I peek outside to glimpse what looks like snow on the ground. I go out to get a closer look and thump! I slip and fall to the ground.

- **The writing uses precise words and phrases to develop the topic.**

Merritt clearly worked hard at using strong, specific words and phrases to describe her experience. *Numbing* is more powerful and accurate than *cold. Puffs of white* is a more colorful and creative phrase than *my breath.* Precise words and phrases add clarity and energy to her story.

I push myself up with my bare hands. The ice on the ground is numbing, and my fingers get a chill. I blow on them and see the puffs of white come out of my mouth.

Using the Scoring Guide to Study the Model

- **The writing uses a variety of sentence lengths and types.**

I like how Merritt uses both short and long sentences throughout her writing. It's more enjoyable and easier to read a variety of sentence structures.

> The air is cold and damp and feels as though it's going right through my body. Carefully, I navigate my way back inside. I'd rather view the ice storm from the warmth of our house.

- **The writing has correct grammar, punctuation, capitalization, and spelling.**

I can tell that Merritt has edited her story and made sure that there were no mistakes. I know how important it is to check for mistakes in my own work, and I will be sure to keep that in mind as I write. Don't forget to check for mistakes in your work, too! Be sure to check for proper grammar and mechanics at every step of the writing process so you can avoid having errors on your final test.

Planning My Time

Before giving us a writing test prompt, my teacher tells us how much time we'll have to complete the test. Since I'm already familiar with the writing process, I can think about how much total time I need and then divide it up into the different parts of the writing process. If the test takes an hour, here's how I can organize my time. Planning your time will help you, too!

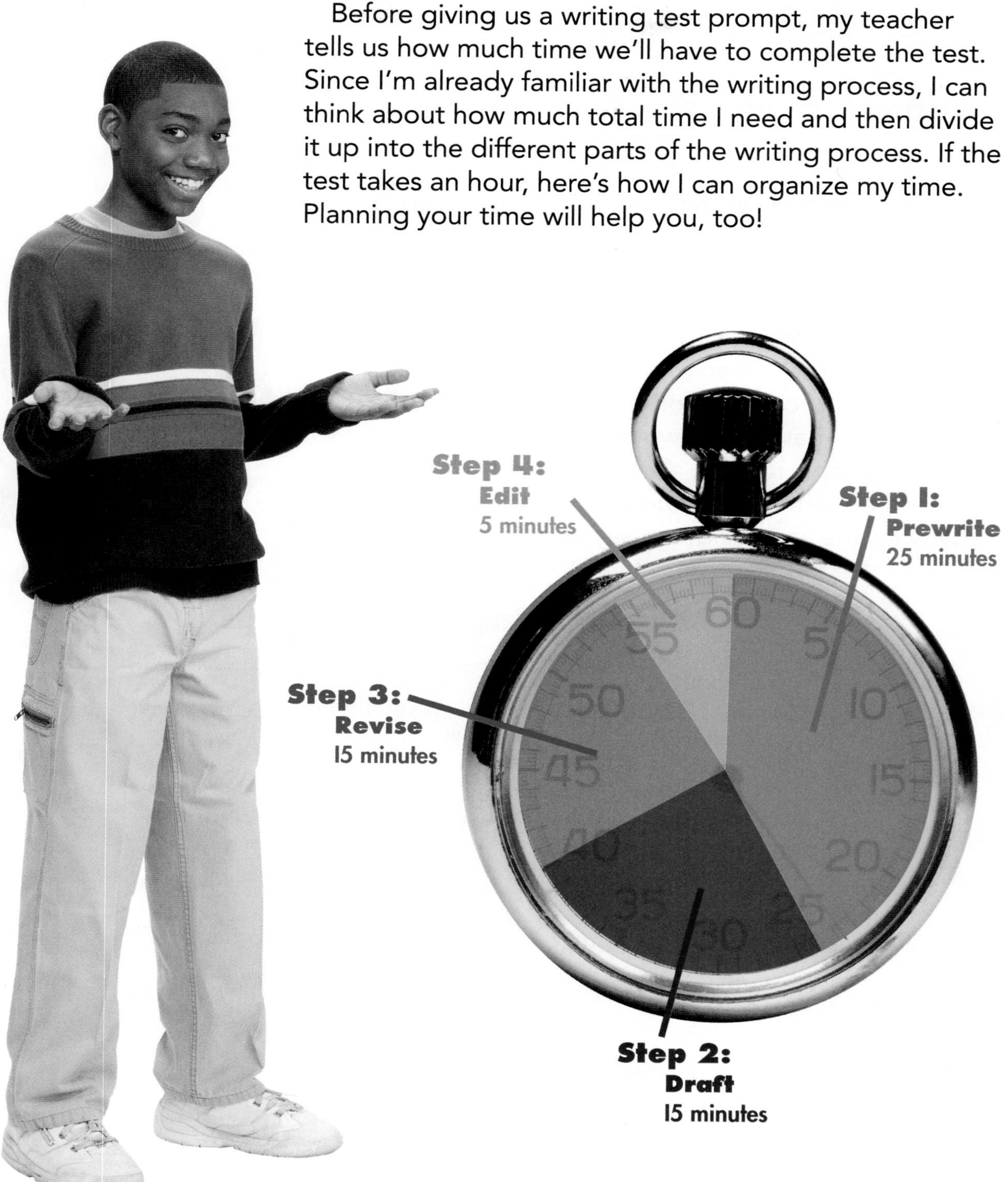

Prewrite

Focus on **Ideas**

Writing Strategy Study the writing prompt to be sure I know what to do.

Once I receive my writing prompt, I study it to make sure I know exactly what I'm supposed to do. A writing prompt usually has three parts, even though they aren't always labeled. Take a closer look at the prompt, though, and you should be able to find the setup, task, and scoring guide. I labeled all three of those in my writing prompt. You'll want to circle key words in the setup and the task that tell what kind of writing you need to do. I circled my topic in blue. You'll also want to circle what kind of writing you'll be doing, as I did, and study what the scoring guide says.

My Writing Test Prompt

Setup

Think about your favorite meal. Where do you go to get it, what does it look like, what does it smell like, and how does it taste?

Task

Write an observation report about experiencing your favorite meal that will make your reader practically be able to taste it.

Scoring Guide

Be sure your writing

- has sensory details that paint a visual image.
- has details arranged in a natural and logical order.
- uses a voice that suits the audience and purpose.
- uses precise words and phrases to develop the topic.
- uses a variety of sentence lengths and types.
- contains correct grammar, punctuation, capitalization, and spelling.

Before you get started, think about how the scoring guide relates to the writing traits you've studied in the rubrics. Even though not all of the traits may be included in every scoring guide, you'll want to remember them all in order to write a good essay.

- **Be sure your writing has sensory details that paint a visual image.**

I want my reader to be able to almost smell and taste my favorite meal. Using lots of sensory details will help.

- **Be sure your writing has details arranged in a natural and logical order.**

I'll introduce my subject, and then provide details in an order that makes the most sense.

- **Be sure your writing uses a voice that suits the audience and purpose.**

I'll keep my voice casual and entertaining. Reading about food should be fun, not boring and dry.

- **Be sure your writing uses precise words and phrases to develop the topic.**

I want to give my reader a "taste" of my favorite meal, so I'll be sure to use precise words and phrases.

- **Be sure your writing uses a variety of sentence lengths and types.**

Using a mixture of short and long sentences will help my writing flow smoothly.

- **Be sure your writing contains correct grammar, punctuation, capitalization, and spelling.**

I'm going to need to leave time to check my grammar, punctuation, and capitalization. I'll be sure to check and double check my spelling, too!

Prewrite

Focus on Ideas

Writing Strategy Respond to the task.

One thing I've learned about writing is that writers gather information before they begin writing. So to get started, I'll take a look at the information that's provided in the writing prompt. You can get a lot of information from the writing prompt! You won't have forever to finish a test, so it's important to think about how you're going to respond before you start writing.

My task is to write an observation report describing my favorite meal. Choosing my favorite meal is easy: I'll talk about the hamburgers at the Tick Tock Diner. Speaking of tick-tock, the clock is ticking on my test time so I'd better get going!

Task — Write an observation report about experiencing your favorite meal that will make your reader practically be able to taste it.

Notes

- ✔ Tick Tock has the best burgers in town!
- ✔ They're big and juicy and loaded with toppings.
- ✔ The place is great, too.

Apply

Before you start writing, think about how you'll respond to the task part of the prompt. Next write down notes to help you gather information.

Prewrite

Writing Strategy Choose a graphic organizer.

Time is limited, so I need to get my ideas on paper fast! Since I know what I'm going to be writing about, my next step is to organize all the details. Because sensory details are so important, it feels natural to organize my observations according to the five senses. I'll use an Observation Chart to keep them all straight.

I'll start out by writing down the topic of my essay, which came out of the setup and task in the writing prompt. Then I'll write down five columns and label them Sight, Sound, Touch, Taste, and Smell.

TOPIC: Tick Tock Diner's Tasty Burgers

SIGHT	SOUND	TOUCH	TASTE	SMELL
-counter with the grill behind it -a few booths along the window -mostly red and white inside -vinyl-covered stools -burgers served on white plastic plate with fries on side -old-fashioned	-kind of noisy -people talking -wait staff and cooks yell orders back and forth -burgers sizzling on the grill -jukebox plays old music	-buns are always soft when you pick up your burger -slightly warm since they put them on the griddle	-juicy, slightly salty, and delicious! -tangy ketchup and creamy mayo -comes with crisp lettuce, sweet tomato, and sour pickles	-whole place smells like a burger -smell the grease from the fries and the grill

Reflect

What do you think? Did Andre record enough details in his Observation Chart?

Apply

Choose a graphic organizer that helps you organize the information you need to appeal to your reader's senses.

Prewrite

Focus on 

Writing Strategy Check my graphic organizer against the scoring guide.

During a test, you won't have a lot of time for revising. That makes prewriting an essential part of your test writing process. Before I even begin writing my draft, I'm going to check my Observation Chart against the scoring guide in the writing prompt.

TOPIC: Tick Tock Diner's Tasty Burgers

SIGHT	SOUND	TOUCH	TASTE	SMELL
-counter with the grill behind it -a few booths along the window -mostly red and white inside -vinyl-covered stools -burgers served on white plastic plate with fries on side -old-fashioned	-kind of noisy -people talking -wait staff and cooks yell orders back and forth -burgers sizzling on the grill -jukebox plays old music	-buns are always soft when you pick up your burger -slightly warm since they put them on the griddle	-juicy, slightly salty, and delicious! -tangy ketchup and creamy mayo -comes with crisp lettuce, sweet tomato, and sour pickles	-whole place smells like a burger -smell the grease from the fries and the grill

- **Be sure your writing has sensory details that paint a visual image.**

My Observation Chart has all the senses covered!

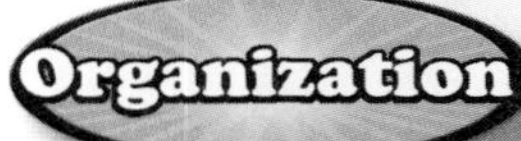

- **Be sure your writing has details arranged in a natural and logical order.**

I'll state my topic early on and then give the details in a logical order according to the five senses.

- **Be sure your writing uses a voice that suits the audience and purpose.**

I'll keep my voice friendly and energetic.

- **Be sure your writing uses precise words and phrases to develop the topic.**

As I look at my Observation Chart, I see some precise and descriptive words and phrases I'll use in my writing.

- **Be sure your writing uses a variety of sentence lengths and types.**

I want to hold my reader's attention, so I'll use a variety of sentences to keep my writing interesting.

- **Be sure your writing contains correct grammar, punctuation, capitalization, and spelling.**

I'll pay attention to this as I write, but I'll be sure to double check things when I edit my draft.

Reflect

What do you think? How will Andre's Observation Chart help him write a good report?

Apply

The steps you take before you start writing your draft will ensure that you have a well-organized and well-written observation report!

Draft

Focus on 

Writing Strategy Draw the reader in with sensory details that paint a visual image.

According to the scoring guide, I need to include sensory details that paint a visual image. My Observation Chart has a lot of information about what the diner looks like, and I think that'll help to draw the reader into my story.

The Tastiest Burger

by Andre

Four oclock is always burger time. That's the time the old broke clock above the Tick Tock Diner has displayed for as long as anyone can remember. But even though the clock no longer functions, the burgers inside are much appreciated by all the customers.

The aroma of burgers cooking on the grill and fries cooking in the deep fryer grabs me from the moment I walk into the old-fashioned diner on saturday night. Its packed. I can hear the buzz of people talking. I hear the wait staff and cooks yelling orders to each other

The diner is decked out in red white, and chrome. Red vinyl covers the seats of the booths and stools, while white-topped tables have chrome legs. An old jukebox rests in one corner of the diner, with tunes from a previous decade. Even the employees there look as though they came from another time, seeing name tags that display names like "Betty" and "Midge" and "Johnny" and "Suzy."

[sensory details]

Proofreading Marks

- ⌐ Indent
- ≡ Make uppercase
- / Make lowercase
- ∧ Add something
- Take out something
- ⊙ Add a period
- ¶ New paragraph
- (SP) Spelling error

[DRAFT]

Norma, my server, doesn't need to ask what I want. My order is always the same burger, fries, and a soda. I take an empty seat at the counter, which puts me closer to the kitchen action. Here, I can hear the burgers sizzling on the grill, inviting me to order. Soon, she places the white plastic plate in front of me. On it sits perfection: a juicy burger and fries still glisening with grease and salt.

[sensory details]

The bun is soft and slightly warm as I lift it to take my first bite. The burger is juicy, salty, and delicious. Crisp lettuce, a thick slab of tomato, and sour pickles surround the patty. While tangy Ketchup and creamy mayyonaise make perfect-tasting accompaniments.

I take a sip of the cold soda, which leaves me ready for a salty fry. I bite into one. Its crisp and salty on the outside, concealing the soft potato inside. Then I go to back the burger, which seems to get messier and harder to eat with every delicious bite I take. I suddenly remember—I have a math quiz in three days!

Before I know it, all that's left on my plate are a few splatters of Ketchup, mayyonaise, and burger grease, along with one lonely fry. On second thought, I devour that as well and leave full and satisfied.

Reflect

What do you think? Can you practically smell and taste the burgers Andre has described?

Apply

Use vivid words and details to make the experience real for your reader. Make sure to include these in your observation report.

Revise

Focus on Organization

Writing Strategy **Make sure details are presented in a logical, natural order.**

The scoring guide says details should be presented in a logical and natural order. I accomplished that by focusing on one sense at a time as I lead readers through a meal at the Tick Tock Diner. It makes sense to let readers experience the meal through a different sense in each paragraph. Checking my writing, though, I see that I've put one detail out of place. In my draft, Norma takes my order before I even sit down! I'll fix that now.

[DRAFT]

[placed sentence in logical order]

Norma, my server, doesn't need to ask what I want. My order is always the same burger, fries, and a soda. I take an empty seat at the counter, which puts me closer to the kitchen action. Here, I can hear the burgers sizzling on the grill, inviting me to order. Soon, she places the white plastic plate in front of me. On it sits perfection: a juicy burger and fries still glisening with grease and salt.

Apply

When you reread your writing, make sure details are organized logically and naturally.

Revise

Focus on 

Writing Strategy **Connect with the readers.**

For this paper, I used first person to help pull the readers into my experience. It's the best way to connect with them when sharing a personal experience. I also want to keep my voice friendly and casual for my audience—my classmates and teachers. But as I read my paper aloud to myself, I heard some words that just don't sound like me. I'll revise them so that my writing sounds more like my speaking voice.

[DRAFT]

[used casual voice]

An old jukebox rests in one corner of the diner, with tunes from ~~a previous decade~~ another era. Even the ~~employees~~ servers there look as though they came from another time, seeing name tags that display names like "Betty" and "Midge" and "Johnny" and "Suzy."

Reflect

How do Andre's revisions help strengthen his voice?

Apply

You want to connect with your readers. Be sure to use a voice that's appropriate for both your audience and your purpose.

Revise

Focus on 

Writing Strategy **Replace vague words and phrases with precise ones.**

Now I'll reread my paper to be sure I've used specific words, as the scoring guide says to do. I think some of my descriptions about the restaurant are a little too vague. I'll add more precise and specific words.

[DRAFT]

[added specific words]

Red vinyl covers the seats of the booths and stools, while white-topped tables ~~have~~ [stand supported by] chrome legs. An old jukebox rests in one corner of the diner, ~~with~~ [belting out] tunes from ~~a previous decade~~ [another era]. Even the ~~employees~~ [servers] there look as though they came from another time, ~~seeing~~ [their white shirts emblazoned with] name tags that display names like "Betty" and "Midge" and "Johnny" and "Suzy."

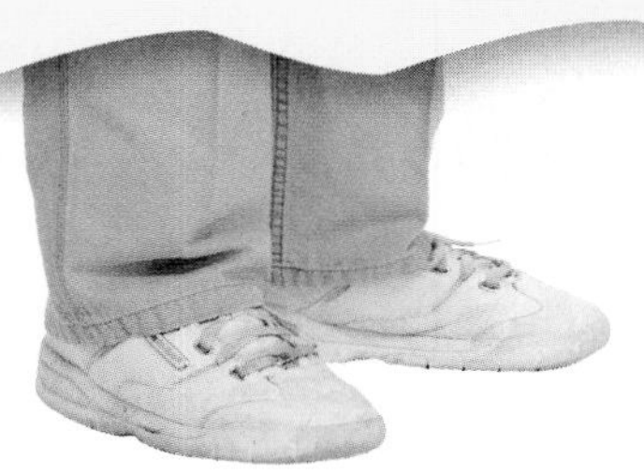

Apply

Word choice is important. Vague words and phrases don't help your reader get a clear picture of what you're describing, so replace them with precise ones.

Edit

Focus on **Conventions**

Writing Strategy **Check my grammar, punctuation, capitalization, and spelling.**

Before I turn in my paper, I'll need to do a final check for grammar, punctuation, capitalization, and spelling.

FINAL DRAFT

The Tastiest Burger

by Andre

[revised choppy sentences]

Four oclock is always burger time. That's the time the old broke clock above the Tick Tock Diner has displayed for as long as anyone can remember. But even though the clock no longer functions, the burgers inside are much appreciated by all the customers.

The aroma of burgers cooking on the grill and fries cooking in the deep fryer grabs me from the moment I walk into the old-fashioned diner on saturday night. Its packed. I can hear the buzz of people talking. I hear the wait staff and cooks yelling orders to each other

The diner is decked out in red white, and chrome. Red vinyl covers the seats of the booths and stools, while white-topped tables have chrome legs. An old jukebox rests in one corner of the diner, with tunes from a previous decade. Even the employees there look as

and

and

stand supported by

belting out

another era

servers

Apply

Check your grammar, punctuation, capitalization, and spelling every time you write for a test.

[FINAL DRAFT]

though they came from another time, ~~seeing~~ their white shirts emblazoned with name tags that display names like "Betty" and "Midge" and "Johnny" and "Suzy."

Norma, my server, doesn't need to ask what I want. My order is always the same: burger, fries, and a soda. I take an empty seat at the counter, which puts me closer to the kitchen action. Here, I can hear the burgers sizzling on the grill, inviting me to order. Soon, she places the white plastic plate in front of me. On it sits perfection: a juicy burger and fries still ~~glisening~~ glistening with grease and salt.

The bun is soft and slightly warm as I lift it to take my first bite. The burger is juicy, salty, and delicious. Crisp lettuce, a thick slab of tomato, and sour pickles surround the patty, ~~W~~while tangy ~~K~~ketchup and creamy ~~mayyonaise~~ mayonnaise make perfect-tasting accompaniments.

I take a sip of the cold soda, which leaves me ready for a salty fry. I bite into one. It's crisp and salty on the outside, concealing the soft potato inside. Then I go back to the burger, which seems to get messier and harder to eat with every delicious bite I take. ~~I suddenly remember I have a math quiz in three days!~~

Before I know it, all that's left on my plate are a few splatters of ~~K~~ketchup, ~~mayyonaise~~ mayonnaise, and burger grease, along with one lonely fry. On second thought, I devour that as well and leave, full and satisfied.

Reflect

When writing for a test, remember to use your time wisely. Be sure to use your writing prompt's scoring guide to check over your writing and make any necessary revisions. Good luck!

Time's up, and it wasn't bad at all. Keep in mind these important steps when you write for a test.

1. **Study the writing prompt before you start to write.** Most writing prompts have three parts: the setup, the task, and the scoring guide. The parts probably won't be labeled. You'll have to figure them out for yourself!
2. **Make sure you understand the task before you start to write. Remember to:**
   - Read all three parts of the writing prompt carefully.
   - Circle key words in the task part of the writing prompt that tell what kind of writing you need to do and who your audience is.
   - Make sure you know how you'll be graded.
   - Say what you need to do in your own words.
3. **Keep an eye on the clock.** Decide how much time you will spend on each part of the writing process and try to stick to it. Don't spend so much time on prewriting that you don't have enough time to write!
4. **Reread your writing. Compare it to the scoring guide at least twice.** Remember the rubrics you have used in the chapter? A scoring guide on a writing test is like a rubric. It can help you keep in mind what's important.
5. **Plan, plan, plan!** You don't get much time to revise during a test, so planning is more important than ever.
6. **Write neatly.** Remember: If the people who score your test can't read your writing, it doesn't matter how good your story or essay is!

Appendix A
Grammar Practice

Compound Subjects and Compound Predicates

Know the Rule

A **compound subject** is two or more subjects joined by a conjunction (*and, or*).

Example:

Both **adults** and **children** wear cotton clothes.

A **compound predicate** is two or more verbs joined by a conjunction.

Example:

American farmers still **grow** and **harvest** large crops of cotton.

Practice the Rule

Each sentence below has either a compound subject or a compound predicate. Write each sentence on a separate sheet of paper. Underline the words that make up each compound subject. Circle the verbs in each compound predicate.

1. Cotton and polyester are used in many articles of clothing.
2. Manufacturers buy and use huge quantities of cotton from Asia.
3. Most shirts and dresses contain some polyester.
4. A cotton blouse or shirt is comfortable in hot summer weather.
5. Farmers pick cotton by hand or use modern machines.
6. My class researched and discussed the leather industry.
7. Shoes and belts are often made of leather.
8. Baseball mitts and footballs are usually leather items.
9. Cars and trucks often come with leather seats.
10. Some people dislike and boycott the use of leather products.

Direct Objects and Indirect Objects

Know the Rule

The **direct object** is the noun or pronoun that receives the action of the verb. Only action verbs can have a direct object. To find the direct object, say the verb and then ask *What?* or *Whom?* The **indirect object** tells to whom or for whom the action of the verb is done.

Example:

The librarian showed **me** interesting **websites** for my report.
(The direct object is *websites*. The indirect object is *me*.)

Practice the Rule

Number a sheet of paper 1–10. Write each sentence. Underline the direct object. If the sentence has an indirect object, circle the indirect object.

1. Our teacher gave us an interesting assignment.
2. Each group will write a report about an extinct animal.
3. Latoya researched information about dinosaurs.
4. She showed me an interesting book about dinosaurs.
5. One website provided my group with colorful drawings of extinct animals.
6. On the island of Bali, people hunted a species of tiger to extinction.
7. The woolly mammoths possessed extremely long tusks.
8. Each group will present its report next week.
9. My group assigned Thomas the task of finding photographs or drawings of the dodo bird.
10. We learned many interesting facts about each group's topic.

Predicate Nouns and Predicate Adjectives

Know the Rule

A **predicate noun** follows a linking verb and renames the subject of the sentence. A **predicate adjective** follows a linking verb and describes the subject. A linking verb does not show action. Rather, it "links" a subject with either another noun or an adjective. The forms of the verb *be* are commonly used as linking verbs. Other verbs that may be linking verbs include *become, seem, feel, taste, look,* and *appear*.

Example:
The Music Man is a famous **musical** from the 1950s. (predicate noun)
Our class seems **excited** about seeing *The Music Man*. (predicate adjective)

Practice the Rule

Number a sheet of paper 1–10. Write each sentence. Underline the subject of the sentence. Then circle the predicate noun or predicate adjective in the sentence. At the end of each sentence, write whether the word is a predicate noun or a predicate adjective.

1. The songs in the play are very entertaining.
2. A small town in the state of Iowa is the setting of the play.
3. In 1957, the show was a great success on Broadway.
4. Broadway is a famous avenue in New York City.
5. It is the site of many large theaters.
6. In 1962, a movie of *The Music Man* was very popular.
7. The film actually became one of the biggest hits of the year.
8. In the beginning of the play, the main character appears honest.
9. He is, however, really a scoundrel after everyone's money.
10. In the end, though, the scoundrel becomes an honest man.

Kinds of Sentences

Know the Rule

A sentence always begins with a capital letter and ends with a type of punctuation. A **declarative sentence** makes a statement and ends with a period. An **interrogative sentence** asks a question and ends with a question mark. An **imperative sentence** gives a command and ends with a period or an exclamation point. An **exclamatory sentence** shows excitement and ends with an exclamation point. When you write, use the punctuation mark based on the effect you want to convey to your readers.

Examples:

Please tell me the year in which the Second World War ended. (imperative sentence)

The Second World War, often written as World War II, ended in 1945. (declarative sentence)

Practice the Rule

Number a sheet of paper 1–10. Write each sentence, adding the correct end punctuation. Then write the kind of sentence it is.

1. World War II lasted from 1939 to 1945
2. Which countries were involved in this war
3. Many powerful countries as well as less powerful countries from around the world were involved
4. Name the countries that were allies of the United States during the war
5. A principle ally of the United States was the United Kingdom
6. Did the United States really fight against Japan and Germany
7. How unbelievable that Germany was once our enemy
8. Have you ever seen the famous photograph taken in New York City on the day that Japan surrendered
9. That photograph shows a sailor kissing a nurse
10. Wow! Everyone must have been happy that the war had finally ended

Dependent Clauses and Independent Clauses

Know the Rule

An **independent clause** is a group of words with a subject and a predicate that expresses a complete thought. An independent clause can stand alone as a sentence. A **dependent clause** has a subject and a predicate, but it does not express a complete thought and cannot stand alone as a sentence. Independent clauses and dependent clauses can be used together to form sentences. A dependent clause often begins with a subordinating conjunction such as *although, as, because, if,* or *when.* When a dependent clause begins a sentence, it is separated from the independent clause by a comma.

Examples:
after we eat lunch (dependent clause)
We will go to the museum. (independent clause)
After we eat lunch, we will go to the museum. (complex sentence with a dependent and an independent clause)
We will go to the museum after we eat lunch. (complex sentence with an independent and a dependent clause)

Practice the Rule

Number a sheet of paper 1–10. Identify the underlined clause in each sentence by writing **independent** or **dependent** after the appropriate number.

1. James wanted to go to a science museum <u>because he is interested in dinosaurs</u>.
2. Because Felipe is studying the history of ships, <u>he suggested a maritime museum</u>.
3. <u>As Lauren had hoped</u>, the class decided to visit an art museum.
4. We looked at some modern sculptures, <u>which not all of my classmates liked</u>.
5. Although the photography exhibit was free, <u>we didn't have time to go</u>.
6. <u>While we walked past the old paintings</u>, a guard watched us closely.
7. <u>We ate lunch in the museum cafe</u> because it was raining outside.
8. This is the same museum <u>that I visited last year with my parents</u>.
9. <u>When my father goes to a museum</u>, he quickly becomes bored.
10. Although I am often bored in museums, <u>I always find something of interest</u>.

Adjective Clauses

Know the Rule

An **adjective clause** is a dependent clause that, like an adjective, describes a noun or a pronoun. An adjective clause always follows the word it describes and often begins with a relative pronoun such as *who, whom, whose, which,* or *that.*

Example:
Women **who have made outstanding accomplishments in sports** inspire all of us.

Practice the Rule

Number a sheet of paper 1–10. Write each sentence. Underline the adjective clause. Circle the noun that each adjective clause describes.

1. Mildred Didrikson, who earned honors in basketball, track and field, and golf, was a famous twentieth-century athlete.
2. She was born in Port Arthur, which is a city on the southeastern coast of Texas.
3. In 1932, she won two gold medals in the Olympics, which were held in Los Angeles.
4. Wilma Rudolph, who was born in 1940, was another Olympic gold medalist.
5. The library has a Wilma Rudolph biography that I want to read.
6. The three gold medals that Rudolph won during the 1960 Olympics in Rome made her an international celebrity.
7. Mia Hamm, who was a world-class soccer player, is now retired.
8. Hamm is a woman that many young women think of as a role model.
9. She has written a book and has appeared in a television documentary, which was produced for cable television.
10. The accomplishments of these admirable athletes have helped women gain opportunities that were not available to them a hundred years ago.

Adverb Clauses

Know the Rule

An **adverb clause** is a dependent clause that tells about a verb, an adjective, or an adverb. Adverb clauses tell *where, when, why,* or *how much*. They often begin with a subordinating conjunction such as *than, although, because, if, as, as if, while, when,* or *whenever*.

Example:
Mrs. Stone planted some flower bulbs in the fall **because she wanted flowers to bloom in the spring**.

Practice the Rule

Number a sheet of paper 1–10. Write each sentence. Underline the adverb clause. Circle the verb, adjective, or adverb that each adverb clause tells about.

1. When the cold winter weather has finally gone, many people plant their gardens.
2. Some people grow flowers because they enjoy the beautiful blossoms.
3. My uncle's garden is much larger than my family's garden.
4. After a person plants a garden, he or she must work in it diligently.
5. Rabbits and chipmunks will eat the vegetables if they get half a chance.
6. Some gardeners spray their plants with chemicals so that harmful insects will stay away.
7. These gardeners are confident because they believe the chemicals will protect their plants.
8. Last year, my mother's tomatoes grew better than her onions.
9. When all the flowers and vegetables do well, the hard work seems worthwhile.
10. A person can start a garden wherever there is enough room and sunlight for the plants.

Run-on Sentences and Comma Splices

Know the Rule

A **run-on sentence** results when no punctuation is used between two complete sentences. A **comma splice** results when two complete sentences are separated by only a comma. You can correct a run-on sentence or a comma splice in several ways. You may decide to add a conjunction, such as *and* or *but*, after the comma. You may decide to separate the two sentences by a period. You may join the sentences with a semicolon.

Examples:

Incorrect:

Vaccinations help to immunize people against diseases, they have not always been popular with the general population.

Correct:

Vaccinations help to immunize people against disease**, but** they have not always been popular with the general population.

Vaccinations help to immunize people against disease**. T**hey have not always been popular with the general population.

Vaccinations help to immunize people against disease**; they** have not always been popular with the general population.

Practice the Rule

Correct sentences 1 and 2 with a semicolon. Correct sentences 3 and 4 by adding a comma and a conjunction. Correct sentence 5 by making two sentences.

1. We heard at the beginning of the school year that we needed flu vaccinations, medical agencies warned parents and students that a flu epidemic was on the way.
2. Many people objected to having vaccinations, their objections were often based on ethical, religious, or medical reasons.
3. Some people were afraid that the flu shot was dangerous they thought that they could avoid the flu by washing their hands and not coughing in other people's faces.
4. The flu and the vaccination were constantly in the news they disappeared from the news when the actual number of cases was much lower than expected.
5. Nevertheless, over the years vaccinations have been extremely beneficial to people vaccinations have helped control dreaded diseases such as polio and smallpox.

Common Nouns and Proper Nouns

Know the Rule

A **common noun** names a general person, place, thing, or idea (*girl, park, painting, freedom*). Common nouns are not capitalized. A **proper noun** names a particular person, place, thing, or idea (*Cindy, Yellowstone National Park, Mona Lisa*). Proper nouns are capitalized. A proper noun that consists of several words (*Yellowstone National Park*) is considered one proper noun.

Practice the Rule

Number a sheet of paper 1–10. Write each sentence. Underline each common noun. Circle each proper noun.

1. Throughout the United States, you can find monuments created by very early Native American cultures.
2. Such a monument is Serpent Mound, located in the state of Ohio.
3. My pal Gus told me that the mound, which is made of earth, is over 1,370 feet long and about one yard high.
4. It winds back and forth through the landscape for about 800 feet.
5. Seen from an airplane, the mound has the shape of a giant snake.
6. Our science teacher, Mr. Pryor, told us that the mound is the largest of its kind in the world.
7. Serpent Mound does not contain any artifacts, such as pottery, jewelry, or graves.
8. Aunt Martha told me that scientists think that the mound was built to serve some religious purpose.
9. The Serpent Mound Museum is located near the mound.
10. You can find information and photographs of Serpent Mound at various websites or by contacting the Ohio Historical Society.

Singular Nouns and Plural Nouns

Know the Rule

A **singular noun** names one person, place, thing, or idea. A **plural noun** names more than one. For most nouns, add *-s* or *-es* to form the plural. The spelling of some nouns changes when *-es* is added to form the plural (*baby/babies; knife/knives*). A few nouns do not add *-s* or *-es* to form the plural; instead, the spelling changes (*child/children*). A few other nouns have the same form in the singular and plural (*sheep*).

Examples:

Many of the **children** in the fourth grade class have **pets**.
Two **girls** own pet **mice**.
Birds can make the **lives** of their **owners** more musical.
Geese would probably not make good **pets**.

Practice the Rule

On a sheet of paper make two columns. Label the left column **Singular Nouns**. Label the right column **Plural Nouns**. Number both columns 1–5. Then list the singular nouns and plural nouns in each sentence.

1. You should regularly check your dog for fleas and ticks.
2. Dogs can pick up these harmful pests in a pile of leaves.
3. Some ticks can cause diseases with their bite.
4. Certain kinds of combs can help you find a tick or flea on your pet.
5. A flea can jump from puppies onto the children playing with them.

Number your paper 6–10. Copy the following chart. Write the missing singular or plural form of each noun.

	Singular Nouns	Plural Nouns
6.	country	_______
7.	_______	women
8.	belief	_______
9.	_______	mice
10.	moose	_______

Personal Pronouns

Know the Rule

A pronoun can take the place of a noun. **Personal pronouns** can be used to stand for the person speaking, the person spoken to, or the person spoken about. **First-person pronouns** refer to the speaker (*I*, *me*) or include the speaker (*we*, *us*). **Second-person pronouns** refer to the person being spoken to (*you*). **Third-person pronouns** refer to the person, place, or thing being spoken about (*he, him, she, her, it, they, them*).

Examples:

I want to learn more about the medical profession. (first person)
The speaker told **us** about the training required for doctors. (first person)
Have **you** ever been to a hospital? (second person)
She must be a determined medical student. (third person)

Practice the Rule

Number a sheet of paper 1–5. Write the personal pronoun in each sentence. Then write whether it is first person, second person, or third person.

1. An ambulance driver talked to us about some different jobs in medicine.
2. Jack asked her if the job as an ambulance driver was very demanding.
3. Can you believe that Jack asked such a question?
4. Carol's two brothers are the two doctors I know.
5. They operate on patients with heart problems.

Number your paper 6–10. Rewrite each sentence using the appropriate personal pronoun in place of the underlined words.

6. <u>Thomas and Cheryl</u> want to become nurse's aides.
7. Thomas was telling <u>Tracy and me</u> all about that job.
8. <u>Tracy and I</u> think the job sounds pretty interesting.
9. <u>Steven</u> doesn't agree with that opinion at all!
10. The librarian told <u>Thomas, Cheryl, Tracy, and Steven</u> to quiet down as they discussed jobs.

Compound Personal Pronouns

Know the Rule

Pronouns formed by adding *-self* or *-selves* to the personal pronouns are called **compound personal pronouns**. Depending on how they are used in a sentence, they are also known as reflexive or intensive pronouns.

- A **reflexive pronoun** reflects back on the subject.

  Example:
  Mike left a message for **himself** to check his voicemail.

- An **intensive pronoun** emphasizes the subject. It often appears right after the subject.

  Example:
  Katie **herself** arranged the plans for the band's rehearsal.

Practice the Rule

Number a sheet of paper 1–5. Write the compound personal pronoun in each sentence. Then write the noun, nouns, or pronoun to which the compound personal pronoun refers.

1. Having decided to give a rock concert for the seventh grade, Mike and Katie found themselves faced with a lot of responsibilities.
2. Mike decided that he himself would find the necessary amplifiers and microphones for the band.
3. The principal herself lent Mike two microphones.
4. I myself thought that my two friends would never succeed at their task.
5. They must have asked themselves many times if they had made a smart decision.

Number your paper 6–10. Rewrite each sentence by replacing the underlined word or words with the appropriate compound personal pronoun.

6. Courtney and Kurt bought <u>Courtney and Kurt</u> tickets for the concert.
7. Courtney had convinced <u>Courtney</u> that the concert would be fun.
8. Ethan and I gave <u>Ethan and me</u> plenty of time to get to the concert.
9. The band presented <u>the band</u> with great style.
10. The students at the concert enjoyed <u>the students at the concert</u>.

Possessive Pronouns

Know the Rule

Possessive pronouns show ownership. The possessive pronouns *my, your, her, his, its, our,* and *their* can replace possessive nouns. These possessive pronouns can stand alone or before a noun. Other possessive pronouns always stand alone. These include *mine, yours, hers, ours,* and *theirs.*

Examples:

Kevin and Kayla's poster is about the planet Mars.

Their poster is about the planet Mars. (possessive pronoun before a noun)

The poster about Saturn is Maya's.

The poster about Saturn is **hers**. (possessive pronoun standing alone)

Practice the Rule

Number a sheet of paper 1–5. After each number, write the possessive pronoun in each sentence. Some sentences may have more than one possessive pronoun.

1. Our recent knowledge about the planets can be attributed mainly to the U.S. space program.
2. Interplanetary spacecraft track planets and record details about their movements.
3. For their report, Jerome and Anna decided to concentrate on Earth.
4. The idea to write about the rings of Saturn for our group's report was mine.
5. I enjoyed Jason, Tanya, and Bill's project on Venus. Theirs was my favorite.

Number your paper 6–10. Write the possessive pronoun that could take the place of the underlined word or words in each sentence.

6. <u>Galileo's</u> observations of the planets in the 17th century supported the idea that the planets orbited the sun.
7. <u>The planets'</u> orbits about the sun are not exactly circular.
8. <u>Tara's</u> planet poster was colorful but not as informative as <u>Tim's</u>.
9. Did you know that <u>Saturn's</u> rings are made up almost entirely of ice?
10. I think that the best planet report was <u>Jill and Shaniqua's</u>.

Relative Pronouns and Interrogative Pronouns

Know the Rule

The **relative pronouns** *who, whom, which, that, what,* and *whose* are used to introduce dependent clauses. The **interrogative pronouns** *who, whom, which, what,* and *whose* are used to introduce questions. Notice that the same pronouns may be either relative pronouns or interrogative pronouns. You must determine how the pronoun is used in the sentence.

Examples:

What does the mayor propose to do about the traffic congestion in our town?

The solution **that** I believe would help involves banning cars on certain days.

Practice the Rule

Number a sheet of paper 1–5. Write each sentence. Underline the relative pronoun and circle each interrogative pronoun.

1. Which traffic problem in the United States are you studying?
2. The problem that I want to write about is intercity traffic.
3. What do you think causes the traffic congestion in cities?
4. Whom do you think we should contact about this problem?
5. The people who live in the cities must help solve the traffic problems.

Number your paper 6–10. Write the relative pronoun or interrogative pronoun that completes each sentence.

6. ______ agency did you contact for traffic information?
7. ______ should I ask for data concerning the number of cars in our town?
8. Do you know the candidate ______ party supports carpooling?
9. Margot asked the speaker ______ she thought about banning cars on Saturday.
10. I believe ______ carpooling will help alleviate the traffic problem.

Articles

Know the Rule

Adjectives describe nouns. The words *a, an,* and *the* are adjectives called **articles**. Use *a* or *an* to refer to a general noun. Use *a* before a word that begins with a consonant sound. Use *an* before a word that begins with a vowel sound. Use *the* when you refer to a specific item or items. Articles can appear before nouns or before an adverb or adjective.

Examples:

I need to get **a** book about reptiles for my report.
This is **an** interesting book about alligators.
Hand me **the** books on the table.

Practice the Rule

Number a sheet of paper 1–10. Write each sentence, using the article or articles in parentheses that correctly complete the sentence. Then underline the article **the** each time it appears and the word to which it refers.

1. One of the traits of (a/an) reptile is that it lays eggs.
2. (A/An) alligator is (a/an) well-known reptile.
3. The saltwater crocodile is (a/an) example of (a/an) large reptile.
4. The encyclopedia gives (a/an) extensive description of this crocodile.
5. One photograph at the website I visited shows (a/an) hind leg of a lizard.
6. When (a/an) crocodile is threatened with danger, it bares its teeth and hisses.
7. How can scientists determine if (a/an) reptile is as intelligent as (a/an) bird?
8. Curled up, (a/an) adult thread snake can fit on the face of (a/an) quarter.
9. This photograph shows (a/an) snake swallowing (a/an) egg.
10. The reptile is certainly (a/an) interesting class of animals.

Demonstrative Pronouns and Demonstrative Adjectives

Know the Rule

This, these, that, and *those* can be either **demonstrative adjectives** or **demonstrative pronouns**. *This* and *these* refer to a thing or things nearby. *That* and *those* refer to a thing or things farther away.

Demonstrative adjectives are used with nouns. They tell "which one."

Examples:

I like **these** cartoons in my book.

That book isn't very funny.

Demonstrative pronouns take the place of nouns or pronouns.

Example:

This is a much funnier collection of early comics.

Practice the Rule

Number a sheet of paper 1–10. Write the demonstrative adjective or demonstrative pronoun in each sentence. After each demonstrative adjective, write the noun that it describes. After each demonstrative pronoun, write the noun or pronoun it takes the place of.

1. I love this cartoon by Dr. Seuss.
2. That artist must have been really talented.
3. This is the book on cartoons I requested last week from the library.
4. Do these websites describe the history of cartoons and comic strips?
5. This series of panels makes up a comic strip.
6. These are reproductions of drawings from *Hogan's Alley,* one of the first newspaper comic strips in the United States.
7. That is the funniest cartoon I have ever seen.
8. Among the cartoons you've shown me, this one is the most colorful.
9. It's difficult to understand the point of these old political cartoons.
10. If it hadn't been for those early cartoonists, we might not have today's animated cartoons.

Prepositions

Know the Rule

A **preposition** is a word that shows a relationship between the noun or pronoun that follows it (object of the preposition) and another word or group of words in the sentence. A **prepositional phrase** is a group of words beginning with a preposition and ending with a noun or pronoun.

Example:

Rain pounded **on the roof**.

Practice the Rule

Number a sheet of paper 1–5. Write the prepositional phrase or phrases in each sentence.

1. Thunderstorms in the Midwest can be frightening experiences.
2. You can usually see the dark clouds of the storm approaching.
3. The lightning begins, and you can hear the deep rumbling of thunder.
4. Throughout the storm, bolts of lightning flash across the sky.
5. Luckily, the thunderstorms quickly pass into the distance.

Number your paper 6–10. Write a preposition from the box to complete each sentence. Try to use each preposition only once.

above	across	from	in	of

6. Having come ______ Los Angeles, experiencing a midwestern thunderstorm was a completely new experience.
7. Lightning seemed to explode ______ our heads.
8. We took refuge ______ my grandfather's barn.
9. The powerful thunder rattled the windows ______ the barn.
10. When the rain stopped, we ran ______ the yard to the house.

The Simple Tenses

Know the Rule

The tense of a verb tells when the action happens. The **present tense** indicates that something happens regularly or is true now. *(fly)* The **past tense** tells that something has happened in the past. The past tense is usually formed by adding *-ed* to the verb. (*call/called*) The past tense of some verbs has a different spelling. *(flew)* The **future tense** tells that something is going to happen. The future tense is formed with *will*. *(will fly)*

Practice the Rule

Number a sheet of paper 1–5. Write the verb in each sentence. Then identify the tense of the verb by writing **present tense, past tense,** or **future tense.**

1. Over six hundred species of birds nest in North America.
2. Not all birds migrate to warmer climates before winter.
3. I will ask the guide at the nature preserve about these birds.
4. Our bus to the nature preserve finally rumbled to a stop at the front gate.
5. On the way, my friends and I thought of questions for our guide.

Number your paper 6–10. Write the present-, past-, or future-tense form of the verb that correctly completes each sentence.

6. Last week in class, we ______ bird flight and migration. (study)
7. We heard about and ______ lots of interesting things about birds. (discover)
8. For example, a bird's feathers ______ very little. (weigh)
9. In the first part of our tour, we watched as a bird ______ seeds from the guide's hand. (eat)
10. Next Monday, we ______ the different habitats of birds. (explore)

Progressive Verb Forms

Know the Rule

Progressive forms of verbs show continuing action. The **present-progressive** form of a verb consists of the helping verbs *am, is,* or *are* and the present participle of that verb. (*I am reading.*) The **past-progressive** form consists of the helping verb *was* or *were* and the present participle. (*They were reading.*) The **future-progressive** form consists of the helping verbs *will be* and the present participle. (*You will be reading.*)

Practice the Rule

Number a sheet of paper 1–5. Write the verb in each sentence, including its helping verb. Then identify the verb form by writing **present progressive, past progressive,** or **future progressive.**

1. Our class is studying different genres of fiction.
2. Joaquin is reading an English mystery novel.
3. I was considering a science fiction novel as my choice.
4. Two of my friends were searching the library for gothic horror stories.
5. My classmates and I will be presenting oral reports about our books next Wednesday.

Number your paper 6–10. Rewrite each sentence using the progressive form of the verb in parentheses.

6. I _____ information about the author of my book today in the library. (future progressive form of *research*)
7. Nicole _____ her oral presentation with a friend. (present progressive form of *practice*)
8. Our teacher _____ us on the content of our report as well as on our presentation. (future progressive form of *grade*)
9. Ashley _____ her book just before lunch. (past progressive form of *finish*)
10. Both David and Ana _____ on historical fiction books. (present progressive form of *report*)

Emphatic Verb Forms

Know the Rule

Emphatic forms of the present tense and the past tense show emphasis. These forms are made by using the present or past form of the verb *do* with the base form of a verb.

Examples:

I **do like** making some money during school vacations.
Caitlyn **did refuse** the position in the school library.

Practice the Rule

Number a sheet of paper 1–5. Rewrite each sentence, changing the verb to the emphatic form of the present tense.

1. I work part-time at the bookstore during my spring vacation.
2. Kelly wants a job like that for herself this summer.
3. I think I'm old enough for a part-time job.
4. Yes, my parents agree with me about my getting a job.
5. I appreciate your offer of work at the library.

Number your paper 6–10. Rewrite each sentence, changing the verb to the emphatic form of the past tense.

6. My mother suggested the possibility of my working during summer vacation.
7. Yes, I accepted the job mowing Mrs. Dolan's lawn.
8. I volunteered a few hours each weekend at a local park.
9. Yes, I finished the assigned tasks.
10. I anticipated having several hours of free time last weekend.

Transitive Verbs and Intransitive Verbs

Know the Rule

Action verbs may or may not need an object to complete the action of the verb. An action verb that has an object is called a **transitive verb**. An action verb that does not have an object is called an **intransitive verb**. Many verbs can be either transitive or intransitive, depending on their use in a sentence.

Examples:

In 2005, a terrible natural disaster **occurred**. (intransitive verb)
We **researched** Hurricane Katrina on the library computers. (transitive verb)

Practice the Rule

Number a sheet of paper 1–10. Write the verb in each sentence. Then write whether the verb is transitive or intransitive. If the verb is transitive, write the direct object.

1. A powerful hurricane battered the city of New Orleans.
2. Huge waves pounded the walls that protected the city from floodwaters.
3. Eventually, the walls, called levees, collapsed.
4. Floodwaters rose higher and higher in the city streets.
5. Thousands of people evacuated their homes.
6. Government officials and volunteers rescued stranded inhabitants.
7. Thousands of college students volunteered.
8. The high winds and flooding caused terrible damage throughout the city.
9. In the years after the flood, parts of New Orleans have recovered.
10. People repaired the damaged streets and buildings.

Conjunctions

Know the Rule

Coordinating conjunctions (*and, but, or, so*) connect words or groups of words (including independent clauses) that are of equal importance in a sentence.

Subordinating conjunctions (such as *although, because, since, if, after*, and *before*) show how one clause is related to another more important clause. Subordinating conjunctions are used at the beginning of adverb clauses.

Practice the Rule

On a separate sheet of paper, write the conjunction in each sentence and identify it as a coordinating conjunction or a subordinating conjunction.

1. Many sports have dishonest players, and baseball is no exception.
2. Although the 1919 World Series scandal happened long ago, it lives on.
3. Several Chicago players joined together to throw the World Series because they were dissatisfied with their low salaries.
4. The poorly paid players disliked the team's owner, but they also disliked the players making better salaries.
5. The players wanted more money, so they contacted local gangsters.

On a separate sheet of paper, choose the conjunction in parentheses that best completes the sentence.

6. The gangsters agreed to pay the players ______ they would lose the World Series. (if/although/but)
7. The White Sox lost three of the first four games against the Cincinnati Reds, ______ the gangsters refused to pay the players any money. (if/or/but)
8. ______ they had not been paid any money, the dishonest White Sox players decided that they would not throw the series. (Because/If/Although)
9. ______ Chicago won the next two games, the gangsters paid the players a visit. (Although/After/If)
10. The gangsters scared the players into throwing the eighth game, ______ the Cincinnati Reds won the World Series. (but/and/since)

More Conjunctions

Know the Rule

Correlative conjunctions always appear in pairs. They connect words or groups of words and provide more emphasis than coordinating conjunctions.

Examples:

Both bats **and** flying squirrels are mammals.

Neither bats **nor** flying squirrels have wings like those of birds.

Common Correlative Conjunctions

both…and
either…or
neither…nor
whether…or
not only…but (also)

Practice the Rule

On a separate sheet of paper, write each sentence. Underline the correlative conjunctions in it.

1. A flying squirrel may be hunted at night by either owls or coyotes.
2. Its tail helps the flying squirrel both control its flight and stop before landing.
3. Active at night, bats spend the daylight hours either grooming or sleeping.
4. Bats are threatened by both disease and the presence of wind turbines.
5. We associate bats with both heroes, such as Batman, and villains, such as Dracula.
6. A hound is a type of dog that helps hunters not only track the prey being hunted, but also chase the prey.
7. There are many kinds of hounds, including both the beagle and the dachshund.
8. Most hunting hounds use either sight or scent to track prey.

On a separate sheet of paper, combine each pair of sentences by using the correlative conjunctions in parentheses that follow each pair.

9. Do you know if the whippet is a hound? Do you know if the whippet is a spaniel? (whether…or)
10. Poodles are not classified as hounds. Border collies are not classified as hounds. (neither…nor)

Irregular Verbs

Know the Rule

The past and past participle of regular verbs are formed by adding *-ed* to the present form. (*climb, climbed, have climbed*) The past and past participle of **irregular verbs** are not formed by adding *-ed*. The best way to learn the past and past participle of irregular verbs is to memorize them. This chart shows the forms of a few irregular verbs.

Present	Past	Past Participle
do	did	(has, have) done
fly	flew	(has, have) flown
have	had	(has, have) had
ring	rang	(has, have) rung

Practice the Rule

Number a sheet of paper 1–5. Write each sentence using the correct form of the verb in parentheses.

1. I (have knowed/have known) about Amelia Earhart since reading about her last month.
2. She (flied/flew) by herself across the Atlantic Ocean in 1932.
3. No woman (had done/had did) that before her historic flight.
4. Earhart also (wrote/written) best-selling books about her adventures flying.
5. With each new accomplishment as a pilot, Earhart's fame (growed/grew).

Number your paper 6–10. Write each sentence using the past or past participle of the verb in parentheses.

6. In 1935, Earhart ______ more famous by flying from Hawaii to California. (become)
7. In 1936, she ______ planning for a flight around the world. (begin)
8. No woman had ______ around the world before. (fly)
9. Earhart and her navigator never ______ it around the world. (make)
10. Sometime on July 2, 1937, their plane crashed and ______ in the ocean. (sink)

Subject-Verb Agreement

Know the Rule

The **subject** of a sentence and its **verb must agree in number**. Use a singular verb with a singular subject. Use a plural verb with a plural subject.

• A **collective noun,** such as *family, group, team,* or *flock,* names more than one person or thing acting together as one group. Collective nouns are almost always considered singular and require a singular verb.

Example:

My **family enjoys** hiking.

• Most **indefinite pronouns,** including *everyone, nobody, nothing,* and *anything,* are considered singular. These pronouns require a singular verb.

Examples:

Everybody is excited about the dance this Friday.

• A few indefinite pronouns, such as many and several, are considered plural.

Several are going early to decorate the gym.

Practice the Rule

Number a sheet of paper 1–10. Write each sentence, using the correct form of the verb in parentheses. Then underline the simple subject.

1. Nobody (want/wants) to miss the homecoming football game this Friday night.
2. My family (look/looks) forward to the game every year.
3. Nothing (excite/excites) my father more than the thought of attending the game.
4. Of course, our school's team (expect/expects) to win the game.
5. The crowd at the homecoming game (is/are) always very noisy.
6. Everyone (attend/attends) expecting a close, exciting game.
7. Our class always (yell/yells) the loudest at the school pep rally on Friday afternoon.
8. A group of cheerleaders usually (lead/leads) us in cheers for the team.
9. Several from the high school often (visit/visits) the middle school for the pep rally.
10. For a few hours, everything related to schoolwork (are/is) happily forgotten.

Grammar, Usage & Mechanics

Auxiliary Verbs

Know the Rule

An **auxiliary verb**, or **helping verb**, works with a main verb. Auxiliary verbs serve a variety of purposes. Some auxiliary verbs, such as *could, should, might,* and *may,* show how likely something is to happen. Other auxiliary verbs, such as *did, is, will,* and *would,* indicate the tense of the main verb. Sometimes other words can appear between the auxiliary verb and the main verb.

Examples:

Just about anything that produces some kind of sound **can serve** as a musical instrument.

A bluegrass musician **might** even **play** a pair of spoons during a song.

Practice the Rule

Number a sheet of paper 1–10. Write the auxiliary verb and the main verb in each sentence.

1. Knowing the characteristics of musical instruments should influence an aspiring musician's choice of instrument.
2. One person may want an instrument with a soothing sound.
3. That person probably would avoid the electric guitar.
4. Someone with good rhythm might enjoy the drums.
5. Which kind of stringed instrument would suit me best?
6. Someone thinking about learning the harp should know about the instrument's large size.
7. A piano will require a large financial investment.
8. Is the flute always used in an orchestra?
9. Can you devote several hours each week to practicing an instrument?
10. A person must consider many factors when choosing a musical instrument.

Conventions **Grammar, Usage & Mechanics**

Titles

Know the Rule

When writing, **underline** the titles of longer works, such as books, magazines, newspapers, and movies. If using a computer, use italics because such titles appear in italics in printed material. Use **quotation marks** around the titles of shorter works, such as songs, stories, and poems. Capitalize the first word and the last word in titles. Capitalize all other words except articles, short prepositions, and coordinating conjunctions. Also, capitalize short verbs, such as *is* and *are*.

Practice the Rule

Number a sheet of paper 1–10. Rewrite each sentence, punctuating and capitalizing each title correctly.

1. The famous poem the raven was written by the American author Edgar Allan Poe who lived in the first half of the nineteenth century.
2. Poe also wrote many well-known horror stories, including the masque of the red death and the fall of the house of usher.
3. The 1962 horror movie premature burial was based on a story by Poe.
4. Poe's poem annabel lee is about the early death of a beautiful woman.
5. Poe wrote only one novel, the narrative of arthur gordon pym of nantucket.
6. Lois Lowry's novel number the stars takes place during World War II.
7. Folk singer Woody Guthrie wrote the song this land is your land.
8. Don't you just love Billy Collins's poem introduction to poetry?
9. In sixth grade, I memorized the poem stopping by woods on a snowy evening.
10. My little brother's favorite song is Hakuna Matata from The lion king.

Commas

Know the Rule

Commas tell a reader where to pause. Use a comma to separate a noun of direct address from the rest of a sentence. Place a comma after a subordinating clause when it is used at the beginning of a sentence. Set off nonessential, also called nonrestrictive, clauses with commas. A nonessential clause provides information that may be interesting but not necessary to the meaning of the sentence.

Examples:

Mr. Diaz, will we have any homework tonight?

If I've learned anything this year, it's that we have homework every night.

I was hoping that**, because of today's soccer tournament,** we would have a break from homework.

Practice the Rule

Number a sheet of paper 1–8. Write each sentence, adding commas where needed. After each sentence, write the reason for the comma.

1. Ms. Stewart is soccer the most popular game in the world?
2. People play soccer which is sometimes called the world game in almost every country in the world.
3. Although few points are scored during a game soccer matches are consistently exciting.
4. The English professional soccer league which is called the Premier League scored an average 2.48 points per game in 2005.
5. Whereas the goalkeepers may use their hands to stop an attempted goal and to throw the ball back onto the field the other players are not allowed to touch the ball with their hands or arms.
6. World Cup Soccer games have been held every four years since 1930 except 1942 and 1946.
7. When the World Cup games are on TV people around the world gather to watch and cheer on their favorite teams.
8. Do you have any more questions Anthony?

Grammar, Usage & Mechanics

More Commas

Know the Rule

Use a **comma** between coordinate adjectives that describe the same noun, but never place a comma between the final adjective and the noun itself. Coordinate adjectives are "equal" adjectives. Ask these questions to determine whether the adjectives are coordinate:

- Does the sentence make sense if the adjectives are reversed in order?
- Does the sentence make sense if the word *and* comes between the adjectives?

Examples:

The library is a gray stone building.

The chattering**,** noisy crowd of children burst through the doors.

Practice the Rule

Number a sheet of paper 1–10. Write each incorrect sentence, placing commas as necessary between coordinate adjectives. Write **Correct** if the sentence is correct as is.

1. Jake loves the old musty smell of the town library.
2. Ms. McMichael is the new children's librarian.
3. She told Jake that he would find longer more interesting books in the young adult section.
4. Jake climbed the creaky wooden stairs to the second floor.
5. The second floor was a whole new world for Jake.
6. Jake entered a clean spacious room.
7. A row of new desktop computers lined one wall.
8. Mr. Gomes extended a friendly warm welcome to Jake.
9. He pointed out a large extensive collection of CDs and DVDs.
10. Jake selected a new best-selling book to take home.

Grammar, Usage & Mechanics

Semicolons and Colons

Know the Rule

A **semicolon** (;) can be used instead of a comma and conjunction to separate the independent clauses in a compound sentence. A **colon** (:) can be used to separate two independent clauses when the second explains the first. Be sure to capitalize the first letter of the second sentence. A colon can also be used to introduce a list at the end of a sentence, to separate parts of references in a bibliography, and to separate hours and minutes in an expression of time.

Examples:

Science fiction books may be set in outer space**;** they may also take place in the distant future.

Our summer reading list includes the following books**:** *A Single Shard, A Year Down Yonder,* and *Lily's Crossing.*

The article on poetry appeared in *World Book Encyclopedia* 12**:**125–127.

Practice the Rule

Number your paper 1–8. Rewrite the sentences using semicolons and colons correctly.

1. Historical fiction requires that the reader know a little bit about the setting of the story science fiction does not require this of the reader.
2. Science fiction stories are my favorite kind of stories they are exciting and challenge my imagination as I read.
3. I can't meet you at the science museum until 4 30 P.M.
4. H.G. Wells is a science fiction author who lived over a hundred years ago he wrote my favorite science fiction book, *The Time Machine.*
5. My favorite science fiction authors include the following Frank Herbert, Ursula K. Le Guin, and William Gibson.
6. Ray Bradbury has published more than 500 titles short stories, novels, plays, screenplays, television scripts, and verse.
7. "All Summer in a Day" is an often-read short story it was published in 1954.
8. The original *Star Wars* movie will be shown at 7 00 P.M.

Brackets and Dashes

Know the Rule

Use **brackets** to set off an interruption to a direct quote.
Use **dashes** to show a sudden break in thought. A dash can also be used instead of the words, *in other words* and *that is* before an explanation.

Examples:

Today at Cooperstown—there's no better place to be today—five players were inducted into the Baseball Hall of Fame.

"I am honored by this [his induction into the Hall of Fame] and honored to be standing in such company," said the great left-handed pitcher.

Practice the Rule

Number a sheet of paper 1–8. Write each sentence, adding brackets or dashes where they are needed.

1. Hall of Fame Weekend that will be quite a celebration will be the last weekend in July this year.
2. "He the great pitcher Robin Roberts was one of the nicest guys I ever met," said his former teammate.
3. The famous Detroit Tigers announcer Ernie Harwell I can hear his voice in my imagination died in 2010.
4. "Sandy Koufax the superstar Los Angeles Dodger pitcher from the 1960s retired early," explained our coach, "because he had arthritis."
5. Hank Aaron the great homerun champion was inducted into the Hall of Fame in 1982.
6. In his speech, Aaron said, "They Jackie Robinson and Roy Campanella proved to the world that a man's ability is limited only by his lack of opportunity."
7. My dad's baseball card collection it must be worth thousands of dollars is kept locked in a drawer in his office.
8. Baseball America's pastime is a well-loved sport.

More Practice

Compound Subjects and Compound Predicates

Write the compound subjects or the compound predicates in each sentence. Then write the conjunction that connects them.

1. Coal and oil are important energy sources around the world.
2. Does West Virginia or Kentucky provide most of America's coal?
3. The sun and wind are other potential energy sources.
4. Some environmentalists prefer and promote solar energy.
5. Solar panels look unattractive but are useful.

Direct Objects and Indirect Objects

Write the direct object in each sentence and label it **direct object**. If the sentence has an indirect object, write it and label it **indirect object**.

1. Our teacher gave the class a quiz this morning.
2. The test required an understanding of the American Revolution.
3. The second essay question gave me considerable trouble.
4. I collected the finished tests at the end of the period.
5. Mr. Erikson took the tests from me.

Predicate Nouns and Predicate Adjectives

Write the subject of the sentence. Then write the predicate noun or predicate adjective and label it either **predicate noun** or **predicate adjective**.

1. Ted Williams was a superstar for the Boston Red Sox from 1938–1960.
2. He became the greatest hitter of his generation.
3. Williams's final appearance as a player was astonishing.
4. His last hit was a home run to deep center field in Boston's Fenway Park.
5. Fenway Park is well known to baseball fans.

More Practice

Kinds of Sentences

Write **declarative, interrogative, imperative,** or **exclamatory** to identify the type of each sentence.

1. Please point to Puerto Rico on the classroom map.
2. What are the main crops grown in the fields of Puerto Rico?
3. Baseball, boxing, and volleyball are popular sports in Puerto Rico.
4. The beaches of Puerto Rico are so beautiful!
5. How far is Puerto Rico from Florida?

Dependent Clauses and Independent Clauses

Copy the sentences. Underline each dependent clause once and each independent clause twice.

1. Just after they first take office, presidents are usually very popular.
2. If America's economy is strong, most people will approve of the president's actions.
3. Public approval can quickly disappear if the public loses confidence.
4. When presidents become unpopular, they risk losing the next election.
5. A candidate will win an election if he or she connects with the voters.

Adjective Clauses

Copy the sentences. Underline the adjective clause in each sentence. Circle the noun or pronoun that each adjective clause describes.

1. Valerie volunteered to work one weekend at a city park that is four blocks from her apartment building.
2. Her mother, who also wanted to volunteer, accompanied Valerie.
3. Ms. Sanchez, who is a park official, was in charge of cleaning up.
4. Her crew, which worked very hard for two days, picked up the trash.
5. City residents appreciate having a park that is free of litter.

More Practice

Adverb Clauses

Copy the sentences. Underline the adverb clause in each sentence. Circle the verb, adjective, or adverb that the adverb clause tells about.

1. My uncle goes bird watching whenever he has some spare time.
2. He is always hopeful that he will spy a rare or unusual bird.
3. Whenever he sees such a bird, he writes about it in his journal.
4. He keeps a journal of his hikes so that he can remember the birds.
5. He always has his journal with him unless he forgets it.

Avoiding Run-on Sentences and Comma Splices

Correct sentences 1 and 2 by adding a comma and a conjunction. Correct sentences 3 and 4 with a semicolon. Correct sentence 5 by making two sentences.

1. People recycle bottles and cans there are other things to recycle.
2. Recycling is one solution to the problem repairing and reusing things that can be fixed is another.
3. Magazines and newspapers can be recycled computers and cell phones can be recycled as well.
4. Department stores throw away tons of clothes and shoes that are not sold, these stores could donate the clothes to charities.
5. After sporting events, some arenas donate left-over food they give it to homeless shelters.

Common Nouns and Proper Nouns

Copy each sentence. Circle each common noun. Underline each proper noun.

1. Lake Erie is part of a group of large freshwater lakes in eastern North America.
2. The five large lakes are collectively known as the Great Lakes.
3. During the winter, the lakes cause heavy snowfall in states such as Ohio and Michigan.
4. Our teacher, Mr. Stevens, was born in the city of Rochester, which is located on the shore of Lake Ontario.
5. A large amusement park in Ohio is right on Lake Erie.

More Practice

Singular Nouns and Plural Nouns

Write the plural form of each singular noun.

1. item
2. city
3. knife
4. man
5. notebook
6. life
7. train
8. house

Personal Pronouns

Write the personal pronoun in each sentence. Then write whether it is first person, second person, or third person. A sentence may have more than one personal pronoun.

1. Last week, we began studying about South America.
2. You made a list of the countries on that continent.
3. Jake told us that Liberia and Morocco were in South America.
4. He is wrong because they are both countries in Africa.
5. I can't wait until we start our unit on China.

Compound Personal Pronouns

Write the appropriate compound personal pronoun to refer to each underlined noun or pronoun.

1. <u>I</u> reminded ______ to exercise thirty minutes today.
2. <u>Mr. Greene</u> bought ______ a membership at a gym in our neighborhood.
3. <u>Marie</u> has asked ______ why she doesn't exercise more.
4. If <u>people</u> would force ______ to exercise more, they would be healthier.
5. <u>We</u> have to be careful not to hurt ______ when we exercise.

More Practice

Possessive Pronouns

Write the possessive pronoun in each sentence.

1. I was very nervous about giving my first oral report before the class.
2. Maya had given hers about the early American colonies the day before.
3. Her oral report was extremely interesting and well organized.
4. After Maya's report, most of us were nervous about giving our reports.
5. Ethan gave his report about John Adams, which was excellent.

Relative Pronouns and Interrogative Pronouns

Write each sentence. Underline each relative pronoun. Circle each interrogative pronoun.

1. Whom do you consider the most important scientist of the last century?
2. Stephen Hawking, whose theories about stars are mind-boggling, has to be on the list.
3. What is Albert Einstein famous for having discovered?
4. Einstein is a famous mathematician who actually failed math one year in high school.
5. Can you believe that such a brilliant person could fail a math course?

Articles

Write each sentence, using the correct article in parentheses. Then underline the article **the** each time it appears and the word to which it refers.

1. The Greeks of ancient times were (a/an) amazing race of people.
2. The Parthenon is (a/an) example of their achievement in architecture.
3. Built as (a/an) temple over two thousand years ago, the building is considered (a/an) enduring symbol of Greek civilization.
4. Located on (a/an) hill above the city of Athens, the ruins of the Parthenon are (a/an) important tourist attraction today.
5. (The/A) Greek islands would be (the/a) wonderful place to visit.

More Practice

Demonstrative Pronouns and Demonstrative Adjectives

Write the demonstrative adjective or demonstrative pronoun in each sentence. After each demonstrative adjective, write the noun that it describes. After each demonstrative pronoun, write the noun or pronoun it replaces.

1. This is the website on volcanoes the librarian told me about.
2. These links lead to photographs and interesting data related to volcanoes.
3. You can sit at that computer and log on to the same website.
4. This is the information on famous volcanoes that I used in my report.
5. You can print out the information on those printers over there.

Prepositions

Write the prepositional phrase or phrases in each sentence.

1. Throughout history, gold has been a sign of wealth.
2. It is used in coins and expensive jewelry.
3. Artists applied gold to the surfaces of paintings during the Renaissance.
4. The presence of gold in the paintings made them very valuable.
5. Alchemists tried to make gold from many different kinds of common metals.

The Simple Tenses

Write the sentences. Use the present-, past-, or future-tense form of the verb that best completes each sentence.

1. In 1861, John Carlton ______ a patent for a small card people could mail without an envelope. (obtain)
2. Today we ______ these small cards postcards. (call)
3. Postcards ______ less to mail than letters. (cost)
4. Tomorrow I ______ a postcard from Los Angeles to my family. (send)
5. Maybe someday I ______ a postcard from someone. (receive)

More Practice

Progressive Verb Forms

Write the verb in each sentence, including its helping verb. Then identify the verb form as present progressive, past progressive, or future progressive.

1. My brother and I were reading about the environment.
2. He was concentrating mainly on the environment in our city.
3. Air pollution is becoming a problem in our city.
4. My brother and I will be planting a tree on the roof of our building.
5. More people are doing things to improve the environment.

Emphatic Verb Forms

Write each sentence, changing the underlined verb to the emphatic form of the present tense or the past tense.

1. I <u>think</u> that our hockey team played very well yesterday.
2. The team <u>made</u> a few mistakes, though.
3. Coach Novak <u>admonished</u> several players.
4. Nevertheless, I'm sure the team <u>appreciates</u> the school's support.
5. Everyone at school <u>enjoys</u> having a hockey team.

Transitive Verbs and Intransitive Verbs

Write the verb in each sentence. Then write whether the verb is transitive or intransitive. If the verb is transitive, write the direct object.

1. The Mississippi River originates at Lake Itasca in Minnesota.
2. The waters of the river flow slowly to the Gulf of Mexico.
3. The river transports tons of sediment to the Gulf of Mexico.
4. From north to south, many famous bridges span the great river.
5. Ships of all types carry cargo to cities along the river.

More Practice

Conjunctions

Write the conjunction in each sentence and identify it as a coordinating conjunction or a subordinating conjunction.

1. Although I was prepared to give my oral report, I was relieved that school was cancelled.
2. Classes were cancelled because heavy snow had fallen during the night.
3. I did the visuals, and my partner prepared the written report.
4. We are both ready to give the report, but we're also a little nervous.
5. Much to our surprise, everyone clapped after we gave our report!

More Conjunctions

Underline the correlative conjunctions in each sentence.

1. The novels of Mark Twain include both *The Prince and the Pauper* and *The Adventures of Tom Sawyer.*
2. Generally, readers find Twain's novel *The Adventures of Huckleberry Finn* either obnoxious or funny.
3. Whether people like Twain or hate him, they usually acknowledge that he is a major American author.
4. Twain wrote not only novels but also short stories.
5. I enjoyed reading both *The Adventures of Tom Sawyer* and *Life on the Mississippi.*

Irregular Verbs

Write the sentences. Use the correct form of the verb in parentheses.

1. Our class (has began/has begun) a lesson on the American Revolution.
2. Elena (chose/choosed) a book about George Washington.
3. Washington (leaded/led) the colonial forces against the British army.
4. I (have wrote/have written) a poem about the brave soldiers on both sides.
5. Vikram (read/readed) a book about the Marquis de Lafayette.

More Practice

Subject-Verb Agreement

Write each sentence, using the correct form of the verb in parentheses. Then underline the simple subject.

1. Everyone (need/needs) to keep up with technological advancements.
2. New products (appear/appears) almost every month.
3. Families (replace/replaces) computers and cell phones all the time.
4. People (spend/spends) lots of money on electrical products.
5. Used electronic devices (take/takes) up space in landfills.

Auxiliary Verbs (Helping Verbs)

Write the sentences. Underline the auxiliary verb once and the main verb twice in each sentence.

1. Can you repair a leaky faucet?
2. Someone with some understanding of plumbing could help you.
3. Hiring a professional plumber can cost lots of money.
4. We all should know a little bit about home improvement.
5. Do you have a basic set of tools?

Titles

Write each sentence, punctuating and capitalizing each title correctly.

1. Released in 1981, raiders of the lost ark is a famous American adventure movie.
2. The first movie based on William Shakespeare's play romeo and juliet was made in 1936.
3. Has Ambrose Bierce's famous short story an occurrence at owl creek bridge ever been turned into a movie?
4. Lewis Carroll's poem jabberwocky is funny but uses lots of made-up words.
5. Fairy tales by the Grimm brothers include cinderella and little red riding hood.

More Practice

Commas

Write each sentence, adding commas where needed.

1. Though Lin was only thirteen she knew that she wanted to be an airline pilot.
2. Ms. Hall can you tell us what education an airline pilot needs?
3. Learning to fly a plane which requires hours of practice can be expensive.
4. A student pilot has to take difficult intensive classes.
5. Would you rather fly a jet a propeller plane or a helicopter?

Semicolons and Colons

Rewrite the sentences using semicolons and colons correctly.

1. The swim meet is scheduled to start at 130 this afternoon.
2. The competition should start on time the predicted rain could, of course, delay the start.
3. The teams competing include the following Bayside's Sharks, Marengo's Fish, The Middletown Blue, and The Morgantown Streaks.
4. The short races are always exciting the high diving competition usually follows these races.
5. All the events should be over by 5 00.

Brackets and Dashes

Write the sentences. Add brackets or dashes where they are needed. Hint: Use brackets when additional information is added to a direct quotation.

1. "I am honored by this award the school literary prize, and I'm glad you liked my story," said Camilla.
2. The school literary prize given every year for the best student writing has become a prestigious award among students.
3. "I wish," added Camilla, "that I could share the prize with all of you the other student writers."
4. Next year's literary contest will include new categories essay and blog each of which will be awarded a prize.
5. The English teachers hope that everyone and they do mean everyone will enter the contest.

Transitions

Certain words and phrases can help make the meaning of your writing clearer. Below are lists of words and phrases that you can use to help readers understand more completely what you are trying to say.

Time Order

about	first	today	later
after	second	tomorrow	finally
at	to begin	until	then
before	yesterday	next	as soon as
during	meanwhile	soon	in the end

Cause and Effect

and so	as a result	because	besides
consequently	once	since	so
therefore			

Compare and Contrast

Compare:	also	as	both
	in the same way	like	likewise
	one way	similarly	
Contrast:	although	but	even though
	however	still	on the other hand
	otherwise	yet	

Words and phrases that can show location:

above	across	around	behind
below	beneath	beside	between
down	in back of	in front of	inside
near	next to	on top of	outside
over	under		

Words and phrases that can conclude or summarize:

finally	in conclusion	in the end	lastly
therefore	to conclude		

Appendix B
Rubrics

Narrative Writing Rubric

	4	3	2	1
Ideas	An engaging topic, experience, or series of events is supported by relevant details. Memorable descriptions develop the narrative. Carefully selected ideas completely satisfy the reader.	Most of the details are relevant and supportive. Descriptions are adequate. The ideas selected by the author frequently meet the needs of the reader.	The narrative is not supported by enough relevant details. Descriptions are inadequate. The ideas selected by the author sometimes meet the needs of the reader.	The topic is not clear. Details are unrelated to the topic.
Organization	The narrative has an engaging beginning and an ending that leaves the reader thinking or feeling. Events are logically and creatively sequenced. A variety of effective transition words, phrases, and clauses signifies shifts in the setting and plot.	The beginning and the conclusion are functional, but one may be stronger than the other. The sequence of events is logical, but may have a flaw or two. More or better transitions may be needed to guide the reader.	The beginning does not get the reader's attention, or the ending does not satisfy. Some events are out of order. Transitions are needed.	The writing is not organized into a beginning, middle, and ending.
Voice	The voice, mood, and tone are perfect for the purpose and audience. Dialogue, if used, is realistic and fits all the characters.	The voice, mood, and tone are appropriate in places, but inconsistent. Dialogue, if used, usually fits the characters.	The voice sounds disinterested. Mood and tone are weak. Dialogue, if used, is unrealistic or does not fit the characters.	Voice, mood, and tone are not established.
Word Choice	Clear and precise nouns and verbs consistently capture the imagery and action of the story. Descriptive language clearly conveys the experiences and events. Modifiers are strong.	Some nouns and verbs are strong, but others are weak. Descriptive language conveys most of the imagery, experiences, and events. Modifiers are satisfactory.	Many nouns and verbs do not capture the imagery or action of the story. The descriptive language is overly dependent on modifiers, and many of these are weak.	Words are overused, very weak, or incorrect. Descriptive language is not used.
Sentence Fluency	A variety of sentence structures and sentence beginnings makes the narrative flow smoothly. To read this paper aloud with inflection and feeling is effortless.	A few sentences share the same structures, lengths, or beginnings. The writing flows reasonably well. It is possible to read this writing aloud with inflection and feeling.	Many sentences have the same structures, lengths, or beginnings. The flow is robotic or rambling. It is difficult to read this writing aloud with inflection and feeling.	Sentences are incorrectly written or incomplete. The writing is difficult to follow.
Conventions	The narrative has been carefully edited. Grammar, usage, and mechanics are correct.	The narrative contains some minor errors that may distract the reader, but meaning remains clear.	The narrative contains many errors. Line-by-line editing in specific places is needed.	The writing has not been edited. Serious errors affect or alter the meaning.

Informative/Explanatory Writing Rubric

	4	3	2	1
Ideas	The topic is introduced clearly. It is developed and supported with relevant facts and concrete details. If included, quotations are relevant, accurate, and insightful. Carefully selected ideas completely answer the reader's main questions.	The topic is introduced adequately. Some facts, details, and quotations (if included) support the topic adequately. The reader's main questions are frequently answered.	The topic is introduced. Facts, details, and quotations (if included) do not develop and support the topic effectively. A few of the reader's questions are answered.	The topic is not clear. The topic is not supported by facts and details. The author did not think about what questions the reader might have.
Organization	The ideas, concepts, and information are organized into a strong introduction, body, and conclusion. Varied, appropriate, and unique transitions connect and clarify relationships among ideas.	The ideas, concepts, and information are organized into an introduction, body, and conclusion. More or better transitions may be needed.	An introduction, body, and conclusion are present. Some transitions may be inappropriate or incorrect.	The text is not organized into an introduction, body, and conclusion. It is hard or impossible to follow the ideas.
Voice	The writer's voice is appropriate for the purpose and audience. The tone is informative, respectful, and consistent.	The writer's voice is mostly appropriate for the purpose and audience. The tone is mostly informative and respectful, but may be too informal in some places.	The writer's voice is not very appropriate for the purpose or audience. The tone is inconsistent.	The writer's voice is very weak or absent. The tone is not established.
Word Choice	The language is exact and concise. Domain-specific vocabulary is used correctly and explained, as needed. Nouns and verbs are clear and precise, supported by a few carefully selected modifiers.	Some of the language is exact, but some is too general or vague. Some domain-specific vocabulary is used but not explained. Some nouns and verbs are weak, requiring too much help from modifiers. Modifiers are satisfactory.	Some language is confusing. Domain-specific vocabulary may be used incorrectly. Nouns and verbs lack clarity and precision. Too many or too few modifiers are used, and many of these are weak.	Many words are repeated or used incorrectly. Domain-specific vocabulary is not used.
Sentence Fluency	The sentences vary greatly in length and structure, adding style and interest. Almost all sentences begin differently. The text flows smoothly and is effortlessly read aloud with inflection.	Sentence length and structure vary somewhat, with some sentences adding style or interest. Some sentence beginnings are repeated. Parts of the text flow smoothly. The paper can be read aloud with inflection.	In many places, the writing does not flow smoothly because sentences are the same length or begin the same way. The paper is difficult to read aloud with inflection.	Sentences are incomplete or incorrect. The text does not flow smoothly.
Conventions	The text has been carefully edited. Grammar, usage, and mechanics are correct.	The text contains some minor errors that may distract the reader, but meaning remains clear.	Many errors are repeated. Line-by-line editing in specific places is needed. The errors interfere with meaning in some places.	The text has not been edited. Serious errors affect or alter the meaning.

Argument Writing Rubric

	4	3	2	1
Ideas	The writer's claim is stated clearly. Counterclaims are anticipated and addressed very well. Accurate reasons and evidence from reliable sources support the claim.	The writer's claim is stated adequately. The author may fail to anticipate or address one or more common counterclaims. One or two reasons or pieces of evidence may not be from reliable sources.	A claim is stated. Counterclaims are not anticipated or are not addressed well. There is little accurate support for the writer's claim.	The writer does not state a claim. Reasons and evidence are not provided.
Organization	The argument is organized logically, including a strong introduction. A compelling conclusion restates the thesis and includes a call to action. Clear and unique transitions clarify the relationships between the claim, reasons, supporting evidence, and counterclaims.	The argument is organized logically, including an introduction. The conclusion may not restate the thesis or may not include a call to action. More or better transitions may be needed to clarify the relationships between the claim, reasons, supporting evidence, and counterclaims.	The argument is not organized logically. The introduction or conclusion is missing (or problematic). Transitions are not appropriate or effective. Counterclaims are not addressed effectively.	The writing is not organized as an argument. The introduction and conclusion are missing. Transitions are not used. Counterclaims are not addressed.
Voice	The voice strongly supports the writer's purpose and consistently connects with the audience. A respectful, confident tone is maintained.	The voice mostly supports the writer's purpose. The tone is mostly respectful and confident, but may be too informal in some places.	The voice is fairly weak or passive throughout the piece and fails to connect with the audience. The tone is inconsistent.	The voice is flat or absent.
Word Choice	Compelling language conveys the writer's ideas and engages the reader. Nouns and verbs are clear and precise, supported by a few carefully selected modifiers.	Some of the language is compelling, but some is vague or ineffective. Some nouns and verbs are strong, but others are weak, requiring too much help from modifiers. Modifiers are satisfactory.	Much of the language is vague or ineffective. Nouns and verbs lack clarity or precision. Too many or too few modifiers are used, and many of these are weak.	The language is not compelling. Words are weak, negative, or used incorrectly.
Sentence Fluency	The sentences vary greatly in length and structure, adding style and interest. Almost all sentences begin differently. The text flows smoothly and is effortlessly read aloud with inflection.	Sentence length and structure vary somewhat, with some sentences adding style or interest. Some sentence beginnings are repeated. Parts of the text flow smoothly. The paper can be read aloud with inflection.	In many places, the writing does not flow smoothly because sentences are the same length or begin the same way. The paper is difficult to read aloud with inflection.	Sentences are incomplete or incorrect. Sentence beginnings are repeated over and over again. The text does not flow smoothly.
Conventions	The writing has been carefully edited. Grammar, usage, and mechanics are correct.	The writing contains some minor errors that may distract the reader, but meaning remains clear.	Many errors are repeated. Line-by-line editing in specific places is needed. The errors interfere with meaning in some places.	The writing has not been edited. Serious errors affect or alter the meaning.

Descriptive Writing Rubric

	4	3	2	1
Ideas	The topic is focused and exactly the right size. Sensory details clearly develop, describe, and reveal the subject. Carefully chosen ideas help the reader to completely experience what is being described.	The topic may need to be more carefully focused. Some sensory details reveal the subject. The author's ideas sometimes help the reader experience what is being described.	The topic is not well focused. Too few sensory details reveal the subject. The ideas fail to consistently help the reader experience what is being described.	The topic is unfocused or unclear. Details are random or missing. The ideas do not support the reader's experience of the topic.
Organization	The description is organized logically and creatively, including an engaging introduction and a thoughtfully crafted conclusion. Varied and appropriate transitions clarify relationships between ideas.	The description is organized logically, including a functional introduction and conclusion. More or better transitions may be needed to clarify relationships between ideas.	The description is not well organized. The introduction or the conclusion is weak or missing. Transitions are weak or confusing. Some of the ideas are hard to follow.	The writing is not organized. The introduction and the conclusion are missing. Transitions are not used.
Voice	An authentic, clear voice conveys the writer's purpose and connects with the reader. The mood is perfect, and the tone conveys respect for the subject and the audience.	The voice connects with the reader in some places. The tone is appropriate but inconsistent. An appropriate mood is somewhat established.	The voice may convey purpose but does not connect with the reader. The mood and tone may not be appropriate.	The voice is weak or absent. Mood and tone are not established.
Word Choice	Precise, descriptive words (including nouns, verbs, and modifiers) bring the subject to life. Figurative language and comparisons create a clear, coherent picture.	Some words are precise and descriptive, but others are not. Some nouns and verbs may rely too heavily on modifiers for clarity. Figurative language and/or comparisons sometimes create a clear picture.	Nouns and verbs lack precision and clarity. Too many or too few modifiers are used, and many of these are weak. Figurative language and/or comparisons do not create a clear picture.	Words are basic and very limited. Figurative language and comparisons are not used.
Sentence Fluency	A variety of sentences and/or lines adds interest and energy to the description. The writing flows very smoothly. Reading this aloud with inflection and feeling is effortless.	Some sentences and/or lines are varied and interesting. The writing flows smoothly some of the time. It can be read aloud with inflection and feeling.	Many sentences and/or lines are not varied or interesting. Most of the writing does not flow smoothly. It is difficult to read aloud with inflection or feeling.	Sentences and/or lines are incomplete or incorrect. The writing does not flow.
Conventions	The description has been carefully edited. Grammar, usage, and mechanics are correct.	The description contains some minor errors that may distract the reader, but meaning remains clear.	Many errors are repeated. Line-by-line editing in specific places is needed. Errors interfere with meaning in places.	The writing has not been edited. Serious errors affect or alter the meaning.

Narrative Writing Rubric

	5	4	3	2	1
Ideas	An engaging topic, experience, or series of events is supported by relevant details. Memorable descriptions develop the narrative. Carefully selected ideas completely satisfy the reader.	Most of the details are relevant and supportive. Most descriptions are memorable. Carefully selected ideas satisfy most of the reader's needs.	Some of the details may be unrelated or marginally supportive, but descriptions are adequate. The ideas selected by the author frequently meet the needs of the reader.	The narrative is not supported by enough relevant details. Descriptions are inadequate. The ideas selected by the author sometimes meet the needs of the reader.	The topic is not clear. Details are unrelated to the topic.
Organization	The narrative has an engaging beginning and an ending that leaves the reader thinking or feeling. Events are logically and creatively sequenced. A variety of effective transition words, phrases, and clauses signifies shifts in the setting and plot.	The narrative has an interesting beginning and satisfying ending. Events are logically sequenced. Most transitions are effective, especially as they signify shifts in the setting and plot.	The beginning and the conclusion are functional, but one may be stronger than the other. The sequence of events is logical, but may have a flaw or two. More or better transitions may be needed to guide the reader.	The beginning does not get the reader's attention, or the ending does not satisfy. Some events are out of order. Transitions are needed.	The writing is not organized into a beginning, middle, and ending.
Voice	The voice, mood, and tone are perfect for the purpose and audience. Dialogue, if used, is realistic and fits all the characters.	The voice, mood, and tone are appropriate. Dialogue, if used, is realistic and usually fits the characters well.	The voice, mood, and tone are appropriate in places, but inconsistent. Dialogue, if used, sometimes fits the characters.	The voice sounds disinterested. Mood and tone are weak. Dialogue, if used, is unrealistic or does not fit the characters.	Voice, mood, and tone are not established.
Word Choice	Clear and precise nouns and verbs consistently capture the imagery and action of the story. Descriptive language clearly conveys the experiences and events. Modifiers are strong.	Most of the nouns and verbs are clear, capturing the imagery and action of the story. Descriptive language conveys the experiences and events well. The majority of the modifiers are strong.	Some nouns and verbs are strong, but others are weak. Descriptive language conveys most of the imagery, experiences, and events. Modifiers are satisfactory.	Many nouns and verbs do not capture the imagery or action of the story. The descriptive language is overly dependent on modifiers, and many of these are weak.	Words are overused, very weak, or incorrect. Descriptive language is not used.
Sentence Fluency	A variety of sentence structures and sentence beginnings makes the narrative flow smoothly. To read this paper aloud with inflection and feeling is effortless.	Most sentence structures and sentence beginnings are varied and flow well. Most of the sentences are well crafted. It is easy to read this writing aloud with inflection and feeling.	A few sentences share the same structures, lengths, or beginnings. The writing flows reasonably well. It is possible to read this writing aloud with inflection and feeling.	Many sentences have the same structures, lengths, or beginnings. The flow is robotic or rambling. It is difficult to read this writing aloud with inflection and feeling.	Sentences are incorrectly written or incomplete. The writing is difficult to follow.
Conventions	The narrative has been carefully edited. Grammar, usage, and mechanics are correct.	The narrative contains one or two minor errors that are easily corrected.	The narrative contains some minor errors that may distract the reader, but meaning remains clear.	The narrative contains many errors. Line-by-line editing in specific places is needed.	The writing has not been edited. Serious errors affect or alter the meaning.

Informative/Explanatory Writing Rubric

	5	4	3	2	1
Ideas	The topic is introduced clearly. It is developed and supported with relevant facts and concrete details. If included, quotations are relevant, accurate, and insightful. Carefully selected ideas completely answer the reader's main questions.	The topic is introduced well. Almost all the facts and details support the topic well. If included, quotations are relevant and accurate. Almost all of the reader's main questions are answered.	The topic is introduced adequately. Some facts, details, and quotations (if included) support the topic adequately. The reader's main questions are frequently answered.	The topic is introduced. Facts, details, and quotations (if included) do not develop and support the topic effectively. A few of the reader's questions are answered.	The topic is not clear. The topic is not supported by facts and details. The author did not think about what questions the reader might have.
Organization	The ideas, concepts, and information are organized into a strong introduction, body, and conclusion. Varied, appropriate, and unique transitions connect and clarify relationships among ideas.	The ideas, concepts, and information are organized into an introduction, body, and conclusion. Most transitions are appropriate and helpful.	The ideas, concepts, and information are organized into an introduction, body, and conclusion. More or better transitions may be needed.	An introduction, body, and conclusion are present. Some transitions may be inappropriate or incorrect.	The text is not organized into an introduction, body, and conclusion. It is hard or impossible to follow the ideas.
Voice	The writer's voice is appropriate for the purpose and audience. The tone is informative, respectful, and consistent.	The writer's voice is appropriate for the purpose and audience most of the time. The tone is almost always informative and respectful.	The writer's voice is mostly appropriate for the purpose and audience. The tone is mostly informative and respectful, but may be too informal in some places.	The writer's voice is not very appropriate for the purpose or audience. The tone is inconsistent.	The writer's voice is very weak or absent. The tone is not established.
Word Choice	The language is exact and concise. Domain-specific vocabulary is used correctly and explained, as needed. Nouns and verbs are clear and precise, supported by a few carefully selected modifiers.	Most of the language is exact and concise. Domain-specific vocabulary is used correctly and usually explained, as needed. Most nouns and verbs are clear and precise. Most modifiers are carefully selected.	Some of the language is exact, but some is too general or vague. Some domain-specific vocabulary is used but not explained. Some nouns and verbs are weak, requiring too much help from modifiers. Modifiers are satisfactory.	Some language is confusing. Domain-specific vocabulary may be used incorrectly. Nouns and verbs lack clarity and precision. Too many or too few modifiers are used, and many of these are weak.	Many words are repeated or used incorrectly. Domain-specific vocabulary is not used.
Sentence Fluency	The sentences vary greatly in length and structure, adding style and interest. Almost all sentences begin differently. The text flows smoothly and is effortlessly read aloud with inflection.	Most of the sentences vary in their beginnings, lengths, and structures. Several add style or interest. Most of the text flows smoothly and is easy to read aloud with inflection.	Sentence length and structure vary somewhat, with some sentences adding style or interest. Some sentence beginnings are repeated. Parts of the text flow smoothly. The paper can be read aloud with inflection.	In many places, the writing does not flow smoothly because sentences are the same length or begin the same way. The paper is difficult to read aloud with inflection.	Sentences are incomplete or incorrect. The text does not flow smoothly.
Conventions	The text has been carefully edited. Grammar, usage, and mechanics are correct.	The text contains one or two minor errors, but the meaning remains clear.	The text contains some minor errors that may distract the reader, but meaning remains clear.	Many errors are repeated. Line-by-line editing in specific places is needed. The errors interfere with meaning in some places.	The text has not been edited. Serious errors affect or alter the meaning.

Argument Writing Rubric

	5	4	3	2	1
Ideas	The writer's claim is stated clearly. Counterclaims are anticipated and addressed very well. Accurate reasons and evidence from reliable sources support the claim.	The writer's claim is stated clearly. Counterclaims are anticipated and addressed. Most of the reasons and evidence are accurate and from reliable sources.	The writer's claim is stated adequately. The author may fail to anticipate or address one or more common counterclaims. One or two reasons or pieces of evidence may not be from reliable sources.	A claim is stated. Counterclaims are not anticipated or are not addressed well. There is little accurate support for the writer's claim.	The writer does not state a claim. Reasons and evidence are not provided.
Organization	The argument is organized logically, including a strong introduction. A compelling conclusion restates the thesis and includes a call to action. Clear and unique transitions clarify the relationships between the claim, reasons, supporting evidence, and counterclaims.	The argument is organized logically, including a good introduction. The conclusion restates the thesis and may include a call to action. Most transitions clarify the relationships between the claim, reasons, supporting evidence, and counterclaims.	The argument is organized logically, including an introduction. The conclusion may not restate the thesis or may not include a call to action. More or better transitions may be needed to clarify the relationships between the claim, reasons, supporting evidence, and counterclaims.	The argument is not organized logically. The introduction or conclusion is missing (or problematic). Transitions are not appropriate or effective. Counterclaims are not addressed effectively.	The writing is not organized as an argument. The introduction and conclusion are missing. Transitions are not used. Counterclaims are not addressed.
Voice	The voice strongly supports the writer's purpose and consistently connects with the audience. A respectful, confident tone is maintained.	The voice supports the writer's purpose and almost always connects with the audience. A respectful, confident tone is maintained.	The voice mostly supports the writer's purpose. The tone is mostly respectful and confident, but may be too informal in some places.	The voice is fairly weak or passive throughout the piece and fails to connect with the audience. The tone is inconsistent.	The voice is flat or absent.
Word Choice	Compelling language conveys the writer's ideas and engages the reader. Nouns and verbs are clear and precise, supported by a few carefully selected modifiers.	Most of the language is compelling. Nouns and verbs are mostly clear and precise. Most modifiers are carefully selected.	Some of the language is compelling, but some is vague or ineffective. Some nouns and verbs are strong, but others are weak, requiring too much help from modifiers. Modifiers are satisfactory.	Much of the language is vague or ineffective. Nouns and verbs lack clarity or precision. Too many or too few modifiers are used, and many of these are weak.	The language is not compelling. Words are weak, negative, or used incorrectly.
Sentence Fluency	The sentences vary greatly in length and structure, adding style and interest. Almost all sentences begin differently. The text flows smoothly and is effortlessly read aloud with inflection.	Most of the sentences vary in their beginnings, lengths, and structures. Several add style or interest. Most of the text flows smoothly and is easy to read aloud with inflection.	Sentence length and structure vary somewhat, with some sentences adding style or interest. Some sentence beginnings are repeated. Parts of the text flow smoothly. The paper can be read aloud with inflection.	In many places, the writing does not flow smoothly because sentences are the same length or begin the same way. The paper is difficult to read aloud with inflection.	Sentences are incomplete or incorrect. Sentence beginnings are repeated over and over again. The text does not flow smoothly.
Conventions	The writing has been carefully edited. Grammar, usage, and mechanics are correct.	The writing contains one or two minor errors, but the meaning remains clear.	The writing contains some minor errors that may distract the reader, but meaning remains clear.	Many errors are repeated. Line-by-line editing in specific places is needed. The errors interfere with meaning in some places.	The writing has not been edited. Serious errors affect or alter the meaning.

Descriptive Writing Rubric

	5	4	3	2	1
Ideas	The topic is focused and exactly the right size. Sensory details clearly develop, describe, and reveal the subject. Carefully chosen ideas help the reader to completely experience what is being described.	The topic is focused and the right size. Many sensory details develop, describe, and reveal the subject. The ideas selected usually enable the reader to experience what is being described.	The topic may need to be more carefully focused. Some sensory details reveal the subject. The author's ideas sometimes help the reader experience what is being described.	The topic is not well focused. Too few sensory details reveal the subject. The ideas fail to consistently help the reader experience what is being described.	The topic is unfocused or unclear. Details are random or missing. The ideas do not support the reader's experience of the topic.
Organization	The description is organized logically and creatively, including an engaging introduction and a thoughtfully crafted conclusion. Varied and appropriate transitions clarify relationships between ideas.	The description is organized logically, including a strong introduction and a strong conclusion. Most of the transitions clarify relationships between ideas.	The description is organized logically, including a functional introduction and conclusion. More or better transitions may be needed to clarify relationships between ideas.	The description is not well organized. The introduction or the conclusion is weak or missing. Transitions are weak or confusing. Some of the ideas are hard to follow.	The writing is not organized. The introduction and the conclusion are missing. Transitions are not used.
Voice	An authentic, clear voice conveys the writer's purpose and connects with the reader. The mood is perfect, and the tone conveys respect for the subject and the audience.	The voice is clear and connects with the reader most of the time. The mood is appropriate, and the tone conveys respect for the subject and audience most of the time.	The voice connects with the reader in some places. The tone is appropriate but inconsistent. An appropriate mood is somewhat established.	The voice may convey purpose but does not connect with the reader. The mood and tone may not be appropriate.	The voice is weak or absent. Mood and tone are not established.
Word Choice	Precise, descriptive words (including nouns, verbs, and modifiers) bring the subject to life. Figurative language and comparisons create a clear, coherent picture.	Most words (including nouns, verbs, and modifiers) are precise and descriptive. Figurative language and comparisons create a clear, coherent picture most of the time.	Some words are precise and descriptive, but others are not. Some nouns and verbs may rely too heavily on modifiers for clarity. Figurative language and/or comparisons sometimes create a clear picture.	Nouns and verbs lack precision and clarity. Too many or too few modifiers are used, and many of these are weak. Figurative language and/or comparisons do not create a clear picture.	Words are basic and very limited. Figurative language and comparisons are not used.
Sentence Fluency	A variety of sentences and/or lines adds interest and energy to the description. The writing flows very smoothly. Reading this aloud with inflection and feeling is effortless.	Most sentences and/or lines are varied and interesting. The writing flows smoothly most of the time. It is easy to read aloud with inflection and feeling.	Some sentences and/or lines are varied and interesting. The writing flows smoothly some of the time. It can be read aloud with inflection and feeling.	Many sentences and/or lines are not varied or interesting. Most of the writing does not flow smoothly. It is difficult to read aloud with inflection or feeling.	Sentences and/or lines are incomplete or incorrect. The writing does not flow.
Conventions	The description has been carefully edited. Grammar, usage, and mechanics are correct.	The description contains one or two minor errors that are easily corrected. Meaning is clear.	The description contains some minor errors that may distract the reader, but meaning remains clear.	Many errors are repeated. Line-by-line editing in specific places is needed. Errors interfere with meaning in places.	The writing has not been edited. Serious errors affect or alter the meaning.

Narrative Writing Rubric

	6	5	4	3	2	1
Ideas	An engaging topic, experience, or series of events is supported by relevant details. Memorable descriptions develop the narrative. Carefully selected ideas completely satisfy the reader.	Most of the details are relevant and supportive. Most descriptions are memorable. Carefully selected ideas satisfy most of the reader's needs.	Some of the details may be unrelated or marginally supportive, but descriptions are adequate. The ideas selected by the author frequently meet the needs of the reader.	The narrative is not supported by enough relevant details. Descriptions are inadequate. The ideas selected by the author sometimes meet the needs of the reader.	The topic may not be clear. Many details are unrelated. The author did not consider the needs of the reader.	The topic is not clear. Details are unrelated to the topic.
Organization	The narrative has an engaging beginning and an ending that leaves the reader thinking or feeling. Events are logically and creatively sequenced. A variety of effective transition words, phrases, and clauses signifies shifts in the setting and plot.	The narrative has an interesting beginning and satisfying ending. Events are logically sequenced. Most transitions are effective, especially as they signify shifts in the setting and plot.	The beginning and the conclusion are functional, but one may be stronger than the other. The sequence of events is logical, but may have a flaw or two. More or better transitions may be needed to guide the reader.	The beginning does not get the reader's attention, or the ending does not satisfy. Some events are out of order. Transitions are needed.	The beginning and ending are weak. The sequence of events is seriously flawed. Transitions are not used.	The writing is not organized into a beginning, middle, and ending.
Voice	The voice, mood, and tone are perfect for the purpose and audience. Dialogue, if used, is realistic and fits all the characters.	The voice, mood, and tone are appropriate. Dialogue, if used, is realistic and usually fits the characters well.	The voice, mood, and tone are appropriate in places, but inconsistent. Dialogue, if used, sometimes fits the characters.	The voice sounds disinterested. Mood and tone are weak. Dialogue, if used, is unrealistic or does not fit the characters.	The voice, mood, and tone are inappropriate for the audience. Dialogue, if used, is unrealistic.	Voice, mood, and tone are not established.
Word Choice	Clear and precise nouns and verbs consistently capture the imagery and action of the story. Descriptive language clearly conveys the experiences and events. Modifiers are strong.	Most of the nouns and verbs are clear, capturing the imagery and action of the story. Descriptive language conveys the experiences and events well. The majority of the modifiers are strong.	Some nouns and verbs are strong, but others are weak. Descriptive language conveys most of the imagery, experiences, and events. Modifiers are satisfactory.	Many nouns and verbs do not capture the imagery or action of the story. The descriptive language is overly dependent on modifiers, and many of these are weak.	Words are not powerful or precise. Descriptive language is not used.	Words are overused, very weak, or incorrect.
Sentence Fluency	A variety of sentence structures and sentence beginnings makes the narrative flow smoothly. To read this paper aloud with inflection and feeling is effortless.	Most sentence structures and sentence beginnings are varied and flow well. Most of the sentences are well crafted. It is easy to read this writing aloud with inflection and feeling.	A few sentences share the same structures, lengths, or beginnings. The writing flows reasonably well. It is possible to read this writing aloud with inflection and feeling.	Many sentences have the same structures, lengths, or beginnings. The flow is robotic or rambling. It is difficult to read this writing aloud with inflection and feeling.	Sentences have little variation. The narrative does not flow well.	Sentences are incorrectly written or incomplete. The writing is difficult to follow.
Conventions	The narrative has been carefully edited. Grammar, usage, and mechanics are correct.	The narrative contains one or two minor errors that are easily corrected.	The narrative contains some minor errors that may distract the reader, but meaning remains clear.	The narrative contains many errors. Line-by-line editing in specific places is needed.	Serious errors affect or alter the meaning.	The writing has not been edited.

Informative/Explanatory Writing Rubric

	6	5	4	3	2	1
Ideas	The topic is introduced clearly. It is developed and supported with relevant facts and concrete details. If included, quotations are relevant, accurate, and insightful. Carefully selected ideas completely answer the reader's main questions.	The topic is introduced well. Almost all the facts and details support the topic well. If included, quotations are relevant and accurate. Almost all of the reader's main questions are answered.	The topic is introduced adequately. Some facts, details, and quotations (if included) support the topic adequately. The reader's main questions are frequently answered.	The topic is introduced. Facts, details, and quotations (if included) do not develop and support the topic effectively. A few of the reader's questions are answered.	The topic is not introduced, or more than one topic is introduced. Details are not relevant. Facts are not included. The author did not think about what questions the reader might have.	The topic is not clear. The topic is not supported by facts and details.
Organization	The ideas, concepts, and information are organized into a strong introduction, body, and conclusion. Varied and unique transitions connect and clarify relationships among ideas.	The ideas, concepts, and information are organized into an introduction, body, and conclusion. Most transitions are appropriate and helpful.	The ideas, concepts, and information are organized into an introduction, body, and conclusion. More or better transitions may be needed.	An introduction, body, and conclusion are present. Some transitions may be inappropriate or incorrect.	The text is not well organized. The introduction and conclusion are weak or missing. Transitions are not used.	The text is not organized into an introduction, body, and conclusion. It is difficult to follow the ideas.
Voice	The writer's voice is appropriate for the purpose and audience. The tone is informative, respectful, and consistent.	The writer's voice is appropriate for the purpose and audience most of the time. The tone is almost always informative and respectful.	The writer's voice is mostly appropriate for the purpose and audience. The tone is mostly informative and respectful, but may be too informal in some places.	The writer's voice is not very appropriate for the purpose or audience. The tone is inconsistent.	The writer's voice is not appropriate. The tone is too informal.	The writer's voice is very weak or absent. The tone is not established.
Word Choice	The language is exact and concise. Domain-specific vocabulary is used correctly and explained, as needed. Nouns and verbs are clear and precise, supported by a few carefully selected modifiers.	Most of the language is exact and concise. Domain-specific vocabulary is used correctly and usually explained, as needed. Most nouns and verbs are clear and precise. Most modifiers are carefully selected.	Some of the language is exact, but some is too general or vague. Some domain-specific vocabulary is used but not explained. Some nouns and verbs are weak, requiring too much help from modifiers. Modifiers are satisfactory.	Some language is confusing. Domain-specific vocabulary may be used incorrectly. Nouns and verbs lack clarity and precision. Too many or too few modifiers are used, and many of these are weak.	The language is very basic and limited. Domain-specific vocabulary is used incorrectly. Nouns and verbs are vague, unclear, or confusing. Modifiers may be missing.	Many words are repeated or used incorrectly. Domain-specific vocabulary is not used.
Sentence Fluency	The sentences vary greatly in length and structure, adding style and interest. Almost all sentences begin differently. The text flows smoothly and is effortlessly read aloud with inflection.	Most of the sentences vary in their beginnings, lengths, and structures. Several add style or interest. Most of the text flows smoothly and is easy to read aloud with inflection.	Sentence length and structure vary somewhat, with some sentences adding style or interest. Some sentence beginnings are repeated. Parts of the text flow smoothly. The paper can be read aloud with inflection.	In many places, the writing does not flow smoothly because sentences are the same length or begin the same way. The paper is difficult to read aloud with inflection.	Most sentences are the same length and structure. Sentence beginnings are repeated over and over again. The flow is too robotic or rambling.	Sentences are incomplete or incorrect. The text does not flow smoothly.
Conventions	The text has been carefully edited. Grammar, usage, and mechanics are correct.	The text contains one or two minor errors, but the meaning remains clear.	The text contains some minor errors that may distract the reader, but meaning remains clear.	Many errors are repeated. Line-by-line editing in specific places is needed. The errors interfere with meaning in some places.	Serious errors affect or alter the meaning.	The text has not been edited.

Argument Writing Rubric

	6	5	4	3	2	1
Ideas	The writer's claim is stated clearly. Counterclaims are anticipated and addressed very well. Accurate reasons and evidence from reliable sources support the claim.	The writer's claim is stated clearly. Counterclaims are anticipated and addressed. Most of the reasons and evidence are accurate and from reliable sources.	The writer's claim is stated adequately. The author may fail to anticipate or address one or more common counter-claims. One or two reasons or pieces of evidence may not be from reliable sources.	A claim is stated. Counterclaims are not anticipated or are not addressed well. There is little accurate support for the writer's claim.	The writer's claim is not stated clearly. Counterclaims are not addressed. Reasons and evidence are unrelated or inaccurate.	The writer does not state a claim. Reasons and evidence are not provided.
Organization	The argument is organized logically, including a strong introduction. A compelling conclusion restates the thesis and includes a call to action. Clear and unique transitions clarify the relationships between the claim, reasons, supporting evidence, and counterclaims.	The argument is organized logically, including a good introduction. The conclusion restates the thesis and may include a call to action. Most transitions clarify the relationships between the claim, reasons, supporting evidence, and counterclaims.	The argument is organized logically, including an intro–duction. The conclusion may not restate the thesis or may not include a call to action. More or better transitions may be needed to clarify the relationships between the claim, reasons, supporting evidence, and counterclaims.	The argument is not organized logically. The introduction or conclusion is missing (or problematic). Transitions are not appropriate or effective. Counterclaims are not addressed effectively.	The argument is not organized logically. The introduction and conclusion are missing. Transitions are not used. Counterclaims are not addressed.	The writing is not organized as an argument.
Voice	The voice strongly supports the writer's purpose and consistently connects with the audience. A respectful, confident tone is maintained.	The voice supports the writer's purpose and almost always connects with the audience. A respectful, confident tone is maintained.	The voice mostly supports the writer's purpose. The tone is mostly respectful and confident, but may be too informal in some places.	The voice is fairly weak or passive throughout the piece and fails to connect with the audience. The tone is inconsistent.	The voice is weak or inappropriate for the purpose and audience. A respectful, confident tone is not established.	The voice is flat or absent.
Word Choice	Compelling language conveys the writer's ideas and engages the reader. Nouns and verbs are clear and precise, supported by a few carefully selected modifiers.	Most of the language is compelling. Nouns and verbs are mostly clear and precise. Most modifiers are carefully selected.	Some of the language is compelling, but some is vague or ineffective. Some nouns and verbs are strong, but others are weak, requiring too much help from modifiers. Modifiers are satisfactory.	Much of the language is vague or ineffective. Nouns and verbs lack clarity or precision. Too many or too few modifiers are used, and many of these are weak.	The language is not compelling. Many words are very basic. Nouns and verbs are vague, unclear, or confusing. Modifiers may be missing.	Words are weak, negative, or used incorrectly.
Sentence Fluency	The sentences vary greatly in length and structure, adding style and interest. Almost all sentences begin differently. The text flows smoothly and is effortlessly read aloud with inflection.	Most of the sentences vary in their beginnings, lengths, and structures. Several add style or interest. Most of the text flows smoothly and is easy to read aloud with inflection.	Sentence length and structure vary somewhat, with some sentences adding style or interest. Some sentence beginnings are repeated. Parts of the text flow smoothly. The paper can be read aloud with inflection.	In many places, the writing does not flow smoothly because sentences are the same length or begin the same way. The paper is difficult to read aloud with inflection.	Most sentences are the same length and structure. Sentence beginnings are repeated over and over again. The flow is too robotic or rambling.	Sentences are incomplete or incorrect. The text does not flow smoothly.
Conventions	The writing has been carefully edited. Grammar, usage, and mechanics are correct.	The writing contains one or two minor errors, but the meaning remains clear.	The writing contains some minor errors that may distract the reader, but meaning remains clear.	Many errors are repeated. Line-by-line editing in specific places is needed. The errors interfere with meaning in some places.	Serious errors affect or alter the meaning.	The writing has not been edited.

Descriptive Writing Rubric

	6	5	4	3	2	1
Ideas	The topic is focused and exactly the right size. Sensory details clearly develop, describe, and reveal the subject. Carefully chosen ideas help the reader to completely experience what is being described.	The topic is focused and the right size. Many sensory details develop, describe, and reveal the subject. The ideas selected usually enable the reader to experience what is being described.	The topic may need to be more carefully focused. Some sensory details reveal the subject. The author's ideas sometimes help the reader experience what is being described.	The topic is not well focused. Too few sensory details reveal the subject. The ideas fail to consistently help the reader experience what is being described.	The topic is not focused. Details are scarce, or may relate to more than one subject. The ideas do not support the reader's experience of the topic.	The topic is unfocused or unclear. Details are random or missing.
Organization	The description is organized logically and creatively, including an engaging introduction and a thoughtfully crafted conclusion. Varied and appropriate transitions clarify relationships between ideas.	The description is organized logically, including a strong introduction and a strong conclusion. Most of the transitions clarify relationships between ideas.	The description is organized logically, including a functional introduction and conclusion. More or better transitions may be needed to clarify relationships between ideas.	The description is not well organized. The introduction or the conclusion is weak or missing. Transitions are weak or confusing. Some of the ideas are hard to follow.	The description is not organized. The introduction and the conclusion are missing. Transitions are incorrect or missing. The ideas are hard to follow.	The writing is not organized. Transitions are not used.
Voice	An authentic, clear voice conveys the writer's purpose and connects with the reader. The mood is perfect, and the tone conveys respect for the subject and the audience.	The voice is clear and connects with the reader most of the time. The mood is appropriate, and the tone conveys respect for the subject and audience most of the time.	The voice connects with the reader in some places. The tone is appropriate but inconsistent. An appropriate mood is somewhat established.	The voice may convey purpose but does not connect with the reader. The mood and tone may not be appropriate.	The voice does not convey purpose or connect with the reader. The mood and tone are inappropriate.	The voice is weak or absent. Mood and tone are not established.
Word Choice	Precise, descriptive words (including nouns, verbs, and modifiers) bring the subject to life. Figurative language and comparisons create a clear, coherent picture.	Most words (including nouns, verbs, and modifiers) are precise and descriptive. Figurative language and comparisons create a clear, coherent picture most of the time.	Some words are precise and descriptive, but others are not. Some nouns and verbs may rely too heavily on modifiers for clarity. Figurative language and/or comparisons sometimes create a clear picture.	Nouns and verbs lack precision and clarity. Too many or too few modifiers are used, and many of these are weak. Figurative language and/or comparisons do not create a clear picture.	Words are vague or confusing. Figurative language or comparisons are incomplete or missing.	Words are basic and very limited. Figurative language and comparisons are not used.
Sentence Fluency	A variety of sentences and/or lines adds interest and energy to the description. The writing flows very smoothly. Reading this aloud with inflection and feeling is effortless.	Most sentences and/or lines are varied and interesting. The writing flows smoothly most of the time. It is easy to read aloud with inflection and feeling.	Some sentences and/or lines are varied and interesting. The writing flows smoothly some of the time. It can be read aloud with inflection and feeling.	Many sentences and/or lines are not varied or interesting. Most of the writing does not flow smoothly. It is difficult to read aloud with inflection or feeling.	Sentences and/or lines are very basic, limited, or repetitive. The writing is predictable and dull.	Sentences and/or lines are incomplete or incorrect. The writing does not flow.
Conventions	The description has been carefully edited. Grammar, usage, and mechanics are correct.	The description contains one or two minor errors that are easily corrected. Meaning is clear.	The description contains some minor errors that may distract the reader, but meaning remains clear.	Many errors are repeated. Line-by-line editing in specific places is needed. Errors interfere with meaning in places.	Serious errors affect or alter the meaning.	The writing has not been edited.

Index

Q

R

S

T